Palace Car Prince

PALACE CAR PRINCE

A BIOGRAPHY OF
GEORGE MORTIMER PULLMAN

LISTON EDGINGTON LEYENDECKER

UNIVERSITY PRESS OF COLORADO

The University Press of Colorado is a cooperative publishing enterprise supported, in part, by Adams State College, Colorado State University, Fort Lewis
College, Mesa State College, Metropolitan State College of Denver, University of
Colorado, University of Northern Colorado, University of Southern Colorado,
and Western State College.

Library of Congress Cataloging-in-Publication Data

Leyendecker, Liston E.
    Palace car prince : a biography of George Mortimer Pullman /
Liston Edgington Leyendecker.
        p.   cm.
    Includes bibliographical references and index.
    ISBN 0-87081-337-4
    1. Pullman, George Mortimer, 1831–1897. 2. Businessman—United
States—Biography. 3. Industrialists—United States—Biography.
4. Pullman's Palace Car Company—History. I. Title.
HE2754.P85L49 1992
385' .22—dc20
[B]   91-37716
                                                               CIP

The paper used in this publication meets the minimum requirements of the
American National Standard for Information Sciences—Permanence of Paper
for Printed Library Materials. ANSI Z39.48–1984

∞

10 9 8 7 6 5 4 3 2

*Cover photo courtesy of the Chicago Historical Society. Cover illustration and design
by Kristin Geishecker*

To Florence Lowden Miller

CONTENTS

Preface		ix
Acknowledgments		xi
Introduction		1
1.	The Family of Lewis and Emily Pullman	11
2.	Early Chicago Enterprises	29
3.	The Colorado Interlude	51
4.	Moving Up	71
5.	Pullman Branches Out	97
6.	The Pullmans of 1729 Prairie Avenue	109
7.	Pullman Expands to England and Italy	127
8.	Growth and Tragedy During the 1870s	145
9.	Pullman, Illinois	163
10.	Consolidation and Growth During the 1880s	179
11.	Troubled Times	201
12.	The Last Call	239
Appendix: Members of the Board of Directors,		
Pullman's Palace Car Company, 1867–1897		265
Notes		267
Bibliography		307
Index		317

PREFACE

The myth developed sometime in Colorado's past that George Mortimer Pullman conceived the idea for sleeping car berths from the miners' bunks he saw during the years he spent in Gilpin County, Colorado. Actually, he already had three sleepers operating in Illinois when he arrived in Denver in July 1860, after a hard week's journey from St. Joseph, Missouri. (He traveled by stagecoach, a vehicle that was a far cry from the sumptuous conveyances he would provide for his own traveling customers.)

While in Colorado, he played a prominent role in the business and social life of Central City and Denver. In the course of my own work with preservation in these two communities and with the gold rush era, I encountered his name frequently and learned that he was highly regarded by his contemporaries in both the supply town and the mining camp. These references led me to wonder what sort of person he was and why he had come to Colorado. Like most American historians, I knew George Pullman as a major developer of the railroad sleeping car and as a man whose name was anathema to labor because of the 1894 Chicago railroad strike. But that was virtually all I had ever learned about him.

Very little research had been done on his Colorado career — a gap in the state's history that I proposed to fill by means of an article — and I was surprised to learn that no lengthy biography existed.[1] To be sure, there were several accounts of the strike and one excellent book about the town he founded, but these works dealt with him only in peripheral fashion. The longer I studied his Colorado sojourn, the more interested I became in the story of his life. Then, thanks to the cooperation of the Colorado State University Foundation, I was able to secure funding for a sabbatical leave that enabled my family and me to spend nine wonderful months in Chicago as I began broader research on George Pullman.

This study, the result of fifteen years' work, derives mainly from George Mortimer Pullman's correspondence to various members of his family, chiefly to his mother and wife; his wife's correspondence to him, interspersed with occasional missives to and from other family members; his Colorado diary; and the diaries kept by his mother and his wife. Most of these materials are in the collection of the late Florence Lowden Miller (Mrs. C. Phillip Miller, Pullman's granddaughter) or at the Chicago Historical Society. Because Pullman's business records were destroyed many years ago, I supplemented these personal documents with Pullman Company scrapbooks and board minute books, lodged in the Manuscript Room of Chicago's Newberry Library. Various newspapers of the era have filled in many of the gaps.

George M. Pullman's biography will interest those who want to learn about the man and his career — beyond his roles as creator of a town, as a curmudgeonly company head who refused to deal with striking employees, and as the perfecter of a very luxurious line of railroad cars. Readers who wish to know more about the strike, the town, or his cars should consult books by Almont Lindsey, Stanley Buder, and John H. White, Jr.

LISTON E. LEYENDECKER

ACKNOWLEDGMENTS

Many people were instrumental in creating this work and certainly deserve mention for their yeomanly service in my behalf. First and foremost, Florence Lowden (Mrs. C. Phillip) Miller graciously opened her family archives to me; not only did she provide a place for me to work in her house, but also did much to make my family and me feel at home in Chicago. Her sons, Phillip and Warren, and their families did a great deal to make our numerous Chicago interludes well worth remembering. Distant members of the family who also helped are George McGinnis of Oceanside, California, and Henry A. Pullman of Long Beach, California.

The cooperative staffs of the Chicago Historical Society are legion, including Clement M. Silvestro and Harold K. Skramstad, Jr., former directors, and Isabel Grosner and Fania Weingartner, former editors of *Chicago History*. Librarians Grant T. Dean, Larry A. Viskochil, Neal Ney, Archie J. Motley, and Linda Evans, together with John Tris and Julia Westerberg, have all been of great service throughout the years. At the Newberry Library, John Aubrey, Susan Dean, Mike Kaplan, and Richard Buchen have always stood ready to help by bringing in another stack of material. Constance Gordon and the staff of the Chicago Public Library's Special Collections Division also aided in the search for Pullman material. And Mary Carey of the New York Historical Society Library was most helpful in solving at least one New York City problem.

Acknowledgments

Richard D. Johnson, formerly of Pullman Incorporated, helped extensively in my early days as I tried to get a handle on George Pullman's railroad career. Charles M. Knoll, a Pullman expert himself, helped out on several occasions.

George Behrend, Anthony J. Bower, Charles Long, the late Brian Haresnape, and Julian Morel, all English scholars who have published and done a great deal of work on Pullman in England, not only furnished me with information but read and commented on the manuscript of Chapter 6. Across the Channel, Philip Jefford, inspecteur general honoraire, Compagnie Internationale des Wagon-Lits et du Tourisme, Paris, provided me with insights into Pullman's activities on the Continent.

At the National Archives and Records Service, Denver Federal Center, Robert Svenningsen always had just the document I needed, and at the Colorado State Archives and Records Service, George E. Warren, former chief archivist, Terry Kettelson, present chief archivist, and Linda Snyder always found another place to look as we traced Pullman's life in Colorado.

At the Stephen H. Hart Library of the Colorado Historical Society, Enid Thompson and Maxine Benson, former heads, Katherine Kane, present head, Laura Sharpe, Katherine Englert, Alice Sharpe, and the late Laura Eckstrom, did all in their power to ease the pain of difficult research. Across the street at the Denver Public Library's Western History Department, Alyss Freese, former head, Eleanor Gehres, present head, Opal Harber, Kay Kane, Hazel Lundberg, Pamela Rose, Lynn Taylor, Sandra Turner, Kay Wilcox, Augie Mastrogiuseppe, Jim Davis, Fred Yonce, and Donald Dilley rendered invaluable assistance. Special Collections Librarian John G. Newman, at Colorado State University, and the late John Brennan, former head of the Western History section of Norlin Library at the University of Colorado, uncovered several items of great use. Douglas Ernest of Colorado State University's Morgan Library helped unravel the intricacies of Missouri railroads at the outbreak of the Civil War, and Richard Stevens, his colleague, rendered great service in response to my questions about Pintsch lights.

In Clear Creek County, Margaret Chiles, former county clerk, and her staff, together with Christine Bradley, the present Clear

Acknowledgments

Creek County archivist, did much to fill in Pullman's Colorado career. The same was true in Gilpin County, where the late F. Morgan Gray, former county clerk, and his assistants Phillis Powers and Nadine Snyder fetched and toted a good many heavy property books as I ran down Lyon, Pullman and Company and studied George Pullman's place in Central City.

At Colorado State University, the Faculty Improvement Committee and the Colorado State University Foundation, including Susan Waggoner, Tom Grip, Jan Carroll, and Glenda Lightburn, greatly eased the problem of finances for this project.

My own graduate students, such as Dennis Means, Brian Moroney, Gordon Hendrikson, Robert L. Hinckle, and Lee Sachs, performed nobly when it came to running down obscure bits of information. Douglas Bridewell, another student, placed early chapters of the manuscript on disk. Saundra Francis put in an outstanding performance in getting the entire manuscript on disk and readying it for the publisher.

The late Robert G. Athearn at the University of Colorado came up with several suggestions concerning early railroads, and James E. Fell, Jr., manager of communications of United Banks of Colorado, Inc., acquainted me with the Dun Collection at Harvard. Robert W. Larson of the University of Northern Colorado read and commented on an early draft of this book, and Duane A. Smith of Fort Lewis College also commented and made useful suggestions on the manuscript. My personal colleagues at Colorado State University, Charles J. Bayard, James E. Hansen II, and John Clark Pratt, also read and criticized portions of the manuscript. Special thanks goes to my *buen amigo* and colleague Mark T. Gilderhus, who read every chapter and made most valuable suggestions. Deborah Ann Clifford not only typed many drafts of this piece but also lent her expertise as editor to this work, thereby improving it immensely. Jody Berman at the University Press of Colorado came to the rescue on numerous occasions.

Finally, my wife, Barbara, and my daughter, Jessica, both endured a great deal and rendered much support while I spent my life in libraries, in my study, and at my typewriter.

To each and all of you, my heartfelt thanks.

Palace Car Prince

Introduction

On the whole, the 1880s treated American businessmen well. During those years, the surrender at Appomattox passed its twentieth anniversary, Indian wars were on the decline, and, although labor conflicts increased, they remained sporadic and isolated, unlike those of the 1870s and incidents that would occur in the 1890s. Depressions came, but they were mild when compared to that of the preceding decade and the one that would plague the next. Politics was becoming a field that attracted men of "the better sort," and the excesses of Ulysses S. Grant's administration were little more than bad memories.

America was building, its cities growing upward as new construction technology allowed contractors to build their structures higher than the traditional eight stories. Commercial streets were paved, albeit crowded, though residential thoroughfares remained dusty in dry weather and became muddy banes to the existence of good housekeepers in wet seasons. Nevertheless, urban areas appeared prosperous; their residents dodged both private and public conveyances, adapted to public utilities, and talked of additional civic improvements. Of course, they acknowleged, blighted sections existed in every city, but wasn't the residents' distress their own fault? After all, everyone had an equal opportunity to rise, and there must be something basically wrong with those who did not respond to the incentive.

Chicago exemplified postwar America for it was home to many of the new monied princes of business, despite the fact that their choice of residence forced a commute to financial centers such as Boston, New York, and Philadelphia, and to Washington, D.C., the nation's political core, to secure backing. Luxurious palace cars, placed on the railroads by men like Webster Wagner and George Pullman, made their peregrinations far more comfortable.

Most of the entrepreneurs shared a similar heritage. Nearly all had come from good rural homes, perhaps not overly opulent but certainly far from poverty stricken. Although these men liked to claim that they had pulled themselves out of the mire of indigence by their own perseverance and pluck, they sometimes forgot that others had helped them along the way. When they did acknowledge external aid, they usually pointed to their mothers, whose love, training, and encouragement spurred them on to great deeds.

Unlike his grandfather and father, who had dealt in dollars and hundreds of dollars, the mature businessman of the 1880s talked in terms of thousands, hundreds of thousands, and even millions. He was a man in a hurry; time was money, and the slightest hesitation on his part courted disaster.

The new capitalists competed fiercely with each other, a form of gambling that appealed to men destined to lead their country into the twentieth century. And in an era when money could be lost overnight and a titan be reduced to beggary in a matter of hours, they fought hard to keep their fortunes. As they grew older and more financially secure, a few remembered their employees in an approach that blended acquisition and philanthropy: They believed that a man would appreciate something more if he worked for it rather than if it were simply given to him. "Self-help" was the phrase used to describe the donations these capitalists made, and even then, many were criticized for their softhearted thinking.

Beyond that, the financial leader of the era paid little attention to his employees (unless their actions cost him money) for he rarely interacted with them. The new entrepreneur or industrialist left his great home each day and traveled to his office in a coach or buggy drawn by a pair of matched horses. At noon, he dined with his peers at the most exclusive club he could afford, discussing business affairs or the latest scandal. After the midday meal, he might stroll back to his office and remain there until his driver came to return him to his dwelling. A short time later, he would attend some cultural, social, or charitable function, accompanied by a wife who likely had helped to arrange the event.

Even when he was not running his empire, he did not mingle with or observe "lesser" Americans because he spent his free hours with his family or others in his social class. The servants who waited on these aristocrats worked as unobtrusively as possible so they would not disturb them as they relaxed, conversed, or ate and drank. In fact, they often did their jobs so well that their employers were not even conscious of their presence.

Under the supervision of his wife, the industrialist's residence — actually, many were palaces — operated as efficiently as his business; she gave orders to a corps of skilled maids, governesses, and the other minions that were so essential to their way of existence. Clearly, his luxurious home life was a far cry from what he and most of his cronies had known as children.

As head of the household, he adopted a paternal manner toward both his offspring and his servants, and generally, his approach failed with his children, though it worked with the domestics. Between his business life and his wife's social life, neither parent spent much time with their progeny, who were raised by a succession of governesses and tutors.

The barriers these men created between themselves, their children, and their employees were not intentional; rather, they were a side effect of a way of life. But later, they would find it difficult to understand the rebellion they faced in their homes, a lesser manifestation of what they would encounter at their places of work. Nevertheless, during the early 1880s, wealthy men luxuriated in a world that seemed created for them alone.

Business forced them to travel much of the time, but transportation was vastly better than it had been during their childhood and adolescent years before the Civil War. Thanks to men such as Theodore Woodruff, Wagner, and Pullman, wealthy Americans could travel in comfort that rivaled the accommodations offered by the nation's best hotels. They arrived at their destinations in a matter of days rather than weeks, and they were refreshed, rested, and ready to enter into a day's business, not dirty, exhausted, and sluggish after a night spent on the "cars." Now, too, their wives could accompany them on journeys without the fears and inconveniences that had been their traveling companions prior to the war. Highly successful people could even travel in the complete privacy of a private car they either owned or rented. More and more availed themselves of these conveyances, so that "private varnishes" (as these vehicles were called) truly evolved into marks of prestige in the 1880s.[1] Passengers could hurry from north to south and east to west as though they were in their homes — waited on by their own servants, dining with their own china, crystal, and silver, and sleeping on their own linen. Even their less prosperous contemporaries shared a modicum of such luxury when they traveled in public conveyances. Certainly, all fared better than their parents and grandparents, who had suffered the rigors of stagecoach travel and endured the discomforts of early trains.

George Pullman, a man who understood the benefits of advertising and an early practitioner of the art of public relations, was one of the men responsible for this new mode of travel. Some seven hundred of his cars — including sleepers, diners, parlor cars, and day coaches — ran on the nation's railroads in 1880, and their numbers increased as the decade progressed.[2]

A survivor of the economic vicissitudes of the 1870s, Pullman had a home on Chicago's posh Prairie Avenue and a summer "cottage" at Long Branch, New Jersey; a pretty and talented wife, Harriet, who ranked as a lioness of Chicago's social elite; four children — two girls and twin boys; a fine reputation among business associates and social acquaintances; and a better-than-nodding relationship with Washington nabobs, including several presidents. The Pullmans, for example, stayed at the White House during Grant's terms, and Harriett assisted Grant's wife in the receiving line. Later, in the 1890s, President Benjamin Harrison, impressed by Pullman's sartorial perfection, would ask him the name of his tailor — a high compliment, indeed.

Famous for his railroad cars on this continent (although not overly successful in Europe), Pullman gained further renown when, on Saturday, 2 April 1881, he and fifty guests rode in his private car to the town of Pullman, Illinois, which he had built several miles south of Chicago's Loop. There his daughter, Florence, started the mighty Corliss engine (purchased from the Centennial Exposition at Philadelphia) that signaled the beginning of car manufacturing in the new community. The industrialist had created the suburb for his workers, hoping to provide better living and working conditions and thereby improve their productivity. Consequently, he was hailed as an innovative employer, as well as a practical businessman. Few American men who appeared more typical of their class than George Mortimer Pullman.

Yet all was not easy. Like other financially successful men of his era, Pullman fought constantly to retain his fortune. In the process, he gradually sequestered himself from his employees and learned of their complaints from mid-level supervisors who often were more interested in pleasing him than in conveying any sense of actual conditions. This ultimately increased his ignorance of labor's changing situation and fostered his paternalistic proclivities toward his employees.

A subtle undercurrent throughout this study, although hard to prove, suggests that Pullman's older brother, Albert (who helped him get started and then served as Pullman's Palace Car Company's second vice president), probably acted as George's public relations man in dealing with both employees and the outside world. Had Albert's poor health and subsequent death not forced him to leave the Pullman Company, perhaps his sibling's name might not have been as badly besmirched when his employees launched their famous strike in 1894.

During that crisis, George chose to stand on principle. In this, he much resembled his father. Lewis Pullman had adhered to his Universalist religious beliefs in spite of their unpopularity in New York's heavily revivalistic, evangelical district, and he had been respected for it. To be sure, their situations varied: Lewis Pullman had faced residents in small towns in western New York, whereas George took on the business establishment of a large city and at the national level. When George assumed a rigid attitude in 1894 and refused to deal with employees he no longer knew who had problems he no longer understood, he was adopting an approach that he had used successfully against previous work stoppages.

Actually, Pullman had been unfriendly to labor even in the 1870s, and he had dealt with his workmen through his managers during the 1880s. Then, following the 1886 Haymarket riot, he, together with store owner Marshall Field, meat packer Philip Armour, and reaper manufacturer Cyrus McCormick, Jr., had supported attempts to secure the maximum penalty for the anarchists who led this riot.[3]

Nevertheless, times were changing, and the general misery caused by the 1893 depression forced Americans to alter their opinions of the aging industrialists they had idolized for several decades. As upheavals in the corporations created by these men affected the general populace, not just the founders and their employees, the public saw that these men, once the personification of the American dream, had feet of clay. Chicagoan George C. Sikes believed Pullman workers had chosen a poor time to strike but admitted they possessed a basic right to bargain with their employer through authorized representation. Sikes agreed that Pullman acted within his rights in this affair, but he noted that people blamed him for not yielding when doing so would have done much to diffuse the situation.[4]

Pullman's defenders argued that any softening of his position would have been a poor business tactic: His company would have lost its stockholders' money (a carnal sin at that time) had he bowed to worker desires. They also pointed out that, strict as he was, Pullman nevertheless pitied and sympathized with his men because he himself had been an impoverished worker in his youth (a portrayal that was less than accurate).[5]

Pullman was astonished, hurt, and even shocked to learn that his stern position on the strike gained him the opprobrium of both his suffering workers and his angry peers because each group lost money due to his stubbornness. His refusal immediately after the strike to heed Governor John Peter Altgeld's plea to aid the poverty-stricken workers — many were starving — also tarnished his reputation.[6] The man many Americans had hailed, perhaps mistakenly, as a friend of labor, had now become an ogre.

Once fallen from grace, Pullman was among the first industrialists to be attacked by reformers. He was particularly vulnerable because his personal life-style and the town he created had been highly publicized. In addition, the service his company provided was used by many citizens — individuals who were directly inconvenienced when this service and railroad facilities in general were halted because of the strike. Suddenly he and others who had risen to affluence and power during the 1870s and 1880s learned they were not beyond criticism, and they were at a loss to explain why the world they had created during those decades had begun to collapse as the turn of the century approached. Wiser members of this group — men such as Andrew Carnegie, the steel magnate, and John D. Rockefeller, the oil baron — stepped aside, although they did not relinquish all power, as new management was replacing the individual heads of corporations who had lost control of their behemoth creations. The new directors, whether they liked it or not, soon had to acknowledge the efforts of labor, even though workmen still faced many years of heartbreaking struggle before they received full boardroom recognition for their contributions.

Pullman was deeply affected by the strike. But his bitterness and distress over what he considered the ingratitude of his workers and the lack of understanding displayed by fellow citizens gradually diminished as he struggled to maintain his company's position of leadership in the field. Publicly, he remained self-assured, self-satisfied, cold, calm, and correct — a prime example of the Victorian gentleman, who served his community as a board member of numerous public charities and institutions. He did, however, heed a few of the strike's warnings: He stopped seeking the limelight and relinquished more power to his subordinates. He began to consider taking life easier, and, in the end, he appeared to make a genuine effort to be more pleasant company. Certainly, the strike marked him, but its lessons came too late for him to change his image to any great extent.

Known for his short temper and irritability, he treated his family — when he took time to be with them — to periodic fits of fury; later, he would try to atone by being very attentive and overindulgent. But there were two people who seldom witnessed his anger: his mother, whom he adored and upon whom he lavished every imaginable luxury, and his eldest daughter, Florence, unquestionably his favorite child. Florence could humanize him in a moment's time and return him to good humor after one of his fits of pique.

George Pullman was kind to his wife, whom he loved and spoiled. But over the years, Hattie Pullman grew more concerned about her health, spending much of her husband's money at spas, health resorts, and sanatoria as she, like many women of her class with few diversions, fruitlessly passed her time trying to regain her health. Hattie's illnesses, which included colds, headaches, rheumatism, and general disability, may have been caused by too tight corsets, too much rich food, and too little exercise, all aggravated by excessive nervousness. The latter malaise was likely due in part to her husband's quick temper. At the same time, his protective attitude that shielded her from unpleasantries and his financial affluence that released her from most worries connected with housekeeping and child-rearing left her with too much time to think about herself. Whatever their origins, her ailments (both real and imagined) forced the Pullmans to spend much of the time apart, although they filled their correspondence with expressions of deep and undying love.

Did their often lengthy periods apart lead George, a healthy and active man, to keep a mistress or engage in occasional extramarital liaisons, as many of his contemporaries reputedly had? Such activities are, of course, difficult to substantiate, especially because American Victorians, like their English cousins, kept their bedroom doors tightly closed. But for all his irascibility, Pullman loved and respected his family, and if he did engage in such relationships, he kept them very quiet. Occasionally, Hattie's diaries and letters intimated that he may have had an affair, but she never accused him directly. Moreover, a man who stayed as busy and complained as much about overwork and fatigue as Pullman did would not have had much time or energy for such pastimes.

The Pullmans' younger children — Harriet, George, Jr., and Walter Sanger — added a great deal of worry to their parents' lives. The twins, Georgie and Sanger, particularly disappointed their father and frustrated their mother as they grew to manhood. This might not have been the case had Pullman been willing to tear himself from his business and spend time with them. But he did not, and with their mother overly preoccupied with her health and raising her daughters, the boys grew into troubled men. Ultimately, their spendthrift habits earned them their father's displeasure and a mere pittance in his will. In this, Pullman differed from other men of his class, who were generally more tolerant of their grown sons.

George Pullman emerges, then, as a prominent figure whose financial success was due, in his opinion, to his own efforts; he seldom, if ever, credited anyone with assistance. His attempts to expand his business in England and Europe were less successful, due perhaps to his inflexibility that, in time, did much to deface the successful image he had created for himself in the United States. Toward the end of his life, other men expressed respect for him publicly, but this may not have been the case privately.

Pullman's money bought him a lavish life and permitted him to remove himself and his family from unpleasant scenes like strikes. It also gained him public admiration for two-and-a-half decades. But he never achieved the universal esteem he would have enjoyed. Pullman understood public relations when it came to selling his products, but he never learned to apply such techniques on a personal level; as a successful businessman who headed a large company, he was above such matters. Nevertheless, as he grew older, he, like other public figures, sought to change his image through publicizing his charitable endeavors. He died before he truly succeeded.

Thus, George M. Pullman exemplified the prosperous, self-made man in the American business milieu of his era. In fact, he was so much a part of it that he did not survive. Plagued by angina pectoris that was aggravated by overwork, a habit he was only starting to overcome, he passed from the scene just as the world he had helped create was giving way to an age of reform. In a sense, he had been a pioneer of the new epoch when he sought to improve his employees' living conditions by building the company town of Pullman; however, his earlier successes were overshadowed by the 1894 strike that exposed his true philosophy concerning labor and tarnished his reputation, just as it aged and embittered him. Although the incident forced him to reassess his life and fostered his attempts to change aspects of his way of operating, it occurred too late. As a consequence, later generations came to associate his name not only with luxurious travel accommodations but with industrial tyranny.

1

The Family of Lewis and Emily Pullman

George Mortimer Pullman was born on 3 March 1831, in what is now known as Brocton, New York, outside of Buffalo. He was the third child and third son of James Lewis and Emily Caroline (Minton) Pullman. His father's ancestors settled in America during the late 1620s or 1630s when an English mariner named Joseph Pulman moved to the area that became York, Maine. Gradually, his descendants left there, going first to Boston (where the family name acquired the second *l*) and then, in the early eighteenth century, to Rhode Island. Most of these early Pullmans were farmers who doubtless embraced the faith or at least a variation on the beliefs of their Puritan ancestors.

The wanderlust did not forsake the Pullman family after they arrived in Rhode Island; Psalter Pullman (born 1760) and his wife, Elizabeth (born 1780), left their home in West Greenwich for a farm in Onondaga County, New York. Their son, James Lewis (born 26 July 1800), accompanied them to New York.[1]

James Lewis Pullman (or Lewis, as he was commonly called) was a sturdily built young man. He turned from farming to carpentry and by 1825 had moved westward to the next county, where he established himself in the community of Auburn, New

York. There, on 4 September 1825, he married Emily Caroline Minton, a slender, dark-haired woman born 14 August 1808, the eldest daughter of James and Theodosia (Reeve) Minton. The couple and their first two children, Royal Henry (born 30 June 1826) and Albert Benton (born 16 October 1828) remained in Auburn for several years. In January 1830, the family moved to an area immediately south of Buffalo, close to Lake Erie, known first as the Corners, next as Salem Cross Roads, and finally as Brocton, New York.[2] There, land could be had that would give "healthful exercise and profitable employment to a growing family of somewhat vigorous boys." In 1831, Lewis Pullman purchased a parcel of land known as Budlong farm and built a small frame house, where Emily soon presented him with a round-faced baby they named George Mortimer.[3]

When the Pullmans decided to move closer to Lake Erie, times were prosperous in that section of New York. The principal reason for the region's growth was the South's increasing demand for food, which encouraged westward expansion to virgin farmlands and higher prices for goods. Prospective settlers also required sustenance and other necessities of life that called for better transportation facilities. This meant that existing waterways had to be made more navigable and that new ones had to be built. And as a result, new communities developed along their courses, together with requisite warehouse and residential facilities.[4] All this made the area a bonanza for skilled workers like Lewis Pullman.

The great commercial catalyst in western New York was the Erie Canal. Completed in 1825, at a cost to the state of $7 million, it stretched 363 miles between Albany and Buffalo. The new waterway stimulated the growth of many new settlements along its route, and it contributed to an increase in the size of existing cities, such as Buffalo and New York City. During the years from 1830 to 1850, it became a popular artery for passenger and freight traffic between the northeastern states and the new western commonwealths and territories. As unsettled New Englanders and Middle States residents left their native regions to find better farmland in the West, they chose the Ohio country or the old northwest. The Erie Canal deflected immigrants from the Ohio Valley to the Great Lakes by providing cheaper, safer, and more comfortable transportation that also reduced both freight costs and shipping time.[5] Certainly, its completion and subsequent popularity did much to dispel the lingering effects of the depression brought on by the panic of 1819.

The 1830s would witness increased commercial activity throughout the country, and the Pullmans were an optimistic young couple willing to take their chances in a new home farther west. A thrifty man, Lewis probably chose the area immediately south of Buffalo for several reasons. First, Buffalo was growing, which meant that work was readily available. Second, land was cheaper beyond the city limits and less expensive than real estate along the Erie Canal; for once the great conduit passed through a region, farms situated beside it doubled and quadrupled in value.[6] Yet, such land would be close enough to the waterway to enable Pullman to profit from the prosperity the canal was creating in that area.

Lewis Pullman's skills as a carpenter entitled him to command top wages of $3 per day, a tidy sum for an ambitious worker in those times. Unquestionably, he stayed busy, for Americans were obsessed by a sense of urgency — a need to get things done in a hurry — that was reinforced by a desire to do their projects well. A man's diligence indicated his worth, and the rewards for his efforts were reflected in his material wealth. That, in turn, determined his social standing. In addition to carpentry, Lewis began moving buildings, a business that often kept him away from home. Nevertheless, the craftsman-entrepreneur found time to grow wheat, corn, and potatoes, while Emily cultivated daffodils, geraniums, and roses. A creek flowed through their property, which also possessed a sulphur spring, and the family owned hogs, a couple of horses, and a "brood of hens with only one old rooster."[7]

Here, George and his brothers spent their early years, during which all of the boys were healthy and encountered their share of mishaps and close calls. On one occasion, the lively young George was saved from an old, angry sow only through the intervention of his uncle James Minton. George's older brother Henry watched over him and saw to it that he had strawberries in season; Henry also absorbed several "lickings" for his younger brother "as father had to trounce around once in a while to strengthen the home government." At Christmas time, the children hung their stockings

George Pullman's early childhood home in Brocton, New York. *Courtesy Charles M. Knoll.*

by the fireplace with a two-tined, bone-handled iron fork and were delightfully happy.[8]

Lewis Pullman was raised a Baptist, and Emily was a Presbyterian. Shortly after their marriage, however, Lewis, who inherited intense religious beliefs from his parents, attended a revival meeting where, for the first time, he gave serious consideration to the preacher's doctrines. "He was horrified by these awful descriptions of the wrath of God. Every night men, women and children shrieked in terror and cried out in wild and piteous pleadings to be saved from the burning fires of hell. This was the approved way in those days to make Christians." He turned away in disgust; "Something within him . . . whispered of a better God, a fairer justice, a sweeter mercy, a stronger love and a brighter hope." Thereafter, he stayed away from church and became known as a Universalist. Members of his Baptist sect attempted to boycott him, but they were unsuccessful because others shared his feelings. Such folk included his parents, Elizabeth and Psalter Pullman, who forsook the Baptist creed for that of Mormonism.

14

Lewis Pullman continued to read his Bible and to be a negative Universalist, one who followed no systematic religion. He and his wife taught their children certain object lessons regarding beauty and strength. For them, lying was one of the world's most hateful acts, so they instructed their children to be honest and instilled habits of frugality, thrift, and industry. They kept the Sabbath and used those hours to educate their children.[9] Thus, although they were unorthodox, the Pullmans remained practicing Christians.

A Universalist church had been organized at Portland, New York, in 1821 and incorporated by 1824 as the First Universalist Society in Portland. But after several years, its membership had declined. Attempts to reactivate it were made from time to time, and as the older Pullman boys grew into their teens, a Universalist evangelist, the Reverend Timothy C. Eaton, began missionary work in the Pullman's neighborhood. He established regular monthly meetings, and many who had quarreled with the more orthodox religions were drawn to his preaching of "God is love" and universal salvation. Lewis Pullman was among those who joined the newly created First Universalist Church of Portland. By common consent, he became the group's leader on Sundays when there was no preacher. His children received formal religious education through the Church: On many Sunday mornings, Lewis Pullman, Bible in hand, led his boys to Sunday School. He also offered prayers in the home as the family knelt about the fire at bedtime; these evening services through the years were considered by the Pullman offspring as some of their most precious memories of childhood. Years later, Henry, by then a Universalist minister, fondly recalled "the old red school house and the people who gathered for Conference and Praise Meetings — Grandma's placid face, Uncle James leading the singing, and Bill Jackson by his side. Aunt Maria and mother with their sweet soprano voices, and then father leading the meeting."[10]

Lewis continued to work as a carpenter and to move buildings. About 1835, he invented a machine for transporting buildings upon wheels, which proved eminently practical for many years thereafter, and in 1841 he secured a patent for his invention. His sons were absorbed in their father's teachings and, following his example, took pride in showing their well-done work to their father

15

upon his return from his buildings operations.[11]

Lewis and Emily had five other children in this period: Frances Carolan (born 2 July 1833; died 16 October 1834); James Minton (born 21 August 1835); William Eaton (born 2 May 1837; died 16 October 1839); Charles Lewis (born 24 April 1841); and Helen Augusta (born 11 May 1843). The older boys completed their education in the local schools and went into business as partners in Salem Cross Roads. George attended Mr. Corell's school, where he completed the fourth grade; then in the spring of 1845, he left education behind to take a position in Buck and Minton's General Store in Westfield, at a salary of $40 per year. His uncle, John H. Minton, was one of the proprietors, along with Edwin Buck. George performed well from the beginning and pleased his uncle by his hard work.[12]

For several years, Lewis Pullman's trade frequently took him away from home for long periods. Because many of his contracts were located along the Erie Canal, the town of Albion, fifty-nine miles east of Buffalo along the east-west artery's south bank (the north side was occupied by the tow path) seemed a better place to locate. It boasted numerous warehouses and grocery stores, all designed and stocked to supply the many canal boat passengers and boatmen who patronized them day and night. In addition, there were countless small variety stores with every item imaginable and a flour mill and two sawmills. Albion also stood on a main overland highway, the Oak Orchard Road, which ran north and south through the town's boundaries just as the canal ran east and west. The village's status as the seat of Orleans County attracted a larger and more varied assortment of dwellers who energetically followed an array of callings, making it attractive to an industrious man seeking a central location for his business as he supported a growing family.[13]

Emily was willing to make the move to Albion, but there were several questions she wanted answered before taking the step. Was the place healthy? Was the water pure? Did Lewis have a residence in mind to buy? She hoped for positive responses to such queries because she preferred a permanent home to frequent moves. She soon told Lewis that if he would send her some money, she would be happy to go look the town over. Apparently, all her questions were answered satisfactorily for the family moved there in the early fall of 1845; Emily insisted on being settled before cold weather set in.[14]

Henry and Albert remained in Salem Cross Roads, where they had enough work to keep them busy all winter, and George continued to work at Buck and Minton's store in Westfield. He sounded a bit homesick when he described his life at Westfield in a letter to his parents. Noting that he sawed all the wood for two fires where he boarded and performed a similar task at his uncle's store, in addition to all his other chores, he told them that so much work was more than he could "stand comfortably" and that shortly he would bolt. Many years later, Henry recalled that another of George's chores at the store was to water the stock in the liquor barrels. During the winter when business was slack, young Pullman, like many clerks his age, probably used the time to read books sold by the store or labored to improve his penmanship (which became very legible), thus supplementing his somewhat meager formal education. Occasionally, he would spend a Sunday with Henry and his wife, Harriet, in Westfield, interludes Henry later remembered as being exceedingly pleasant.[15]

George remained with his uncle's general store for three years, gaining a good knowledge of contemporary merchandizing procedures. Finally finding such work unsuited to his purposes, he rejoined the family in Albion by early January 1848.[16] Meanwhile, Henry and Albert also moved to Albion and started a cabinetmaking shop, which interested the whole family. (George had become an apprentice cabinetmaker himself, which may have been one of the reasons he returned to the family circle.) Unfortunately, Henry developed an allergy that affected his eyes and kept him from his work in the shop for several months. During his illness, Lewis and his boys (probably Albert, George, and James), together with six other men, worked in the shop from six in the morning until nine at night. Three of the additional helpers boarded at the local tavern, and the remaining three lived with the Pullmans (a far from customary arrangement, but not unusual), making a household of eleven. This created extra burdens for

George Pullman's childhood home in Albion, New York. *Courtesy Charles M. Knoll.*

Emily Pullman, who attempted to get by with a "cheap girl." But sewing and knitting fell so far behind that she eventually decided to hire a girl who could do all the housework while she herself sewed. They employed an Irish girl who, after a fortnight, not only did all the housework but also helped Emily with her handiwork.

Because of unusually bad traveling weather, the winter of 1847–1848 proved rather dull for the family in Albion. Fewer people visited the Pullman shop to buy furniture, and the ware-room became filled with their products.[17] But the following October, George wrote his maternal grandmother that, though times were tough, business was good enough to enable them to build a hundred-foot addition to their shop and to think about hiring twelve to fifteen hands; if nothing went wrong, he said, they could make some money. He added that Albert did piecework and boarded with Henry, while his wife earned $3 or $4 per week making caps.[18]

The move to Albion brought increased prosperity for the Pullmans and an enlargement of the family, with Emily "Emma"

Caroline (born 25 September 1846) and Frank William (born 11 May 1848). Lewis Pullman continued his work as a carpenter and house-mover, assisted by his sons in the latter endeavor, and labored in the family cabinet shop during the winter months when bad weather prevented him from following his own trades. He became interested in local politics and served two terms on the board of trustees of Albion Village in 1849 and 1852. A regular Democrat, he kept informed about political matters in his former home in Chautauqua County. In 1848, he and others who shared his political philosophy were "about to commence raising *Hickory Poles*" during the elections that fall.[19]

Pullman chair manufactured in Albion, New York. *Courtesy Harriet G. Frohberg.*

In spite of popularity in the community, the Pullmans still espoused the Universalist creed and suffered for it because Universalism was despised by more orthodox Calvinists and evangelists who did their best to discredit the sect and its members. Basically, Universalists believed that all mankind would eventually be saved and that no one would be condemned to eternal punishment for earthly misdeeds. After death, those who had strayed from the path of righteousness might be disciplined for a period of time, but sooner or later, God would extend them forgiveness and eternal salvation. This was a welcome doctrine, indeed, to men like Lewis Pullman, distressed as they were by the canting of evangelistic western New York Baptist preachers who concentrated on man's depravity as they terrorized their congregations with images of the horrors of God's wrath. Universalists also supported many reform movements of the period, but their moderation did not endear them to more militant advocates of causes such as abolition and temperance. And though Universalism attracted increasing numbers during the 1830s and 1840s, its followers continued to be regarded as odd by more conservative neighbors.[20] Nonetheless, Lewis Pullman's family endured these trials and occasionally joined other Universalists for services in the local courthouse or in members' homes, and the children, even those who were nearly adults, became more interested in the sect's philosophy. Forty years later, Henry Pullman recalled the services held in the old court house: He remembered that when Lewis Pullman was deeply moved by a service, his countenance "shone with an almost divine radiance" and that Emily Pullman's "heart was always in her songs of praise."[21]

Universalism continued to attract followers throughout the nineteenth century, and by 1888, it was said to be the sixth largest denomination in the United States. Among those who preached its doctrines were Henry and James Pullman, both of whom became doctors of divinity and Universalist ministers. Henry served as pastor of the Second Universalist Church in Baltimore, Maryland, and James held a like office for the First Universalist Church at Lynn, Massachusetts.[22]

Though Lewis Pullman was a member of both the International Order of Odd Fellows and the Renovation Lodge A.F. and A.M., he spent many evenings at home with his family. On these occasions, Henry, his wife, Harriet, and their baby would stop by, followed shortly by Albert and Emily, his wife, and then George, like as not in a dither over some project. Their father might greet them with his youngest child, Frank, in his arms. During these gatherings, the men probably discussed business conditions and politics, while the women recounted the latest exploits of the younger Pullmans, swapped recipes, and compared notes on happenings in Albion. As the evening's visit drew to a close, all likely joined together for a few moments of prayer before departing.

By this time, James had begun work in the local printing office. But after 1850, the family began to separate, probably due to slow times in the cabinet shop. Albert and Emily moved to Grand Rapids, Michigan, to become established in furniture manufacturing. James joined Albert in August 1852, so two of the sons left the family circle.[23]

In the fall of 1852, Lewis began making additions to the home, and by late November, he had completed the front yard and fence, built hall stairs, finished five chambers, and lathed and plastered the downstairs hall and bedroom. He wrote to his mother-in-law, Theodosia Minton, to invite her to visit them, noting that "we have all things fixed up to make you comfortable." All she had to do was take the railroad cars from Salem Cross Roads to Albion and then direct the driver of a waiting carriage to their home. He further informed her that business had been much better than he had anticipated — sales had been great, profits fair — and that the boys (Henry and George) had rented an adjoining shop to the north and filled it with chairs.

Emily wrote that the remodeling had thrown her behind in her sewing and that she did not see how she would get to the bottom of her basket. Frank was standing beside her as she wrote, she said, Helen was at seminary, and Emma and Charley were at district school. George had just returned from New York, and Henry and his family were well. Reports from Grand Rapids stated that all were in good health, and "if life and health are spared," she and Lewis planned to travel there the following summer.[24] In this and other correspondence, she and her husband reflected their middle-class prosperity and their keen interest in their numerous offspring.

Over the years, Lewis Pullman concentrated increasingly on his building-moving business. From time to time, he received assistance from his three older sons, although it became more and more obvious that George was the one following in his father's footsteps. He was the firm's "trouble man," and during working hours, his muddy garments distinguished him. However, once work

The Lewis Pullman family, from a daguerreotype probably taken about 1850. Top row, left to right: Albert, Henry, and James; middle row: Charles, James Lewis Pullman, Emily Caroline Pullman, and George; bottom row: Frank, Emma, and Helen. *Courtesy the Chicago Historical Society.*

ended, he cleaned up, put on stylish clothes, and "promenaded in all his glory, with high top hat and longtailed coat."[25]

Then, one evening in December 1852, Lewis Pullman was stricken by apoplexy. The seizure at first seemed fatal, but Lewis, a strong man, rallied, though he was never again his formerly active self. He lived very quietly until 1 November 1853, when he died peacefully, whispering to those of the family who were at his bedside, "I am not going far away; I will always be near and be in waiting for you."[26]

Both Pullmans must have attributed their material success to their Universalism. Although dissenting Christians, they believed their faith was the object as well as the foundation of their way of life, a view they held in common with most of their contemporaries, and they imbued their children with such doctrine. As noted earlier, two of the older sons, Henry and James, became Universalist ministers, and Albert remained a devout layman throughout his life. The other children, including George, followed Universalism's precepts less enthusiastically, but religion was never too far from the surface throughout their lives. Thus, if one reviews the general characteristics of middle-class Americans during the 1830s and 1840s, Emily and Lewis Pullman certainly fitted the mold quite well.[27]

In their time, American commerce was humming. It had emerged from its post-1837 economic doldrums during the second half of the 1840s and continued to be vigorous into the first years of the 1850s. The impetus came as the United States opened new areas to exploitation and settlement by rounding out its western and southwestern boundaries through conquest and purchase. Territorial expansion led New Englanders to step up their output of manufactured goods — goods that were readily absorbed by westerners, who responded by sending gold and agricultural produce to the northeast. This interaction established even greater bonds between the two sections and swelled the flow of traffic over the Erie Canal.[28] However, the good times stemming from its augmented use were only temporary since railroads were beginning to make an impact in the area. This new form of transportation, unlike waterways, could run just about anywhere and was not hampered by the droughts or freezes that could delay or even halt canal and river transit.

By 1850, several small independent railroads known collectively as the Central Line provided rail service between Albany and Buffalo, paralleling the big canal. Their freight-carrying capacities were limited by the New York legislature so the separate little lines depended upon passenger traffic and ran commuter-like trains between small towns, all the while publicizing their none-too-efficient express service between Albany and Buffalo. They finally merged as the New York Central in 1853, becoming a potential rival for the great route of humanity and goods, the Erie Canal.[29]

In 1853, Henry was ordained a Universalist minister, and Albert, the skilled cabinetmaker in the family, was still struggling to establish himself in Grand Rapids, Michigan. Both men were married and raising families. James, a bright young lad of seventeen, entered Albion Academy in preparation for college and then followed Henry into the Universalist ministry. Helen, Charles, Emma, and Frank were too small to fend for themselves, and their mother was busy caring for them. Thus, when Lewis Pullman died, twenty-two-year-old George, the eldest unmarried son, seemed the logical person to support the family, a responsibility he was quite willing to assume.[30]

Lewis Pullman had been a good provider, but the size of his family prevented any substantial accumulation of great wealth; his legacy was little more that some real estate and his contracting business. The cabinet shop, hardly a flourishing concern, did not generate enough profit to clothe and feed two adults and several growing children, and George was not a craftsman; indeed, he found it difficult to work with his hands. Beyond that, the state of New York had obtained funds from a sympathetic legislature to continue its off-and-on project to widen the Erie Canal,[31] which could provide new opportunities for building-movers. Therefore, after long discussions with his mother, whose judgment he valued, George decided to abandon the furniture-making business. He soon took over his father's moving firm, which he had managed and expanded since the onset of Lewis Pullman's final illness.

Shortly afterward, in 1854, George Pullman contracted with the State of New York to move twenty or more buildings, mainly warehouses, back from the new right-of-way along the Erie Canal in the vicinity of Albion. He obtained some financial backing from Noah Davis, a fellow Albion resident, and entered into partnership with yet another Albionite, Charles Henry Moore. Young Pullman's dedication to his work impressed his fellow citizens, one of whom, writing many years later, recalled that when the rollers under a warehouse jammed, George, unmindful of his clothes, promptly dived into the ankle-deep mud under the structure. Next, he would squirm into the cramped underspace armed with a bar and attack the recalcitrant roller or the projecting beam, all the while directing those who wound the hauling capstans to "check'er," "stop'er," or "go ahead" until the building moved freely.[32]

He employed anywhere from six to a dozen men for a six-day week and, by 1858, paid them $1.00 to $1.25 per day. His

George M. Pullman, from a daguerreotype taken in 1857. *Courtesy the Chicago Historical Society.*

contract lasted three or four years, and he made several thousand dollars (one account placed the exact amount at $5,700). He supported the family but realized his work for New York eventually would run out; therefore by 1857, as another depression settled in, he journeyed as far away as Chicago in search of new projects.[33]

25

Finally, in early January 1859, Pullman learned of additional opportunities in Chicago through Mrs. Joel A. Matteson, wife of the proprietor of the Matteson House in Chicago. She and her daughters had visited Albion and, in the normal course of social events, became acquainted with the young building-mover. She soon mentioned a project to raise portions of Chicago's business district by eight feet in order to build a sewage system.[34]

George Pullman traveled to Chicago before the end of the month. While waiting for some business papers, he spent his leisure time attending *Uncle Tom's Cabin*, visiting family friends, and traveling to and from Harvard, Illinois, where he called on his maternal aunt and her husband, Mr. and Mrs. Richard R.W. DaLee. He also made side trips to Galena, Illinois, and to Milwaukee, Fond du Lac, Racine, and Whitewater, Wisconsin, using Chicago as his base of operations.[35]

George spent two days in Grand Rapids, Michigan, with Albert and his family, whom he found in rather straitened circumstances. He also dickered for some property in Grand Rapids (close to Albert's) that would make a pleasant home for his mother, who was giving some thought to moving there.[36]

He returned to Albion and, on 20 February 1859, wrote his mother that he was leaving for Chicago the following day "on urgent business connected with a contract for raising the Matteson House, which I am endeavoring to secure." If he obtained the job, it would insure the permanence of his business and permit him, once again, to establish a comfortable home for his mother and siblings. He was not sure he would be awarded the contract, but, certain it was worth the effort, he arranged to have one thousand screws (screw jacks) shipped to Chicago if he secured the work. If unsuccessful, he told his mother, he would be home in about ten days.[37]

George Pullman did win the contract to raise the Matteson House, one of Chicago's better-known hotels.[38] In short order, he journeyed homeward by rail from Chicago to arrange for his transfer to that mud-saturated young city growing rapidly along the western shore of Lake Michigan.

On the eve of his departure for Chicago, George Pullman was nearly twenty-nine years old. The product of a middle-class home, he inherited that class's love of status and its virtues. He also felt a great sense of responsibility toward his younger siblings and was their chief means of support. Just as he had striven to please his father, he would continue to honor his memory. However, like many young men of his generation, he adored his mother and remained dependent on her advice and strength, cherishing her presence and support for most of the remainder of his life. Outwardly, he followed the religious precepts his parents had instilled in him: He was a regular church attendant and an honest, hardworking man who stuck to the job, fulfilling his contracts rapidly and well. George Pullman appreciated the nicer things in life — nice clothing, good food, and cultural offerings — that were the product of individual efforts. And he had earned the respect of the community by his dedication to business. Though he had not inherited his father's ability to work with his hands, at least he had performed manual labor and understood its problems. He did inherit his mother's practicality, and this was reinforced by his creative and strong-principled mind, business sense (a trait of his prosperous maternal uncles, as well), ambition, energy, and imagination. His formal education, coupled with his experience as a shop clerk, craftsman, business traveler, and building-mover, equipped him to pursue a commercial career, and through his assumption of Lewis Pullman's established business he gained much-needed expertise in management. A budding entrepreneur, he could raise money, manage it, and use it. Self-confident, he was also a good salesman who was accustomed to dealing with people seeking his expertise both in his native region and beyond.

Undoubtedly, he sensed that his future did not lie along the Erie Canal. A young man as alert and ambitious as he was would have observed the potential of railroads even as he labored to move buildings back from the waterway's banks. The depression probably lent urgency to his decision to leave the area. Thus, like many of his contemporaries, he left his roots in small town, antebellum America. He was ready to pursue his fortune in the burgeoning midwestern city of Chicago.

2

Early Chicago Enterprises

The *Chicago Press and Tribune* on 28 February 1859 announced the contract to raise the five-story, brick Matteson House, located at 97 Randolph on the northwest corner of Randolph and Dearborn streets — the largest building elevated up to that time. The block on which it stood was reputedly the city's most valuable, bounded by Randolph, Clark, Lake, and Dearborn streets. Its frontage of eighty feet on Randolph and ninety feet on Dearborn made the hostel's ground floor a prime business space, and its management rented to stores on both thoroughfares. Erected at a cost of $20,000 and opened in August 1851, the Matteson House was considered second only to the city's famed Tremont House.

S. B. Cobb, executor and manager of the Matteson estate, dealt with the contractors who would raise this building — Pullman and Moore. The project was to be completed within forty-eight days. The hotel, to be raised five feet or more to street grade, would then be painted and prepared for the spring travel season. Slightly more than a month later, well ahead of schedule, the first turn had been made upon the eight hundred screw jacks under the Matteson House, and after ten days, on 3 April, the structure stood completely raised. Reports stated that within a week, piers would be placed under it and the basement finished.[1]

Chicago was one of America's most dynamic cities. Founded in the late 1820s, its rapid growth began during the years following the Mexican War. The Illinois and Michigan Canal and the Illinois River gave the community a continuous waterway to the Mississippi and strengthened commercial ties with St. Louis.[2] A variety of grains and southern produce were transported to Chicago via the canal, as were the passengers, lumber, hardware, groceries, and clothing destined for communities south of Chicago. But though it contributed greatly to the city's bustling economy and growth, it (like other water routes in the 1850s) faced the ever-increasing threat of railroads like the Galena and Chicago Union, the Illinois Central, and the Chicago, Burlington and Quincy — all of which had begun to make inroads on its business. Nevertheless, these transportation facilities, together with their extensions, helped to make Chicago the commercial center of the region and gave it an aura reminiscent of the area where George Pullman had grown to manhood.

By 1854, the town had become a huge grain reception point that supported speculators and others engaged in warehousing and processing grain and financing its shipments. This also stimulated other enterprises and commodities, including milling, distilling, brewing, cattle, and hogs. Grain speculation peaked when England and France went to war with Russia in the Crimean War (1853–1856) but dropped shortly afterward because of the panic of 1857. It rose again briefly during 1859, only to subside until the outbreak of the Civil War.[3]

The financial crisis of 1857 served as a dividing point between the post–Mexican War boom years and those that commenced with the outbreak of the Civil War. Nationally, between 1846 and 1854, times were prosperous as both domestic and foreign capital financed an unprecedented growth through industrial construction, railroad development, and land speculation. Gold discoveries in California, the completion of railroad lines from the East to Chicago, a resurgence in cotton prices in the South, and a tremendous growth in northeastern manufacturing made the years between 1849 and 1854 a high point of economic expansion in the nineteenth century. But the boom ended in the United States during 1854, although a major financial debacle was staved off until England's postwar depression in 1857 adversely affected this country.[4]

The three-year period that followed the panic of 1857 was not one of booming expansion in any section of the country.[5] The slackening of business was very serious in the West, a region plagued by low wheat prices, poor crops, and declines in land sales, coupled with a slowing in western migration and in railroad construction and a decrease of eastern and foreign cash flow.

Chicagoans felt the pinch by the summer of 1857, when money became scarce and loans were difficult to obtain. Bank runs and failures among lumber and wholesale dealers began in the fall. As autumn gave way to winter and then to spring, more and more workers were laid off as the city vainly attempted to institute relief measures. Many of the unemployed left the city, and those who remained did so under very straitened circumstances, for wages continued to be low in Chicago until 1860. The exodus left many residences and stores empty, which not only reduced rent income but impoverished property owners.[6]

Hard times devastated the land boom in Chicago's business district in 1857, and things worsened over the next two years when owners could no longer make the required time payments on their buildings and real estate. Building construction stopped immediately, and several commercial structures remained unfinished for several years. Nevertheless, a contemporary report stated that the panic only "staggered" Chicago: Its businessmen supported each other, so that while some lost money, only a few failed completely. By December 1858, several of its banks had survived the two critical years, although 204 businesses had gone to the wall during 1857–1858. On the positive side, the slack period gave Chicagoans an opportunity to take stock of their rapidly growing community and to attempt improvements where needed, which included raising their city's street grades.[7]

Even during the boom period, Chicago arteries had been an ongoing source of complaint because of their muddiness, which often rendered them nearly impassible. In 1855 and 1857 the city council adopted plans to drain the thoroughfares and raise their grades. Thus, in 1859 and 1860, laborers were hard at work filling roadways with mud and sand, digging sewers, and laying gas and water pipe. As streets went up, buildings and sidewalks also rose out of the mud, thanks to contractors like Pullman and Moore.[8]

Although he went to Chicago to raise buildings, Pullman took on any contract that paid. He soon discovered that the community's residents were leaving its business district to move south, many actually transporting their wooden residences from sites on which they planned to erect brick business blocks. Chicago movers performed their work slowly to prevent damaging the house interiors, but Pullman soon developed a faster procedure, using skids to slide the structures along the ground. As a result, homes arrived at their destinations more rapidly, their interiors intact.

In part because he handled the big contracts personally, Pullman's business prospered. Before long, he had earned a reputation as a hard worker among his new neighbors; when they approached him about a job, he would take a couple of minutes to calculate its cost and then arrive at a figure "done to a nicety." They also appreciated his constant efforts to improve and system-atize operations and insure that all ran smoothly.[9]

But his primary occupation remained building-raising, and in May, Pullman and Moore elevated the Democratic Building, named for the influential city newspaper within its walls. After that came Jackson Hall and the New York House (227 Randolph). By the end of summer, Pullman and Moore felt well enough established to inform Chicagoans that hoisting brick structures was their specialty; their offices were now located at 200 Washington.[10]

At the outset of 1860, Pullman and Moore bought the build-ing-raising concern of Samuel B. and Charles S. Abbott, probably because lifting structures continued to be a popular enterprise during the early part of that year. And the firm of Pullman and Moore secured a good portion of that business, including J. H. Dunham's brick store on the corner of south Water and Dearborn streets, along with three brick stores on Wells Street, between Lake and the alley, that belonged to P. and J. Casey and Edward Taylor. Such an auspicious beginning brought contracts in at a great rate, and George was forced to call in his brother Albert at the end of

February.[11] Albert was no doubt glad to join George for his Grand Rapids venture had not been overly successful. By the middle of March, Pullman also brought in his partner, Charles H. Moore, to furnish help.[12]

At the end of that month, Pullman and Moore, along with two other firms — Brown and Hollingsworth, and Ely and Smith — undertook a job that involved lifting an entire block of buildings, weighing an estimated 35,000 tons and measuring 320 linear feet. Each partnership contracted to raise a different section: Ely and Smith would lift the east 140 feet, Pullman and Moore the west 100 feet (for $3,100), and Brown and Hollingsworth the remaining 80 feet. Working jointly, the firms would accomplish the biggest undertaking of its kind ever attempted in Chicago, at a total cost of about $17,000. The architectural firm of Carter and Bauer superintended the project, slated to raise the block four feet in about four weeks. Located on the north side of Lake Street (Chicago's business thoroughfare) between Clark and LaSalle streets, the block housed a number of the city's best stores at street level, as well as the Marine Bank; the upper floors accommodated offices, bookbinderies, printing shops, manufacturers, and other businesses. The job was done expertly, to the delight of the many people who watched. And not only did they observe, they bought; tradesmen in the block reported increased sales while their structures were lifted. Once the preliminaries were completed, six hundred men turning six thousand screw jacks lifted the block four feet and eight inches in five days. Naturally very proud of their work, the three firms decided to commission artist Edward Mendel, of 162 Lake Street, to execute a lithograph of the undertaking. Copies were soon available at McNally's on Dearborn Street, opposite the post office. During April, Pullman and Moore once again joined forces with Brown and Hollingsworth to lift a row of eight, four-story brick stores immediately across the street from their greatest endeavor.[13]

Contemporary accounts and reminiscences relate that Pullman and Moore followed a fairly standard raising procedure. After signing the contract to elevate a structure, workmen dug near the existing foundation and cut holes into it in order to place heavy timbers or blocks under the building. Next, they set screw jacks

A lithograph of Pullman's building-raising project between Clark and LaSalle streets in Chicago, 1860. The contractors were Brown and Hollingsworth, Pullman and Moore, and Ely and Smith. *Courtesy the Chicago Historical Society.*

Marine Bank Building, Chicago, 1866–1867. This was one of Pullman's more publicized building-raising projects. *Courtesy the Chicago Historical Society.*

Tremont House at Lake and Dearborn streets in Chicago, 1861, probably after Pullman and Moore raised it. *Courtesy the Chicago Historical Society.*

in place and adjusted them. The size of the jacks depended on the job; for instance, those used to raise the block that included the Marine Bank ran three inches in diameter and had a three-eighths-inch thread. Once the screw jacks were set, Albert, equipped with a whistle, would join the roustabouts beneath the building, while George would stand in the street, whistle in mouth. When Albert whistled and George answered, each laborer followed a prear-ranged sequence: He gave each of his screw jacks a quarter turn, returned to his original position, and repeated the procedure. New timbers replaced old each day as the buildings rose. Meanwhile, other employees built up the foundation to the floor sill or installed temporary supports until masons installed permanent footings at completion.[14]

Pullman left for the Pike's Peak region, soon to be Colorado Territory, shortly after raising the two city blocks, leaving Moore and Albert to handle the building elevation segment of his business. During January and February 1861, while George worked in Central City, Colorado, Pullman and Moore, together with Ely and Smith, received the contract to raise by six feet the Tremont House (on the corner of Lake and Dearborn). This was one of Chicago's

Tremont House in 1866–1867. *Courtesy the Chicago Historical Society.*

best-known hotels, a six-story brick building on an acre of ground. All Chicago became interested as this massive hotel rose to grade by 17 March 1861. But though George received credit in later years for having done the job, Albert was the one most responsible for its elevation.[15]

Building-raising occupied most of Pullman's working hours in Chicago, but his seemingly boundless energy, coupled with his entrepreneurial instinct, led him to another endeavor — the fabrication of railroad sleeping cars. He had developed an interest in manufacturing such vehicles before he left New York. In fact, one of his close friends and neighbors in Albion, former State Senator Benjamin C. Field, had organized a group to build and operate several sleeping cars. The senator, using his political influence, helped the New York Central secure permission to employ the new cars at a price above the standard rate of 2 ¢ per mile. Because Pullman spent a great deal of time traveling in connection with both the cabinet shop and his building-raising business, it is not surprising that he showed considerable enthusiasm for his friend's scheme to make railroad journeys more comfortable: George was accustomed to the hardships one encountered, particularly with regard to sleeping accommodations on board canal boats and railroad trains. He and Field apparently had discussed these new cars in the Pullman home at Albion.

During a trip to Buffalo shortly before he left for Chicago, Pullman decided to visit his mother's family in Westfield and discovered that one of the new sleeping cars was connected to the train that would take him there. He wanted to examine the vehicle as well as ride in it, so he paid $1 for a berth he did not plan to use (Westfield lay a mere sixty miles outside Buffalo). He later described the cars as having ceilings so low that a tall man's head might have brushed against them. Furthermore, the cars were unventilated, so that when totally occupied, "on a winter day, with a big stove fire at each end the atmosphere was something dreadful."[16] They contained three tiers of berths, with the lowest at floor level. Travelers paid $1 to occupy the lowest berth, 75¢ to climb into the second, and 50¢ to sleep in the upper.[17]

In spite of his previous decision not to use the bunk, he did crawl into it, completely dressed (as was customary). But he did not sleep: He was far too uncomfortable. Instead, he passed the time reflecting on how the car could be improved. He did admit that "one of the great luxuries of the trip was the opportunity to wash your hands and face the next morning."[18]

Pullman continued to ponder the matter of improving sleeping cars even after he left New York for Chicago early in the spring of 1859. Quite possibly, Field may have accompanied him on that journey because they formed the partnership of Pullman and Field just prior to leaving Albion.[19] Shortly after he arrived in Chicago, Pullman approached the Chicago, Alton and St. Louis Railroad about certain sleeping car improvements he had begun to formulate. Officials of the little road received his ideas so favorably that Pullman traveled to Bloomington, Illinois, a community southwest of Chicago, where the Alton shops were located. There he hired an Alton mechanic, Leonard Seibert, to help him implement his plan. Pullman and Seibert examined all the Alton passenger cars and finally chose coaches 9 and 19 for their experiment. Seibert spent most of the summer of 1859 gutting and reconstructing them, without blueprints, under the supervision of master mechanic

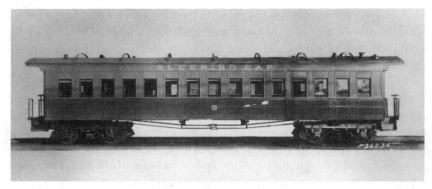

This probably was a reproduction of the original Car No. 9, which was made for the Pullman exhibit at the Chicago World's Fair in 1893. *Courtesy Pullman Incorporated.*

William Cessford and master car builder David Shield, while Pullman hovered in the background directing and scrutinizing the work.[20]

By the time Field and Pullman began their sleeping car endeavor, such vehicles had become indispensable adjuncts to a first-class railroad's operations, although certain difficulties persisted. The biggest was how to equip a car for night travel without detracting from its comfort and space as a day coach. A second problem was how to convert the carriage for day or night use. Because other car builders had begun to arrive at solutions to these obstacles, Pullman had to work carefully to avoid infringing on their patents. Unfortunately, little or no information survives concerning the two converted conveyances, even though Pullman built a replica for the 1893 Columbian Exposition at Chicago. Consequently, historians must rely on glowing but vague descriptions furnished by journalists who observed and rode in the vehicles shortly after they were introduced to the public.[21]

The forty-four-foot-long, flat-roofed conversions, measuring just over six feet from floor to ceiling, were mounted on four-wheeled trucks equipped with iron wheels. Their cherry-wood interiors, containing ten sleeping sections, were so compact, perfectly arranged, and well assembled that these cars were difficult to distinguish from ordinary first-class cars. Plush upholstery, oil lamps, and box stoves supplementing the "various saloons and closets" (actually a linen closet and two restrooms, one at each end of the car) would have done credit to a steamboat, the epitome of luxurious travel in the United States at that time. And like contemporary railroad cars, their lower berths could be fashioned from two seats. Beyond that, the differences between these and other sleepers became apparent. Trusses, placed in the roof to support the upper tier of berths, permitted Pullman to dispense with "the upright iron bolts" used as props by traditional sleepers.[22] Roomy and wide upper berths, slung close to the ceiling, also served as storage areas for bedding when not in use. When the time came for passengers to retire, the couches were lowered "by a peculiarly unique contrivance, not yet patented" that made them accessible, provided occupants with pure air, and, when bedding and berths were put away the following morning, left each car prepared for a day's travel. The upper berths were the most touted attractions of these earliest sleepers, each of which cost Field and Pullman about $1,000. Brakemen made up the sleeping couches, for there were no porters as yet.[23]

The first run took place during the afternoon of 15 August 1859 when George Pullman and his partner Field invited several Alton officials, along with a representative of the New York Railroad Bureau and a group of Chicago reporters, to accompany them on Car No. 9. They rolled out of Chicago's Van Buren depot at 5:30 P.M., en route to Summit Station, some twelve miles outside the city. Once there, the party witnessed a demonstration of how the berths were prepared, and they strolled about the gravel pits of "Summit Farm." Things got more lively as the hosts began to pour champagne, and all were in high spirits when they returned to their point of origin about 8:00 P.M. Superintendent A. D. Abbott of the Alton made a short speech, and the group then gave Pullman and Field three cheers and a tiger, with an additional one for Abbott, and returned home.[24]

Pullman and Field experienced numerous troubles with their sleepers in the spring of 1860, but they managed to get a third in operation nonetheless, this time on the Dixon Air Line. This road, also called the Galena Air Line, was a branch of the Galena and Chicago Union Railroad, which ran between Freeport, Illinois, and Fulton, Illinois, a town just across the Mississippi River from Clinton, Iowa.

Interior of Car No. 9, a remodeled day coach that made its first trip from Bloomington, Illinois, to Chicago on 1 September 1859. This car was George Pullman's first attempt to implement his own ideas in sleeping car construction. *Courtesy the Chicago Historical Society.*

Pullman had thus begun to make a name for himself in two fields of endeavor in the city where he would make his home for nearly forty years. Both his businesses prospered, although sleeping cars would eventually absorb his total attention.[25] His hard work paid off during the spring of 1860: Financial transactions recorded in his diary showed that Pullman and Moore took in $10,431.47 for building-raising work between January and the middle of May, and Pullman's sleeping cars earned $1,539.75 between January and June.[26] Naturally, not all of the income was clear profit, for there were car repairs and general maintenance costs, not to mention washings and other minor items. In addition, Pullman and Moore paid numerous bills connected with their building-raising and business trips. Yet the partnership emerged with some profit after paying expenses and wages, and the owners felt prosperous enough to treat employees to special refreshments on at least one occasion.[27]

George Pullman turned twenty-nine on 3 March 1860. Although he had no mustache, he sported whiskers on his chin and along his jaw in the manner of many men of that period. A nice-looking fellow, he continued to dress well and comported himself in a gentlemanly manner. And despite business pressures, he managed to relax periodically. He ate at smart places like the Revere House and the newly opened Hyde Park Hotel, where he invariably treated himself to oysters. He also kept up with the news, reading such Chicago newspapers as the *Democrat, Daily Herald*, and the *Daily Times*. One of his favorite pastimes appears to have been whirling southward on Michigan or Wabash past the fine houses that wealthier Chicagoans were building or driving by the mansions of the well-to-do living in the northern part of the city. In addition, he attended the theater several times in the spring of 1860. On Sundays, he went to St. Paul's Universalist Church. When possible, he attended both morning and evening services, and he wrote his mother that he was enjoying religious worship more than ever. This was unusual for a young businessman in a city whose residents reputedly paid little heed to religion or other niceties of life, so devoted were they to commerce.[28]

Universalist Church, Chicago, where Pullman worshipped when he first moved to the city; photograph dated 1866–1867. *Courtesy the Chicago Historical Society.*

His personal expenses included clothing, washing, shaving (at $1.50 per month), and a hair invigorator. His board cost him about $15.00 a month, and though the record does not show where he lived when he first moved to Chicago (it was probably in the Pullman and Moore office building), he and Albert began boarding at the Garden House in early May 1860.[29]

Thus, a little more than a year after arriving in Chicago, Pullman was one of that city's established young businessmen. However, he soon became sidetracked by events taking place in the foothills of the Rocky Mountains, some thirty miles from a struggling frontier community known as Auraria or Denver City.

Gold was discovered in sizable quantities at various spots throughout the section of the Rockies that would soon become Colorado Territory. Traces of the yellow metal had been found in the vicinity of the present city of Denver during the summer of 1858, causing a rush to the area the following spring. But no major strikes were publicized until late spring. Among those finds was one made on 6 May 1859 between today's Black Hawk and Central

City; the lucky miner was a redheaded Georgian named John Hamilton Gregory. The validity of the strike, attested to by well-known journalists Horace Greeley, Albert Richardson, and Henry Villard, encouraged more frequent and increasingly optimistic reports from the goldfields.[30] By 1860, Chicago newspapers contained many accounts of life in Denver and the mines.[31]

Like other Americans, Chicagoans were interested in the new goldfields. Enthusiastic correspondents fired barrages of information concerning new strikes and ensuing wealth into Chicago's newspaper columns. But these optimistic reports were tempered when miners discovered very shortly that the gold they found in Colorado differed greatly from that in California. Once they exhausted the free gold on the surface and pursued outcroppings into the mountainsides, they found the precious metal was encased in base rock from which it had to be separated in order to be marketable. Therefore, by the fall of 1859, crushing mills were coveted pieces of equipment. Many of the earliest mills were homemade *arrastres*, which served to recover some ore but not in the quantities said to exist by assayers. A very ancient type of crusher introduced by the Spaniards to the New World, the *arrastre* consisted of rocks tightly positioned into a circular flooring surrounded by a raised edge. A wood post, set on a pivot, rose from the center of the floor with one or two wooden beams extending horizontally from the post. One or two very heavy drag stones hung down from each of the beams. One beam extended over the raised outer edge of the *arrastre*, so that a draft animal (or a human, in some cases) could turn the post and drag the rocks over ore spread on the floor of the crusher; the ore was ground to a pulp or slime when a trickle of water was added onto the floor as the crushing began.[32]

A more sophisticated mill began operating in Gregory's Diggings that September. Then, in late November, C. B. Clark and John F. Vandevanter introduced the first foundry-built mill in the region, manufactured by the Eagle Iron Works of P. W. Gates and Company, in Chicago. Vandevanter escorted the dismantled mill to Colorado and also served as the authorized agent for P. W. Gates and Company, which had been building stampers for the copper mills in the Lake Superior area.[33]

Industrially produced mills were much more efficient, much heavier, and more expensive than their homemade predecessors. Depending on the number and size of stamps they featured, the machines weighed anywhere from several hundred to several thousand pounds. Different manufacturers produced their own versions, but all stamp mills operated on the premise that ore placed in a mortar could be pounded to a pulp by a battery of stamps, each weighing between three hundred and seven hundred pounds. The stamping reduced the quartz to the consistency of sand in the streams where gold might be found. Once the reduction took place, the precious metal could be mechanically separated from base rock to obtain the same result that placer miners working by hand achieved. The manufactured mills were powered by water or steam engines.

In December 1859, Clark and Vandevanter moved their stamp mill to Nevada Gulch, where it did so well that by mid-March, John Vandevanter returned to Chicago bearing orders for more Gates crushers, ranging in size from three hundred to five hundred pounds per stamp. That same month, Clark and Vandevanter disposed of their Gates mill for $15,000, a substantial profit — since they had originally paid $1,500 for it at the Eagle Iron Works. Gates mills were among the most highly regarded crushers taken to the Clear Creek mines west of Denver that season. By 3 April, Gates and Company had sold twenty-one of their stamp mills to "Pike's Peakers." The firm began advertising in Denver's *Rocky Mountain News* and planned to open a foundry in that city.[34]

Vandevanter wrote letters to the *Chicago Press and Tribune* describing the goldfields and how well his mill handled the region's ore. Furthermore, Gates and Company assembled and operated such machines in its shops so that interested parties could see practical demonstrations of company products; George Pullman must have been among the observers at one such exhibition, held early in 1860. Vandevanter returned to Chicago on 17 March, armed with bona fide orders and promises from miners interested in purchasing mills. He remained in Chicago for several days, telling those interested in mining what equipment and supplies they would need and what route to follow. He made his headquarters at the P. W. Gates and Company offices, and Pullman probably was one of those who sought his advice.[35]

Newspaper correspondents from the Kansas goldfields, as the Colorado mines also were known, continued to couch their reports in such glowing terms that Pullman and Moore must have considered the appealing opportunities offered by the western area. Such information would have been reinforced by conversations with John Vandevanter himself. Finally, on 5 May, Pullman succumbed to the gold fever and ordered a quartz mill from the Eagle Iron Works. Pullman and Moore also took on Robert Graham as a partner, and on 9 May, Graham left Chicago for St. Joseph, Missouri, to escort the new machinery to the mines.[36]

Pullman was selected to represent the firm in the mining region, and he may have been chosen for several reasons. First of all, he was young, unmarried, energetic, and experienced at operating in a boom area. A hard worker, he knew how to supervise gangs of men, how to deal with people, and how to make himself prominent — talents that could help Pullman and Moore become established in a new locale. Furthermore, Chicago still suffered from the effects of the panic of 1857, as evidenced by the slow increase in population and business.[37] A bonanza area therefore was likely to appeal to a man with Pullman's burdensome family obligations: His two sisters, Helen and Emma, were in finishing school, brother Frank's education was in the offing, and George's mother still depended on him for support. Finally, Pullman possessed a young man's natural desire to see new country; this, supplemented by a spirit of adventure, probably influenced his decision to venture into a new and exciting region.

On 17 May, George Pullman departed Chicago for a three-week visit to his family in New York. There, he settled his affairs and looked after his mother's interests before boarding a train that returned him to Chicago on 7 June.[38] As Pullman prepared to leave for the goldfields, Benjamin Field (who was becoming more involved in his first love — New York politics) assigned his interest in the sleeping cars to George as security for endorsements and money advanced. There were other financial arrangements to be settled before Pullman felt free to depart. Meanwhile, he bought a revolver and cartridges, traveling blankets, a belt and flask, medicine, a portfolio and stationery, a carpet bag, more cartridges, a rubber suit, a knife, and a satchel. He paid his dentist $20.00, settled a $49.00 bill with his clothier, paid a pew assessment, sent his mother a $30.00 draft, and withdrew $87.50 from his personal account plus $600 from the Pullman and Moore account before boarding a Pullman car on the Chicago, Alton and St. Louis Railroad, bound for St. Louis, on 19 June 1860. His cousin, William Minton, was the conductor on the car, and Pullman passed a restful night on the first leg of his trip to Denver. He spent the following day in St. Louis, attending to business and visiting with William before the latter returned to Chicago.[39] The next day, he boarded the North Missouri Railroad, which took him to St. Joseph, a favored spot for the most direct route between Chicago and the Pike's Peak region.[40] He arrived in St. Joseph at 9:30 P.M. on Thursday, 21 June 1860, and took a room at the recently built Patee House.[41]

A bustling community filled with entrepreneurs and promoters, St. Joseph also had numerous storekeepers anxious to furnish Pike's Peakers with supplies for the journey to the Rockies. But in spite of the city's nervous activity — much of it caused by the Pike's Peak excitement — the more solid element of the population erected sturdy buildings (many of which would not have been out of place in Chicago) and gave the city its impression of substance. The Patee House, for example, located at 12th and Penn streets on the outskirts of town, had been built between 1856 and 1858 and was one of the largest and best-equipped hotels in the country. Reputedly equal to Chicago's Tremont House in size, it also housed business offices, including those of the Pike's Peak Express and the Pony Express.[42]

In St. Joseph, Pullman arranged for passage to Denver, cashed a check at Beattie and Company (the oldest bank in the community), and wrote his mother another letter. Actually, he had not anticipated leaving St. Joseph as quickly as he did, but on arrival, he learned that a Central Overland California and Pike's Peak stagecoach, leaving for Denver on Saturday, had space for a party of eight. Each member of the party contributed an additional amount to the ticket fee ($100 to Denver) to purchase the ninth seat in the coach so that they would have more space. At 10:00

A.M. on Saturday morning, 23 June 1860, Pullman walked out the front door of the Patee House, deposited his letter to his mother in the mail box, and boarded a stagecoach for Denver City.[43]

Pullman availed himself of the best means of travel — a stagecoach would take him to the Rockies more quickly than any other conveyance, and speedy travel was a matter of prime importance to his generation. It was also the most comfortable way to get there, and it required less personal effort: Unlike many of his less fortunate contemporaries, Pullman did not have to fend for himself or for animals as he whirled across the Great Plains. The vehicle itself, from Concord, New Hampshire, was constructed of white oak, making its red or green body strong and safe yet light enough to move rapidly. Atop wheels spaced to prevent overturning, the frame rested on leather springs that eased the jarring of rough roads more efficiently and made repairs simpler than their steel counterparts. The driver sat on top of the carriage with a conductor or passenger for company. Those who traveled inside found two or three movable benches, each wide enough to seat three people, that were softened with leather cushions and equipped with hinged and padded reversible backs. Passengers thus could face each other or forward if the coach were filled to capacity. In the case of the stage Pullman rode, all benches must have been used, arranged so that the eight passengers faced forward, a much more crowded and less comfortable accommodation than those he was manufacturing at the time.

The coaches also carried mail along with the passengers' luggage, all carefully packed because space was at a premium; an improperly loaded conveyance gave a bumpy ride, often causing its occupants to suffer nosebleeds. Pulled by twelve horses or, preferably, mules, these carriages were regarded throughout the prerailroad West as efficient transportation for humans. More importantly, they traversed the region at speeds ranging from five to eight miles per hour, between stations located about twenty-five miles apart.[44]

George Pullman's route took him across the Missouri River, through a corner of northeastern Kansas, and into Nebraska. The coach reached Fort Kearny on Tuesday, 26 June, and, after a two-hour rest and breakfast stop, it departed on the second leg to the base of the Rockies. On the morning of 28 June, the coach and its weary passengers entered Colorado at Morrell Crossing (Old Julesburg) and pursued a southwesterly course to Denver, arriving there at 3:00 A.M. on Saturday, 30 June 1860.[45] Pullman must have collected his baggage and walked the two blocks from Bradford's Corner (Denver's stage station) to the Broadwell House, the town's leading hostelry, where he remained for several days. At that time, Denver boasted close to a thousand unpainted clapboard structures, along with a few wooden edifices that would have looked good anywhere and several brick buildings.

On the stagecoach, Pullman had struck up an acquaintance with James E. Lyon, a native of Ogdensburg, New York, who had been in business in Racine, Wisconsin, and St. Joseph, Missouri, for several years. They became friends and agreed to a joint venture in freighting and storekeeping after they had examined the possibilities in the Denver area. They chose to locate their store in Central City, whereupon Lyon immediately returned to the United States (that part of the country lying east of the Missouri River) to purchase supplies and get them back to the mining region before the onslaught of winter. They named their firm Lyon, Pullman and Company, although they included Charles Moore as a silent partner.[46]

Here, as he had done in New York and in Chicago, Pullman conducted much of his business through partnerships, a common type of business organization during the antebellum period. By the time he arrived in Colorado, he had gained some business sophistication and was acquainted with the ramifications of partnerships. Basically, people entered into such an arrangement for a specified period of time, and each partner was liable for the financial obligations of the other. This last factor was the weakness of the arrangement and no doubt prompted each member of a partnership to scrutinize the commercial activities of the other. This probably explained why Pullman had carefully subordinated Field's power to his own in the firm of Pullman and Field before he left Chicago. Field's increasing interest in New York politics made George Pullman very apprehensive about the havoc his partner might wreak on their sleeping car business when he, Pullman, was not there to oversee affairs. The arrangement between Pullman, Moore, and Graham probably was a limited partnership in which Graham invested capital (or, more likely, his effort and time) in the firm. Graham was not liable for any funds beyond those he had invested per his agreement with Pullman and Moore, but he could not withdraw his money until the partnership was dissolved, nor could he transact any of the firm's business.

Of course, Pullman maintained his principal partnership with Charles Moore; nevertheless, Moore's relationship as a silent partner in the fledgling Lyon, Pullman and Company doubtless meant that he provided much of the capital that Pullman needed to start the operation. This donation entitled him to a share of the profits and enabled him to act as Pullman's adviser concerning the early phase of their Colorado venture. As was customary, Pullman's work and investment earned him a portion of the take, while both men shared liability for any financial difficulties or obligations that Lyon, as their partner, might incur.[47] Thus, there was risk involved as James Lyon departed to buy supplies and George Pullman prepared to make his mark on the Colorado goldfields.

3

The Colorado Interlude

After leaving Denver for Chicago and St. Joseph, Lyon purchased goods to stock the shelves of the proposed firm of Lyon, Pullman and Company, while Pullman settled himself and erected the dismantled stamp mill that had arrived on 2 July. He wrote his mother that he had become a "rough looking subject," dressed in a gray flannel shirt and gray pants tucked into stoga boots, all of which was topped off with a "slouched hat." He added that he had not shaved since leaving the "States" and therefore sported a very "respectable moustache."[1] But though Pullman's family might have been shocked at his appearance, he would not have stood out in any way from most of the men with whom he was dealing at that time.

Pullman had already been to Mountain City, a collection of log cabins strung out along Gregory Gulch that served as the center of mining activity in the area. There he stopped at the Tremont House, which was owned by a Chicagoan named Hop Martin and was one of the log cabins that still lacked doors and windows. As Pullman noted, it was a "pretty rough establishment," where he slept on a bed of hay on the floor, but food there was first-rate. Mountain City was the new name for what had been known as

George M. Pullman during his Central City career. *Courtesy the Colorado Historical Society.*

Gregory Diggings, the camp that had grown up along Gregory Gulch close to the original strike in the area.[2] When Pullman arrived, placer operations in the gulch continued to produce, and other miners were engaged in lode mining on the hillsides. Located immediately to the east of Mountain City, where Gregory Gulch joined North Clear Creek, was Black Hawk, a camp that served as the entry to the mining area that was just emerging as the region's milling center. The boundaries between Black Hawk and Mountain City remained most unclear at that early date, although Mountain City extended westward up Gregory Gulch to its intersection with Spring Gulch.

At the junction of those two gulches, another community (which absorbed the western end of Mountain City) was springing to life — Central City. According to Frank Hall, author of Colorado's first multivolume history, it contained "only a few scattered cabins and sheeted wagons" in June 1860. That summer, however, Central City would grow into the new mining area's commercial center, catering to the hardworking populace with hotels, boardinghouses, saloons, cafes, grocery stores, and supply houses. Central City soon fanned out along the banks of Eureka, Nevada, and Spring gulches, all of which united within its limits to form Gregory Gulch.[3] The town's false-fronted, log business structures faced Main Street, a north-south thoroughfare. That street connected with the east-west road running from Black Hawk and Mountain City and continued on past mills and placers along Eureka Gulch to join with another road being built to Georgetown, a little mining camp some eighteen miles beyond. The new denizens of Mountain City and its sister communities had already begun building cabins up the sides of ravines, rendering them almost treeless as they cut timber to furnish building materials and fuel. Such energy gave the whole area an aura of great activity.

Once he and Lyon had explored Mountain City and its environs, Pullman returned to Denver, where he moved from the Broadwell House to Mrs. Lane's boardinghouse on Larimer Street.[4] He spent the next two days in Denver, but after seeing Lyon off on the coach, Pullman went back to Mountain City and the Tremont House. For the next several days, he worked out of Mountain City as he pursued the tiresome task of finding a suitable

Central City as it appeared in 1860. *Courtesy the Colorado Historical Society.*

location to assemble his mill. Graham was with him, as was a former
employee named Gilbert Noble, and all three men explored various
gulches in their quest for the right site.[5]

Graham and Pullman finally selected Russell Gulch, about a
mile and a half to the south and parallel to Gregory Gulch along
a road between that camp and another soon to be known as Idaho
Springs. Originally discovered and opened in early June 1859 by
William Green Russell, the Georgian whose strike near Denver had
set off the Pike's Peak gold rush, Russell Gulch proved to be one
of the better-producing areas in 1860. On 18 July 1860, Pullman
and his partner staked a piece of ground two hundred feet square
— the required size for a mill site in Russell District — and
recorded it.[6]

Shortly after staking the site and moving the stamp mill to
Russell Gulch, Pullman had to walk several miles in the mountains
on a rainy night and caught a severe cold. That, coupled with the
fatigue he suffered after looking for a sawmill site, brought on a
bout of mountain fever, a typhus-like complaint common among

miners of the period. Too sick to continue working, he returned to Denver and placed himself under Mrs. Lane's care. Ill for the next ten days, Pullman "thought of *home and mother pretty often.* However with good nursing, plenty of water and homeopathy," he recovered so thoroughly that his health was better than it had been in years. When he finally informed his mother of his illness in September, he hastened to add that his appetite was splendid, that he had gained weight, and that he was again working hard with no sign of headache in over three weeks.[7]

Meanwhile, the partners erected a building to house their Gates nine-stamp quartz mill. Pullman and Graham employed fifteen men and six yokes of cattle at this mill, run day and night except on Sundays.[8] Unlike many of their contemporaries, the partners actually made some money because their mill produced about $5,000 worth of gold during the first seven weeks of operation. Pullman noted that fewer than one out of twenty operators had even covered expenses, and many made the best deal they could to sell their crushers before returning home disgusted. Pullman believed that those who replaced these departed miners would be men with the necessary ingredients for success — energy, perseverance, and money — who, within a year, would develop the area's resources to such a point that even the most skeptical would be convinced that "Pikes Peak *is not all humbug.*" But Pullman's elation at his own success was dampened by his dislike for his associate — a "regular wooden man," as he called Graham. Toward the end of October 1860, he acquired a new partner, Dr. J. W. Morris of Leavenworth, Kansas, and became the sole operator of the mill. There he made his headquarters and established an office, his cabin being only some fifty feet from the mill.[9]

Pullman's dismissal of Graham, followed by his acquisition of a new partner in the stamp mill venture, was a very typical scenario in that area and era: Most of the miners and businessmen formed and dissolved partnerships in a rather casual manner. Pullman's varied activities in the goldfields soon led him to acquire partners in several ventures, another common practice. He no doubt entered into most of these arrangements as the partner who furnished the financing, and his junior partners probably handled the production end. Like many of the gold camp merchants, he seems to have extended some credit and used a bit himself, but apparently, he never did this to any great extent and thus was never embarrassed financially, as many merchants and brokers were.[10]

Pullman chose to erect his mill and dwelling in an area now known as Gilpin County. The topography of his site was typical of the county — heavily timbered and rugged hills, steep mountains, and ravines. However, much of its pristine aspect changed during 1860 as great numbers of immigrant families arrived to build homes and stores and establish businesses that not only brought eastern amenities to the communities but increased their sizes when newcomers settled along the entire length of many gulches. At the end of October, Pullman observed hundreds of cabins dotting the mountainsides. His personal contribution to Russell Gulch was a two-cabin complex: One housed his mill, and the other was a residence for Pullman and several of his employees. He also had a barn, begun in October to shelter his horse, mule, and cattle for the winter. Like others in the area, Pullman used local pine for building, cut and stripped of its bark and converted to logs roughly squared by axes. Later, when he enlarged his structures, he likely followed local custom by nailing clapboards, produced in his own steam sawmill, over exterior walls for a more finished appearance.[11]

Presided over by Mrs. Scott, the housekeeper he hired at the end of July for $45 per month, Pullman's one-story, sixteen-foot-square dwelling was a rough cabin roofed with bark, rather than shingles. A large stone fireplace and chimney completed the outside. Occupants entered through a front door "composed of an old piece of rag carpet hung over a hole in the wall." The dining table, also of rough pine, nearly reached across one side of the room; there, sixteen people ate their meals, for Pullman fed most of the employees at the mill. Two rough bedsteads, constructed of round poles, occupied the other side of the room around which they hung bed quilts in place of curtains. One was used by Mrs. Scott and her husband, and Pullman and Graham used the other on a hay mattress. They rolled their coats up for pillows and covered themselves with Indian blankets. Another two men slept on the dining table until Mrs. Scott awakened them each morning so she could set the table for breakfast. She cooked on a little sheet-iron stove located on what Pullman called the "piazza" in front of the cabin. Everyone ate from tin plates, drank coffee and tea from tin cups, and used "quite ordinary knifes [sic] and forks" and pewter spoons. Their fare generally consisted of fried bacon and mush, baked beans, and biscuits. Occasionally, they feasted on hash, considered a luxury because potatoes cost 20 ¢ a pound. There was always plenty of hot coffee.[12]

By the end of October, Pullman had placed a two-story building over the quartz mill and enlarged and fitted up the cabin (which by then he called a house), making it very respectable. He now lived in a private room with a pine bedstead, table, and chair. The bed frame would soon be enhanced by a feather mattress and plenty of bedding, and the room would be carpeted with gunny-sacks, all of which would arrive with the wagon train Lyon had dispatched from St. Joseph. Mrs. Scott also had a separate room with rag carpeting, considered quite aristocratic during that period. In his elegant surroundings, Pullman celebrated Sundays by putting on a white shirt.[13]

Lyon returned just as Pullman disassociated himself from Graham, and the two friends concentrated on the proposed store because their wagon train would soon arrive from the Missouri River. They chose two lots, each of which had a forty-foot front and a back extension one hundred feet in depth (the regulation size for building lots in Gregory District), together with a building frame that was measured twenty feet wide and one hundred and ten feet long. The land, purchased from Charles L. Brown for $440 on 5 November 1860, was located on Lawrence Street close to the place where the head of Spring Street would one day be cut.[14]

Their wagon train, touted as the finest and largest to leave St. Joseph that season, amounted to twenty-six or twenty-eight wagons loaded with groceries and provisions and drawn by 100 yokes of oxen. When it arrived on F Street (today's Fifteenth) in Denver during the forenoon of 11 November, workers unloaded a few of the wagons, but the majority creaked on, destined for the Lyon, Pullman and Company store in Central City. In addition to the train, 250 healthy head of cattle followed along. Everything looked promising — until the sudden onslaught of a furious snowstorm, the worst that season. Yet in spite of the inclement weather that continued for several days, the partners managed to get their goods into the store and return the train to the foot of the mountains by 23 November. Nevertheless, cattle losses, plus the extra expense incurred in moving the train twenty-eight miles under such conditions, amounted to about $1,300. Lyon and Pullman, however, were able to announce the opening of their store in Central City on 6 December 1860. Lyon chose this place as his headquarters, selecting a pleasant suite of rooms on the second floor.[15]

In June 1861, the *Denver Republican* noted that Lyon and Pullman were erecting two buildings to accommodate stores, offices, and saloons. One of these — a two-story frame structure on Main Street very close to the Clark-Vandevanter mill that they had acquired earlier that year — reached completion in July 1861. The partners also acquired a second piece of Main Street realty, which they used as a rental, on the south side of the present intersection of Main and Gregory streets.[16]

The other building, erected on their Spring Street property, measured forty feet across, thirty feet deep, and twenty feet tall. Designed with a balloon frame covered by dressed siding, the building featured a platform along the entire front and an outside stairway that permitted access to the second story.[17] By constructing these buildings Lyon and Pullman demonstrated their familiarity with boomtown trends and their belief that Central City would be a permanent community.

The firm also rented a dwelling located almost opposite the Lawrence Street store on 5 November 1861, secured by a six-month lease on the house and furniture. Margery Chase, the lessor, charged Lyon and Pullman $40 per month, with the understanding that the partners could put $80 worth of repairs in the house if they deemed it necessary — a sum they could withhold from the final two months' rent.[18]

In January 1861, Lyon, Pullman and Company acquired the Clark-Vandevanter mill, by then one of the most famous crushers in Gilpin County. The plant stood between Main and Spring streets at the junction of Eureka and Spring gulches. This mill, brought to Central City early in 1860 by John Vandevanter, worked so well that he and Clark sold it on 31 March 1860 to J. H. Alexander and Company for $15,000. It was then used to process ores from

Alexander and Company claims on the Gunnell lode through the spring and summer. Although some experienced miners noted that it was not saving even half the gold that passed through it, the mill processed an average of $275 worth of gold per day in June.[19]

In September, Alexander and Company made extensive repairs and added six stamps; on the first run after the overhaul, the mill yielded $858 worth of gold in thirty hours. Yet even this spectacular production, which continued into October, could not save the owners, who had never paid Clark the entire purchase price. Hence the mill was sold to the highest bidders, Lyon, Pullman and Company, on 24 January 1861 at a sheriff's sale for $4,200; several pieces of mining property were included in the deal as well.[20]

Lyon sold his interest in the mill the following March to George T. Clark, Emory J. Sweet, and Cady Hollister, and the plant passed to the control of Pullman, Sweet and Company. Clark was a very popular express agent, and Hollister and Sweet were reputable operators in Gold Dirt, a mining camp north of Central City. The *Rocky Mountain News* prophesied that the mill would enhance its good reputation under Sweet's supervision. With that, the new owners added a few improvements and went to work.[21]

Sometime later, James P. Brown began mining at the east end of the quartz mill and went underground ten feet. He employed a large force of men and reached a point six feet from the eastern boundary of the mill building. Lyon and the members of Pullman, Sweet and Company became uneasy about Brown's motives and sought an injunction to prevent him from undermining their property. The plaintiffs claimed that their tailings pile outside the mill was worth $1,000. They also stated that defective sluices, aprons, and mortar boxes, used throughout most of the mill's operation, had laid a constantly increasing deposit of quicksilver amalgam underneath and around the mill that was of great value, although they did not know how great. They charged that Brown's work threatened to undermine the building, the mill, and the machinery and that he intended to mine out the pay dirt, quicksilver amalgam, and tailings beneath and around the mill buildings. They added that his operations would damage both the claim and the structure. Gorsline, Johnson, and Teller represented the plaintiffs, and Morse and Cavanaugh counseled the defendant when the case was taken before Judge Charles Lee Armour on 8 September 1862. He heard the arguments and granted the injunction, thus stopping a somewhat unorthodox method of obtaining mineral wealth.[22]

Lyon, Pullman and Company preempted and purchased many pieces of property, did some mining, operated their freight business, kept their store, and engaged in an unsophisticated type of banking by dealing in gold dust. And if there were not enough storage facilities in Central City for all their goods, the partners could stow them at the Cold Spring Ranch just outside Golden; Pullman had purchased the ranch that fall for use as a stopover during his periodic trips to Denver, and he kept a buggy and team there.[23]

Pullman also owned a steam sawmill that he bought from the Fond du Lac Mining and Lumbering Company of Oshkosh, Wisconsin, shortly after his arrival. Several of the Wisconsinites, disillusioned with their existence at the foot of the Rockies, had already gone home by the time the others sold Pullman their operation and plant for $1,200, much less than they had paid for the machinery in the States.[24]

Pullman and his partner in this venture, John W. Medberry, soon had the mill in operation on North Clear Creek. After about three weeks, John Vandevanter purchased a one-third interest in it, and on that same day, 15 September, Medberry and Pullman arranged for C. A. Shaw to manage the mill. They employed a second crew of fifteen men and twelve yokes of oxen at this steam mill, which ran day and night except for Sundays.[25] Medberry and Pullman furnished Shaw with enough logs to stock the operation for eight months — the length of his contract — although they could cancel the agreement after two months by giving Shaw thirty days' notice.

Vandevanter released his interest in the mill on 19 May 1861 as Pullman was arranging his Colorado affairs before going to the East. Later, the mill was moved to Missouri Gulch, where Medberry, Charles H. Wheeler, and John S. Harris ran it. But the operation did not fare too well in Missouri Gulch, and on 26 May 1862, Medberry, Harris, and Wheeler forfeited it at a sheriff's sale for $1,000. Lyon, Pullman and Company then leased the mill on 9 June 1862 to Benjamin O. Russell for three months. In one final business arrangement for the mill on 15 April 1863, the company quitclaimed the mill to J. H. Hayford and James W. Richards for $500.[26]

Pullman did not confine his interests solely to the mining camps located west of Denver; he also engaged in the haying business some sixty to seventy miles north of his usual area of operation. On 6 August 1860, a writer for the *Rocky Mountain News* commented that hay would be pretty cheap in Mountain City that winter judging from the numbers who were entering the business. The residents of Gregory and other gulches, hoping to avoid a shortage of fodder for the second winter in a row, began to purchase and cut feed in the natural hayfields along the Cache la Poudre River, close to the present communities of Fort Collins, La Porte, and Loveland. John Vandevanter, Spafford C. Field (a relative of Pullman's partner Benjamin Field), and a man named Rawson already were purchasing hay and hauling it to Denver when Pullman joined them. He first bought an interest in their load and later became Field's partner. By September, they had three mowing machines cutting hay on the Poudre and were running seventeen wagons between there and the mining camp. Pullman, who enjoyed his trips to the region, described them in glowing terms. But though his correspondence showed that he made quite an investment in the business, he did not record the date when he withdrew from it.[27]

By the start of 1861, George Pullman had pursued many business ventures; two quartz mills, a sawmill, two stores, a rental building, a business to buy gold dust, freighting and haying operations, and numerous mining schemes. Small wonder that he had trouble extricating himself from all his endeavors, which meant that his departure for the East was delayed for several months.

Pullman's letters to his family indicate that he had anticipated staying in Colorado only for several weeks or, at most, two or three months. At the outset, he wrote of returning home before winter or no later than October. As he came to know the country, he wrote several times of bringing his mother, sisters, and brother Frank to the area for vacations.[28] In keeping with contemporary business philosophy, he apparently wanted to become established, hire

George Pullman, seated on right, with friends Lewis N. and John E. Tappan in Denver.
Courtesy the Colorado Historical Society.

dependable people to run his enterprises, and then return home. Capable persons were not lacking, for he encountered numerous Chicago acquaintances in Colorado, including Frank H. Angevine, Charles S. Abbott, S. H. Gill, and Gilbert C. Noble, who had worked with and for him in that city. As early as the end of August, he wrote his mother that he would know in two weeks whether he would go east in the fall or wait until winter. His business would determine when he could get away.[29]

That September, Pullman confided to his mother that he had "pitched in *pretty deep*" in business and was just beginning to see his way out. He noted that even though hundreds of disappointed settlers were still leaving Colorado, the territory's prospects had brightened a great deal in the last month, so much so that he anticipated the spring water would bring an even greater influx of a better class of people with more capital. Furthermore, at the end of October, once he had rid himself of Graham, Pullman found his business matters progressing much more satisfactorily. As he grew increasingly optimistic about the area, he informed his family that he expected to continue his business there for another year or longer. He was uncertain whether he would get home for the holidays but said he would go if Lyon, Pullman and Company's trade warranted outfitting another wagon train for Central City that season. By December, his enterprises had become too complicated to permit a journey east for Christmas; he had celebrated Thanksgiving by giving his workmen in Colorado an oyster dinner.[30]

He wrote his mother in January 1861 that a letter from Moore in Chicago probably would determine when he left for home. His departure also hinged on the weather, even though Moore wanted him in Chicago if their firm received the contract to raise the Tremont House. Pullman was anxious to travel home even if only for a short time, and he had spent the preceding six weeks arranging his business affairs so he could be absent for two or three months. In keeping with this plan, he had closed the Russell Gulch quartz mill until spring and had discharged all the men except the superintendent.[31] Thus, only four people remained in the cabin, a situation that permitted them to use a linen tablecloth and white crockery at meals.

Pullman's work schedule allowed him to spend three hours each morning attending to his accounts, handling business calls, and looking after miscellaneous matter at the quartz mill. Then he rode his pony over to the store where he helped out until the mail

arrived about 3:00 P.M. After that, unless detained, he returned
to the mill in time for supper. Once every two weeks or so he went
to Denver, and at least once a month he traveled over the road to
the Cache la Poudre River to check on the hay train. Although his
business demanded close attention and caused some anxiety, he
lived comfortably. But things became even busier after the purchase
of the Clark-Vandevanter mill in Central City; many times he
reached home at nine or ten o'clock at night, too tired to do anything
but eat a bowl of johnnycake and milk before going to bed.[32]

Bad weather, accompanied by tales of travelers' suffering, led
him to postpone his trip east a little longer. Moreover, with spring
approaching, he wanted to decide whether to spend another year
in Colorado. In mid-March, he announced he would continue
operations there for another year and was busily refitting and
preparing the quartz mills for spring operations. By then, he had
sold a half interest in the Central City quartz mill to Hollister and
Company, who would manage it, and had begun to dispose of his
interest in both the sawmill and lumber business.[33]

The bad weather had actually worked to his advantage. As he
admitted, it would have been an unpleasant season in which to
vacation, and his Colorado interests would have suffered a great
deal in his absence. Now he was far more satisfied with his business
arrangements and much more confident about Colorado's future
than he had been just two months earlier. In addition, the extra
time in the territory had given him the opportunity to attend two
parties in Denver, where he had relaxed and enjoyed himself.[34]

Because Lyon, Pullman and Company was preparing to send
its freight train eastward to obtain goods about 1 April, Pullman
planned to be in St. Joseph when the train arrived to purchase the
supplies and see the train off to Colorado. Once that was done, he
could go home. Unfortunately, further delays, complicated by the
outbreak of the Civil War, meant that Pullman did not leave
Denver for the East until 22 June 1861.[35]

He remained in the East until the following March, apparently
testing ores to determine why they did not produce the gold
indicated by their assays — a problem that continued to haunt
Colorado operators until Nathaniel P. Hill adapted European
smelting processes to Gilpin County ores in 1868. Many matters

required Pullman's attention once he was back in the States, including family affairs and the house-raising and sleeping car business in Chicago that he had left for a year. During this period, he also arranged to become P. W. Gates and Company's representative in Colorado.[36]

When he returned to Colorado in March 1862, Pullman found that Lyon had not managed the company to his liking. Lyon was too much of a speculator for Pullman's tastes; further, Moore had uncovered information that cast doubts on Lyon's reliability, all of which strained the partnership.[37] Pullman had good reason to entertain misgivings about his Central City partner because Lyon's returns of gold did not correspond with the reports of high production maintained by Gilpin County mines. Besides that, Lyon had purchased a great deal of property in the firm's name during Pullman's absence. Nevertheless, Pullman did not dissolve the partnership, in spite of Moore's constant admonitions to do so. Later that fall, Lyon did send between $3,000 and $6,000 worth of gold to Pullman, predicting that returns would soon rise to a high of $2,000 per week. Unfortunately, his optimistic predictions never came to pass, and matters beyond his control finally caused him to issue drafts on Pullman's Chicago bank account, for which he apologized.[38] Meanwhile, their firm appeared to be operating at a profit from income on the Gregory lode and Pleasant Valley Mining District claims, the crushing operations, the building rent on Central City's Main Street, the mercantile enterprise, and the gold dust purchasing business.

Nearly every Colorado firm purchased gold dust because that commodity, prior to 1862, was the chief circulation medium in the territory. Each concern weighed the dust paid them by customers, then graded and shipped it to towns along the Missouri River. Lyon, Pullman and Company forwarded its dust to their Chicago office via express or with a trusted friend who might be traveling east. Once the dust arrived in Chicago, William H. Waite, secretary of the Western Marine and Fire Insurance Company, forwarded it to the Metropolitan Bank in New York City for sale to either the mint or an exchange.[39]

Pullman maintained his reservations concerning Lyon's casual approach to their affairs until late in 1862, when he requested H.

D. Towne to examine the Central City firm. Towne saw to it that a new bookkeeper was hired and settled several disputes between Lyon, Hollister, and Sweet, even while he convinced Lyon to forsake speculation and devote his energy to managing the company. Though a bad manager, Lyon ultimately proved he was not dishonest.[40]

Pullman did not stay long in Colorado after he had set his affairs straight. On 29 July 1862, he again boarded a stagecoach for the East, having previously sent to New York several pieces of very valuable ore that he contemplated testing as he had done with other Gilpin County rock the preceding summer.[41] But he was not able to return to Colorado until the first days of 1863; shortly thereafter, he wound up his affairs and left the territory on 14 April 1863.

Although Pullman never recorded his reasons for leaving Colorado, several were apparent. In the first place, like many of his contemporaries, he considered his residence in the territory to be temporary. Secondly, managing totally unrelated businesses in two parts of the country proved most difficult, and he finally had to make a choice. In Colorado, he faced unreliable partners and mills that were not giving miners a full recovery of gold from their ores. And by 1863, steady mining production had declined due to the difficulties encountered in separating gold from the matrix. Colorado mill operators were in trouble; Pullman knew this from his own investigations with Colorado rock. Nonetheless, he had made some money — how much is unknown, but estimates run between $20,000 and $100,000. This was probably enough to finance his experiments with sleeping cars, which seemed a more stable way to achieve the goals he had set for himself.[42] One suspects that he made little, if any, money from mining: What assets he took with him when he departed Colorado probably came from his entrepreneurial and merchandising activities rather than from mineral production. Fundamentally, Pullman understood promotion and marketing, but he was not comfortable in mining, an unstable industry at best. He was also astute enough to see that his future lay in a city where he could control his product, rather than in a mining camp whose existence was constantly threatened by loss of good ore. There were personal considerations, as well, including the long, hard stagecoach ride back and forth across the plains, accompanied by an ever-increasing danger of Indian attack. Moreover, Pullman missed his family and wanted to be closer to his mother and siblings in Chicago. It was time to leave.

George Pullman's sojourn in Colorado fit a rather common pattern. His Chicago concerns required capital, in short supply due to the depression that lasted from the outbreak of the panic of 1857 until the commencement of the Civil War in 1861. Like many others, Pullman went to Colorado expecting to remain there just long enough to make a sizable amount of money; specifically, he planned to establish a money-making concern that could then be entrusted to capable managers while he returned to his major interests in Chicago. He typified the American businessmen who followed the miners to Colorado and sought to profit by furnishing them with goods and services they could not — or would not — provide for themselves. He accomplished this through partnerships, business structures that were common both in the eastern United States and in the West. Although he entered into several mining schemes, his main interests were clearly commercial, and it is doubtful that he ever did any actual pick-and-shovel work in a mine. His *modus operandi* in Colorado, along with his style of life, reflected the civilization that he and his contemporaries brought with them. This, in turn, began to change Denver, Central City, and their environs from frontier towns to mature, urbanized communities.[43] Even his living arrangements symbolized the transition that was taking place in the territory by the end of 1860. He lived in a well-appointed cabin that was presided over by a housekeeper, as opposed to the crude huts and lean-tos of his predecessors. Pullman dined with plates, cups, and saucers, using silverware to consume his sophisticated fare; earlier miners had wolfed down a basic diet of flapjacks and bacon, often eating with their knives straight from a frying pan.

Although Pullman resided in a mining camp, his merchandising and entrepreneurial activities placed him in a different milieu from that of the ordinary miner. Had he chosen to remain in Colorado, he likely would have made his mark there, hobnobbing as he did

The office of the Tappan brothers on 15th Street in Denver, 1865. George Pullman would have been well acquainted with this area, although he had left Colorado more than a year earlier. *Courtesy the Colorado Historical Society.*

with bankers, other entrepreneurs, and merchants, many of them men who made places for themselves in Colorado history. His sense of timing was good, and, had Colorado's ore been easy to handle instead of expensive and stubborn to separate from its matrix, his scheme would have been more successful. As it turned out — he knew when to leave, after he had garnered some money and just before Colorado plunged into a four-year depression that lasted until 1868. Finally, the Colorado interlude served to broaden his knowledge of the United States and the needs of its citizens, particularly the traveling public.

As he arranged to leave Colorado, George Pullman began to exhibit certain traits that would characterize him for life. Chief among them was an all-consuming passion for business. In an age when most young men devoted at least a modicum of time to politics, Pullman did not appear interested in such matters, not even when residents of Denver and the gold camps were excitedly speculating about whether the Pike's Peak region would achieve territorial status. Never in his letters to his family or in his diary did he note any of the anticipation and subsequent jubilation that reigned in the area as settlers in Jefferson Territory (created illegally during the fall of 1859) resumed legal citizenship when Colorado Territory was formed on 28 February 1861. True, that spring, he alluded to his fellow Pikes Peakers' concern over the incipient Civil War, but that was all. As a rule, his missives emphasized his business endeavors and schemes.

Another institution that he relegated to minor status in favor of business was religion. Although he attended church services the day after his arrival in Denver, Pullman made little or no further mention of having done so over the next three years. Religious services abounded in the area, although they were informal gatherings under trees or in saloons, schools, or business blocks because few regular houses of worship had been erected. Certainly, their unconventionality would not have offended Pullman, raised as he was in a sect whose meeting places generally were schoolrooms or homes. He doubtless worshipped during his long sojourns in the East, but religion was not prominent in his life at the foot of the Rockies.

Examining Pullman's life during these years, one cannot help but sense that he was beginning to consider himself a cut above most of his contemporaries. For example, he occasionally wore a white shirt in an area where such a practice was relatively rare, he rode a pony or mule between Russell Gulch and Central City while others walked, and he lived on a higher plane than many of his contemporaries.[44] Such comportment tended to separate him from the area's more ordinary dwellers.

Finally, an irascibility began creeping into his dealings with others during this period, exemplified by his impatience with Robert Graham, his less-than-cordial treatment of miners who called on him at his stamp mill in Russell Gulch, and his shortness with Helen, his sister, when she improperly addressed a letter to him.[45] All indicated a curtness not evident in the young adventurer who had set out for Colorado almost three years before. It was too soon to tell what these outbursts indicated. Perhaps he was frustrated that his endeavors in the goldfields had not been more profitable. Maybe he was overwhelmed by so much work in areas so far removed from each other. Possibly he was simply tired out by too much stagecoach travel and worry over family and business affairs in New York and Chicago. Whatever the cause, he was beginning to show signs of strain.

Following his return to Chicago, Pullman dissolved his partnership with James Lyon in the fall of 1863. Charles Moore, in spite of his earlier misgivings, retained his interest and joined Chicagoans Franklin Parmelee, David A. Gage, and Henry D. Towne in Lyon's new enterprise, James E. Lyon and Company (later renamed the Consolidated Gregory Company). Lyon maintained an office in Central City but operated out of the Milwaukee Mill at the entrance to Black Hawk, which the partners had purchased and refurbished in late May and June 1862.[46] Meanwhile, Lyon, who experimented with ore and for several years was considered the leading mill man in the territory, remained friendly with his former partner.

Pullman also retained an interest in Colorado minerals, serving as director of the Eagle Gold Company, which was formed by his friends Cady Hollister and Emory J. Sweet to operate the Gold Dirt lode in Gilpin County. He had established a good reputation for himself in the mining camps, and his old acquaintances always welcomed him on his periodic visits to Colorado in later years. As he grew older, Pullman often reminisced about the years he spent there and collected all the literature he could find that dealt with the period when he resided in the Rockies.[47] Nevertheless, early in the spring of 1863, he put all this behind him and returned to Chicago, where he again began constructing luxurious railroad sleeping cars.

4

Moving Up

George Pullman departed Denver on Thursday, 9 April 1863. He reached Atchison, Kansas, the following Wednesday morning and went on to Chicago via St. Louis, arriving on Saturday morning, 18 April. Once back in that city, he resumed his hectic business life.[1]

Chicago was more vibrant than it had been three years before. The onset of the Civil War brought the young metropolis unprecedented prosperity as its residents won numerous contracts for army supplies, as well as large orders to furnish beef to the Union army. In 1861, a quartermaster depot was established to supply troops from Illinois, Iowa, Minnesota, and Wisconsin, and Chicago soon became an important warehouse for government supplies that furnished Northern armies with food, fodder, horses, lumber, uniforms, and vehicles. It was ideally located — far enough from the front lines to be safe from attack yet serviced by connecting railroads so that troops and equipment could be transported wherever they were needed easily and quickly. Chicago's role as an important supply base stimulated manufacturing, which attracted workers and speculators and large amounts of capital. Continued production, although accompanied by the gradual

71

diminution of the work force as men were called for military service, led to the manufacture of great quantities of machinery to satisfy the increased needs of western farms. The city grew from 109,263 dwellers in 1860 to 187,446 by 1865, and its commerce nearly doubled during the same period.[2]

Chicago building construction multiplied after the real estate market began its recovery during the final months of 1862. Land prices continued their moderate but steady climb through 1863 and 1864. The largest group of purchasers were merchants, followed by lumber dealers, packers, and manufacturers whose wartime profits enabled them to acquire good residential and commercial sites. Soon, large homes, warehouses, mercantile establishments, and churches began to appear, together with many smaller dwellings. Many Chicagoans boasted increased currency flow and large cash balances, which they invested in other areas destined to improve their financial positions as they enriched their city.

Close to twelve thousand new buildings (many constructed of brick and stone) were erected during 1863 and 1864. Gas companies developed, contractors dredged a passage to admit larger vessels to the city's docks, and the Great Lake Tunnel was begun to give Chicagoans an adequate supply of water. At the same time, cultural institutions began to dot the scene: The Chicago Museum opened in 1863, the rebuilt McVickers Theatre in 1864, and an opera house in 1865.[3] With his good sense of timing, George Pullman had left one area whose boom was declining to return to another whose prosperity was resurfacing.

At first, he spent much of his time settling his mining affairs and working with other enterprises, such as the Eagleton Wire Manufacturing Company in New York (of which he was a main owner). He also served as a director of the Third National Bank in Chicago. That fall, he disposed of his interest in Lyon, Pullman and Company but promptly invested in mining interests represented in New York that were more satisfactory and would not require his personal attention. Such purchases demonstrated Pullman's emerging business acumen, for he needed few, if any, distractions as he enmeshed himself in Chicago's highly competitive and scintillating commercial world, especially that segment dealing with transportation.[4] One distraction he avoided was service in the Union army — he hired a substitute during the late summer of 1864.[5]

The 1850s had been years of expansion for American railroads, even though construction had been slowed by financial embarrassments emerging from the panic of 1857 and by sectional controversy that doubtless caused the federal government to cease granting lands to railroads by the end of the decade.[6] During those ten years the more prominent, east-west railroads recorded marked increases in both freight and passenger receipts. Rail profits were stimulated by growth in states like Illinois, whose fertile soils enticed enough settlers to double its population. Newcomers cultivated the lands, spawning an agricultural boom. This boom received a great deal of support from railroads that gave the area access to eastern markets and, in turn, made the region a readily available outlet for eastern manufacturers.

Then came the Civil War, the first conflict in which the nation's railroads played a vital role, proving that they could move thousands of people and tons of freight efficiently and rapidly. The Illinois Central, probably the most important of the rail lines serving Chicago and Illinois during the 1850s, typified rail service during the conflict. It transported 626,000 soldiers, which caused passenger revenues to outdistance those earned by hauling freight. The war years served the Illinois Central well: The rail service the company provided for the national government was but a small fraction of its total new freight and passenger business. In fact, passenger revenues doubled, and though some of the increase was due to troop train service, much resulted from civilian activity. Moreover, the war's end did not bring any major decline in traffic on the Illinois Central; during the three years following Appomattox, passenger receipts dipped to approximately their midwar level. Consequently, wartime and postwar prosperity enabled the Illinois Central to reduce its debt and examine new options, thanks to steady expansion in freight and passenger traffic tied to Illinois's rapid growth.[7]

In addition, a new generation of men were anxious to exploit the resources of the western states once the specter of sectionalism had been vanquished. They went into banking, industry, trade,

and transportation, often backed by Americans who had learned
investment procedures during the war and who were eager to place
their surplus funds in growing new firms. Railroads were ideal
investments for such people: They would link the resource-rich
West to the factory-supported East, and they were encouraged by
various segments of the population, including the national government, new communities seeking rail connections, and capitalists
interested in long-range investments.[8] Americans traveling to these
newly opened areas demanded more comfortable means of transportation. George Pullman, a young entrepreneur with firsthand
knowledge of the frontier, Chicago's business conditions, and
western travel, stood ready to fulfill their requirements with his
luxurious conveyances.

Thus, Pullman continued to pursue his interest in sleeping
cars. Earlier, he and Field had ordered a new sixteen-wheeled
palace car from the Wason Car Company in Springfield, Massachusetts, for use on the Chicago, Alton and St. Louis. In January
1863, while Pullman was still in Colorado, Ben Field wrote that
the car was progressing nicely; workmen and painters were hard
at work. However, Field also informed Pullman that the ironwork
on the car had already cost over $3,500 and would cost more that
$5,000 before the master car builder, a man named Wood, was
finished. Moreover, the builder said he believed the conveyance
would be a poor one because a proper method of installing the iron
covering had yet to be discovered. In late May, Pullman wrote his
mother that there had been an unexpected delay in finishing the
new car. Nevertheless, he said, he hoped to have it in Troy, New
York, about 15 June.[9]

The $6,500 fifty-eight-foot vehicle rested on two double trucks
with a total of sixteen wheels that, together with a compound lever
and several sets of springs, reduced bumps and helped eliminate
the rocking motion of the car on the tracks. The interior of highly
polished black walnut contained fourteen sections, each capable
of accommodating four people, or fifty-six in all. The carriage's
double doors and windows deadened the sound, so passengers
could converse easily while they observed the passing countryside
through plush mohair curtains. During the day, the berths were
arranged along the sides, and camp chairs were available for those

who wished them, making the car a very pleasant salon. At night, couches were formed by sliding out the sofas and letting down the cushioned backs. About three feet of space remained in the aisles once the beds were made and screened with damask curtains from ceiling to floor. Eight Westlake patent ventilators in the ceiling provided excellent air circulation and eliminated cinders and dust. At each end was a very pleasant stateroom equipped with doors and windows, as well as a writing table with space for three or four persons. Throughout the day, the entire apartment slid back into the side of the coach; it was drawn out at night with its soft bed let down so that its occupant might sleep totally apart from other travelers. Field and Pullman's latest offering possessed all the conveniences of a first-class hotel room, including brilliant lighting furnished by six large kerosene lamps suspended from the ceiling. Finally, it offered passengers two very desirable features not found in ordinary sleeping cars — mattresses made of the very best material and berths with clean, white counterpanes, pillowcases, and sheets that were changed daily.[10]

That summer, Pullman took the new car to St. Louis, where he was negotiating a sleeping car contract under highly competitive circumstances. People there commented very favorably on this latest addition to Pullman and Field's fleet, first called Car 40 but later changed to *Springfield* in honor of the town where it was built.[11] The Chicago, Alton and St. Louis Railroad was also pleased with George Pullman's products: In 1864, the president of the line, Timothy Blackstone, stated that the young car manufacturer had spared no pain or expense to turn out the best-furnished and most comfortable cars, which were kept neat and wholesome. He noted that all of this had added to the popularity of the Alton as a passenger line and went on to credit Pullman with "having constructed and placed upon the line some new sleeping cars which in all their appointments" were the most perfect ever built. Blackstone concluded with the hope that Pullman's great attention to detail and financial outlay would prove highly remunerative.[12]

Perhaps the delays encountered during the *Springfield*'s construction led Pullman to consider building a car himself. Accordingly, he secured a shed from the Chicago and Alton that stood on the site of the present Union Station. Then he expended $20,000 to install a workshop, hired the necessary workers, and purchased the requisite materials. By 1864, he and his crew were prepared to begin building a much larger, more elegant sleeping car. But George could not spend all his time overseeing the work on his creation because other business matters and family responsibilities intervened. For instance, in 1864, he enrolled his youngest brother, Frank, in the Poughkeepsie Military Institute, made several journeys to Ohio, and secured contracts in Detroit.[13] Nonetheless, his main concern lay with the construction of the new car.

Although he employed a practical car builder to supervise the work, both he and Albert kept a close watch over the car's progress during the fall of 1864 and early 1865. When the vehicle, which they called Car A and then the *Pioneer*, emerged in the spring of 1865, it was fifty-four feet in length, ten feet in width, and nearly ten feet in height. It did not differ greatly from other first-class sleepers, though it might have been a bit larger. The well-appointed sleeping cars of the era all approached oriental opulence with their expensive wood-paneled interiors, exquisitely upholstered furnishings that easily converted into soft, comfortable beds, lavish carpeting, curtains, draperies, and convenient washroom facilities. And though Pullman's latest vehicle was luxurious, the sleepers put out by Wagner and Woodruff, his leading competitors, were equally sumptuous.

Unfortunately, there are no extant descriptions that mention this car by name. But several newspaper clippings in the Pullman Company scrapbooks dated May 1865 contain descriptions of a new car Pullman was showing in Chicago, St. Louis, and other communities throughout the region.[14] Built in his Chicago shop, the car had made a trial trip to St. Louis on 26 May 1865. These accounts must refer to the *Pioneer* because the car's dimensions fit those originally given for that legendary car; in addition, the price of $18,000 matches that quoted for the famous conveyance.[15]

The glowing descriptions of Pullman's new car included, for example, that of a reporter writing for the *Daily Illinois State Register*, who noted: "It were useless to attempt to enumerate, in so brief a notice, even a few of the many improvements which have been introduced . . . into this carriage, rendering it . . . superior to any that we have ever inspected." And a reporter with the *St. Louis Despatch* wrote, "The superiority of this car, over any other in the world, is that it will answer for a night or day car, and is well ventilated. . . . Mr. Pullman has built thirteen sleeping cars, which he runs on different roads, but this last (thirteenth) eclipses all others." Such reports may have been due to a journalistic afterglow from imbibing too much of George Pullman's wine. Or perhaps many of the local newsmen had not seen the gorgeously appointed transports that ran on eastern roads and thus compared Pullman's car to the sleepers of their youth.[16]

Tradition states that the *Pioneer* was part of Abraham Lincoln's funeral train between Chicago and Springfield. But recent scholarship has cast doubt on this and suggests that the story may have been a sales pitch used at a later date. The questions stem from the fact that the car's dimensions would have necessitated pruning railway station platforms, extending the sides of railway bridges, and raising some viaducts so it could pass on the funeral journey. Clearly, there was comment at the time about its greater size: Several reports that described it in the clippings from the Pullman scrapbooks alluded to its enlarged proportions. According to these accounts, the car was destined to run on the Chicago, Alton and St. Louis as soon as necessary modifications could be made, but there is no indication that they had been carried out at the time of President Lincoln's funeral.[17]

The official Pullman Company version agreed with a statement made almost thirty-five years later by J. W. Stockton, an assistant superintendent for the firm — a version he said Pullman himself had related to him. Though many people monitored its construction very closely, when the *Pioneer* was completed, it was still too wide to clear the station platforms belonging to the Chicago, Alton and St. Louis Railroad. But Pullman had spent all his money building the vehicle and could not secure backing to build a similar car on a smaller scale. Somewhat disheartened, he stored the car in Chicago until people in charge of Lincoln's funeral cortege suggested it be included. The person who made the suggestion could only have been James H. Bowen, a prominent Chicago developer, who was deeply involved with the arrangements for carrying President Lincoln's body back to Springfield. (As president of the

Third National Bank of Chicago, of which George Pullman was a director, Bowen must have known about the *Pioneer* and Pullman's difficulties with it.) The car builder hurried to get his carriage readied, and the Chicago and Alton immediately detailed groups of workers to cut down station platforms and take out other obstacles in order to permit passage of the *Pioneer*. Once that was accomplished, the car was placed in the train. As J. W. Stockton recalled, "Mr. Pullman's car became the subject of universal comment. From that moment its success was assured."[18]

Visitors who progressed down the wide central aisle obviously appreciated the rich Brussels carpeting, the chandeliers with exquisitely ground shades hanging from the ceiling, the numerous French glass mirrors separating the various sections within the car, and the black walnut interior. Overhead, murals on the ceiling were painted on an azure background, and the paneling that concealed the upper berths was painted the same color. The effect was an opaline light, said to be most pleasant during the summer.

Marble-topped washbasins stood by water closets at each end of the carriage. In addition, there were two staterooms at each end partitioned by handsome folding doors, the upper parts of which were filled with enameled glass. These rooms with berths could be partitioned to form smoking rooms accommodating six to eight passengers; they could also be further rearranged to create two rooms, both with access to the outer door.

Broad blue panels concealed or encased the upper berths against the sides of the car, making the beds scarcely noticeable. Their upper sides pulled down with little effort, thanks to a system of hinges and weights. Once down, an iron elbow that resembled those used on buggy tops held the berths in place. The lower berths were made from the seats: The seat backs, hinged to the bottoms, came down, and the underpinnings were pulled out to form beds. Pillows were stored in boxes beneath the seats, but the expensive hair mattresses, linen sheets, coverlets, and blankets were in a closet at the center of the car. They were brought out as travelers (fifty-two could be accommodated for sleep) prepared to retire at nightfall. They were assured privacy when curtains were drawn, turning each berth into a cozy sleeping compartment with its own

French plate mirror and light so that occupants might dress correctly before drawing back the curtains and emerging the next morning.

Unlike the wood stoves that had stood at each end of the older sleeping cars, a central furnace located under the center of Car A provided passengers with heat in winter. In summer, windows in the raised roof at the center of the car furnished ventilation. Even the running gear was improved: The car stood on sixteen instead of twelve wheels, and each set turned independently. Such a system permitted both greater safety and better weight distribution, making the vehicle's motion much easier on the track. In fact, passengers could read newspapers or books with no difficulty; as one journalist noted, "A man must be troubled with tooth-ache or treason who fails to fall to sleep pleasantly in this elegant compartment."[19]

The car cost $18,000 at a time when sleeping cars usually cost about $4,000; its painting alone ran to more than $500. What impressed everyone was the vehicle's daily linen change, which added to its comfort and cleanliness. Others pointed out that its adaptability as a day or night car made it superior to similar conveyances, and the ventilation system did much to increase its attractiveness to the traveling public. The $18,000 price tag seemed extravagant in an age when many people could buy a home, "with a little to spare for horses and carriages," for a like amount.[20] Nevertheless, Pullman set about promoting his creation with all dispatch.

At the end of May 1865, he took the car to St. Louis for exhibition and, while there, treated a party of residents from that city to an hour's run to Mitchell, Illinois. Naturally, newsmen joined the group that lounged on the cushioned sofas and partook of a substantial lunch, washed down with several bottles of "green seal" (champagne). Pullman's guests thoroughly enjoyed the ride, the meal, and the wine and returned to St. Louis in high spirits.

The young entrepreneur also offered the car to a committee of the St. Louis Chamber of Commerce that had received an invitation to visit Boston by the city's board of trade. Such publicity would not injure either him or his car, the thirteenth he had produced.[21]

The *Pioneer* after it had been retired. *Courtesy the Chicago Historical Society.*

But in spite of all the publicity it received in later years, the newer *Pioneer* seemed to be little more than a heavier, more elaborate version of its predecessor, the *Springfield.*

In September 1865, Pullman also placed his cars on the Michigan Central Railroad after the *Pioneer* came to the attention of James F. Joy, president of that line. He admitted it took some arguing to convince Joy that the cars were worth the extra charge, but once the magnate believed that the public was willing to pay more for better accommodations, he withdrew his objections. Other railroads took an interest toward the close of 1865; the Chicago, Burlington and Quincy (CB&Q) a subsidiary of the New York Central, and a Canadian line, the Great Western, soon acquired his cars.[22] Passengers thus could remain in their berths while the car they rode was switched to another track, a highly desirable feature.

Pullman did not forget his fellow Chicagoans in his publicity efforts. In May 1866, for example, he organized a picnic at Haare's Park, twelve miles west of Chicago. Five hundred prominent citizens rode to the affair in Pullman cars, and food, chairs, and tables were unloaded from the train and set up. Kinsley's Restaurant, Chicago's finest eating place, catered the hot meal. White-jacketed waiters served the guests, who selected their choices from silk menus. They drank champagne with the meal and afterwards sipped cognac and puffed on cigars while they listened to Thomas Drummond, judge of the United States Circuit Court of Appeals, resolve that Pullman's efforts deserved the thanks of the entire traveling public. George Pullman made a brief speech thanking his guests for their kind words, after which the party climbed back on the cars for the return trip to Chicago.[23]

Pullman and Field continued to turn out new cars; by the end of 1866, they had forty-eight operating in the Midwest. These included the *Omaha*, a sleeper they had built in Chicago and North Western Railway shops, and the *City of New York*, which the CB & Q constructed for them.[24]

Pullman also entered the southern railway system in 1866. Railroad companies were very anxious to place sleeping cars on night trains in the South, particularly on the Nashville and Chattanooga road. George Pullman, in conjunction with H. I. Kimball (Kimball also was a veteran of Central City's early days) and Robert Ramsey, formed Pullman, Kimball and Company under Tennessee state law, with a capitalization of $300,000 for thirty years. In 1867, they established their headquarters in Atlanta, Georgia, with George Rice, a well-known southern banker, at its head. Pullman charged the firm $150,000 for the use of his rights and patents.[25]

He was unable to make much headway in the East because the railroads in that area already used luxurious sleeping cars, built by either the Wagner Car Company (supported by Commodore Cornelius Vanderbilt, the New York railroad baron) or the Central Transportation Company (CTC) (owned principally by Thomas A. Scott, vice president of the Pennsylvania Railroad, and Andrew Carnegie, the recently resigned superintendent of the Pennsylvania Railroad's Western Division who was now a budding capitalist). Such a situation would not stymie Pullman for long, but other pressing matters had to be settled first. For example, Benjamin Field bowed out of the partnership in 1866. Over the years, Field had become increasingly involved in New York politics and left more and more of the work connected with sleeping cars to George Pullman. Thus, by January 1867, the firm's official letterhead reflected its true ownership — Pullman's Sleeping Car Lines, Central Office, 92 Lake Street in the Tremont House.[26]

Another important landmark in Pullman's life came on 22 February 1867 when the Illinois legislature granted him a charter for Pullman's Palace Car Company. To accumulate the large amount of capital this new venture required, he formed a corporation and once again, his actions neatly coincided with changes occurring in American commerce. Basically, a corporation gave a group of businessmen certain legal powers, rights, privileges, and liabilities once they had secured a charter. More enduring than the partnership, the corporation offered its founders distinct advantages: The death or withdrawal of one shareholder did not cause the demise of the firm; individual stockholders could limit personal liability to the amount they had ventured in the organization; and shareholders could dispose of their shares in any way they pleased. Finally, the organization's stocks and bonds were a most effective way of consolidating the subscriptions of numerous investors into an aggregate amount of money for large-scale endeavors.[27] Of course, there were also disadvantages: For instance, when a firm incorporated, its officers, answerable to their stockholders, had to keep thorough minutes of business decisions, and in most instances, they also found it wise to hire lawyers to advise them about their negotiations. Yet the corporation was a more permanent, more substantial business establishment with the stability and potential for growth that Pullman's generation sought in its institutions.[28] In 1867, the corporation was becoming very popular with the new industrialists, especially those in manufacturing and transportation, who were creating a commercial world that was more compatible with their needs.

Pullman was a member of that new group of industrialists. Unlike his predecessors, he was not a production manager; instead, he hired people (his brother Albert, for example) to build his sleeping cars. And like his contemporary Andrew Carnegie, George Pullman preferred to devote his energies to managing his business, distributing his cars, and establishing and maintaining good relationships with his customers. His chief clients were the railroads that were the true pioneers in corporate expansion and increased owner participation.[29] Therefore, his financial environment practically dictated that he incorporate Pullman's Palace Car Company.

At the first meeting, a group of men agreed to purchase shares of stock in the new firm at $100 per share. They executed their options in Chicago on 30 March 1867. The original subscribers were:

> George M. Pullman 500 shares
> John Crerar 100 shares
> Norman Williams, Jr. 50 shares
> J. Irving Pearce 100 shares
> Schuyler S. Benjamin 100 shares
> H. E. Sargent 100 shares
> Robert Harris 50 shares[30]

John Crerar was president of Crerar, Adams and Company, a prosperous manufacturer of railroad supplies and contractor's materials. He served as a member of the board of directors of the Chicago, Alton and St. Louis Railroad, and also had been one of the backers of the *Pioneer*. When Pullman decided to incorporate his sleeping car venture, Crerar, a close friend, introduced him to Norman Williams, Jr., a young and upcoming Chicago lawyer and member of the firm of Williams and Thompson; Williams drew up the corporate charter. Homer E. Sargent, another prominent young Chicagoan, was general superintendent and general manager for the Michigan Central Railroad and an incorporator of Chicago's Union Stockyards and Transit Company. Robert Harris was general superintendent of the Chicago, Burlington and Quincy Railroad Company until March 1876, when he assumed the presidency. Schuyler S. Benjamin and J. Irving Pearce were partners who owned the Adams House, one of Chicago's better-known hotels. Harris and Sargent proved useful to Pullman at a later date, seeing to it that he placed his cars on their lines.[31] Like Pullman, Crerar, Pearce, Sargent, and Williams all went on to become very prominent Chicagoans, often serving on the same boards of that city's benevolent associations. Thus, Pullman was careful to surround himself with ambitious, public-spirited men who were likely to help him as he organized his corporation.

The subscribers gathered again on 15 July in George Pullman's Lake Street office. There they perused the act to incorporate Pullman's Palace Car Company, which listed Pullman, Crerar, and

Williams as the incorporators. Capital stock in the firm amounted to $100,000; its directors were to hold office for one year. The corporation would manufacture, construct, and purchase railway cars for sale or use and obtain or issue permission to use them as the company thought proper. The subscribers approved all such matters.[32]

The bylaws of the new firm stated that the company's offices would be in Chicago and that its business would be managed by a board of directors elected by stockholders at annual meetings each September. The directors would be stockholders, and they would elect a president, who had to be both a stockholder and a director, for one year; like the directors, he would hold office until the board chose his successor. Board members also would elect the secretary, who would hold office at their pleasure but did not have to be a stockholder. The bylaws also called for a general manager to be appointed by the board, who would act as the company's fiscal agent and general superintendent. In addition to the quarterly board meetings each year, the president was empowered to call special meetings; the first annual meeting was to take place in September 1868. The stockholders had one vote for each share they owned, and the board would determine dividends from the net earnings of the company. Shares continued to cost $100 each and were transferable. Finally, George Pullman became president and general manager of the company, and Charles Angell was elected secretary.[33]

In his new role, Pullman traveled to various cities to convince railroad executives that his cars, though more expensive, were more desirable and worth the added expense. He used his same sales abilities when dealing with prospective shareholders, sometimes selling them his personal stock in the new organization, which he replaced with shares held in its treasury. He also contracted with manufacturers to build his vehicles and at the same time, designed new types of cars that he had constructed and then placed before the traveling public. The mundane day-to-day operations of the company were handled by Albert, who was general superintendent, and by Charles Angell, the secretary. Whatever his title, George Pullman was still the company front man.

At a special meeting called on 27 July 1867, stockholders increased the company's stock from $100,000 to $1 million and elected Homer Sargent and Robert Harris directors. A directors' meeting followed immediately, wherein it was announced that Pullman sleeping cars were now running on the Michigan Central Rail Road [sic], the Chicago, Burlington and Quincy Railroad, the Great Western Railway of Canada, the Chicago and Great Eastern Railway, the Chicago, Alton and St. Louis Railroad, and the Chicago and North Western Railway. There were thirty-seven cars at the time, ranging in price from $4,000 to $28,000. Pullman purchased all of them, together with their fixtures, later that fall with company funds, at a total cost of $991,695.79.[34] His reasoning for such a purchase probably was tied to his desire for complete control over anything bearing his name.

In a special meeting on 1 November 1867, the directors voted to pay a dividend of $3 per share to stockholders of record at the close of business that day. The board repeated this practice over the next several years, voting each time to pay a $3 per share dividend. The stockholders also increased the capital stock of the firm from $1 million to $1.25 million at a special meeting on 2 April 1868. They did so for two reasons: The directors had ordered construction of eighteen additional sleeping cars to meet increased demands by lines already using Pullman conveyances, and they wanted to extend business to other railroads, as well. The company first offered the new shares to stockholders of record at the proportion of one share of new for every four shares of original stock they held. Any stock not taken would be sold for no less than par whenever the company saw fit to do so.[35]

At the August 1868 meeting, the directors permitted Pullman to subscribe for 114 shares of the new issue because his current account against the company exceeded the total par value of the stock. They also resolved that four cars, costing $35,981.43, would be placed in the firm's service and that the company would reimburse Pullman for money spent to purchase them. Three months later, the board allowed Pullman to have the remaining 670 shares of stock in the treasury at par; again, his current account against the company exceeded their value. The directors also resolved that three dining cars, the *Delmonico, Southern, and Tremont*, along with two dining cars under construction, would be accepted and paid for by the company.[36]

Attendees at the special stockholders' meeting held on 24 April 1868 learned that company directors had contracted with several railroads for exclusive use of the sleeping cars. The company would therefore need additional cars to fulfill those contracts and to handle increased business on the other lines serviced by Pullman. Twenty-five cars were already on order, and the Board believed it should increase capital stock to pay for the additional vehicles. The directors recommended creation of a sinking fund from surplus earnings to cover depreciation of cars and equipment during the present contracts; thus, they increased capital stock from $1.25 million to $1.75 million by issuing five thousand new shares. Their action meant that $62,500 (5 percent of the present capital stock) would be paid into the fund out of the company's surplus earnings prior to 1 May 1869. From then on, the firm would set aside a sum equal to 5 percent of the existing stock at the end of each fiscal year to be paid into the fund.[37]

At a special stockholders' meeting held in August 1869, the group decided against issuing new capital stock faster than necessities or company expenditures dictated in order to avoid increasing the firm's obligations to pay interest or dividends on such stock. Then, at another special meeting on 31 December 1869, the directors permitted Pullman to buy 576 shares of company stock at $110 per share. They reasoned that Pullman occasionally had sold some of his personal stock to people the company believed should become stockholders and that this stock should be replaced by company shares in the treasury. George Pullman paid market price for the shares, the amount at which he had parted with his personal paper.[38]

Although Pullman was preoccupied with the formation of his new company during the final years of the 1860s, he also began to build different types of cars and introduce them for public inspection. In March 1867, he exhibited a new kind known as a hotel or drawing room car. More drawing room cars soon appeared and, by the middle of August 1867, one of these "palaces" left

Chicago's Michigan Central depot daily on a through-run to Rochester, New York, without transfer. As an added convenience, the trains, traveling at forty miles an hour, were served by a customs officer who prevented way passengers from entering the through cars; thus, passengers to Rochester did not have to have their baggage checked at the Canadian border. The springs of the eight-wheeled trucks on which the cars ran were adjusted so that travelers felt scarcely any vibration as they rode over the track.[39]

Not content with the success of his drawing room cars, Pullman placed another luxury car on the tracks in the spring of 1868 — the palace dining car. He named the first of these the *Delmonico* after the great New York City restaurateur. Built at the Chicago, Burlington and Quincy shops in Aurora, Illinois, at a cost of $20,000, it measured sixty feet long and ten feet wide. It was divided into two spacious and airy dining rooms, each presided over by two waiters, and seated a total of forty-eight people at a time; a full train of passengers could dine without inconvenience within two hours. The movable tables, each set for four, were placed between the Moroccan leather seats along the sides of the car so that diners could enjoy the passing view. A mirrored glass door above each table disclosed a closet that contained full silver place settings for four people, each piece monogrammed with PPEC — Pullman's Palace Eating Car. The car's center aisle was carpeted, but the flooring under each table was covered with oil cloth to ease the labors of the cleaning crews. At night, *Delmonico* personnel slept on the seats that converted into bunks.[40]

The vehicle's ventilation system precluded "all foul air, smoke and dust." Water warmed by a Baker's heater — an ingenious, detachable furnace located beneath the car — circulated through pipes under the seats to heat the car during the winter.[41]

The eight-foot-square kitchen, a "marvel of compact conveniences," stood between the two dining areas, and an outside door made it easy to load supplies. Two cooks directed their richly ornamented, imaginatively assembled domain, whose central scheme was economy of space; every canister and tool had its proper spot. Cooking was done on a three-tiered range, built especially for the car, that included one area for baking, another for broiling, and a third for boiling water and other purposes. A series of pipes connected a steam boiler to the carving table to keep food hot. On each side of the range, shelves and cupboards stored kitchen equipment and supplies, and there was ample storage, for meats and vegetables lay in huge, metallic boxes beneath the car. Beside them, a large water tank connected to a pump in the kitchen forced water into two receptacles in the roof; from there it flowed into hot or cold water pipes, released when the cooks turned stopcocks. Another pump furnished the cooks with ice water stored in a large container beneath the kitchen floor. With these facilities, the chefs could turn out 250 meals per day.

Pullman introduced the *Delmonico* to the traveling public at a reception in East St. Louis at the Chicago and Alton depot. There a group of prominent people, including railroad personalities and several newsmen, quaffed generous portions of champagne as they enjoyed entertainment "interspersed by speeches and songs." All guests were convinced that George Pullman was a master at keeping a "hotel on wheels."[42] But despite the elegant praise they received, the first diners were not money-makers, and it was not until the 1880s that dining cars became standard parts of a train.[43]

By the summer of 1869, Pullman's Palace Car Company owned over seventy cars and maintained workshops in several communities. The principal shop was in Aurora, Illinois, but others were located in Dayton, Ohio; Detroit, Michigan; Fond du Lac, Wisconsin; and Hamilton, Ontario. Although the company did not own these establishments, workers built cars to Pullman specifications and sent them to Chicago. However, that policy changed during the summer of 1870 when the Pullman Company bought the Detroit Car and Manufacturing Company. This move was made after Pullman and his assistants researched potential sites (even California) for their car-manufacturing operation.[44] From then on, Pullman built his own vehicles in the Detroit works.

Pullman turned to manufacturing for several reasons. First, there was a constant demand for new vehicles. To meet this demand, the company not only had cars built, it also purchased others and revamped them to its specifications. Throughout 1868, nearly every directors' and stockholders' meeting called for the construction or purchase of additional drawing room cars, diners, and sleepers. And by April of the next year, new contracts for exclusive use of Pullman sleeping cars on several railroads, together with an increase in existing business, resulted in orders for new conveyances and a request for 5,000 more shares of stock to pay for them. This expansion raised Pullman stock to 1.75 million shares, 830 of which were reserved for the Chicago and Northwestern Railway Company to pay for sleepers acquired from them and for others under construction in their shops. Such purchases were in keeping with company philosophy: By January 1870, Pullman's Palace Car Company believed its operations depended largely upon maintaining continuous lines of sleeping cars throughout the country and absorbing as many sleeping car facilities upon trunk railway lines as possible to prevent competition.[45]

Pullman also entered into a fifteen-year contract with the Pennsylvania Railroad Company, securing exclusive rights to run drawing room cars, sleeping cars, and reclining chair cars over the entire line and all lines and trains the railroad might control by lease, purchase, running arrangements, or other means. Once again, additional vehicles would be needed to fulfill these contracts with the Pennsylvania and others with the Hannibal and St. Joseph and North Missouri Railroad companies, as well as increased demand on other lines served by Pullman. Seventy cars were already under construction for these purposes, and the directors increased capital stock to $3 million to pay for them.

Meanwhile, negotiations were pending with other railroads that owned and operated between 1,000 and 2,000 miles of road and needed drawing room and sleeping cars. Therefore, the board voted an additional 10,000 shares of stock to be issued at such times and in such amounts as the directors deemed appropriate and in the best interest of the company. In July 1870, on the eve of its purchase of the Detroit Car and Manufacturing Company, the firm approved a 5,000-share issue of new stock to cover equipment costs and production for new contracts.

The company also sought to terminate existing litigation involving the ownership and validity of patents in sleeping car construction. For example, the Pullman Company purchased the property, equipment, contracts, and seventeen patents of the Central Transportation Company.[46]

The Pullman Company's rapid expansion led its leaders to seek direct supervision over equipment production. Obviously, complete adherence to Pullman standards could only be achieved in a plant totally controlled by the company. Such control would also prevent patent violations and allow the firm to produce exactly the cars it needed under the direction of its general superintendent, Albert Pullman. Doubtless, an interest in saving money was also involved in the decision for the company would no longer have to bargain with an outside firm to manufacture its palaces.

In sum, then, business demands, production control, avoidance of legal problems, and the opportunity to save money and begin consolidation of the firm all entered into the decision to acquire the manufacturing plant in Detroit.

By the middle of 1870, the company was turning out several styles of cars — the sleeping car, the drawing room car, the hotel car, and the dining car. The sleeping car contained two staterooms, each of which housed two double berths and twelve "open sections"; both made up into two more double berths one above and one below. Altogether, there were twenty-eight berths, maintained by a conductor and a porter. The drawing room car contained two drawing rooms, each furnished with a sofa and two large easy chairs that became two double and two single berths at night. There were, in addition, three staterooms, each having two double berths and six "open sections" with two double births each — in all, twenty sections of two double berths per, making a total of twenty-six such sleeping compartments. These vehicles also employed a conductor and a porter. The hotel car had two drawing rooms furnished as above and one stateroom with two double berths and six "open sections" of two berths. Each hotel car had a large kitchen built in one end, equipped to dispense food that compared favorably with that of the most exclusive restaurants of the era. Hotel cars carried a conductor, a cook, and two waiters.[47]

If excursionists renting the cars required aid, conductors stepped in to make arrangements with the railroads for transporting the particular carriage wherever its occupants wished it to go.

Conductors on hotel cars also acted as stewards and purchased all that was required for the table. Eventually, the hotel car evolved into the private car and the diner, and the drawing room car became the parlor car used for daytime travel.[48]

Another Pullman vehicle, similar to the two described above, was mentioned in early accounts of the transcontinental trains. One of these commissary cars, the *Young America*, featured a "refreshment saloon" at one end, containing a well-stocked, neat bar with a black walnut counter. Chairs and settees in the car accommodated sixteen people, but the car could handle twenty-four comfortably at bedtime. The arrangements of closets, tables, looking glasses, and general ornamental work was quite similar to that on other Pullman cars. At the other end of the car stood the kitchen, a model of compactness and convenience. The cook, a man named Dan Brown, stated that he would have no difficulty using its facilities to produce daily meals for anywhere from 120 to 150 persons. The kitchen contained space for dishes and other items necessary for table use, and a large icebox ran along one side. "The commissary department [was] directly underneath the center of the car, and compris[ed] a compartment for vegetables, wines, condiments etc."[49]

One wag suggested that there was only one more car Pullman needed to manufacture to make his train complete — a nursery car. "A *nursery car*, adapted to the wants of families with children; this could be easily arranged with cradles, and furnished with toys etc., and doubtless it would be well patronized." After all, every traveler knew how disturbing it was to have one crying child on a sleeping car, and there were often a half dozen or more in one coach. Also, he suggested, such a car would prevent youngsters from wiping their sticky hands on other travelers.[50]

Another traveler, an Englishman named A. G. Dudley Ward, suggested that Pullman put on a bath car, especially during the summer months. Ward had traveled from San Francisco to New York by train and was most happy to board a Pullman at Ogden, Utah.[51]

In spite of his busy work schedule, George still found time to spend with his family. Increasing affluence led him to think of bringing his mother, younger sisters, and brother to Chicago, where they could set up housekeeping. The youngsters were thrilled at such a prospect, as the letters that flowed from Frank to Emma and back (with an occasional missive from Helen, now graduated from the Clinton [N.Y.] Liberal Institute) revealed.[52] Certainly, such a move would have pleased their mother: Not only would she have a home of her own again, she would be close to her sister Hannah Maria DaLee, who lived with her family in Harvard, Illinois, and her sons Albert and Charley resided in Chicago, as well.

Things became more definite when, early in 1865, Helen accompanied George to Chicago and stayed at the Sherman House, a hotel where he had lived for several years. But George's business affairs occupied most of his time, and, though Helen enjoyed herself, she was quite lonely. Then, on 24 February 1865, they drove out to see a house located at 811 Wabash Avenue. The Pullmans soon arranged to take possession on 1 May, after which George planned to raise the house, install a cellar, and select furnishings.[53]

That month, George brought Frank to Chicago, where he worked as a clerk in the Third National Bank.[54] By mid-September, Frank reported to his mother that the house was finished and that the painting would be done that week. George was seeing to the house's furnishings, although he was very busy with the contract for running sleeping cars on the Michigan Central and the Chicago, Burlington and Quincy. In November, the house was almost totally decorated, and by then, all of Emily and Emma's goods had arrived in Chicago from Fulton. They called the house "811," and Emily, George, Emma, and Frank lived there for several years, until early October 1868.[55]

During this period, George began courting a young Chicago woman named Harriett ("Hattie") Amelia Sanger. According to family tradition, he met her at a celebration honoring the completion of the first hotel car in 1867; however, this date seems a bit late — other information indicates he had known Hattie for some time. In any case, by February of that year, they were planning to marry although the date had not been set.[56]

Hattie was born in Chicago on 18 April 1842, the daughter of Mary Catherine McKibben Sanger and James Y. Sanger, a builder who helped construct railroads in Illinois, Missouri, and California. She finished her formal education at the Episcopal convent in San Francisco about 1860, after which she returned to Chicago when her father was working on the new Illinois penitentiary at Joliet.[57]

An energetic young woman, she did a great deal of volunteer work during the Civil War. In 1862, she visited all the hospitals in Memphis, with Mary Logan (wife of prominent Illinois politician and Civil War general John A. Logan), passing out delicacies and dispensing comfort to wounded Union army soldiers. Later that year, when they were ordered back to Chicago, she joined other women working for the Union Soldiers of the Sanitary Commission.[58] An attractive woman, Hattie commanded a retinue of ardent admirers.

In 1867, while her father's firm — Sanger, Steel, and Company — was excavating the rock sections of the Illinois and Michigan Canal, the family lived on Wabash Avenue in Chicago. During the winter of 1866–1867, James Sanger, constantly exposed to the cold and wet, contracted a disease (probably pneumonia); by early summer 1867, he was a very sick man.[59] Nonetheless, as a good Victorian father interested in his daughter's future welfare, he likely paid close heed to her suitor's rising fortunes.

Although ill himself twice that spring, George Pullman remained ambitious, hardworking, and vigorous as he entered his thirty-sixth year on 3 March 1867. Still struggling financially, he was partially recompensed by glowing kudos from the press and his contemporaries for his various railway carriages. Obviously, he was a young capitalist to be reckoned with, supplying an ever-increasing number of products and services to a growing industry that was starting to affect the lives of countless Americans during the expansive postwar years. Many Chicago mothers, hoping to marry off their eligible daughters to promising men, no doubt viewed him as a good risk. Something of a romantic figure because of his early career in moving and raising buildings on the Erie Canal and in downtown Chicago (a job that was not without risks), his time in the Colorado goldfields gave him an additional aura of adventurousness. Another side to his many-faceted character was revealed by his continued care for his aging mother and younger sisters and brother. Clearly he appeared to be a model of dependability and propriety, and no hint of scandal had touched his private life. By then, Pullman's clear, clean-cut face was growing a bit fuller, set off by his well-kept, ever-present chin whiskers and complemented by his penchant for correct dress. All these factors likely helped bolster his image as an up-and-coming young businessman and furthered this cause with Harriett Sanger.

The scant record of their courtship in notations Harriett made in her diary during the spring of 1867 indicates that they spent a great deal of time together — sleigh riding, visiting friends, going around town, and being with each other in their homes. And like lovers throughout history, they seemed content with one another's company. Hattie spent some time with Helen and Emma Pullman and became well acquainted with their mother. When apart, as they were several times that spring, George and Hattie sent letters back and forth, and George occasionally splurged on a wire to her. She also spent quite a period of time in St. Louis, visiting friends and seeing doctors (an early sign of the hypochondria that would haunt her the rest of her life) while George remained in Chicago or traveled in the East.[60]

They were married at her father's bedside at 11:30 P.M. on 13 June 1867.[61] The young couple remained in Chicago for several days, presumably to see how James Sanger was progressing and to permit George to settle his own affairs before departing on a Canadian honeymoon. They journeyed by way of Niagara Falls and then took a boat down the St. Lawrence River to Montreal, where they spent a day before boarding a steamer for Quebec. They passed a day in Quebec and returned to Montreal the next morning, where they learned that her father's condition was very grave. They returned to Chicago immediately, and arrived there on 2 July. James Sanger died the following morning. Whether they ever completed their honeymoon is conjectural.

George and Harriett Pullman soon were part of the younger social set in Chicago. And over the next eight years, they had four children: Florence, born 11 August 1868; Harriet, who arrived 17 September 1869; and finally, twin sons, George, Jr., and Walter Sanger, who were delivered on 25 June 1875. Thus, George

Pullman added a young family to his obligations as he led his company into a period of further expansion.

The years immediately following his return from Colorado were busy ones for Pullman, who assumed full leadership of his firm as Ben Field bowed out and Albert faded into the background, content to supervise the construction of cars. George used funds he had acquired in Colorado to build his most famous early car, the *Pioneer*, and he increasingly associated with Chicago's leading businessmen. It was George himself who publicized his company's products and secured the backing necessary to incorporate Pullman's Palace Car Company in 1867. He also emerged as the firm's president and general manager, assuming titles to match the jobs he already performed. In his new position, he continued to travel, negotiating with railroad executives beyond the Illinois borders to place sleeping cars on their lines. He also planned and built new types of conveyances and introduced them to the public. To raise additional operating capital, Pullman approached selected members of the general public that he wanted as stockholders in his company, if need be selling them his personal stock. Finally, he purchased a car manufacturing plant in Detroit, giving him more control over production of his vehicles. Now, he was ready to branch out and begin to compete seriously against other firms that also sought a more national market.

5

Pullman Branches Out

George Pullman was not the only man experimenting with
sleeping car design over the years — others had worked just as
hard at improving the old sleepers so disliked by American
travelers. Toward the end of the 1850s and throughout the 1860s,
at least fourteen men, most of whom operated independently,
patented various devices for such coaches.[1] Of these, Pullman's
greatest competitors were Webster T. Wagner and Theodore T.
Woodruff. Because of his association with Andrew Carnegie of the
Pennsylvania Railroad Company, in a sleeping car firm known as
the Central Transportation Company, Woodruff was Pullman's
toughest competitor.

Woodruff had been a master car builder for the Terre Haute
and Alton Railroad. After some twenty years of sketching and
building sleeping car models, he had obtained two patents for what
he termed a railway-car seat and couch, in December 1856. In
the next year, he placed his first sleeping car on the night express
train from New York to Albany, and by 1858, several of his
carriages were running on other lines, as well.

That same year, Woodruff showed a model of his invention
to J. Edgar Thomson, president of the Pennsylvania Railroad

Company, who referred Woodruff to Thomas A. Scott, his general superintendent. Scott agreed to incorporate Woodruff's invention into the Pennsylvania line's rolling stock, and Woodruff signed a contract with the railroad on 15 September 1858. Scott then cut his friend and assistant, Andrew Carnegie, into the deal for an eighth interest, and four years later, Carnegie organized the Central Transportation Company to succeed T. T. Woodruff and Company.[2] Woodruff demonstrated little ambition or aptitude for administrative detail and became little more than a figurehead, while Carnegie ran the new company and constantly upbraided Woodruff to improve his vehicles and thus increase profits. Carnegie, along with other sleeping car manufacturers, sensed that the firm which secured a contract with the Union Pacific — the eastern portion of the proposed transcontinental line — would emerge as the leading sleeping car company. He had arrived at that conclusion as early as 1862, when Congress passed the Pacific Railroad Act, and it was the chief reason why Carnegie had reorganized the Woodruff Company. But in spite of his careful planning and unusual foresight, he faced one competitor who promised to give the Central Transportation Company a good fight in securing the Union Pacific contract — George Pullman.[3]

Talk in sleeping car circles in early 1867 concentrated on which man's organization would convince the Union Pacific to use its cars. Pullman possessed an initial advantage because he was well acquainted with that railroad's board of directors. This familiarity stemmed from 1866, when Union Pacific's vice president, Dr. Thomas C. Durant, decided to celebrate, as well as advertise, his line's completed track to the 100th meridian. He invited many of the country's most important people to the celebration, a great number of whom accepted and traveled from Chicago, via the Burlington Road, to Hannibal and St. Joseph on a train of palace cars furnished by George Pullman.[4] The palaces scored a big hit with their passengers, including Durant, who cast aside his personal railroad car in favor of Pullman's new hotel car, *Western World*.[5]

The new car, built at the Michigan Central shops in Detroit for about $24,000, was the first of ten such vehicles that Pullman planned to use on lines running from St. Louis to Albany by way of Chicago, Detroit, and Niagara Falls. He hoped to appeal to those passengers who desired a more luxurious mode of travel. As usual, he introduced the *Western World* by means of an excursion, on 20 March 1867, this time made on the Chicago, Burlington and Quincy Railroad. He played host to some sixty rather prominent people, including Lieutenant Governor William Bross of Illinois.[6]

The *Western World*, higher and wider than previous Pullman cars, ran on sixteen wheels and featured an exterior decor of frescoes in "good taste and appropriateness." Passengers found the inside "upholstered with purple plush, elegantly painted, heated by a large furnace in cold weather, and cooled by a large ventilator in warm weather." Each of four separate, large drawing rooms set off from the main section of the car contained a sofa and two arm chairs, the latter constructed on pivots so occupants could turn to face the sofa. A table stood between the chairs and sofa. At night, the chairs and sofa became three good-sized and well-ventilated double berths. A corridor ran between both ends of the vehicle without passing through the drawing rooms. Furnishings in the main part of the car were the same as in the drawing rooms, but the area was not partitioned into rooms. In each section, a bell connected to the kitchen could be used to request service. The kitchen featured a miniature stove that had "all the compartments necessary for cooking, making tea and coffee, keeping warm plates, etc. The excursionists . . . were made fully aware of this fact from the choice beefsteaks, fried oysters and other viands, that were served to them hot with iced champagne." Silver cutlery and china plates were set on clean linen, and passengers drank from bulb glasses that did not spill. At last, travelers who rode this car could dine whenever they wished; no longer did they have to face the horrors (and often the resultant indigestion) of wayside eating establishments.[7]

In April, Pullman dispatched the *Western World*, along with a lesser car named the *City of Detroit*, to New York, where directors of the Union Pacific Railroad waited to board them for a trip to Omaha, Nebraska, eighteen hundred miles to the west. At Rochester, a curious horde descended upon them. Pullman employees took the organ out of the commissary car and set it up in one of the staterooms so that a quartet could perform. The coaches, with

George and Albert Pullman aboard, left Rochester at 10:00 A.M.; their guests spent the time smoking and playing the organ as they rumbled by crowds that assembled at every station along the way to observe the new car.

As the train pulled into Syracuse, a group entered the car to watch its passengers dine. Newsmen also clambered abroad and accompanied the travelers to Utica, amusing themselves by singing as they drank champagne and coffee. The train reached Albany that evening; the next morning, great multitudes, including many legislators, flocked to see the *Western World*.

The latest Pullman offering did not proceed beyond Albany because it did not fit the gauge of the Hudson River Railroad. Eastern businessmen and railroad men suddenly faced the fact that, though such a car could run from Omaha to Albany, it could not enter the great metropolis of the East, New York City. Something, they realized, had to be done; a new set of track must be laid before an unbroken line could stretch between Chicago and New York. For that reason, another party of eastern railroad men and capitalists left Albany in late May, headed for the terminus of the Union Pacific that by then was about three hundred miles west of Omaha. They must have received the same red carpet treatment their predecessors enjoyed.[8]

Pullman had invited Dr. Durant, together with Sidney Dillon, John Duff, Oliver Ames, and Timothy J. Carter (all directors of the Union Pacific), and several less prominent people to travel west in his cars in 1867. Ostensibly, they would test the feasibility of establishing a line of hotel cars between New York and the Rocky Mountains. Pullman's guests left on 17 April 1867, riding a train composed of the *Western World*, a commissary car, and a very finely appointed day car. Their destination was the Rockies. As noted earlier, the luxurious ride and sumptuous surroundings led the sybaritic Durant to relegate his personal conveyance to government commissioners who were inspecting the work on his road and to avail himself of a Pullman car.[9] Obviously, Pullman and his products had become very well known to the powers who controlled the destinies and contracts of the Union Pacific.

Several other firms, besides those headed by Carnegie and Pullman, also sought the Union Pacific contract in 1867. Just as

Hattie and George were culminating their courtship, the railroad called a meeting of such entrepreneurs in New York City. Carnegie and Pullman and other hopefuls who gathered there stayed at the St. Nicholas Hotel.

By this time, Pullman's name was becoming known — he had four dozen cars rolling on the Michigan Central, the Chicago, Burlington and Quincy, and the Great Western Railway of Canada. Carnegie understood and appreciated Pullman's mode of operation, which stressed the use of good publicity and giving the traveling public what it wanted, while de-emphasizing worry over patent rights and corporate franchises. Carnegie realized that Pullman was a tough adversary, but he was certain the legal rights of the Central Transportation Company would be upheld in the courts, even though such a victory would be expensive and time-consuming. By the same token, Carnegie also recognized that if Pullman wanted a monopoly in the sleeping car field, he would need the support of the Pennsylvania line plus the great amounts of capital controlled by that road's leaders. Therefore, during the first day's sessions, Andrew Carnegie closely observed George Pullman as he competed with the heads of other sleeping car companies in presenting proposals to place their sleepers on the Union Pacific. In the process, Carnegie assessed the Chicagoan's strengths and weaknesses and soon incorporated this information in a plan of action.

That evening, Carnegie saw to it that he greeted Pullman on the hostelry's main stairway. In what appeared to be an accidental meeting and casual exchange, he suggested that they join to form a company called the Pullman Pacific Palace Car Company (here, Carnegie, a shrewd judge of character, appealed to Pullman's vanity) and thus strengthen their negotiating power with the Union Pacific. After they had conversed for some time in his room, Pullman agreed to the merger.[10]

In actuality, George Pullman probably had little choice but to agree to Carnegie's offer because Woodruff's patent designs antedated those of Pullman and Field; there was also some question of patent infringement that directors of the Central Transportation Company felt confident could be settled in their favor through the courts. Nevertheless, Carnegie (who had a great deal of admiration for Pullman) believed such litigation would take too long; during that time, his competitor might secure other profitable contracts, including the one from the Union Pacific, that would permit Pullman to pay any fines he might incur from patent violations and still continue to operate.

For his part, Pullman was suspicious of Andrew Carnegie and demanded a majority interest in the combined firm. These problems were settled in June 1867, at which time Carnegie drew up a contract stating that he and Pullman would furnish sleeping cars for the Union Pacific, keep the upholstery in repair and the bedding clean, and provide one porter for each car. The Union Pacific agreed to keep the lights and stoves fueled and the car in good running condition. But controversy developed when the directors of the Union Pacific demanded a controlling share of stock in any company organized to furnish sleeping cars for their lines. Chiefly through Carnegie's statesmanship, however, the matter was finally settled; Oliver Ames received 2,600 shares in trust for Union Pacific stockholders, and Pullman and Carnegie each received 1,200 shares. Andrew Carnegie also agreed that the patents owned by the Central Transportation Company would be assigned to the new Pullman firm for $20,000. Pullman, however, was reluctant to pay such a sum at a time when his funds were tied up in constructing new cars for the transcontinental run. Matters dragged on until 27 April 1870, when renewed negotiations led to an agreement whereby the Pennsylvania Railroad leased the Central Transportation Company's entire operation to Pullman's Palace Car Company in perpetuity in exchange for an annual royalty of $264,000. The Pennsylvania's managers believed the new alliance would result in the introduction of a great many improved parlor and sleeping cars on its railroad system. By the close of 1874, the Pennsylvania Railroad owned 1,223 shares of Pullman stock, valued at $123,300, and held $770,000 worth of 8 percent bonds issued by the Pullman Company.

The Central Transportation Company ceased to exist in 1884, absorbed, for all intents and purposes, by the Pullman Company, yet its name continued to haunt the company throughout Pullman's life. Although Carnegie eventually sold his Pullman holdings, for many years he used his stock dividends from that company to finance other ventures and his shares of stock to pay off debts to old friends.[11]

George Pullman emerged as the top man in these negotiations, but he was not totally victorious because the directors of the Central Pacific Railroad, the western counterpart of the Union Pacific, refused to allow him to operate his cars on their lines west of Ogden, Utah, after July 1870. Pullman attempted to negotiate with them, and the traveling public raised a tremendous clamor,[12] but the heads of the Central Pacific preferred to run their own ornate "silver palace cars," which they could operate without paying royalties to Pullman. But their cars, despite their elegant name, lacked the luxury and comfort offered by Pullman's creations, and passengers complained vociferously about this disparity. Pullman eventually overcame the opposition of the Central Pacific's "Big Four" — Charles Crocker, Mark Hopkins, Collis P. Huntington, and Leland Stanford, who were the line's main backers. But his cars did not run regularly on Central Pacific and Southern Pacific tracks until after 1 July 1883.[13] However, in spite of his ultimate triumph in this affair, Pullman's Pacific Car Company would not exist too much longer.

At a special directors' meeting held on Monday, 26 June 1871, Pullman stated that the capital stock of the Pullman's Pacific Car Company totaled 5,000 shares. The firm owned 2,600 of these shares, and the holders of the remaining 2,400 offered to sell them to the Palace Car Company at the rate of $200 per share, accepting payment in ten-year Pullman Company bonds bearing 8 percent interest per annum; the bonds would be convertible after three years into stock in Pullman's Palace Car Company. The board authorized Pullman to buy the stocks on those terms, although such an agreement involved issuing 1,000 bonds, worth $1,000 each, that also were to be used to finance construction of additional equipment.[14]

Meanwhile, the Union Pacific encountered financial difficulties after it connected with the Central Pacific, and by the close of 1871, it seemed headed for receivership. This was by no means the road's first financial crisis. For example, in 1869, its leaders had forestalled a critical problem by using their personal credit.[15] Then, in December 1870, the federal government ordered land grant railways to begin paying interest on their subsidy bonds. When publicized, this action drove the Union Pacific's stock so low that the company could not pay coupons on its first mortgage bonds that fell due New Year's Day, 1871. Some directors began urging the company to default; others started selling their stock.[16]

A few of these men, headed by New York financier Cornelius S. Bushnell, signed personal short-term notes to raise the needed money. Their efforts were heroic, for they thus became personally liable for well over a half-million dollars. Because these notes were due very shortly, Bushnell appealed for aid to Andrew Carnegie, George Pullman, Thomas Scott, and J. Edgar Thomson, all of whom were connected in various ways with the Pennsylvania Railroad Company. Pullman reputedly was the first to see an opportunity not only to advance their fortunes but to assume the management of the troubled road. The four men agreed to help Bushnell clear his debts in return for certain concessions, including relinquishment of control of the Union Pacific to the Pennsylvania.

Bushnell complied, and on 8 March 1871, Carnegie, Pullman, and Thomson took their seats as members of the Union Pacific's executive board, and Scott assumed its presidency. The new directors had extended their credit to the breaking point: Pullman had put up some 1,800 shares in his company, and the other three had traded bonds in the Northern Central Railway. They placed these securities with Drexel, Morgan and Company in return for $600,000 cash, which they augmented with personal funds to relieve Bushnell and his cohorts of their immediate problems. During the year that Scott served as president of the Union Pacific, its affairs improved greatly. Nonetheless, financial exigencies and other responsibilities forced the Pennsylvania group off the board. Scott, Carnegie, and Thomson left in March 1872; Pullman resigned one year later, making way for New York Central interests to take control of the transcontinental line.[17]

Harriett Pullman was probably glad when her husband left the Union Pacific board. In March 1872, when informed that he would not be home for a while due to problems connected with the Union Pacific, she wrote him that she felt "inclined to rebel very strongly at your connection with the road if your cares (and time) are to be greatly increased thereby."[18]

Pullman continued to furnish the Union Pacific with cars, although traffic declined once the first thrill of riding across the country by rail passed and Americans settled back to routine. The waning enthusiasm of the public was another reason why Pullman's Pacific Palace Car Company was in trouble and virtually out of business by 1871.[19]

However, his conveyances had elicited glowing reports from users who remembered traveling the same distances by stagecoach only a few years before. During August 1868, less than a year before the east-west lines were connected, the noted editor and voyager Samuel Bowles forecast that Pullman's railroad cars would soon carry passengers from New York to San Francisco, without having to stop or change, and provide them with excellent beds and food. Bowles and his party rode in a hotel car on a round trip between Chicago and Benton, Wyoming, the end of the railroad track. They spent four days on the car in great comfort and enjoyed the trip immensely. A veteran of a long stagecoach journey over the plains and Rockies in 1865, Bowles especially noted that his Pullman car's organ permitted passengers to spend many hours listening to music and singing as they traversed the endless stretches of the Great Plains.

Bowles also discussed the car's accoutrements and its perfect ventilation, pointing out that passengers were tolerably free from dust and cinders. He was not pleased with everything, but he was enough of a realist to understand that certain problems were inherent in traveling, especially for those accustomed to privacy and to using a great deal of water in their ablutions. He noted that such folk became somewhat annoyed "at the common corner and washbowl and single looking-glass, however elegant and [clean]." He added that when anywhere from "a dozen to forty people" congregated for several days in one car, there was bound to "be some sacrifice of fastidiousness to the spirit of travel. That the Pullman car demands so few is a wonder."[20] Noted author Grace Greenwood, on a similar trip several years later, wrote that when her party was able to retire to their Pullman berths, a lack of worry allowed them "the sleep of the just."[21]

Not everyone who rode Pullman sleepers was totally satisfied with his or her accommodations. One passenger suggested that the company order its porters to stop talking to brakemen because their conversations disturbed sleepers. The same person also requested that porters be taught to remove mud from shoes before they blacked over it (Pullman passengers left their boots or shoes by their berths after retiring, to be shined by the porters). Then there was the matter of feather pillows whose down attached first to the plush seats and then to the black clothing of male passengers. Finally, the writer commented very sarcastically about the filthy train hands who used the toilet facilities paid for by passengers. He wrote that it was a special treat for women, standing in line to use the washbasin, to watch a brakeman "begrimed with smoke and dust making his toilet." They enjoyed seeing "him rinse out his mouth, a moment before befouled with tobacco, with a glass they must use for a like purpose."[22]

Another transcontinental traveler referred to his complaints as "discomforts." The first came at night when people retired to shelves that, when arranged for the night, measured three-and-one-half feet in width and gave their occupants only enough space to sit up. The curtains did a good job of enclosing the berths, he said, but once inside, passengers had to dress and undress and then keep themselves *and* their belongings all on the shelf for the night. Some overcame the problem by partially removing their clothes, but the writer believed this was a poor solution, for there was no greater refreshment than an entire change of wardrobe at night. A second discomfort he noted occurred the next morning as both men and women stood in line to use the two washbasins in the cars: "You see a lady with a sponge and a toothbrush and towel, edging her way along the narrow passage between the curtains, to take her turn at the washstand, where she waits perhaps some minutes for the gentleman to finish who is already in possession. When she gets her turn she is waited for by another gentleman, who is compelled to be an unwilling witness to her ablutions under penalty of losing his place."

Lack of ventilation proved a third discomfort for this passenger. Part of the problem was caused by a canvas covering nailed over the ventilators along the roof to prevent snow from entering the system. As he pointed out, "I fancy there is a little struggle as with us, between those who insist on an occasional change of air and those who prefer heat even at the expense of a poisonous atmosphere." Apparently, this problem was not unbearable, it was an occasional annoyance. As the gentleman added, all these irritations could be avoided in a drawing room car where one had privacy — if one had a drawing room — and could control the ventilation.[23] Such complaints concerning the cramped berths, lines at the washbasins, and poor ventilation seemed to be fairly universal and extended as well to the "silver palace cars" operated by the Central Pacific.

The function that marked Pullman as a promotional genius was a train excursion from Boston to San Francisco at the end of May 1870. The passengers were members of Boston's leading families and its board of trade. At that time, Americans still considered Boston the nation's financial center, and the fact that Pullman secured members of its board of trade for a western excursion was an advertising coup, indeed.

The journey began on 23 May when a luxurious, eight-car train, carrying the nabobs (along with George and Albert Pullman) pulled out of Boston. A model of Victorian opulence, its lavishly upholstered and appointed cars boasted every accessory imaginable to its status-conscious passengers. There was, for example, a baggage car that housed the printing press for the train's daily newspaper, the *Trans-Continental*, along with five large ice chests and a refrigerator that cooled the party's perishable foods and wines. Next came the smoking car, containing the editorial offices of the newspaper, a wine room, and a barbershop. Two sleepers appeared next, succeeded by two specially appointed hotel or parlor cars; a commissary and a dining car brought up the rear.[24]

When the train arrived in Chicago the following evening at about 11:00 P.M., Hattie Pullman was on hand to greet her husband, who left the excursion at that point. Albert Pullman remained with the group for the remainder of the journey to San Francisco.[25] The party received a grand welcome in Chicago and rolled on to similar celebrations in Omaha, Ogden, and San Francisco. Between these receptions, if the riders became bored with sight-seeing, card-playing, and eating and drinking, they could amuse themselves by singing, accompanied by one of two organs on the cars, or they could pick out a book from one of the two splendid libraries on board and read as the train sped them westward at a smashing speed of twenty-two miles an hour.[26]

Pullman's vehicles were becoming part of the Union Pacific lore, and reports from noted writers lent additional support to his efforts in those days when people read books and newspapers for amusement and information. In 1871, Pullman and the Union Pacific negotiated a twelve-and-one-half-year contract, which they renewed in 1884. He also became interested in other western railroads, such as the Great Northern and the Northern Pacific lines. Yet Pullman had other obligations to fulfill, beyond those he owed his stockholders and customers. He also was the head of a growing family.

6

The Pullmans of 1729 Prairie Avenue

Hattie and George Pullman's four children — Florence, Harriet ("Little Hattie"), and twin sons, George Mortimer, Jr., and Walter Sanger — all arrived between August 1868 and June 1875. Their expanding family forced the Pullmans, who owned a building lot as early as 1871, to take serious steps toward planning a suitable dwelling.[1]

This project was interrupted by the disastrous Chicago fire of 8 October 1871, which destroyed the city's downtown and nearby residential districts. On that day, George and Hattie had passed a "lovely quiet Sunday," but sounds of the great conflagration awakened them at midnight. George went directly to his office in the Armour Building at 1:30 A.M., where he remained until the holocaust consumed the Pullman's Palace Car offices about 8:00 that morning. He transported everything of value by freight car to their residence before flames devoured the Armour edifice. As concerned citizens during the subsequent recovery effort, the couple helped those whose plight was far worse than their own.

George served as chairman of the relief committee in October 1871 before becoming treasurer of the Chicago Relief and Aid Society, a position he continued to hold until 1873. He also was a

The George M. Pullman home on Prairie Avenue, Chicago. *Courtesy the Chicago Historical Society.*

member of the first board of directors of the Young Men's Christian Union of Chicago, which began on 17 October 1871. Between 1872 and 1874, he served as that organization's president. Hattie busied herself by working in sewing rooms and collecting money for the relief of victims.[2]

Meanwhile, they continued their search for a new home. At the time they lived at 574 Michigan Avenue, but this abode was only temporary, and during March 1872, they made several inquiries, even though they were uncertain whether to buy or rent.[3] They soon negotiated with Henry S. Jaffray, an architect, who not only made improvements on their current house but also began construction in conjunction with builder John M. Dunphy on a new one.[4] By the fall of 1875, painters were hard at work, which probably brought sighs of relief from the couple. They had been living with their four children at the Palmer House for several months in 1874 and 1875 before moving to the Grand Pacific Hotel at the end of October 1875. They also made daily visits to their house and already were buying furniture and appliances. Records show that Hattie Pullman still received calls in the Grand

Pacific Hotel on New Year's Day of 1876; but finally, on 13 January, the family occupied their long-awaited home at 879 Prairie Avenue (later renumbered as 1729 Prairie Avenue), one of the very posh residential districts of postfire Chicago. Local luminaries such as the Philip D. Armours and the Marshall Fields were among their neighbors. Although they did a great deal of traveling that year, Pullman did find time to try out the new mansion's bowling alley and billiard room.[5]

On New Year's Day 1877, the Pullmans received callers for the first time in their new home and climaxed the day with a party. Enlarged in the late 1870s and again in the early 1890s, the house served their family until Hattie Pullman's death in 1921; it was later demolished. Unfortunately, no complete description of the Pullman home has been located at the present time, although the family had pictures made of its interior just before it was destroyed.[6]

Like many of their contemporaries of ample means, the Pullmans also sought a summer residence, a place to escape the extreme heat of the city and to relax, far from the social and commercial pressures attendant upon people of their means and position. They chose Long Branch, New Jersey, one of the country's better watering spots of the latter nineteenth century, which by 1890 would claim 50,000 summer guests. In fact, it became a very fashionable locale for those who believed that an ostentatious display of wealth symbolized elevated social status.

The Pullmans made their first recorded visit there during the summer of 1871, when they called upon President Ulysses S. Grant and his wife, Julia. After staying with the Grants for several days, they moved to a hotel. George and Hattie also called upon other friends with summer dwellings in the area, including General Horace Porter and his wife, Sophy. But filial duty forced them to leave Long Branch for the Thousand Islands region of the St. Lawrence River. George's mother's family maintained several summer camps on one of the islands, and they celebrated her birthday there each year. Hattie and George reappeared at Long Branch in September 1873 for a two-week stay at the West End Hotel. Then toward the latter part of September, the Pullmans were in New York City, looking at house plans before inviting

111

The George M. Pullman summer home at Long Branch, New Jersey. *Courtesy the Chicago Historical Society.*

architect Jaffray to Long Branch. The following June, Hattie moved into their new house at Elberon, which lay a bit west of Long Branch. Fine summer homes were located there, although most, like the Pullmans', were wooden and thus considered inferior to those in Newport, Rhode Island.[7]

They named their summer mansion "Fairlawn," and they passed the hot months there on a fairly standard schedule. After celebrating the boys' birthday in Chicago, usually with a musicale, they would board the PPC (President's Private Car or Pullman's Private Car) for Long Branch, the servants having preceded the family by about a week in order to ready the house for occupancy. They usually reached Long Branch about 4 July and enlivened the holiday with a fireworks display.[8]

The move was a large undertaking — a newspaper article noted that a "good many cars" were necessary to carry all of Hattie Pullman's impedimenta, including four children, twelve servants, five horses, three vehicles, and an assortment of trunks and other luggage. The Pullmans also used a stable car with six stalls, which provided sufficient room for the carriages and berths and sitting rooms for the grooms and hostlers.[9]

The children enjoyed their summers at Fairlawn, and Florence and Little Hattie celebrated their birthdays in between forays to crab, swim, sail, and ride. Their parents shared these diversions but also engaged in more adult activities, such as lawn parties and receptions where they entertained an endless procession of guests. From New York, Pullman would take a boat or train to Fairlawn as often as he could, sometimes leaving the city in the evening and returning the next morning. Invariably, a friend, relative, or business associate accompanied him. Hattie entertained their friends and members of the family and maintained an active social life among the summer people in the area.

At least once a summer, the Pullman's visited the family property in the Thousand Islands region of New York, where George had spent a few weeks during the summer of 1863 or 1864 with Henry and Helen.[10] An expansion of the St. Lawrence River, the Lake of the Thousand Islands measured forty miles long and four to seven miles wide and contained about seventeen hundred islands.[11] Eventually, the Pullmans acquired title to one of the islands on Alexandria Bay, the chief resort of the Thousand Islands on the U.S. side and famous for its pretty scenery and excellent boating and fishing.[12] They built several cabins on the property, which they named Pullman Island. Their standard arrival date was around 14 August in order to celebrate George's mother's birthday, although he usually opened the island on 26 July, the anniversary of his father's birth. In 1888, on Emily Pullman's eightieth anniversary, George presented her with a summer home named "Castle Rest," which became a focal point of her children's summer visits. After her death in 1892, George kept the house open, and it became something of a shrine where her offspring continued to gather in hot weather, particularly on her birthday.[13] But though George Pullman's family made an annual visit to Castle Rest, they preferred to spend the greater part of the summer at Long Branch.

Actually, Pullman had little opportunity to enjoy his several homes, for he traveled incessantly on business throughout the United States and, on occasion, to Europe. His customary route lay between Chicago and New York, but there were thrusts into Cincinnati, Cleveland, and Louisville, stops in Detroit, and excursions to Boston and other New England cities. Generally, his trips to Europe combined business and pleasure because Hattie accompanied him. In June and July 1878, for example, while Pullman worked in England, Hattie and Florence spent the time in Paris.[14]

Castle Rest, the summer home George M. Pullman built for his mother in the Thousand Islands district on the St. Lawrence River. *Courtesy the Chicago Historical Society.*

In November 1881, the entire family arrived in Paris where they planned to live for two years in order to complete the girls' education.[15] While there, George paid them a visit that culminated in a month-long tour of Italy.

On the day he sailed from the United States, Pullman's Palace Car Company's authorities determined that workmen in the shops would pay 10¢ a day for rides to and from their jobs in Chicago. This decision caused very hostile feelings on the part of workmen. Prior to that time, the company had spent $8,000 per month to furnish free rides; now, workers would pay half of this expense. When management announced the decision, carpenters and painters immediately struck and, together with several hundred fellow workers, held a peaceful meeting during which speeches were made and a committee was chosen to discuss the matter with the manager.

But, though he was friendly to the deputation, the manager voiced little hope that the company would retreat from its new position. Pullman responded that he had paid some $200,000 for employee transportation in the past but was still willing to pay half in the future. When reports of his answer reached the meeting, participants decided on a general strike unless L. M. Johnson, assistant to the president, rescinded the obnoxious order. In any case, the workmen agreed to form a union. The next day, both the company and its employees maintained their standoff; a large force of police was on hand should trouble develop.[16]

A long way off, Pullman doubtless kept informed of events by cable, but there was little he could do. He celebrated his fifty-first birthday while on his European trip and returned to the United States toward the end of April when matters had been settled.

His European schedule did not work out as planned, and George wrote Hattie at the Adelphi Hotel in Liverpool to wish her and the children a safe and pleasant voyage home. He stated that he felt the loss of their society more than ever before and continued that if he could ease the "load of care that weighs upon me so heavily," he could devote more time to his family which would make them all much happier. He told his wife that he intended to work toward this goal and that he hoped she would help him all she could with her "sympathy and love for that will give me more courage and strength than anything else in the world."

Although he permitted his wife to bring three carriages back to the United States, he warned her that he would be unable to do anything to the house at Long Branch other than have it cleaned and put in good order; he could not attend personally to the reupholstering and papering as she had requested. He hoped that the two of them might be able to spend a week or two at the Windsor (a hotel they frequented when in New York City) and perhaps take a short trip to Chicago while the house was being repaired under her direction. All went well, and George Pullman left Chicago on 5 June 1882 to meet his family at the Windsor Hotel.[17] The two-year residence in Paris was over, and the family was reunited at last.

Five years elapsed before members of the Pullman family returned to England. This time, George sailed in June 1887, accompanied by his sister, Helen West, and his cousin, Emily.[18] Hattie remained in the United States but visited the Deeres in Moline and friends in Wisconsin before going to Long Branch during her husband's absence. Pullman enjoyed the voyage; he had occupied the captain's room near the center of the ship (the *Fulden* or *Fulda*), which, in his opinion, outshone any accommodations he had occupied in his several crossings. He spoke of a noticeably "cozy homelike air" that permeated the entire ship. They arrived in South Hampton and went on to London, where the women's friends awaited their arrival and whisked them off immediately; George went straight to the Grand Hotel in Trafalgar Square.

Once in his hotel, Pullman did little but rest for the next four days. He had experienced the "same feeling of extreme weariness both on the ship and since arriving" that he had undergone earlier that spring. Though it passed temporarily, he was plagued by the same miserable condition throughout his stay in England. Fatigue prevented him from doing much in the way of amusement, but he did attend several dinner parties, including one with James G. Blaine (former speaker of the house, secretary of state, and Republican nominee for the presidency), as well as a function at the U.S. minister's home. He also visited with Colonel Georges Gouraud (his firm's European representative), Samuel Elliott (a family friend), and Robert and James Caird (company representatives in England). London, which was celebrating Queen Victoria's jubilee, promised excitement, but Pullman's affliction prevented his participation in the festivities, including the Henley Regatta. Instead, he kept to his room, where he wrote to Hattie, and occasionally went out to pay a few calls.[19]

His one major attempt at relaxation was a visit to the Isle of Wight one weekend after his first meeting with the Midland Railway executives to discuss the continued use of his cars on their line. He took Helen and Emily with him and considered it the loveliest place he had seen in England. But even that outing was marred because he became violently ill and returned to London, not to emerge from his room for two days. He had several meetings with the Midland people, but the trip did little to advance his cause with them.

Except for short excursions to dine and buy a few things, he remained in his room.[20]

He probably felt a great deal of relief when he, Helen, and Emily sailed on the *Auraria* from Liverpool on 16 July 1887. They arrived in New York nine days later to find Mrs. Pullman and Florence waiting to take him immediately to Long Branch. All his family was happy to have him back home again.[21]

As doting and wealthy parents of two very accomplished daughters, the Pullmans followed the custom of their class by sending Florence and little Hattie, now ages twenty and nineteen, on a tour of Europe once they had completed their educations at Miss Brown's School in New York City. The handsome young ladies had to be chaperoned, and the Pullmans chose Hattie's old friend and sponsor, Mary Logan. The trip began on 24 October 1888, at 8:00 A.M. when Mrs. Logan and her charges sailed from New York by steamship. Of course, the Pullmans went on board to see that the party had pleasant rooms, and all were in pretty good spirits, although the leave-taking proved so difficult that Hattie suffered from a headache the rest of the day. Nevertheless, she recovered sufficiently to go to the theater with Samuel Elliott that evening.

George left for Chicago the next evening after quarreling twice with his wife.[22] These were not the first of such scenes, which indicated that Pullman's frustrations in business affairs were starting to intrude upon his personal life. The clashes had begun the year before when, on 30 August 1887, Hattie Pullman reported that there had been quite a "rumpus" about Pullman Island affairs and matters in general. This blowup was followed by two others on 7 and 8 September.[23] George and Hattie seemed to agree less and less on his relationship with his mother's family, and other problems connected with his business entered into the picture. He had just returned from an unsuccessful voyage to England, and he was at grips with his archrival, the Wagner Sleeping Car Company, over attempted patent infringements of Pullman vestibules. In addition, an ongoing problem with the Baltimore and Ohio Railroad (B&O) still plagued him. Also, although Pullman's Palace Car Company was doing very well,

Pullman himself was preparing for a stockholders' meeting on 13 October 1887 at which he would ask for an additional issue of capital stock not to exceed 25 percent.

His flare-up of bad temper in 1888 probably stemmed from his having to bid farewell to Florence for several months, coupled with worry over the formation of the Union Palace Car Company that threatened his organization. Further, his investment in the New York, West Shore and Buffalo Railway Company was reaching a crisis during that season. The ensuing arguments at home, of course, were very unpleasant, but once they occurred, tensions eased.

The girls and Mrs. Logan arrived at Southampton and toured northern Europe, particularly Germany. Little Hattie wrote to her mother, and Florence corresponded with her father; Mary Logan also sent accounts of the trip and the girls' conduct.[24]

Hattie spent part of the winter and spring of 1889 in Hot Springs, Arkansas, while her husband traveled between Chicago, New York, and Washington. Working at a hectic pace, he noted that the pressure discouraged him and made him feel unequal to the daily work that crowded in. However, he told his wife that he did secure beautiful rooms for them in the new steamer *City of Paris* for 16 April, and he was devoting every effort to be ready to sail to Europe on that day; by that time, he believed he needed rest or he might break down.[25]

Unfortunately, when sailing day arrived, he could not go. In fact he was prevented from leaving for Europe for nearly a month because of a stock issue to cover the costs of purchasing the Union Palace Car Company and second-class tourist cars from several railroad firms (see Chapter 10). Despite his delay, Hattie, a friend, Grace Nicholas, and another woman named Emma (probably Hattie's maid) boarded a liner for Liverpool. After spending two days in London they left for Nice, where they met Mary Logan and the girls on 28 April. All appeared to be in fine shape, except that Florence and Little Hattie needed new clothes. Joined by their mother, the girls left for Milan and then Switzerland before returning to Paris to await their father; he arrived on 23 May.

Pullman basked in the company of his wife and daughters until 29 May, when they departed London for Liverpool to sail for home.[26] Back in the United States, they passed the remainder of 1889 at Long Branch, on Pullman Island, and in Chicago, although George traveled constantly.

Hattie took ill at the outset of 1890 and spent most of the year recuperating. On 13 July, she went to the Windsor Hotel in New York and suddenly decided to go to Europe the following week, just for the trip. In the interim, the family left for Fairlawn the next day, and the day after, George, Emily Stuart (Emily Pullman's companion), Henry Pullman, and his wife all departed for Pullman Island. Hattie, accompanied by her daughters, returned to New York City; on 19 July, she sailed for Europe on board the *Etruria*, accompanied only by her nurse, Miss Parmiotti. George stayed at Pullman Island.[27]

Pullman did not see Hattie off; however, before leaving for Castle Rest, he wrote her a note, enclosing round-trip steamer tickets and saying that he had arranged everything for her. Nervous and anxious about Hattie, George did not anticipate much rest or pleasure until he heard from her at Queenstown. He requested that she not take any remedies other than those administered by Parmiotti. Two days later, George wrote Hattie, telling her how important it was to him and the children for her to get well and be her old self again. He added that his nerves were considerably shattered and that he hoped four or five days of absolute rest and quiet would make him feel stronger. He assured her of his love and his desire for her recuperation and ended by saying, "Good bye my *precious Darling*."[28]

Hattie was very weak and inclined to lie down for most of the sea voyage. Her fatigue continued after she arrived at the Victoria Hotel in London, but she was able to dress and receive visitors during her stay, including Robert Lincoln, ambassador to England, Samuel Elliott, a close family friend, and Georges Gouraud. Meanwhile, her husband wrote to report that the children telegraphed him every night and that he looked forward to seeing them. He said he intended to be in New York to welcome her when she returned and concluded that he hoped her strength would be much improved and that she was hardly a moment out of his thoughts.[29] The return trip was stormy, and Hattie must have been glad when she docked at New York City on 10 August. George and the girls were waiting to take her immediately via the private car to Long Branch.[30]

Hattie also spent much time journeying to resorts in the southern United States and California, attempting to relieve her rheumatism. Generally, the California trips were delightful affairs when she visited her girlhood friends, Dan and Nellie Earl, who lived in San Francisco.[31] She almost always secured accommodations at the Palace Hotel in that city. When the Pullmans traveled west together, they were accustomed to stopping in Denver, Colorado, to tour Central City and other scenes of George's young manhood. In Denver, they visited their friends the Walter Scott Cheesmans and Judge George C. Symes and his wife, Sophie. Cheesman, a prominent Denver pioneer, had married Alice Sanger, the widow of Hattie's oldest brother, James Sanger. Symes was another highly placed Denverite, who married Sophie Foster of Chicago, Hattie's good friend. During the 1880s, the Pullmans added Colorado Springs and Manitou Springs, both resorts south of Denver, to their itinerary. They also rode to Leadville, the state's greatest silver mining camp, because, like other Chicagoans, Pullman had investments in at least two silver mines there, the R. E. Lee and the Silver Cord.[32]

In the South, Hattie preferred Hot Springs, Arkansas, and St. Augustine, Florida, although she tried many other resorts through the years. Occasionally, she would prevail upon George to join her for several days, and such brief periods of respite from business cares in the North left him refreshed, as did the trips to California. One trip in the West in 1881, however, was marred when George had to prepare a body for burial at Trinidad, Colorado: The unfortunate man had died on board the train.[33]

Hattie and George began their stays in New York City by headquartering at either the Brevoort House or the St. Nicholas Hotel. The Brevoort House, on the corner of Fifth Avenue and Eighth Street, was "an aristocratic and quiet family hotel" patronized by English tourists on the European plan, with rates of $2 per day. The St. Nicholas, standing on Broadway between Broome and Spring streets, was a paragon of luxury and gaudy splendor when it opened in 1853. Later, the Pullmans went to the Fifth Avenue Hotel at Madison Square, on the corner of Twenty-third

Street — one of New York's most noted hotels, which could handle up to one thousand guests. A favorite hangout of officials and politicians, its charges on the American plan started at $5 per day. The Pullmans proceeded to the Windsor Hotel, also on the American plan, at Fifth Avenue and Forty-sixth Street, one of the largest and most handsome hotels in the city and a favorite resort of brokers and financiers; rates were $5 to $6 per day. In October 1885, they moved to the Victoria to live there while Hattie consulted several doctors.[34] Located at the intersection of Broadway, Fifth Avenue, and Twenty-seventh Street, close to Madison Square, its rates began at $4.50 per day on the American plan or $2.50 per day European plan. After that time, George and Hattie preferred the Victoria or the Windsor.[35]

Not all of Hattie's trips were in quest of better health, just as those of her husband were not always connected with business. For instance, they traveled to Washington, D.C., on many occasions, spending much of their time visiting General (John A.) Logan and his wife, Mary. Also, during the early and middle 1870s, they were guests of President and Mrs. Grant at the White House and at their cottage in Long Branch. Pullman and Grant had known one another for some time: Quite possibly they met in June 1865, when Grant rode in a Pullman car (some authors state it was the *Pioneer*) from Detroit to his home in Galena, Illinois. Probably the greatest thrill for Hattie came in January 1872 when she and George spent a week at the White House, where she assisted Mrs. Grant as hostess at two White House receptions.[36] The Pullmans reciprocated by entertaining the Grants when they visited Chicago (for example, Hattie gave a reception for the president and his wife, inviting 525 people) and by hosting the Grants at Pullman Island. Throughout the years, the Grants and Pullmans saw each other many times, and in 1885, George and Hattie rented rooms at the Windsor Hotel to watch the general's funeral procession.[37]

Although the Pullmans were acquainted with other presidents (including Grover Cleveland, Benjamin Harrison, and William McKinley), they were never as close to them. Not surprisingly, George Pullman, an active Republican who was well known in Washington and a liberal contributor to his party's coffers, was not an intimate of Cleveland, a Democrat. But during Harrison's administration, Pullman lunched at the White House several times and occasionally spent an hour with the president's family following those meals.[38] Once when Hattie was sick in Washington, Harrison's wife sent her a basket of flowers. And in 1890, President Harrison appointed George a member of the International Railroad Commission, a position he declined after much soul-searching because the appointment would impose too much work and responsibility on his already overloaded schedule.[39] Pullman's death early in the McKinley administration precluded a closer relationship with that chief executive. Perhaps George and Hattie would have been guests at the White House more often had James Blaine won the 1884 election — there was a warm friendship between their families.

Certainly, George and Hattie did not lack close friends, as their guest lists in Chicago, New York, and Long Branch attest. These included notables from all over the United States. The couple obviously played an active part in the Chicago social scene, particularly that of Prairie Avenue. Nevertheless, both were gone much of the time, and such absences prevented their giving as much time to entertaining as did their more sedentary neighbors (although they, too, traveled a great deal). Their intimate friends included leading lights of Chicago's affluent world, as well as prominent figures at the national level.

In spite of his unremitting social and work schedules, Pullman donated time and money to worthwhile causes in Chicago. In 1869, when the Chicago Club came into being, Pullman was among one hundred original members and one of that number who advanced the club $500. When the Chicago Manual Training School got started on the night of 30 January 1883, Pullman was one of its nine trustees. He also helped support the *Weekly Magazine*, a Chicago publication that appeared in 1882 but ceased operations in 1884 because of financial difficulties. In addition, George was a member of the board of counselors of the Chicago College of Dental Surgery. A director of the very social and historically minded Calumet Club, he also officiated as vice president of the Chicago Citizens League in 1885.[40]

Through a love of music, he joined the Chicago Musical Festival Association and subscribed to its guarantee fund. Thus, his money helped back the First and Second May Musical Festivals presented in Chicago in 1882 and 1884. In 1890, with the inception of an Orchestral Association that would become the permanent Chicago Orchestra in 1891, Pullman stood among the original fifty members to handle the financing of the new orchestra. They left the musical technicalities to Theodore Thomas, the director.[41]

Along more commercial lines, Pullman's name appeared as a trustee of the Merchants Loan and Trust Company. He also served as a vice president of the Chicago Baseball Club, formed at a public meeting on 1 October 1869. A charter member of Chicago's Commercial Club, organized in 1877, he became its vice president in 1884. And when the Chemical National Bank failed, Pullman joined those wealthy Chicagoans who gave guarantees against its losses on the deposits of Columbian Exposition exhibitors.[42]

Although the Pullman children accompanied their parents on many of their trips, the twins remained in Chicago much of the time. Florence and Harriet attended Miss Brown's School in New York City, Florence graduating with high honors in 1887, and Harriet in 1888. The boys began their schooling in New York City on 25 January 1883. Their teacher, Miss Jones, charged $1.50 per hour for the two; however, tutors handled much of their education because the family spent so much time traveling. In September 1888, they were enrolled in St. Mark's School in Southboro, Massachusetts, a heartbreaking wrench for them and their mother at the outset, although they apparently enjoyed their time at the school very much. During the summer of 1889, they had a tutor at Long Branch, and that September, they entered the Dobbs Ferry School in Brooklyn. When they were seventeen years old, in 1892, they enrolled at the Hill School for Boys at Pottstown, Pennsylvania. All these institutions were designed to prepare them for college; in addition, they attended the University School of Chicago and the Chicago Manual Training School for one year each.[43]

The Pullmans raised their children in accordance with Victorian standards. In addition to formal educations, their progeny received dancing lessons, attended parties, and enjoyed various other amusements of the time. The girls learned how to be good hostesses and to conduct themselves as young ladies, all of which

123

climaxed with the grand European tour in 1888–1889. The boys learned how to be gentlemen, and both were excellent horsemen, although Georgie seemed the better rider. The twins suffered the usual maladies and mishaps connected with youth: Sanger had an abscessed eye, for example, and Georgie suffered a broken leg when a horse fell on him.[44] Troubled by other childhood plagues and disorders, they still survived and joined the young social crowd in Chicago.

Nonetheless, as time went on, Pullman was not altogether satisfied with three of his children. Florence (or "Nonie" as the family called her) was a great source of contentment and pride to him. But Harriet, George, Jr., and Sanger constantly violated his very proper Victorian concepts of how youngsters should act and how they should treat their elders, their father in particular.[45] Probably, like many fathers before and since, he did not understand teenagers. His style of paternalism had worked to a degree with his younger brothers and sisters during the 1850s and 1860s, but it did not succeed with his own offspring during the 1880s and 1890s. His and Hattie's prolonged absences meant that the children, especially the twins, grew to adulthood under the care of governesses, aunts and uncles, their maternal grandmother, and a succession of tutors before and during their stays in several boarding schools. To be sure, Pullman had been gone much of the time his siblings Charlie, Helen, Emma, and Frank were growing up; yet, their mother had always been with them. Moreover, they had lived in a much smaller community, and money had not been quite so easy. Further, as Charlie and Frank reached manhood, George did not get along with them either; Charlie was forced to turn to his older brother for aid, but Frank had rebelled openly against his paternalism.[46]

Suppressing their misgivings concerning their children, the Pullmans continued their lives as prominent socialites, receiving and visiting friends on holidays and attending dance classes, dinners, and receptions. They reciprocated with similar affairs in Chicago and at Fairlawn: On 1 June 1886, for instance, Hattie held a reception in Chicago at which four hundred ladies and gentlemen were in attendance. Pullman loved the theater (they had a small one in their Prairie Avenue home), and whether in New

York or Chicago, he constantly attended stage productions, taking all available members of his family and any guests staying with them at the time. After the town of Pullman was completed, they took parties (via private car) to the theater there or, in summer, to the regattas on the community's lake. Thus, the Pullmans were known as gracious hosts who entertained frequently in their homes in Illinois, New Jersey, and New York; there were few nights, indeed, that they sat down to dinner by themselves.[47]

Much of this rich style of living, however, still lay in the future, as Pullman began to direct his energies toward European railroads that also seemed likely markets for his luxury cars.

7

Pullman Expands to England and Italy

Word spread as George Pullman continued to make a name for his carriages and himself in the United States, and foreign railroad companies began to take an interest in his cars. People "in influential quarters" approached and even urged him to extend his operations to Europe, yet he preferred to confine them to the United States.[1] Nevertheless, such interest eventually must have whetted his own, for on the afternoon of 10 August 1870, George and Hattie Pullman, leaving their little daughters, Florence and Harriet, with their grandmother Sanger, sailed from New York on board the steamship *Ruskin*. The couple soon discovered several friends among the passengers, who introduced them to others. Among them were Colonel and Mrs. Georges Gouraud; the colonel soon would become Pullman's European representative. The Pullmans enjoyed the second day as much as the first, spending it reading, talking, and consuming five meals. They arrived at Queenstown (today's Cobh) on the southern coast of Ireland on 19 August and immediately went ashore, catching a train to Cork. Several shipmates, including the Gourauds, joined them. At Cork, they kissed the Blarney Stone and spent the night.

127

The following day, they shopped and drove about the city before boarding the train for Killarney. Their next day was filled with more shopping and sightseeing, for there was much to wonder at and do in the Killarney area. The Pullmans then took a train to Dublin, where they watched the comedian Toole that evening. Three days passed quickly in Dublin as they shopped and visited its cultural and historical monuments. The Pullmans left Dublin by boat on 26 August, across the Irish Channel to Holyhead. Both were very seasick during the crossing but thoroughly enjoyed their car ride from Holyhead to London.

They spent two weeks in London, ordering clothes, sightseeing, and calling on and dining with acquaintances, including fellow Chicagoans Potter and Bertha Palmer and Laura Honore (Mrs. Ben Honore). Often accompanied by the Gourauds, they took in Madame Tussaud's Waxworks, the Geological Gardens, the Tower of London, St. Paul's, Cremorne Gardens, and the theater. They visited their bank, J. S. Morgan and Company, whose head, Junius Spencer Morgan, returned their calls on several occasions. The Pullmans even ventured outside London to visit Windsor Castle and drive through Eton.

On 30 August, they toured the Bank of England and the underground railway, where attendants permitted them to ride the engine. On 5 September, Colonel Gouraud accompanied them to Greenwich to attend a twenty-five-course dinner given in Pullman's honor by J. S. Morgan. George had spent a great deal of time with the banker, probably attempting to determine the feasibility of introducing palace cars to England. Backing by Morgan's bank certainly would not harm his cause.

On 9 September, the Pullmans were very seasick crossing the Channel but felt well enough to have lunch in Ostend. That afternoon, a train deposited them in Brussels, where they passed the next two days sightseeing, shopping (spending 2,772 francs for lace), and going to the theater.

The Pullmans followed their usual pattern of sightseeing in Antwerp and Cologne, Hattie noting with interest Cologne's ancient cobblestone streets and sidewalks and people walking in the middle of the thoroughfares.

They pushed on to Frankfort, pausing at Coblenz to take a boat up the Rhine, where they lunched and savored a new wine called Triesteiner. The Pullmans shopped for glass keepsakes in Frankfort before heading to Nuremberg for a hurried day sightseeing and purchasing toys and ivory. In Munich, they saw the Royal Palace and invested in three paintings, one a Murillo copy, while squeezing in visits to a glassworks and foundry. They also saw Schwanthahe, the sculptor from whom they purchased some statuary and ordered more.

In Vienna, they took in the sights, shopped, walked, and attended a play at the opera house before returning to Frankfort to buy glass and china and to gamble at a casino. George spent one morning with a banker named Sultyback. After they returned to Brussels, Hattie remained in her room for one day with a severe headache, while George nursed a bad tooth. Nevertheless, they did buy yards of lace there before boarding a train to Ostend.

Back in London, after an enjoyable sail over the Channel, they did little more than attend plays, although they found time to tour Westminster Abbey and sail on the Thames. During last-minute shopping on 5 October, they purchased dolls for the children just prior to boarding a train for Derby. They found a good hotel at the station there and stayed all night. The next morning, Pullman interviewed James Allport, general manager of the Midland Railway, apparently a preliminary step toward introducing Pullman cars to that line.

After the conference, the Pullmans journeyed to Sheffield to meet General F. A. Starring and Colonel Gouraud, and while Gouraud and Pullman talked business, General Starring took Hattie shopping for scissors. She was not overly impressed by Sheffield, commenting that it was "the most horribly dull smokey place that I ever saw." They were in Liverpool the next day. On Saturday, 8 October 1870, George and Hattie took a small boat to their steamer *Cuba*, accompanied by the Gourauds and General Starring. Hattie was seasick during most of the return voyage to the States, but the Pullmans arrived in Chicago on 22 October 1870 to find their two little girls and Hattie's mother all well.[2]

Although the trip appeared to emphasize pleasure more than business, Pullman must have been assessing the possibilities for his carriages in European travel. Clearly, the time he spent with Morgan was not all social in nature, for Pullman did do business with J. S. Morgan and Company, and Morgan's son, J. P., would serve on the Pullman Company board of directors from 1874 to 1879.[3] And though the Pullman's trip was not unusual for those Americans who sought culture along with relaxation, they *were* traveling deep in the heart of the European railroad country. Finally, George's interview with James Allport must have concerned the future of Pullman's cars in England. One thing was certain: His attitude concerning the introduction of his carriages overseas changed in the early 1870s when the Midland Railway Company, one of the major lines in England, invited him to confer with its stockholders.

Meanwhile, Allport spent several months during 1872 traveling in Canada and the United States. His trip impressed on him the excellent accommodations railroads there offered passengers; in particular, he spent a good deal of time riding Pullman cars, accumulating some six thousand miles as he studied the vehicles and their operation. On his return to England, Allport advised the Midland directors to invite Pullman to introduce his system to the British Isles.[4] Allport was an astute, popular manager, and these men heeded what he said.

On Tuesday, 18 February 1873, the shareholders of the Midland Railway Company gathered for their half-yearly meeting in the Derby Station boardroom. Their chairman, W. P. Price, MP, announced that Pullman was seated in that very room, prepared to discuss introducing modified versions of his cars into Britain on an experimental basis. Price stated that most of those assembled probably were aware that the Pullman system provided accommodations equal to those of a first-class hotel, available day or night to those passengers "willing to pay for [them] by a small addition to the amount of their ordinary fare." This arrangement permitted Americans and Canadians to travel with a modicum of discomfort even on the longest, most tedious journeys. The Midland did not intend to introduce exact replicas of Pullman coaches that operated on the Canadian and American railroads; rather, the cars would be adapted to Midland requirements, although constructed along Pullman principles. They would be imported and tested on the line as soon as possible. Price concluded offhandedly that Pullman was doing this at his own risk.[5]

George Pullman acknowledged Price's introduction and the applause that followed; he then addressed the meeting, using models of his cars to illustrate and reinforce his points. He secured the contract, promising that eighteen new cars would be shipped from Detroit the following September and that he would return to oversee their introduction.[6]

James Allport demonstrated not only prescience but excellent timing. Because Britain's small size and short distances had worked against the use of sleeping cars within its borders, many English businessmen were forced to ride fast trains to various cities to or from London and to arrive at their destinations very late in the evening or early in the morning. By the time they secured suitable lodging in a hotel, it was so late that they slept only a few hours and were barely awake for their appointments the following morning. James Ashbury, chairman of the Ashbury Railway Carriage and Iron Company, observed their problem and, in an attempt to alleviate it, placed the first sleeping car ever run in England on track in late January or early February 1873. He planned to run the conveyance from Glasgow to London, but a heated axlebox forced him to uncouple it from the train. He tried again on 24 February, less than a week after Pullman conferred with the Midland officials; this time, the car ran the course from Glasgow to London successfully, arriving at the Great Northern Railway terminal at King's Cross. But despite its success, one reporter noted that the car was "vastly inferior to the Pullman cars."[7]

Pullman entered into the Midland contract at considerable personal risk, for both parties looked upon the deal as experimental. Not only did he plan to secure the financing for the proposition himself, he also agreed to build as many sleeping, parlor, or drawing room cars as the Midland's traffic could handle. The vehicles would also be designed and built to serve the British loading gauge and equipped with all the recent Pullman improvements. In addition, Pullman's Palace Car Company agreed to provide all the car attendants and to keep the bedding and upholstery in repair (actually, this was standard Pullman contractual procedure). The Midland had the option to purchase a half interest in the cars that Pullman's company operated on its line.[8]

In addition, Pullman agreed to build day coaches to be sold to the Midland Railway Company. These carriages would contain ordinary seats for all three classes of English passengers who did not wish to pay the additional fare or supplement that Pullman charged for the privilege of riding in the sumptuous palaces. Dealing with various classes was something new to Pullman because social classes usually mixed freely on American trains. He would also introduce American baggage cars and the American system of shipping baggage to the Midland lines, using Pullman coaches. Furthermore, his company would build car entrances on all Pullman-built conveyances at the end, not on the sides as they customarily were in England. They would also be six inches lower and eight inches narrower than Pullman coaches in the United States, an accommodation to Britain's lower tunnels and narrower bridges.[9]

The Midland agreed that Pullman would receive exclusive rights to provide dining, drawing room, and sleeping cars on its line for fifteen years (the length of the contract). The rail line would provide two sheds at Derby where Pullman could build his own drawing room and sleeping cars along with the Midland's day cars; he also received additional rights to build cars for other English lines in those sheds.[10]

Pullman consented to allow the Midland to run his cars on its lines free of any charge or payment. His financial return for his outlay of capital and expenses would come via a small additional charge — 2 s. 6 d. for each hundred miles — to those passengers who wished to enjoy the extra comfort provided by his cars. Meanwhile, the railroad would collect the usual fares. Thus, in effect, two trains running each way between London and Liverpool would be American in all respects except for the retention of the compartment system on day coaches and third-class travel accommodations, plus a few other minor features.[11]

Pullman returned to London, where he and his wife had been residing since early January.[12] There he arranged to finance the

Midland contract with three Londoners: Ernest Benzon, Edward Henry Green, and Julius Beer. These men agreed to pay the Pullman Company £20,000 in exchange for a half interest in its contract with the Midland Railway Company. The three Englishmen would also provide half the necessary funds to activate the contract with the Midland. They proposed to expand the Pullman system in Europe; whenever business developed sufficiently to establish a company or companies, Pullman would send four of its cars for experimental purposes, with the English subscribers bearing half the cost. As soon as the Pullman Company executed a contract to run any of its cars over any railroad on the Continent, the Englishmen would pay the company an additional £15,000, as well as half the manufacturing and delivery costs. They signed the necessary documents on 14 March 1873.[13]

The next day, George and Hattie steamed for New York aboard the Cunard liner *Abyssinia*. They arrived in Manhattan on 26 March, spent the following day with his mother, and departed for home on 28 March.[14] There was much to be done.

Back in Chicago, Pullman called a special directors' meeting on 3 April to approve and confirm his contracts with the Midland Railway Company and with Benzon, Green, and Beer.[15] At another special directors' meeting less than a month later, on 26 April, H. E. Sargent's resignation from the board was accepted, and Edward E.L.P. Benzon of London was immediately elected to fill the vacancy. Three months later, on Friday morning, 25 July, the directors convened once again at another special meeting in their office at the corner of Michigan Avenue and Adams Street in Chicago: They affirmed that Benzon, Green, and Beer had paid the Pullman Company $111,410.90 for the privilege of gaining a joint interest in the contract with the Midland Railway Company and in any other contracts that might thereafter be made in Europe.[16]

Meanwhile, George Pullman forged ahead, and by April 1873, his company already was hard at work producing cars destined for service in England. Albert Pullman, by then second vice president of the Pullman Company and the true construction man of the two brothers, left for England on 2 July 1873 to take charge of assembling the carriages once they reached England.[17] A month

later, on 2 August, the Pullman Company shipped the first install-
ment of cars from Montreal. This group consisted of three parlor
cars and three sleepers that the company built and then broke
down into sections for the journey. Arriving in Liverpool, they were
transported to the Midland Company's shops at Derby, where
Albert oversaw their reassembly by a "corps of men from the
Detroit shops." The only problem seemed to be the wheels, since
those used on English trains were larger than those mounted on
American cars, so the workers substituted English wheels, enlarg-
ing the American-style trucks, or "bogies," to fit them. With that
exception, the imported carriages were wholly American in construction. The rest of the vehicles were scheduled to be forwarded
in the course of a month — four day cars, combining first- and
second-class passenger accommodations, and four baggage cars.[18]

On 25 January 1874, the *Midland*, a sleeper, stood ready for
service. The car rested on bogies that were adapted to the larger
British wheels. A second car, the *Excelsior*, issued from the Derby
shops on 15 February, was also a sleeper, but like the *Midland*, it
had some adaptations. The *Midland* was not a standard sleeper
but combined ten sofa sections with two cross sections. A cross
section was the standard Pullman plan of two seats facing each
other, with a folding berth installed above them. A sofa section
differed from the cross section in that the two facing seats were
replaced by a sofa, which made into a berth, backed up to the
window. Sofa sections usually appeared in compartments, and each
Pullman designed for use in England had two at one end and a
corridor that ran to one side. Each compartment's sofa section
stood closest to the windows, and a small cross section nestled
against the corridor side. The *Excelsior* had eight cross sections in
the main sleeping area and two compartments, each of which
contained a cross section and a sofa section. Each section was six
feet long and made into beds that were two feet and nine inches
wide. At one end of each car stood a women's basin and relief
station; a men's toilet and a general washroom were placed at the
other end.

These cars preceded a number of drawing room cars (or
parlor cars, as they were known in the United States) arranged
with a long general seating area, called a saloon, and two private

compartments with a side corridor. The general passenger area contained seventeen chairs, and each compartment had two armchairs and a sofa. The chairs rested on pivots so passengers could turn any way they wished and tilt back until they were comfortably settled.[19] The carriages were luxurious and highly decorated, with the conveniences that Pullman delighted in providing his American clientele.

During the late winter and early spring months of 1874, the Midland Company introduced the American cars to the English by means of several excursions, reminiscent of Pullman's marketing in the United States. The company made up trains of sleeping and drawing room cars, and on one of these occasions, it rigged a sleeper to function as a dining car where passengers enjoyed lunch. Although the meal must have been prepared before the journey began, this was the first time food was served on an English train. The excursion, which drew the usual quota of suitably important people, received a good rating. On a run from St. Pancras Station (London) to Bedford and back, gentlemen of the press were included and were served old sherry, poultry, game, and champagne, with a grand finale of sweet liqueurs compliments of George Pullman. Needless to say, their reactions were most favorable and proved that Pullman knew how to treat the press, no matter what the country.[20]

On 1 June 1874, a complete train of American cars, capable of carrying two hundred passengers, began a regular day and night run between St. Pancras and Bradford. The train was a special express composed of five cars, two of which were actual Pullmans; the other three were common American day coaches for second- and third-class occupants. The train represented several firsts: It was the first English train whose passengers could walk from end to end (although the company discouraged them from doing so); it was the first in which all passengers had washroom facilities; finally, it was the first with universal heating (welcome as this would be in the winter, passengers did not need it during June). Later, on 1 January 1875, the Midland abolished second-class fares and put on a first- and third-class passenger train in April 1875, which it followed with another American train between St. Pancras and Manchester in March 1878.[21]

At the outset, the experiment went exceedingly well. Trains featuring Pullman cars were among the best paying on the Midland by November 1874.[22] The following February, Midland shareholders learned that Pullman cars on their trains earned more per train mile, as did the Pullman train itself.[23] That June, a pleased George Pullman remarked that his success in England had prepared him to put his cars "upon every considerable railway in Europe." He had been in England from December 1874 until February 1875, no doubt observing the progress of his vehicles.

He commented that everything for the cars on the Midland was made in Detroit except the upholstery and trucks. His firm could manufacture the cars in Detroit and ship them to England — paying $400 freight per car — for less than it would cost to make them in England. He prided himself on the fact that he could send products of his home works overseas and still undersell the British manufacturers on their own turf. Bragging that the Midland and Italian roads were "merely the entering wedges," Pullman intended to place his cars on every major European line, using his Detroit works to supply the coaches for shipment abroad.[24]

Of course, the Midland was not the only British railroad interested in Pullman's conveyances; other companies availed themselves of his services after 1875, including the London, Brighton and South Coast; Great Northern; London and South Western; London, Chatham and Dover. A Scottish road, the Highland, tried them, as well.[25] All met with varying degrees of success because the British were not totally satisfied with Pullman cars.

Although some might not have liked his vehicles, blossoming overseas interests led George Pullman to combine business with vacation in England and France during the early summer of 1878. On Sunday, 5 June 1878, he and his wife, accompanied by their eldest daughter, Florence, and a maid named Elise, steamed from New York City on board the *Scythia*. After a pleasant voyage, they disembarked at Liverpool on 15 June. Once ashore, they went immediately to the Adelphi Hotel for a day and a half; a Pullman car then carried them to London.[26] From their lodgings at the Bristol Hotel, Florence, who was nearly ten, wrote her grandmother Pullman that the *Scythia* was a very fine ship and its captain most kind, which made the trip pleasant. She continued that they "stayed one Sunday in Liverpool and came on in Papa's car on Monday and reached London the same evening." Young Florence found England's capital a wonderful city that she thoroughly enjoyed touring with her parents. She informed her grandmother of their impending trip to Paris, where, she supposed, she would have to speak French and concluded by writing that her father was getting a good rest and felt very well.[27]

The Pullmans remained in London for ten days before going to Paris on 28 June. There they took in the sights and visited friends. Pullman undoubtedly used part of the time to negotiate, albeit unsuccessfully, with the French railways. After nearly two weeks in the French capital, he bade his wife and daughter farewell and returned to London to conduct business from the Pullman Company offices in St. Pancras Station. He often traveled to Derby, Leicester, and Brighton.[28]

Hattie remained in Paris, staying in rented rooms and playing whist, shopping, visiting, exploring the city, and attending an exposition. She reported that Florence was happy; her doting father hoped she was perfecting her French. Not all went smoothly, however, for Hattie was forced to seek the services of a dentist who charged her 130 francs, an amount that led her to write, "It is no wonder dentists live in grand style over here."[29]

Finally, Pullman suggested that his wife leave Paris and join him for a ride to Edinburgh on the Great Northern Railway. He had negotiated with that line to place his cars in its service, as well as on the North Eastern Railway.[30] After an all-night ride, Hattie and her entourage found George awaiting them early on 19 July. She went to bed for the remainder of the day with a headache.[31]

The Pullman jaunt to Edinburgh apparently came as something of a surprise and caused hurried correspondence between the Pullman Company and the Great Northern concerning passes to be issued to the conductor and H. S. Roberts, Pullman's general manager in England. A special parlor car, the *Globe*, was taken to London by James Bower, an English conductor who had worked for Pullman in the United States. Bower remained in charge of the *Globe* when it carried the Pullman party to Scotland. Hattie, recovered from her headache, played hostess on the trip to Colonel

Gouraud, Roberts and his wife, and a Mr. Fry. They stopped to visit the York Cathedral and ended a very pleasant journey with comfortable rooms in Edinburgh.[32] The group hired carriages the next day and drove about the city to visit many of its historical attractions.

Next, they ventured into Sir Walter Scott's country, visiting Abbotsford, his home. Bower welcomed them back aboard the *Globe* for the return to London. The Pullmans then settled their affairs in London and readied themselves to leave for Liverpool.[33]

Hattie and Florence spent their final morning in Liverpool shopping with friends until lunch, while George discussed business. Then, they sailed in the *Scythia* for New York, arriving on 6 August.[34] Although the trip was a most important one for business reasons, it nonetheless provided the head of Pullman's Palace Car Company an opportunity to obtain much-needed rest between spates of work.

The Great Northern Railway began serious negotiations with Pullman for use of a car he was remaking into a diner in January 1879, to run between Leeds and London. Known as the *Prince of Wales*, the car went on its maiden run on 18 October 1879, scheduled for a round-trip from King's Cross to Peterborough. It left at 12:20 P.M., and a sumptuous repast was set before notable guests just as the train reached Peterborough at 1:50 P.M. A crowd watched the diners relish a meal of soup, lobster mayonnaise, mutton cutlets, roast beef, green peas, mashed potatoes, dessert, cheese, and celery, topped off with coffee or tea and wine. The train pulled out of Peterborough at 2:35 P.M. and was back at King's Cross by 4:00 P.M. after a most successful run. A second trip on which another group of well-known passengers dined did so well that the *Prince of Wales* became a regular feature on the Great Northern's run between London and Leeds.[35]

Pullman made his mark on English railways in a variety of ways due to the conveniences his cars offered their passengers. Pullman car lighting, provided by Argand lights that did not cast shadows, was a tremendous improvement over the customary lamps found on British vehicles. Pullman also supplied his cars with Baker heaters, popular devices in the United States, to assure his riders a warmth unknown in British cars. Passengers on vehicles other than Pullman's had but one recourse — to rent a foot warmer that was too hot to use when first obtained and that cooled down all too rapidly.[36]

The massive, solidly constructed Pullman cars safeguarded against injury in case of a wreck, as the British traveling public would soon learn. On 2 November 1892 and 4 October 1894, the Pullman cars *India* and *Iona*, respectively, were involved in fearsome wrecks. Nevertheless, the passengers riding in both carriages were saved. Although the *India* was badly damaged, the cars in back of it were relatively safe, and the *Iona* received little damage; English carriages on the same train were destroyed.[37] Pullman cars also gave their occupants a very smooth ride, thanks to the bogies upon which they were mounted. Finally, passengers riding a Pullman car had a lavatory at their disposal — a convenience unheard of on ordinary British trains.[38]

Nevertheless, the British public did not take to Pullman day coaches. People simply refused to ride them, probably because they were too public and did not offer the Victorian English enough privacy. Or they may have been too drafty when compared to the usual closed compartments of English cars. Whatever the reason, Britishers did not like the long, open cars, and the company removed the day coaches from its lines very shortly after their introduction.[39]

The British preferred Pullman's drawing-room cars and sleepers, although they resented the extra fare or supplement (six shillings for sleepers and one to five shillings for day travel). On long journeys, however, they did appreciate being able to rise from their luxurious armchairs to stretch, stand, or move about without disturbing others. If it suited them, they could freshen up in the washroom or eat a meal from their lunch baskets at a table. They must have enjoyed the warm sleepers equipped with comfortable beds, appealing as they were with snowy linen and warm blankets. They appreciated, too, traveling in rooms that were warm in winter and filled with fresh air in summer.[40]

Eventually, Pullman eliminated sleeper and drawing room trains on the Midland and distributed the individual cars among other trains that ran north of London into Scotland. During December 1883, the Midland purchased all the Pullman drawing room cars running on its line from London to Liverpool, Manchester, Glasgow, and Edinburgh. This action stemmed, once again, from customer's objections to paying the Pullman supplement for luxury travel on day cars. Frequently, Pullmans were nearly empty, and they weighed so much that the company lost money simply by pulling them. Then, too, the engineers complained of their great weight, but the company hoped to utilize them without extra charge. Pullman attempted to satisfy these criticisms by building four lightweight sleepers at Derby in 1882–1883. His firm retained ownership of its sleepers and various other cars until 1888, when the Midland finally purchased them.[41]

Pullman was unable to establish himself as securely on the European continent for there he faced an equally astute counterpart, the Belgian, Georges Nagelmackers. As a young man in 1868, Nagelmackers had traveled in the United States to investigate American railroad passenger cars; their standards of comfort had impressed him. He also met George Pullman while in the States.[42] Nagelmackers returned to Europe full of plans, which were frustrated temporarily by the outbreak of the Franco-Prussian War. Nevertheless, he bided his time, and in 1873, he began making improvements on his Compagnie Internationale des Wagon-Lits. Although he came from a wealthy family, Nagelmackers had to disband his company and turn for financial support to Colonel William D'Alton Mann, an American whose firm, Mann's Railway Sleeping Carriage Company, Limited, was headquartered in Paris; and by 1874, he had secured most of the sleeping car contracts on the Continent.

Although Mann's Railway Sleeping Carriage Company's efforts preceded Pullman's on the Continent, both Pullman and Colonel Gouraud, his European representative, continued their attempts to interest several European railroads in a Pullman contract. Among them was France's Nord (Northern) Railway, which believed its customers preferred the greater privacy of Mann compartments to the open Pullman sleeping cars; the sensibilities of French families were not quite equal to sleeping in the midst of strangers. Therefore, in May 1874, the Nord informed Gouraud that Mann's firm would carry its passengers between Paris and Cologne and from Paris to Calais.[43]

140

Colonel Gouraud responded by shipping the English Pullman sleeping car *Midland* over the Channel in June and then traveling in it to Italy, where he placed it on display before enthusiastic crowds and concluded a contract with the Upper Italian Railway. That accomplished, he tried to reopen negotiations with the Nord, which refused to yield. The colonel met defeat, too, in Vienna after trying to establish Pullman service between Berlin and Rome. Nevertheless, in his capacity as deputy administrator for Pullman's Palace Car Company, Gouraud did conclude two sleeping car contracts with Italian railroads. The first, made with the Upper Italy Railroad Company on 24 June 1874, was to run fifteen years, as did the second contract with the Southern Railroad Company, executed on 13 August 1874.[44]

Meanwhile, Mann and Nagelmackers successfully placed one of two boudoir cars in England in June 1875, on a short run between Victoria Station and Dover. Their entry was a type of parlor car with a drawing room, pantry, smoking room, and honeymoon compartment. Mann cars always emphasized luxury, but even more, they stressed privacy as a counter to the more public accommodations of Pullman vehicles.[45]

In December 1876, Georges Nagelmackers bought out Colonel Mann's interest and reincorporated the Compagnie Internationale des Wagons-Lits. The Wagons-Lits organization, which was also headquartered in Paris, became too strongly entrenched for Pullman to overcome. Nagelmackers had all the financial support he needed and was very reluctant to deal with Pullman, who seemed to want control of the Wagons-Lits.[46]

But Pullman's Italian contracts put his cars in service on the northern lakes, a great tourist area, and he did have a contract with Italy's Southern Railroad. He soon opened an office in Milan (although Colonel Gouraud kept the main offices of Pullman Europe in Paris) and set up a plant in Turin where workers could assemble the American-built cars. The Italians liked the Pullman sleeping cars, which were quite similar to those on the Great Northern and Midland railways in England. By 1876, there were twenty Pullman sleepers running on Italian rails. In fact, Pullman cars were so popular that King Humbert of Italy included them among his reasons for knighting Pullman toward the end of the

1880s. Pullman himself made very little of the honor, though it must have pleased him a good deal; unfortunately, it gave journalists a good chance to poke fun at him.[47]

Thus, Pullman kept Nagelmackers out of the greater part of Italy, just as the Belgian prevented him from expanding his interests in the rest of Europe. This situation frustrated both men, who finally resolved the problem when Pullman sold Nagelmackers his Italian interests and operations in 1888. He may have welcomed this opportunity because he had become entangled in legal difficulties with the Meridionale Railway Company in Italy as early as 1881. But it is clear that his inability to gain a major portion of the European sleeping car business became one of the great disappointments of his life.[48]

In spite of George Pullman's difficulties on the Continent, he still managed to use his European connections for occasional business and pleasure trips. On 1 June 1881, Hattie and George left New York for Europe, particularly Paris, and were back in the United States on 30 July. The record does not show the purpose for this journey; later events suggest that they might have made arrangement for a longer stay that commenced in October 1881, when Hattie and the children went to Paris to live. They were in Paris on 6 November and planned their French sojourn to last for at least two years, until the girls had completed their educations.[49]

George Pullman followed them on 14 February 1882. On the eve of his departure, he stated that fifty Pullman cars, representing $750,000, were running on foreign roads. He arrived in Paris on 26 February and likely spent the next few days enjoying his family and the social scene with Hattie, as he continued his fruitless negotiations with unyielding French railroads.[50]

Then on 10 March 1882, the entire family, accompanied by several guests, left Paris on board a special Pullman car headed for Italy. On 11 March they were in Turin, where they probably inspected the Pullman plant as they drove about. Their next stop was Florence for two days of sight-seeing before moving on to Rome, where they spent their time being tourists and where the gentlemen of the party attended the opera. They shopped in Naples, visited Pompei and Sorrento, and then moved on to Venice via Bologna. In Venice, they purchased a sizable quantity of glass but found time to tour the Doges' Palace and St. Mark's Cathedral and take an evening row in a gondola.

They reached Milan on 23 March, and Pullman probably showed them his offices there as they took in the old city's many attractions. That evening, they heard the opera at La Scala. They left Milan the next day and reached Paris on 26 March. Pullman remained there for several days before going on to London with his wife, Samuel Elliott, and H. S. Roberts.[51]

Once in London, George Pullman faced several matters that needed his attention, among them the formation of the British Pullman Palace Car Company that absorbed the English division of the Pullman Palace Car Company (Europe). Although the new firm did not come into being until a meeting on 8 September 1882, Pullman must have laid the groundwork for its inception while in London.[52]

In addition, Pullman was experimenting for the first time with electrical equipment on his drawing room car *Beatrice*, one of a train of Pullman cars running on the London, Brighton and South Coast Railway from London to Brighton. The *Beatrice* boasted a ladies' boudoir, but its great attraction was the electric equipment. The line first tried the new system on 14 October 1881 (with standard kerosene Argand lamps held in reserve in case of failure), and the lights glowed the entire time. Faure batteries, which lasted six hours without recharging, supplied the current for twelve Swan incandescent lamps mounted in the lower decks of the roof. The experiment created great interest at a time when most people still used oil or candles in their homes; as a result, three additional Pullmans running on the London, Brighton and South Coast Railway received electric systems that December.[53]

George Pullman must have spent additional time negotiating with Midland Railway officials because, as noted above, that line absorbed all Pullman parlor cars and two diners in December 1883. Although overbooked with business appointments, he hosted a dinner party at his London hotel on 6 April, and then he and Hattie invited a group of businessmen to ride a Pullman car to Dover. Hattie accompanied her husband and Samuel Elliott to Liverpool on 11 April 1882 and watched them sail that afternoon. Pullman and Elliott docked in New York ten days later.[54]

Apparently, the European plan did not work out for Hattie and the children, for they were back in the United States in the summer of 1882.[55] There may have been some financial constraints behind the change in plans: George was hard-pressed during the early 1880s due to the expenses of his new town of Pullman and because of poor financial conditions in the United States.

Pullman spent a month in England (18 June–25 July) in 1887. Once again, he must have gone there to negotiate with the Midland because his contract with that company was due to expire the following year. As it turned out, the railroad did not renew this contract and took over his remaining operations on that line during 1888, due to the passengers' reluctance to pay the supplement he charged for riding his cars.[56] The Midland then reduced the supplement from eight shillings to five in order to compete with the London and South Western Railway, even though the latter's cars did not have the hot water heating system standard on Pullman cars.[57]

George also may have gone to negotiate with other British railways for the use of vestibules, since he did maintain contracts with other railways besides the Midland. Actually, the Pullman Company continued to operate in Great Britain until 1963, when all lines were nationalized.[58]

Thus, Pullman's ventures overseas were not great successes. Nevertheless, his cars were very popular in the United States, Mexico, and Canada — so much so that the 1870s and 1880s were decades of steady growth for the firm.

8

Growth and Tragedy During the 1870s

By the outset of the 1870s, George Pullman no longer worked closely with the men who labored over his luxurious conveyances. Instead, he dealt with business managers who, like him, were active participants in the rapid expansion and transition of America's financial and industrial systems. During this era, many businesses grew from small concerns, in a country that basically had been rural and agrarian, to large corporations, in a land that was fast becoming urban and industrial.

Times were ripe for such changes following the Civil War. The federal government encouraged men like Pullman to grow by interfering as little as possible with their machinations or by passing legislation that helped, rather than regulated, their industries. In addition, industrial enlargement insured a good market for Pullman's products, thanks to the rapidly expanding railroads (thirty thousand miles of new track appeared between 1867 and 1873), investment capital, and sufficient labor to finance and carry out such development. The recently laid track provided fresh highways for Pullman carriages to carry passengers whose affairs sent them throughout the land. The connection with the Union Pacific lent a decidedly national aspect to Pullman's company, and his alliance with the Pennsylvania Railroad, the second leading transportation system between the East and the Midwest, tied his organization to a second major player in the new era of growth.

Pullman continued to exhibit his organizational talent and good judgment as he headed his growing concern. Like many businessmen of his day, he looked for means to check competition that not only threatened profits (not to mention stockholder dividends) but appeared to be very inefficient and wasteful, although a few years before, such rivalry had been a desirable commercial ingredient.

His energy, drive, resourcefulness, and ambition, along with his desire for wealth and high social status, typified many of his associates as well. His expensive tastes and extravagant way of life did differentiate him from a good number of his contemporaries who were inclined to lead more frugal lives, yet there were many his age who had no qualms about flaunting their success. Pullman's marriage to one of Chicago's well-placed belles assured him prominent social status in that city. And like many members of his group, he observed the social propriety of attending church (the Presbyterian, after his marriage), but he was not a member. Certainly, he was right in step with the times as he oversaw his own expanding operation, of which he was no longer sole owner or even a partner: He now relied on the advice of a board of directors and answered to stockholders for his decisions aimed at increasing the size and income of his corporation.[1]

When stockholders in Pullman's Palace Car Company met on 31 January 1870, they concurred that the firm's business depended on forming continuous lines of sleeping car communications and absorbing sleeping car facilities on as many trunk lines as possible in order to prevent useless competition. More importantly, they maintained that the company should preserve an unbroken line of its own cars from the Atlantic seaboard to connect with the Pullman Pacific Sleeping Car lines. Furthermore, they felt it behooved their interests to terminate existing litigation involving the ownership and validity of patents used in sleeping car construction.

First on the roster was the matter of the Central Transportation Company, which had plagued Pullman's firm since its inception in 1867. By 1870, the Central Transportation had instituted several suits against George Pullman (sole owner of the patents used in construction of the cars sold to Pullman's Palace Car Company and in all the cars since built for it), alleging infringement of patents they owned and used in constructing their own cars. Not only were these suits likely to be lengthy and expensive affairs, but they were liable to impair markedly, if not destroy totally, the value of the patents to both parties, which would seriously damage the Pullman Company.

During the winter of 1869, representatives of the Central Transportation Company approached Pullman's firm with a proposal to 1) consolidate the interests of the two companies or 2) permit Pullman's Palace Car Company to lease the rolling stock, franchises, and equipment and acquire the patents of the Central Transportation Company. Pullman directors determined that a lease would serve their company's best interests because it would dispose of the litigation. Also, it would give their firm complete control of all sleeping car patents and many important sleeping car contracts. These included contracts with the Pennsylvania Railroad Company and all its leased lines from New York to Chicago, St. Louis, Cincinnati, and Louisville, as well as a large number of its valuable interior lines.

The terms offered by the Central Transportation Company included a ninety-nine-year lease for a rental of $264,000 per year and an additional bonus of 3,000 shares of Pullman's Palace Car Company stock. Pullman's board accepted and issued 3,000 shares of stock (par value $300,000) to Richard D. Barclay of Philadelphia, trustee for the Central Transportation negotiators.

In return, Pullman acquired all the property, equipment, contracts, and patents belonging to the Central Transportation Company, consisting of sleeping car contracts with sixteen railway companies that covered some four thousand miles. According to the agreement, the Pullman Company would pay Central Transportation the annual sum of $264,000 for ninety-nine years from 1 January 1870, unless some of the sixteen railways refused to allow Pullman to continue running its cars over their lines, thereby causing the net revenue from such companies to fall below $264,000. In that event, the Pullman Company retained the option to cease the $264,000 payment and to return the property received from Central Transportation or to establish a new payment for a lower yearly amount. The Pullman Company also made a similar arrangement to acquire the entire property, contracts, and equipment of the Southern Transportation Company, along with its five contracts over some fifteen hundred miles of railway. Pullman's Palace Car Company was to pay Southern Transportation $25,000 per year, on the same terms as those with the Central Transportation Company.

In addition, Pullman had contracted with the Pennsylvania Railroad Company for exclusive rights to run drawing room cars, sleeping cars, and reclining chair cars over its entire road and those it controlled by lease.

To provide additional vehicles to fulfill these agreements and separate ones made with the Hannibal and St. Joseph and the North Missouri Railroad companies and for increased business on other lines it operated, Pullman found it necessary to provide additional cars (seventy new cars were under construction). The stockholders, meeting in Chicago on a very busy January morning, voted to increase the capital stock from $1.25 million to $3 million by issuing 12,500 additional shares. They could not afford to pay for such stock personally, so they had to dispose of a majority to people not previously associated with the Pullman Company. They also voted themselves 2,500 shares of new stock for payment of a stock dividend and reserved 2,000 shares of new stock for sale to Central Transportation Company stockholders at par.[2]

Negotiations also were pending with other railroad companies that owned and operated between one and two thousand miles of road to equip the lines with sleeping and drawing room cars. These deals were likely to come to fruition shortly, and the Pullman stockholders also voted that an additional 10,000 shares of stock should be issued at such time and in such amounts as the directors might deem in the best interest of the company; all new stock not taken by stockholders could be sold at the directors' discretion at not less than par.

The board approved these contracts at a special directors' meeting on 16 February 1870. At another such meeting on 27 July, the group voted to issue 5,000 shares of new stock that would be offered to stockholders before the public. The directors also learned that since the meeting held on 31 January, arrangements had been made with the Kansas Pacific Railway Company and the Grand Trunk Railway Company, fully equipping their lines with sleeping and drawing room cars, and with the Michigan Central Railroad Company and the Great Western Railway Company of Canada, outfitting their roads with parlor (drawing room) cars for day use. To meet such commitments, many vehicles were under construction, financed by the latest stock issuance.[3]

By the time the directors assumed their accustomed seats for the meeting on 31 July, George and Hattie Pullman were on the verge of departing for their two-month trip to Europe. Someone had to be left in charge of the firm, so Pullman had approached Henry R. Pierson, vice president of the Chicago and North Western Railway, to serve as vice president of Pullman's Palace Car Company. Pierson accepted on 10 June, and on the following day, the board of directors approved his appointment.[4]

Even though its president was out of the country, the company continued its course of consolidation and expansion. The board met on 17 August to discuss several matters, among them the proposed purchase of the Detroit Car and Manufacturing Company of Detroit, Michigan. The purchase amounted to 1,000 shares at $100 per share based on that firm's balance sheet for 31 March 1870. By 13 September, Charles Angell and Henry Pierson both wrote Pullman in London that his firm had purchased the car works in Detroit for $100,000 and that it could take possession the following week.[5]

Angell traveled to Detroit to settle with the stockholders, who called a special meeting and elected Pierson president in order to keep the organization in order. At the same time, Albert Pullman arranged to put several cars in Detroit shops for repair at once.[6] The Company now had its own manufacturing works and was no longer totally dependent upon other firms for the production of its cars.

Pierson performed well in Pullman's absence. In a letter to his employer, Angell reported, "Mr. Pierson is working hard and faithfully and my confidence in him steadily increases, and I have faith that he will more than meet your fullest anticipations."[7] Pierson kept a rigorous schedule but apparently did not like the

149

breakneck pace he was forced to maintain. In a letter to Pullman, he complained, "I am weary, vexed and most discouraged. I have been on the go every minute since you left, and more is pressing than I can do. You are needed here very much." Even though Pierson did tell Pullman to enjoy himself, he urged him not to delay his return home.[8] And, in fact, the Pullmans were back in Chicago on 22 October: Much work had to be done. Among other things, the board approved on 6 February 1871 Pullman's action in accepting Pierson's resignation as vice president, and board member Amos T. Hall was appointed vice president pro tem. At a special directors' meeting on 26 June 1871, Colonel Charles G. Hammond was elected a director, thus filling the vacancy created by Pierson's resignation; Pullman then appointed him vice president of the company.[9] Nevertheless, in November 1872, Hammond accepted an appointment as assistant vice president, and the board then approved the appointment of General Horace Porter as vice president.

Porter was the sort of man Pullman sought. Ambitious and hardworking, he had attended the Lawrence Scientific School at Harvard before going on to graduate third in his class from the United States Military Academy. Shortly afterward, the Civil War broke out, and the young lieutenant served during its entire duration. He was wounded once and received six brevets for gallant and meritorious service. Eventually, he came to the attention of Ulysses S. Grant, who made him an aide-de-camp, and Porter, by then a lieutenant colonel, gradually grew closer to his commander. He was one of among the witnesses who signed the formal document of General Robert E. Lee's surrender at the war's end.

Following the conflict, Porter remained in the army and, in March 1869, began service as President Grant's private secretary. Although addressed as "General" (a title that would have impressed Pullman) because of his brevets, his permanent rank was major. In his capacity as Grant's private secretary, he met George Pullman when the industrialist visited the president during 1871. Pullman, who was still looking for a man to take some of the burden from his shoulders, offered Porter the position of vice president with the Pullman's Palace Car Company, which he accepted on 26 November 1872.[10]

Although Porter probably was happy to leave President Grant's service because of the scandals plaguing his former commander's administration, he drove a hard bargain. The Pullman's Palace Car Company agreed to appoint him vice president effective 1 December 1872, at an annual salary of $10,000 plus necessary traveling expenses. As additional compensation for his resignation from the army, Pullman was to transfer and place in trust at the Farmers Loan and Trust Company in New York 500 shares of its fully paid stock, as well as 500 shares of fully paid stock of the Pullman Southern Car Company. After five years of service, Porter would have the option of buying the Pullman Company stock at par ($100 per share) and the Pullman Southern Car Company stock at $70 per share. But Porter wanted even more security; hence, Pullman also agreed to purchase Porter's option to these stocks.

Eventually, on 1 December 1877, Porter sold his option on both sets of stock to Pullman for $60,000 because the stock set aside for him did not advance in value as had been expected, due to the depression after the panic of 1873. George Pullman paid Porter the money out of his personal account and then requested the company to repay him, which it did in installments during 1880. In spite of his cautious dealing with the Pullman Company, General Porter served as its vice president for more than twenty years. He maintained offices in New York City and represented the company in the eastern United States and Europe when Pullman could not do so. He was well known in business circles and served as president of the Union League Club in New York for several years.[11] Although he held high offices in other companies, he remained loyal to the Pullman Company and its founder, with whom he apparently enjoyed a very warm relationship.

All was not smooth sailing for the Pullman Company, although strong leadership eased its course. Later, one commentator noted that the reason for Pullman's success was that he had a knack for choosing capable executives.[12] But, the Chicago fire in October 1871, followed by the panic of 1873 and subsequent depression, clearly affected the growth and progress of the firm.

The Chicago fire broke out on the evening of 8 October 1871 and lasted until late the following day. It destroyed some 2,000

151

acres and 18,000 structures, leaving 90,000 people homeless. The Pullman Company headquarters burned to the ground, and though the firm saved its records, it still had to locate new offices and replace stocks and bonds lost in the holocaust. Its founder and head also took time from such work to serve on Chicago's Relief and Aid Society, which assisted those who had lost everything in the flames.[13]

There never was any doubt that the city would rise again, its leadership determined to reconstruct the metropolis even before the fire's embers had cooled. Chicago's commercial base was firm, thanks to its location (which insured continued regional preeminence in both railroad and water transportation), its valuable real estate (which was the base of much of its wealth), and its reputation as a good investment area. All these advantages led to funding from the Illinois legislature, the eastern United States, and Europe that supplemented insurance payments made to Chicago's residents. Within a year, the city had bounced back and could boast about its increased real property values and bustling commerce, due in large part to the current national faith in progress and the ease with which financing was still available.[14]

The same could not be said for the depression of the 1870s, which began two years after Chicago's fire. It was the first nationwide period of hard times since the end of the Civil War, although there had been a retraction of wartime inflation following Lee's surrender. Nevertheless, by the end of the 1860s, as noted above, a period of financial stability, prosperity, and expansion occurred, particularly exemplified by railroad development. Other areas of domestic growth included cattle-raising, agriculture, mining, manufacturing, and foreign trade, much of it financed by overseas capital and inflated credit. However, bad times on the continent by 1872 and 1873 led many Europeans to dispose of their American investments.[15]

In the United States, good times led to increased speculation, price fluctuation, and overexpansion until, on the morning of 18 September 1873, the bank of Jay Cooke and Company in Philadelphia, which was trying frantically to find funds to complete construction of the Northern Pacific Railway, failed and set off a panic that ended investor faith in the nation's unstable economy.

This lack of confidence brought on price drops and declines in foreign trade and manufacturing as the money market tightened drastically; there was also an increase in unemployment. Between 1873 and 1878, interest rates dropped, as did bank clearances, wages for labor (except for foremen), and wholesale prices. Bankruptcies ran rampant among individuals, companies, banks, and industrial corporations. By 1874, almost 6,000 businesses failed, a number that increased to nearly 8,000 in 1875 and to over 9,000 in 1876. In 1875, almost 500,000 men were unemployed, and private charities struggled nobly to help the impoverished. Yet in spite of the adverse effect the depression had on individual firms and people, American production showed an increase nationally during this period.[16]

Despite the fire and the depression, the Pullman Company continued to expand both in numbers of rolling stock and in amounts of paper stock. But during the depression, it did as it had done in the past — it moved cautiously. Actually, much of the company's growth was accomplished through bond issues that began at the end of 1870. The first issue was an outgrowth of the company's absorption of the Union Pacific Railroad's entire interest in the sleeping cars, equipment, and franchises on its line. The Pullman Company gave the Union Pacific 5,200 shares of its stock, reserving the option to purchase the stock within a limited period at par.[17] To enable the Pullman Pacific Car Company to take up the option and raise sufficient money to make payments coming due on fifty cars under construction, the board of directors called a special meeting on 19 November 1870. They resolved that 1,000 bonds of $1,000 each, payable on 15 November 1875 at the Farmers Loan and Trust Company in New York City, be prepared; the bonds would bear 8 percent per annum interest. The board also authorized the president to sign and issue the bonds as they might deem in the best interests of the company.

The bonds would be convertible three years from their issue date into stock of Pullman's Palace Car Company at par and would be offered to stockholders at par. During the four-year term of the bonds or until they were converted into company stock, no cash dividend exceeding an amount of 12 percent per annum or any stock dividend would be made by the company, nor would any other bond or bonds be issued that would fall due prior to the maturity of the bonds so authorized.[18]

At a subsequent special directors' meeting on 26 June 1871, the board authorized Pullman to buy out the shareholders of the Pullman's Pacific Car Company.[19] To purchase that stock and finance the construction of additional equipment, the board ordered that 1,000 bonds of $1,000 each would be payable on 15 May 1881, bearing an annual interest rate of 12 percent. Like the preceding bond issue, this one contained clauses to the effect that there would be no cash dividends exceeding 12 percent per annum and no stock dividends; nor would bonds be issued that would fall due prior to the maturity date of these bonds.[20]

During 1872, the directors authorized two other bond issues similar to those of 1871; one would be payable 15 February 1887, the other 15 August 1892. At a special meeting on 16 September 1873, the directors ordered 1,000 bonds prepared at $1,000 each, payable 15 October 1878 at the Farmers Loan and Trust Company in New York City; these bonds bore interest at 7 percent annually. They also ordered a new stock issue to cover the conversion of debenture bonds authorized at the meetings of 19 November 1870 and 26 June 1871. The stockholders voted an increase in the capital stock of the company from $6 million to $8 million by issuing 20,000 additional shares of stock. Then on Monday, 1 February 1875, the directors voted to rescind the phrase "nor shall any other Bond or Bonds be issued falling due prior to the maturity of the Bonds hereby authorized," which was contained in the bond issues dated 26 April 1871, 10 February 1872, and 16 July 1872.[21]

The following month, the directors authorized the issue of debenture convertible bonds of Pullman's Palace Car Company in the amount of 200,000 sterling (British), which would bear 7 percent per annum interest and would fall due on 1 April 1885 or be convertible at the option of the holder into five fully paid shares of Pullman Company stock. The contract was with J. S. Morgan and Company, London. In September 1875, the stockholders voted to increase Pullman Company stock from $8 million to $9 million by the issue of 10,000 additional shares to cover this transaction.[22]

At a special meeting on 1 November 1875, the directors realized that during the present year, $277,000 of 8 percent bonds would mature, as would $598,000 of 7 percent bonds in 1878. The company needed its current surplus earnings to pay for construction of additional cars, and the board concluded that by limiting the cash dividends to $2 per share quarterly, sufficient money would be reserved to retire and cancel the bonds at or before maturity. Such action was a preferable way for the firm to pay its bonds by appropriating a portion of its current revenue for that purpose, rather than issuing new securities for their redemption. Therefore, they resolved that a dividend of $2 on each share from net earnings be declared payable to stockholders on 15 November.[23]

That year was a bad one for the Pullman Company, for it lost several of its lucrative contracts, particularly the one with the Michigan Central, whose backer, Commodore Vanderbilt, also supported a Pullman competitor, Wagner Sleeping Cars. Although Pullman secured other contracts to compensate for those lost, the business world watched his firm for indications of instability for several months.[24]

On 20 November 1876, Pullman purchased on behalf of his company $65,000 of its debenture bonds of the fourth series at 85 percent of their par value, and on 14 December 1876, he bought $5,000 of its 8 percent debenture bonds of the fourth series at 82.5 percent of their par value. The board ratified and confirmed these purchases and authorized him to buy, with current accruing surplus revenues of the company, any of its securities, up to an amount not exceeding $100,000 whenever he judged it would be in the company's best interests.[25]

On 12 September 1878, the board again resolved to issue 1,000 bonds of $1,000 each, payable 15 October 1888, at the office of the Farmers Loan and Trust Company in New York City, with an annual interest of 7 percent. Their goal was to allow the president, at his discretion, to offer the holders of bonds maturing on 15 October 1878 (which had been issued 16 September 1873) the privilege of taking the new bonds at the rate of 95 percent to an amount equal to their present holding, provided they exercised their option by 5 October 1878. For the further payment of such bonds as were outstanding after 5 October and maturing 15 October 1878, the president was authorized to negotiate the sale of the new bonds or as many of them as would be required to pay off the old bonds, holding the remainder until further direction of the board.[26]

Another matter that Pullman took up with the company was repayment for his investments in the firm. At the annual stockholders' meeting on Thursday, 7 September 1871, he offered to assign all his patents (both original and acquired) and all his claims for litigation expense concerning them to the Pullman's Palace Car Company for $100,000. The stockholders resolved to pay him that amount as cancellation for his interest in the whole matter. Then, on Friday, 25 July 1873, at another directors' meeting, the board paid Pullman $25,000 for his right, title, and interest in patents pertaining to sleeping, drawing room, dining, and hotel cars in various European countries.[27]

Little more than a year later, on 9 September 1874, Pullman presented a letter to the directors that stated that he had never been compensated for his services as the company's president and general manager. He added that, because he had owned the lines that constituted the original basis of the business for several years prior to its organization on 1 August 1867 "and having thereby become thoroughly identified personally with the success of the Pullman cars," he was "disinclined to receive any compensation from shareholders, who have, largely through faith in the system created by me, invested their money in its stock, until I could more fully demonstrate its success and consequent value as an investment."

Pullman wrote that he had devoted the previous seven years to the company's business at some personal inconvenience and at a very considerable personal sacrifice and that he believed that now, with the company established on a permanent and profitable basis both in the United States and Europe, the time had come for the board to institute just and equitable compensation for his past and future services as president and general manager. He left the amount to their judgment. The board resolved that his salary be set at $12,000 per year, effective from the date the company was organized. They also repaid Pullman for two car ventilation patents he had purchased from inventors for the company. At another meeting, the board ordered that Pullman be paid $300 per month for his traveling expenses while absent from Chicago on company business dating from 1 January 1876.[28]

Toward the end of the decade, the board members rewarded themselves. On Saturday, 1 November 1879, they resolved that, commencing with that meeting, each director would receive the sum of $10 per meeting for his services, expenses, and personal attendance.[29] The group also resolved at the end of the year (29 December 1879) that, because Pullman, as president, was occasionally called upon to subscribe to various purposes in the company interest, the firm would pay such receipts out of its general expense funds.[30]

The board also saw to it that the company made money. At a meeting held on 25 July 1873, it noted that the charges made for all work done at the Pullman Company's Detroit shops since 1 August 1872 (the start of that fiscal year) had been made at the cost price without adding any percentage for the capital invested in the shops and the construction materials they contained. Since it was customary for all car-manufacturing companies that had built and were still building cars for Pullman to charge an additional 10 percent to cover interest on their capital, the board therefore authorized the president to add a similar charge on the Pullman Company's books against all work done at its Detroit shops during the current fiscal year. The amount was equal to 10 percent of the average capital invested in the Detroit shops and construction materials during the year and was credited in the company books to an "income account."[31]

R.G. Dun and Company — a credit information firm whose minions watched the activities and growth of businesses, including Pullman's Palace Car Company during the 1870s — wrote cryptic summaries that were usually accurate and in Pullman's case generally favorable. In April 1875, Dun's man in Chicago reported that most of the company's bonds had been converted into stock that consisted of the Pullman patents, carrying a value of $100,000, and U.S. rolling stock, amounting to seven hundred cars (the first of which had averaged $15,000 a piece to build). Although it divided 12 percent on capital stock, the firm still maintained a surplus of several hundred thousand dollars. The Pullman Company paid its bills promptly, and Chicago businessmen looked upon it as an exceptionally good customer. Not all was known about the firm: Its factory was in Detroit, and its heaviest bills were incurred in that city, so if it possessed a floating debt, this was hardly recognized in Chicago.

But there was another, less enthusiastic side to Dun's summary of Pullman activities. It noted that Pullman family members were extravagant in their living outlays and expenses — they traveled constantly, played a major role in the Chicago social scene, and lived in costly rented apartments while awaiting completion of their very expensive new home. Further, the firm's European venture was thought to be injudicious; it appeared that the company was reaching for distant business that it could not handle profitably. In addition, the company's patents were expiring, and some of its railroad contracts were approaching termination.

Never before had Pullman stock been placed on the market. Now, however, several brokers hawked it in Chicago for $91, but there were no buyers. Bostonians responded in the same fashion, although a great many residents of that city held that company's stock. The Chicago, Burlington and Quincy Railroad Company also possessed a heavy interest in the corporation. The stock was down to 80 percent in October 1875, probably due to Pullman's loss of the Michigan Central contract, which was turned over to the Wagner Company. But the Michigan Central contract was only a small part of Pullman's business, and the company was doing well for its receipts had been large. The following week, its stock was selling at $89 in Boston. Then in May 1876, its stock was quoted at $85.40 in Boston; although business was not as profitable as it had been, it was still considered a firm that paid its debts and was good for large contracts. By the end of 1876, things began to escalate, for Pullman was known as a rich concern in spite of its stock depreciations during the last few months, caused by loss of contracts "on one or two of the main trunk lines." Fluctuating stock values affected its stock dividends but seemingly did not affect its credit, which remained high. Few, if any, doubted that the company would survive the minor crisis.

A reporter believed its stock to be worth about $87.90 in January 1877, and later that year, Pullman did a safe if not profitable business, sufficient for its ordinary needs. By October 1878, the corporation's undertakings were steady and should have resulted in a good income, even though an officer of the firm had absconded with over $100,000. The Pullman Company did not appear affected by the loss and continued to turn out sleeping cars, as well as a number of cars for the New York Elevated Railroad Company. The firm did a large business, paid its debts promptly, and maintained a strong relationship with its employees. The same held true through 1879, when Pullman was reputed in good credit for its regular commercial wants (that is, it could pay its debts).[32] The Pullman Company's stable financial condition testified to the fact that the depression was over and had been for some time.

Perhaps the saddest event that occurred in the early history of the Pullman Company came at the end of the 1870s when the firm's secretary, Charles W. Angell, fled to Europe with some $120,000 in money and securities belonging to his employer. Angell had served as secretary of Pullman's Palace Car Company from its inception in 1867 until July 1878. A faithful and loyal worker, Angell became very ill in the early years, and George Pullman supported him during his sickness. Later, during the spring of 1871, when Angell took a two-month trip to regain his health, Pullman gave him $500 before he left.[33]

About 1873, Angell married Eva Badger, a reigning beauty of Chicago's social world. She died on 3 June 1875 after giving birth to twins, one of whom also died very shortly thereafter. The death of his wife distressed Angell so greatly that his friends began to fear for his mental and physical deterioration.[34]

By 1876, Angell was a very respected widower with one child; he held a lucrative position and maintained a reputation for paying his debts. He was considered reliable for any small contract into which he entered because of his good character.[35] Indeed, the Pullman Company thought highly of him; occasionally, he served as its spokesman.

The following year, he began to recover from the effects of his wife's death and started to take an interest in society once again.

He dated a young woman, but when she refused to marry him in April 1878, he began leading a more dissipated life, though he was neither a gambler nor a drinker. In mid-July, he became ill but spent three days and nights with a girl named Sadie, "an inmate of Currie [sic] Watson's establishment, one of the most notorious houses of ill fame in Chicago." After that, he began making plans for his customary summer vacation of two to three weeks in the East.[36]

About 24 July, he informed his office that he was leaving for a short vacation and intended to meet Pullman in New York when the latter returned from Europe. Angell drew $1,200 from the company account, leaving shares of Pullman's Palace Car Company stock that he owned as security; their value more than covered the money he borrowed. At that time, he told the company cashier that he did not feel well and might be taken ill while in the East. He said that he intended to take a restful vacation and did not want his mail forwarded to him.

As it turned out, he also helped himself to about $50,000 in cash and $70,000 worth of bonds and other Pullman Company securities that he then sold in New York. Later reports listed a lower amount, but he apparently had been taking securities from the company vault since April. Meanwhile, Angell sailed from New York, going first to England and Brussels before finally setting in Lisbon. The Pullman Company mounted a great search for him in the United States but was unable to locate him. Then, in October, it printed a circular in five languages, including Angell's photograph and description. Sent in bulk all over North and South America, Europe, Australia, Japan, China, the South Sea and Pacific islands, and to all consuls of the United States, one of these circulars eventually led to his apprehension.[37]

Angell had $80,000 in his possession when the Portuguese government placed him in the custody of the U.S. consul in Lisbon. Word of this was cabled to America, and the Pullman Company sent an agent to receive both the stolen money and Angell himself early in January 1879. He was in Philadelphia by 23 February, where he was turned over to detectives possessing a requisition from the governor of Illinois. They left for Chicago at once.[38]

At his trial, Angell pleaded guilty and received a sentence of ten years in the state prison at Joliet, Illinois, the longest term authorized by Illinois law. Pullman visited Angell in his cell the day before he was transported to Joliet and stated that his former employee seemed very confused in his speech; the magnate added that Angell's troubles had started after his wife died. Angell served his time, marked by an unsuccessful attempt to obtain a pardon from the governor of Illinois in 1883.[39]

The whole Angell episode cast a pall over what amounted to a successful decade for Pullman and his company. One thing seems evident, although difficult to prove: Angell was apparently suffering from some sort of depression when he committed the act, though this was vigorously denied both by the Pullman Company and others who stated his act was premeditated. One long-ranging outcome of the Angell incident may have been that it caused Pullman to grow more distant from his workers. Certainly, reports for the next decade indicated that he no longer felt as close to his employees as he once had. Perhaps Angell's crime against a man who had treated him almost like a son reached farther in its effects than anyone suspected at the time.

The stability of the Pullman Company did not appear to be affected by Angell's theft, and its president went to great lengths to inform the public that it was not hurt by it, even though some thought it might cause problems for the firm. Once Mr. Angell was safely incarcerated, the company turned to other matters.

A. S. Weinsheimer, formerly cashier for the Pullman Company, assumed the position of company secretary and remained there for many years.[40] One of the last acts the board of directors performed as 1879 drew to a close was to pass a resolution calling for the company counsel to prepare a form releasing Pullman's Palace Car Company from liability for employee damages due to railroad casualties; this was to be printed and presented for signature by such employees under the direction of the president.[41] Gone, indeed, were the days when the employer shared the risks and dangers of his employees. Times were changing.

The Pullman Company was now a large organization that boasted 464 cars, gross earnings of $2,196,734.99, and net earnings of \$974,279.09 for the year 1878–1879.[42] This was not bad for a company, founded just twelve years before, that had withstood lawsuits, the worst depression of the century to that time, and a major theft. Ultimately, its sound management had left it intact and known not only nationally but internationally. George Pullman had weathered the initiation rites to join the ranks of the nation's industrial capitalists. Now, as he and his firm and he entered the 1880s, Pullman prepared to take on a venture that would bring him a great deal of fame for at least a decade.

9

Pullman, Illinois

George Pullman's bright star of success continued to shine during the 1880s. His organization prospered through constant attention to passenger comfort and the addition of new features like Pintsch lights, especially designed fixtures with one to six burners fueled by a system of gas that was compressed from petroleum carried on the cars. At the same time, placing vestibules between his cars made the vehicles safer and increased their appeal to travelers. Eventually, almost every major railroad line in the United States would use Pintsch lamps, and vestibules became standard equipment on all trains.

The Pullman Company maintained shops in various parts of the United States, while its energetic president, by then in his early fifties, managed its business affairs from offices on both Michigan Avenue in Chicago and Broad Street in New York City. At the outset of the 1880s, its position apparently secure, the company prepared for a period of solid growth. Meanwhile, Pullman surrounded himself with substantial businessmen who advised him in their capacity as company board members. His own commercial savoir faire, supported by their expertise, enabled him to sustain profitable transactions as demonstrated by the numerous stock increases he and his board requested during the 1880s. They enjoyed the confidence of their stockholders, who raised little or no opposition to the augmentation of capital stock each time the directors requested it.

But Pullman found little time to enjoy his growing wealth. Like many of his contemporaries, he was busy constantly (a fact to which he alluded over and over again in his letters to Hattie), and the affairs of his organization kept him traveling a good deal. He did, however, try to spend time with his spouse — unlike his neighbor Marshall Field, who was so wrapped up in his business that his first wife, a romantically inclined woman, languished as a result of his inattention.[1]

While consolidating and solidifying his empire, Pullman also directed his attention to the condition of his workers as a whole in an attempt to better their lives and thus improve his enterprise and save money. These endeavors added immeasurably to his fame, culminating in the creation of the company town of Pullman, Illinois.

He began considering such a community early in 1879, when expanding railroad production, together with spreading railroad traffic, greatly enlarged the public demand for cars of every description. Amplified business led Pullman and his directors to consider increasing the company's manufacturing and repair facilities. They held many discussions, finally agreeing informally upon a policy of building their own shops and other structures for such a purpose. A large plant would have to be built, but the question was where to locate it? At first, Pullman looked toward St. Louis, but land prices there soared when realtors in that city learned of his interest. Chicago was a logical spot as the hub of midwestern railroading, but, like St. Louis, its property values were very high.[2]

Other reasons for not locating in Chicago proper included the living conditions for workers in poorer sections. The slums, with their overcrowded tenements, flimsy construction, and poor sanitation, were prime breeding grounds for dreaded pestilences such as cholera and tuberculosis and spawning areas for every imaginable crime and act of violence. In addition, during the 1870s, Chicagoans endured annual spectacles of labor unrest, so that by the 1880s, many people considered such disturbances harbingers of European-style revolutions. Alcoholism also ran rampant in these sections, where a worker's only form of relaxation lay in a saloon, drinking with comrades. Pullman's contemporaries Philip D. Armour and Marshall Field did not approve of employee drinking. Field even discharged workers he discovered imbibing when not on the job; Armour was not as severe, although he, like Field, did not drink himself. The meat-packer's dislike of spirits probably stemmed partly from the conventions of the time, which discouraged the use of liquor.[3] George Pullman himself detested alcoholism, which ruined a man's health, led to work absences, and impaired job efficiency — all of which wasted Pullman's money. To remove workingmen to a clean, well-kept setting free from squalor and accompanying vices — a place where they could be taught middle-class virtues and walk to work — seemed a prime solution to the palace car entrepreneur.

Company towns were not a new idea for they had existed since shortly after the War of 1812, established by New England textile manufacturers to house their workers. Earlier in his career, Pullman had read a book entitled *Put Yourself in His Place* that convinced him of the need for cooperation between labor and capital. Although an exponent of the profit motive, he decided the best way to protect free enterprise and benefit employees might be found in time-tested business procedures. Therefore, he proposed to create not only an industrial plant but a town whose planned appearance would be maintained constantly, thus combining aesthetic values with practical purposes. Initially, the company would bear the expenses of construction and upkeep; it would be repaid by means of rents established to return a 6 percent profit on invested capital. In this instance, George Pullman differed from other industrialists who owned such communities, for they sought no profits from rents paid by their employees.[4]

Pullman intended no philanthropy, because he believed the better-class worker he wanted to attract would appreciate the situation more if he were financially committed to it.[5] Certainly, the worker's life would be enhanced, and, from the company's viewpoint, healthier living conditions and superior surroundings would lead to less drinking and, consequently, reduced absenteeism and increased job efficiency. Here, once again, Pullman resembled Marshall Field. Field devoted the ninth floor of his store to gymnasium facilities for employees of both sexes, a music room for all to enjoy, and a restaurant where they might eat for cost. He also offered paid vacations, half pay when sick, and other benefits. But though he portrayed himself as a man interested in the welfare of his workers, he, too, was no philanthropist; all these conveniences, when combined with the firm's high standing and strong reputation, attracted first-rate employees willing to accept lower wages than those paid by Field's competitors.

Pullman also believed that residents of his community, less likely to succumb to the blandishments of labor agitators, would, in turn, shield the company from strikes and other manifestations of labor discontent. In sum, the town would be a monument to Pullman's plan for bettering the conditions within his firm — assisting the organization and aiding the workmen, as well.[6]

Eventually, the board concluded that the best location for this community would be in or near Chicago. Pullman's advisers also believed that a number of dwellings and other improvements should be built near the manufacturing shops for use by company officers and operatives. In addition, sanitary regulations might be more thoroughly supervised under company administration.[7] They appointed as agent a fellow board member, Colonel C. G. Hammond, and authorized him to examine locations for the buildings and determine the number of acres needed for a successful business venture. After several months of a secret search, Hammond selected a site, presented a report on some 310 acres of real estate that included property to be covered by the shops as well as adjoining realty, and showed the board a plat of the area.

Fourteen miles south of Chicago in Hyde Park Township, on relatively isolated, water-soaked prairie where real estate was cheaper, Pullman's community would play an active part in the city's industrial scene. It would be close to Chicago, yet far enough away to avoid many of the city's baneful influences.[8]

Pullman furnished the board a detailed account of the land's cost as of 1 July 1880. Huntington W. Jackson and David B. Lyman, who held the land as trustees, offered it to the company for about $290 per acre. Negotiations were also pending with several other people for an extra ten acres of land.

George Pullman's estimates for the buildings, machinery, and other improvements aggregated to about $1 million. The board, accepting the offer, chose to receive the deed from Jackson and Lyman and to pay its cost price plus 6 percent interest from 1 July 1880 until the date of payment. They also directed George Pullman to purchase the additional ten acres required to complete the acreage depicted on the plat. At the same time, in a directors' special meeting held on 22 July 1880, they approved contracts to construct shops and other improvements at Pullman, as well as to purchase material and machinery.[9]

Pullman bought four thousand acres of land, keeping five hundred for the company and turning the remaining thirty-four hundred over to the Pullman Land Association, formed in the spring of 1880. Early that January, Solon Spencer Beman, architect, and Nathan F. Barrett, landscape designer, both of whom had worked on Pullman's personal dwellings, began collaboration on a master plan for the proposed community. At an office in the Pullman Company headquarters on Michigan Avenue, Beman designed and supervised the construction of the factory buildings and dwellings, while Barrett plotted and landscaped the area.[10]

Surveyors appeared on 24 April 1880, and on 25 May, construction began on the first building, the Allen Paper Wheel factory; by October, that structure's exterior walls were in place. Widely used in the United States (mainly under sleeping cars), the paper wheel supposedly gave a smoother ride. It consisted of a cast iron hub that was fitted on the car axle and surrounded by a disk made of layers of paper glued together and subjected to tremendous pressure. A cast iron outer tire fit around the paper disk on the outside. Chicago businessmen owed nearly two-thirds of the $1 million Allen Paper Wheel Company, a consolidated corporation of all paper wheel interests in the United States. R. V. Allen, inventor of the paper wheel and general superintendent of the works, anticipated hiring about one hundred men to manufacture twenty thousand car wheels annually.[11]

As work commenced on one hundred houses in November, and interest naturally burgeoned in the activities. Consequently, the Illinois Central management arranged excursion trains between Chicago and Pullman so people interested in the new community could watch its progress. In spite of bad weather, the brick houses went up rapidly, and on 1 January 1881, the first resident, a foreman transferred from the Detroit shops, moved his family into a Pullman dwelling.[12]

By 17 March 1881, the company had expended $1.3 million at Hyde Park for land, car works, buildings, machinery, housing for workmen, and other improvements. To provide the additional capital necessary to complete the project, the board decided to increase the company's stock, rather than issue revenue bonds. The directors were reasonably assured that the augmented profits from the larger manufacturing facilities would provide dividends on the supplemental capital. Beyond that, the investment itself would prove of great value to the company by increasing the permanency and stability of its business. Therefore, the board recommended increasing the capital stock of the company by 33.3 percent.[13]

On the morning of 2 April 1881, Pullman and fifty guests looked on and applauded as Florence, his eleven-year-old daughter, activated the Corliss engine powering the equipment in the new plant. Cars could now be produced, as well as repaired, in the shop buildings that the company had been using since the beginning of March. But the complex, though it was a significant addition to the Pullman Company, was rendering the firm's president almost crazy with work pressures as he arranged for increased capital. This might explain why, shortly afterward, Pullman and Florence left Chicago to join Hattie in California.[14]

Much of the material used in the construction of the new community was processed and prefabricated in the Pullman shops, saving both time and money. Except for seventy frame houses located on farms and near the brickyards, the dwellings were made of brick, many with pressed red brick facings. Built along broad, tree-lined streets, the residences were fitted into rectangular blocks laid out in a gridiron pattern. Each structure featured a basement or cellar (many of the tenants used them as kitchens), and all were serviced by gas and water. Some 10 percent had bathtubs. The better homes, along with all the shops, factories, and public buildings, boasted steam heat.[15]

Rents averaged about $14 per month, although half of the dwellings were let for monthly prices between $6 and $10. The company and its house and store tenants executed leases every January, each of which contained a clause permitting the landlord or tenant to terminate on ten days notice. This seemed to be a fairly standard procedure and advantageous for the company: If faced with a work stoppage, it could gain access to the housing for use by strike breakers.[16]

Other buildings in the town included the Florence Hotel, named for Pullman's daughter and opened in November 1881, which contained the town's only bar; the block-long Arcade building, with shops, library, theater, several meeting rooms, and medical and legal offices, among others; a church dedicated in 1882 by the Reverend James M. Pullman; and Market Hall composed of stores and a large room used for revivals and lectures. The new community had its own bank, vegetable farm, park, athletic field, small lake, and stables, all aimed at directing the lives of residents in a subtle, yet forceful way. Most observers responded favorably to the town, where construction continued to be supervised by Solon Beman until 1891.

After Pullman opened his new plant, he returned to Chicago for a 2:00 P.M. stockholders' meeting. There he reported that the works, now partially operating, employed about four hundred men in the manufacture and repair of cars. He expected the complex to be complete by the first of the following August when the company, including the Detroit shops, Elmira car works, and repair shops at Mantua and St. Louis, would be able to employ more than four thousand men and would own "the most complete and extensive car manufacturing and repairing establishment in this country." Such excellent facilities, supplemented by the firm's connections with America's railroad system and those in some European areas, would enable the firm "to control, permanently, a very large and profitable business."[17]

After the stockholders agreed to issue new stock, the directors turned their attention to another matter connected with the new town: a foundry and car wheel works to operate in conjunction with the car works at Pullman. The Union Foundry Company had proposed to unite with Pullman in erecting a foundry large enough to do both its work and Pullman's. The board resolved that the Pullman Company would subscribe in the amount of $150,000 to the capital stock of the new firm, known under the general laws of Illinois as the Union Foundry and Pullman Car Wheel Works.[18]

The board also authorized the acquisition of real estate in St. Louis for shops where employees could varnish and make minor repairs to cars. They allowed $20,000 for the land, buildings, and other improvements and also approved Pullman's purchase of 183 acres (at $205 per acre) to provide a proper outlet for the sewage from company buildings and other enhancements at Pullman.

Large payments for the new stock poured into the company, creating a surplus of funds over and above immediate needs. Desirable as it was to realize interest pending its purposeful use, the board appointed three of its members — John Crerar, Charles Hammond, and Amos Hall — to form a committee to lend funds with proper security when in accordance with the company's interests.

By 31 July 1881, Pullman had spent $2,545,904.96 on the town of Pullman, with board approval. The company combined monies from the increased capital stock and surplus revenues to build its Chicago car works and make other improvements: increase its rolling stock value by some $500,000, add about $7 million to its lumber and construction material, and pay $328,000 of its debenture bonds.

Still, company town interests necessitated a further expenditure of $2 million on railway, water, sewage system, and other amenities, including 750 additional homes for workmen and their families. Income and revenues from rentals would pay a fair rate of interest on the investment. Proposed additions to company property were deemed essential so the firm could promptly supply the large and increasing demand for railway equipment. Therefore, the board authorized a new issue of capital stock in the amount of 25 percent of the company's entire stock to complete the improvements at Pullman and carry out certain other projects. Then, in January 1882, the board announced construction of 115 new sleeping cars and another 25 percent stock increase.[19] In both cases, stockholders received advance notice circulars and were given an option to subscribe to the new issues at par, to an extent of one-quarter of their holdings. All stock not subscribed would be sold or disposed of at the board's discretion.

A second circular, calling for a special meeting of the stockholders to discuss and act upon the stock increase, was quite informative. It stated that the gain for the fiscal year ending 31 July 1881 over that of the preceding year totaled $363,722.25; the increase for the first five months of the current fiscal year was $342,113.40 over the corresponding period of the preceding year. Further, it noted that the company was constructing the 115 new sleeping cars at an average cost of $16,000 each. Finally, expenditures at Pullman were itemized: For car works, machinery, tools, and miscellaneous items up to 1 January 1882, they amounted to $1,311,966.26; for lumber and materials, including cars under construction, $959,108.45; and for real estate, homes for workmen, and other improvements, including seventeen miles of railroad, $2,582,588.85. The grand total was $4,853,663.06. Although work was not yet complete, the resultant revenue at the rate of $320,000 per annum would be greatly increased by the end of the current fiscal year (31 July 1882) when the town of Pullman was expected to have a population of over four thousand people residing in company homes. The sanitary, social, religious, and educational conditions would render the place unusually attractive for better-class mechanics. And the manufacturing interests of the company could not fail to benefit substantially by a contented, skilled labor force drawn by a policy of intelligent and careful attention to employee welfare and comfort. In the process, Pullman's Palace Car Company hoped to counter the tendency of workers to move frequently. Stockholders authorized one further $2,523,600 stock increase, which amounted to 25 percent of the company's stock, at the meeting called for 1 February 1882.[20]

While workmen constructed shops and houses, George Pullman, with two matters in mind, searched for large, profitable contracts for railway equipment to help finance his new manufacturing establishment. First, even though he believed it would take two years for a large organization to compete successfully in the commercial market against other established car builders, he also had to keep his employees at Pullman busy if they were to remain happy in their new surroundings and continue to pay their rents. In 1882, this led Pullman to make large personal subscriptions to securities of both the Northern Pacific Railroad and the New York, West Shore and Buffalo Railway, understanding that his company would receive contracts to build passenger and freight cars at cost plus 10 percent. He also obtained franchises for operating Pullman's Palace Car Company cars on both lines.

There was more to the latter transaction than appeared on the record books of Pullman's company. The West Shore was financed and promoted by Pennsylvania Central men who were opponents of the New York Central, owned by the Vanderbilts. By joining this group, Pullman and his vice president, Horace Porter, registered their irritation with the Vanderbilt family for having substituted Wagner palace cars for Pullmans on the Michigan Central some five years before. The West Shore, which began at Weehawken, New Jersey, paralleled the New York Central all the way to Buffalo and began to compete with the older railroad as soon as it was completed. New York Central managers responded immediately by drastically reducing their prices and beginning construction on a retaliatory line in Pennsylvania that would connect Reading and Pittsburgh. Vanderbilt's new road, the South Pennsylvania, was intended to be a direct rival to the Pennsylvania Central.

The wasteful war between the two powerful transportation companies annoyed New York banker J. P. Morgan, who assembled their leaders on board his yacht, the *Corsair*, in July 1885. The conference lasted all day, as Morgan kept the antagonists negotiating until each faction agreed to buy out the other. Such action halted the needless expenditures that had been Morgan's chief concern.[21]

Soon after Pullman made the subscriptions, financial conditions in the United States became straitened, a situation that imperiled the car manufacturing business and the Pullman Company's large community investment. It also threatened the construction contracts obtained through George Pullman's subscriptions because

both the Northern Pacific and the West Shore encountered difficulties. Eventually, securities of the West Shore and the Northern
Pacific declined so drastically that Pullman had to meet the cash
payment on his subscription — totaling $1 million — as rapidly
as possible. Informing the board of his predicament, he stressed
more than ever the relation of the company to the contracts that
were so vital to the firm's credit and the preservation of the works
at Pullman. His subscription had to be paid in full to retain the
covenants; if the corporation failed to act with dispatch, they could
be lost altogether. The loss of the contracts would involve a fiscal
disaster on the investment at Pullman, a very serious blow to
company credit, and financial loss to the stockholders. Therefore,
it behooved the firm to support its president's actions during this
sudden crisis and preserve compacts to protect its credit and
stockholders. The board rescued Pullman by surrendering 1,800
shares of Pullman's Palace Car Company stock in the treasury to
him so that he might use them to discharge the loans pledged as
collateral security by the company.[22]

As it developed, the contracts Pullman secured with the West
Shore line proved very profitable. The Northern Pacific franchise,
also very lucrative, became a stepping stone toward securing
franchises on the Southern Pacific system. In fact, Pullman would
later comment that these deals led to contracts that, when supplemented by his personal contributions, totaled about $5,065,000.
This sum sustained Pullman "during a critical period of its history
caused by the general depression in railway manufacturing from
the latter part of '82 to the beginning of '85."[23]

In spite of their eventual outcome, matters did not always
progress smoothly for Pullman and his associates. One rocky
stretch occurred in February 1884 when the New York City
brokerage house of McGinnis Brothers and Fearing suspended
operations. One of the oldest and most reputable brokerage firms
in New York, McGinnis Brothers and Fearing closed its doors as
a result of the collapse of Northern Pacific securities the preceding
fall, the depression in West Shore securities, and excessive investment in Pullman's Palace Car Company stock. Although experts
predicted only a temporary suspension, Pullman, one of their best
customers, experienced several anxious days of frantic work to get

his account released. McGinnis Brothers and Fearing owed him $25,000 for securities they could not deliver, but he was comparatively happy once he extricated his funds to find his losses were no more than $15,000. In spite of these financial problems, his personal friendship with the McGinnises obviously survived, for their name appeared often in Hattie's diaries.[24]

The tough financial periods in the 1880s forced Pullman to utilize his best marketing strategies. As noted earlier, he dealt with railroad executives personally, calling upon his good memory and complete command of his product's detail to help consummate each deal. Because he maintained that Americans would pay for quality, he made sure his conveyances were the safest available, that they were equipped with the latest innovations, and that they contained the best of everything, all supplemented with fine services. He saw to it that the public learned about his cars at fairs, by means of excursion trips, and through advertising. Certainly, the town he had created provided a fine introduction to Pullman products. There, he could augment his sales skills by giving people a detailed picture of how his palaces came into existence. Descriptions, pictures, and statistics all helped, but a plant tour that provided firsthand knowledge of the various stages of construction was more convincing and allowed onlookers to witness for themselves the care and attention to detail that went into manufacturing Pullman conveyances.

Thus, Pullman, delighted with his town, took great pride in entertaining many visiting dignitaries there, including potential clients. For example, during July 1882, Collis P. Huntington, head of the Southern Pacific Railway system, spent the night in the town. Pullman was very nervous about the visit. He was most anxious to get his cars placed on lines controlled by Huntington and his partner, Governor Leland Stanford of California. The car builder spared no effort to impress Huntington and his party, who appeared pleased, though they left their host to spend a day at home in a state of mental exhaustion. Nevertheless, Pullman's attempts to see that they enjoyed themselves paid off, for the following year, his firm secured contracts with the Central Pacific, the Southern Pacific, and the Southern Pacific of Arizona. Entry into the lucrative West Coast lines controlled by Huntington and his associates was something Pullman had aimed toward for many years.[25]

His reaction to the Huntington visit was probably indicative of the financial ordeals that beset him during the early 1880s and kept him away from his family much of the time. By the end of August 1882, his wife, a very pretty woman who had celebrated her fortieth birthday in April, wrote that she was worried about him and felt it unnatural for him to spend so much time by himself. She also commented that he appeared far from well and seemed indifferent to her. Her remonstrances led him to reply, eleven days later, that the mental strain upon him was great and that he was "awfully lonesome nights" without her. Nonetheless, he continued his ceaseless work but began using the town of Pullman as a haven. Several times during the 1880s, he spent the night at the Florence Hotel, where a suite was kept in constant readiness for him, and returned to Chicago the following day.[26]

Although it served as a refuge, Pullman's town did cause him problems on occasion. For instance, he was hauled into court at least twice by plaintiffs who charged he had usurped their lands that lay either within or adjacent to the community.[27]

By the early 1880s, Pullman's relationship to his company was changing; it was much different from what it had been when he returned from Colorado to become its head. At that time, he was personally acquainted with his men, and he and his brother Albert took an active part in supervising their work. Now, as manager and president, his control of the organization was undisputed, but his very position removed him from his laborers. His great reserve, coupled with an intolerance for mistakes and an explosive temper, led those employees with whom he worked closely to regard him with fondness and respect mixed with a tinge of fear. But his car builders and other minions, separated from him by layers of bureaucratic management, viewed him as an unapproachable person who consorted with chief executives, ranking politicians, and highly placed socialites at local and national levels. He remained in command of the working details of his firm thanks to his constant need of them, but his territory was now the board-room, not the factory floor. Workers who observed him when he visited Pullman saw an austere and distant man — a man who differed greatly from the one they had known and worked with during the early years.

Thanks to Pullman, architect Solon Beman received other contracts, including one for the company's headquarters, the Pullman Building, on the southwest corner of Michigan Avenue and Adams Street in downtown Chicago. Serious consideration on this project began on Monday, 26 June 1882, when the directors noted that George Pullman had been purchasing the vacant lots on that corner for the purpose of building company offices. On the day of the meeting, his investment in the property, including interest and taxes, amounted to $118,019.87. Pullman announced his readiness to relinquish his title to this land to the company after reimbursement for his expenses and advances and the board believed the time had arrived to save rent payments by erecting a suitable building for the company's offices. The directors resolved to pay Pullman the above amount in full, plus an encumbrance of $2,500 not yet due upon one of the lots in the property he had assumed when he bought the land.[28]

Construction got under way in April 1883, and the completed building adorned Chicago's skyline in the summer of 1884. The Pullman Building stood ten stories high, a modernized, modified Norman, round-arched Gothic structure. Fireproofed from cellar to garret, it stood as one of the principal commercial landmarks in metropolitan Chicago. Its first story was rock-faced, with reddish granite laid up in large blocks, and granite, pressed brick, and terra cotta covered the structure's steel skeleton. Estimated to have cost from $500,000 to $1 million, the edifice became the object of much admiration.[29]

The basement contained steam-heating equipment, but the boilers were housed in a separate building in deference to those occupants who disliked structures equipped with boilers. The basement also had a laundry for the building's apartments and storage areas for the sleeping car company and the stores on street level.

Pullman's Palace Car Company occupied the first three floors, although merchants with stores also traded on the first floor in spaces not devoted to the Pullman purchasing agent's storeroom. People seeking access to the second floor from the business entrance on Adams Street took a broad flight of granite and marble stairs up from the court. Here were the offices of the president, second vice president, cashier, general counsel, purchasing agent, and secretaries, as well as the telegraph office. The general superintendent, division superintendent, and ticket agent offices filled the third floor, together with rooms for conductors and porters. General Philip Sheridan maintained his headquarters on the fourth floor, the telephone company took over the fifth, and professional men rented the sixth. Occupants reached the 125 offices by means of two elevators.

The upper floors were given over to seventy-five first-class apartments, from seven to ten rooms in size, for families; there were also a number of small suites of two to four rooms for bachelors. One of Pullman's goals was to furnish interested company employees with superior living space close to their work, rather than inconveniently located homes in the Chicago suburbs. People not connected with Pullman's Palace Car Company could also rent the apartments.[30]

The dwelling spaces, all with views of Lake Michigan, were arranged for maximum comfort. For instance, even though most rooms had fireplaces, all featured steam heat, as well. Apartment dwellers entered the building by the Michigan Avenue entrance and were whisked to their rooms in two large passenger elevators. Occupants could also avail themselves of the Albion, a fine restaurant with private dining rooms, a parlor, and a reading room, located on the ninth floor.[31]

Thus, by 1885, George M. Pullman had added immeasurably to the fame and the skyline of his adopted city. People came from all over the western world — many riding in railroad cars of his manufacture — to see his workers' town south of Chicago.[32] At hotels in Chicago's Loop and the streets of its commercial district, they could observe the building he created for his company. And those who ventured into the city's elegant residential district on Prairie Avenue would see his palatial home, reputedly one of the most expensive in the city. These were no small accomplishments by the standards of his times for a man who had come there to move buildings some twenty-six years before!

10

Consolidation and Growth During the 1880s

The town of Pullman gave its founder a great deal of pleasure, but it also occupied much of his time. Numerous other matters, too, demanded his attention as his enterprises grew, and he strove to consolidate many of them under the Pullman Palace Car name during the 1880s. Pullman continued to broaden his operations and to deal with more railroad companies as he expanded into the western and southern United States and Mexico. There were few board meetings, indeed, when the members did not approve several contracts their president had made with various lines.

It seemed as though his corporation's expansive growth would never cease. In their reports of 1882 and 1883, Dun's agents complimented the firm, among "the largest and best corporations in America," on its constant acquisition of wealth and extension of business. The company's directors received their share of kudos when another Dun report called the management "brilliant, able and apparently satisfactory to all concerned." The organization paid all its bills each month, and its credit was unquestioned. In August 1883, the Dun representative commented that Pullman's firm ranked beside the mightiest and best-run organizations in

America, and its stock was among those listed that paid the best dividends.[1]

Dun's representatives considered Pullman himself to be one of the Chicago millionaires who possessed a princely income from his regular business, although his true wealth was a matter of speculation. Nevertheless, in financial terms, there was no doubt he was one of the country's substantial men. Even when rumors circulated on Wall Street that he was in financial trouble due to his dealings with the Northern Pacific and the West Shore, no such gossip spread in Chicago, and his company's stock continued to rise while others declined. The reporter noted that Pullman considered himself worth about $5 million although Dun's man placed his value at between $1.5 million and $2 million in October 1883 because his Chicago investments alone were worth almost that amount. His home, "about the finest residence in Chicago," was said to be worth approximately $500,000. In April 1884, the company, according to its secretary, A. S. Weinsheimer, was in better condition than ever, with Pullman, its main stockholder, worth $2 million to $3 million.[2]

Indications that the 1880s would prove to be a decade of continued growth surfaced as early as 1882. And a report to stockholders dated 18 October 1883 stated that contracts had been made for cars with eight additional companies, including the Chicago, Milwaukee and St. Paul; the Central and the Southern Pacific Railroad systems, covering over ten thousand miles of railway; contracts also had been renewed with four important railways, including the Union Pacific and the Louisville and Nashville systems, which had more than seven thousand miles of track. The company constructed and placed in service sixty-five new cars at a cost of $930,315.40. Thirty-seven new cars, costing $529,100, had been completed and placed in service since August 1883, and sixty-nine vehicles were under construction because of recently made contracts, at a cost of $1 million.[3]

Such glowing reports did not, however, mean that all was smooth sailing. Occasionally, Pullman experienced difficulties with his workers. As noted earlier, the first confrontation occurred in 1882, when Pullman refused to continue paying full carfare to transport his employees to and from Chicago on a daily basis. The second disturbance came two years later, when 150 men in the freight car department struck because of a wage slash. The corporation publicly described the trouble as minor, saying it was brought on by "chronic kickers" whom it promptly replaced with workers from Chicago. In October 1885, men ceased work when the company ordered a 10 percent wage cut; however, the cut was effective in only a few shops at a time, so the general strike never came to pass. Then, in the spring of 1886, the shops closed when Pullman workers joined the Knights of Labor in a national strike for an eight-hour day and a 10 percent increase in wages. The manufacturing establishment reopened in ten days with police protection, and the men returned to their work places under the old terms. Once again, they had failed to wring any concessions from their employer. Toward the end of August 1887, a report stated that the company intended to cut trimmers' wages by 10 percent (there were nearly a hundred trimmers). The lateness of the season probably forestalled a strike, but the men believed wage cuts would soon be announced in other departments. Meanwhile, the company stated that declining orders led to the periodic wage cuts, an excuse the workers did not believe.

In January 1888, a foreman's high-handed tactics resulted in a wood-carvers strike, but the men were given a chance to return before they were discharged. Then, in January 1891, strikers in the freight shops were ordered back to work within nine days or they would be fired; only one man complied. Thus, though the company did offer unhappy workers a chance to return to their jobs under former conditions, it did not yield to their demands for relief. George Pullman was the person responsible for this seemingly successful policy, although it was enforced by company officials.[4]

Pullman also faced difficulties from outside because competitors lurked at every crossing, and he constantly had to defend his empire against those who sought to overthrow it. At the outset of the 1880s, he became embroiled in a lawsuit with the Baltimore and Ohio Railroad, a customer for the preceding ten years, that now sought to manufacture its own sleepers for company use. On

25 September 1880, the Pullman Company asked for an injunction against the Baltimore and Ohio to prevent their building and using Palace cars, thereby infringing upon the Chicago company's patents. The B&O had originally contracted with the Pullman organization for use of its cars for ten years; now that that arrangement was about to expire, the railroad had secured an agreement with Barney and Smith in Dayton, Ohio, to begin building cars on 1 October 1880.[5] In fact, several of the new vehicles already stood in Baltimore, ready for operation.

Pullman alleged patent infringement, maintaining that his firm had manufactured enough cars for all the railroads in the United States. He also charged that the B&O was endeavoring to get other roads to cancel their Pullman contracts. Nevertheless, the courts refused to allow Pullman's claims, and the Pullman Company bought the B&O's sleeping car equipment and its franchises in June 1888. The firms also signed a twenty-five-year contract, and Pullman's Palace Car Company agreed to furnish the B&O with all necessary sleeping and parlor equipment.[6]

Among the ongoing and vexing problems confronting George Pullman was that of the Central Transportation Company. As noted earlier, on 17 February 1870, Pullman's Palace Car Company signed a ninety-nine-year lease with the CTC for all its rights, properties, and contracts, including those for operating sleeping cars with sixteen railway companies. Pullman was to pay $264,000 annually; however, if railroads did not renew their contracts and income fell below that amount, Pullman could annul the lease and surrender the CTC property or continue operations at a reduced rental. As a result, the Pennsylvania Railroad Company agreed to use Pullman's services for fifteen years, beginning 27 January 1870.[7]

On 27 January 1885, the contract between the Pullman Company and the Pennsylvania Railroad expired. The railroad declined to renew, except on terms less favorable to Pullman and at largely reduced profits. Pullman then proposed a modified contract that allowed it to reduce its annual payments to $66,000, with 25 percent of the taxes to be paid, an amount equal to 3 percent annually on the CTC's capital of $2.2 million. The new agreement offered Central stockholders the option of exchanging four of their shares in return for one of Pullman stock. If the stockholders approved the contract and exchanged their stock, all the Central assets would accrue to the Pullman Company.[8] But the Central shareholders did not cooperate; instead, they rejected the revised accord by a vote of eleven to one. Next, a newly installed Central board, hostile to Pullman, attempted to compel the Chicago firm to maintain payments of the original rental of $264,000, which, due to the lapse of contracts with other railway companies, placed a burden on the Pullman Company.[9]

Meanwhile, Pullman had negotiated a new contract with the Pennsylvania Railroad on the assumption that his revised agreement with the Central would be accepted. He offered to purchase any Central Transportation Company stock held by persons who wished to sell it. In addition, he sent a signed circular letter to every CTC stockholder in which he explained his position and wrote that the offer to exchange four shares of their stock at a par value of $50 (then selling at about $28) for one share of Pullman stock at a par value of $100 (then selling for about $114) would remain open. As an added inducement, he would pay those who accepted the offer an additional 2 percent dividend, issued in May 1885.[10]

On 11 May, he met with CTC directors, who refused his stock exchange proposal because it amounted to a repetition of the offer the stockholders had already turned down. After further discussion, Pullman offered to buy all the Central stock for $30 a share, which the directors also refused. The meeting ended with an understanding that the CTC directors would prepare a final proposition to submit to the Pullman Company.[11]

Matters rested until 22 August, when Pullman wrote President John S. Stevens of the Central Transportation Company. He reviewed the entire controversy, stating that his bids and attempts to pay quarterly rentals had been rejected. He said that he had been forced to withdraw his offer to exchange stock when he learned that the CTC had illegally issued 1,000 shares. Pullman not only held Stevens responsible as an instigator of the controversy, he also blamed him for failing to offer any practical solution to the problem and for inaugurating what promised to be a long and expensive lawsuit that would deny any dividends to Central stockholders.[12]

Pullman then proposed to terminate relations between the companies and to deliver to the Central its sleeping cars under the terms of the original lease, which had provided for such a contingency. He asked Stevens to inform him as to when his firm was prepared to receive them. Stevens rebuffed Pullman's overtures. The Central executive pointed out that CTC board members had suggested several times that if Pullman would capitalize the $66,000 he proposed as a yearly payment into 5 percent bonds and give Central the principal — $1.42 million in cash — the company would recommend that its stockholders accept the offer. Central would then combine its surplus and divide over $40 per share among the stockholders, thus dissolving the company. But because Pullman would not accede to its wishes, the CTC would not consider his offer either.[13]

Other schemes followed, but the crux of the standoff lay in the fact that the anti-Pullman faction of the CTC agreed to prevent George from gaining control of their company. The Central then brought several lawsuits against the Pullman Company for rents due them, until Pullman secured an injunction against such actions in May 1887.[14]

Litigation continued throughout the 1890s, until finally, on 2 July 1898, in accordance with a Supreme Court mandate, the Pullman Company paid the CTC $1,317,401.16 ($727,846.50, plus interest from 1 January 1885 to 1 July 1898).[15] Obviously, not all of Pullman's ventures were successful.

Another continuing source of frustration to George Pullman was the Wagner Palace Car Company, his chief and most enduring competitor. Like Pullman, Webster Wagner was a native New Yorker, born on 2 October 1817. A trained wagon maker, he followed that trade until hard times forced him to sign on as a station agent for the Utica and Schenectady Railroad in 1845, where he designed his first sleeping car. In 1858, Wagner managed to get four sleepers running on the New York Central Railroad; later, in 1867, he began manufacturing drawing room cars that he also placed on that line. A Republican, Wagner was elected to the New York General Assembly in 1870, and the following year, his constituents sent him to the state senate, where he served until his death some eleven years later.[16]

The Vanderbilts, who owned the largest percentage of his firm, backed Wagner's efforts to place his cars on the New York Central, which pulled them from New York, through Cleveland, and into Cincinnati. But Pullman's cars featured many patents not owned by Wagner. Because the Chicagoan's vehicles were used widely on lines other than the New York Central, Wagner contracted in 1870 to use Pullman's upper berth and other designs on his cars as long as they ran only on New York Central lines. As time passed, however, that railroad's tentacles began inching toward Chicago. By then, the Wagner Company had become a closed corporation called the New York Central Sleeping Car Company. In 1875, Cornelius Vanderbilt gained control of the Michigan Central Railroad and forced Pullman to withdraw his Palaces from the line; furthermore, he coerced the Michigan board of directors to use Wagner's carriages even though they preferred Pullman's. His method was simple and very persuasive: He informed the Michigan Central directors that if they did not avail themselves of Wagner's services, their firm would lose its through-run between New York and Chicago. Pullman, embittered by the commodore's high-handed tactics and his contract with Wagner breached, sued his passenger car rival for patent infringement, although little came of the suits.[17]

Despite all this, by the outset of the 1880s, rumors circulated that Wagner and Pullman interests were about to consolidate. At first, both Pullman and Horace Porter, his vice president, denied such stories, although Wagner had made overtures to Pullman for several years.[18] These advances were ignored until January 1882, when Pullman admitted that negotiations had been under way for two years to explore such a consolidation. Stating his intentions were "wholly for the public comfort and convenience," he noted "that a grand union of sleeping cars running on all passenger railways, in America, would have a happy effect ultimately" — an excellent public statement for a businessman to express in an era when consolidation was considered the best means to end wasteful competition and begin efficient operations.[19]

Throughout January 1882, stories concerning the merger continued to circulate, even alleging that an agreement had been reached but many details still had to be arranged. Pullman admitted attending several meetings where the subject was discussed, but no plan to unite emerged. Senator Wagner's untimely death in a railroad accident on 13 January halted the negotiations, and Pullman was not sure they would continue. Some observers saw little advantage to be gained from such a merger, for neither company would agree to be swallowed by the other. Still, merging the interests of both firms *would* enhance service by furnishing through-cars on all roads to all points.[20]

The stories of consolidation grew out of litigation that was pending between Pullman's Palace Car Company and the Missouri Pacific system, controlled by New York financier and railroad mogul Jay Gould. Apparently, Gould (joined by the Vanderbilts) intended to place Wagner cars on the Missouri Pacific system when its Pullman contracts expired; one of these lines was the Iron Mountain Railroad (whose Pullman contract had run out on 20 November 1881). Pullman resisted, applying to the courts for an injunction and claiming that the Missouri Pacific had given his firm exclusive rights to furnish drawing room and sleeping cars for fifteen years. The injunction was sought to prevent other sleeping cars from being used on the Missouri Pacific.

The Pullman Company's request for an injunction against the Missouri Pacific was refused on 28 April 1882.[21] The case went to the Supreme Court, which held that the Iron Mountain was not obliged to use Pullman cars despite the fact the Pullman firm held an exclusive contract with the Missouri Pacific. Iron Mountain's directors had the authority not only to introduce New York Central Company cars but to cancel those operated by Pullman in spite of the exclusive contract.[22]

By that time, Pullman had sought other means of vengeance by backing the New York, West Shore and Buffalo line, built by the Pennsylvania Railroad to harass the New York Central. Pullman's support earned him a minor part in the dispute and, though he maintained that his involvement with the West Shore was due to his desire to obtain funding for his new community (as discussed in the preceding chapter), the record shows that he was also attempting to settle a grudge with the Vanderbilts.

The Pullman Company confronted its archrival once again during the 1880s, when the two firms clashed over the use of covered passageways, or vestibules, between passenger cars. Vestibules were built at each end of a passenger car to provide a corridor between the carriages. Elastic diaphragms resembling accordions, equipped with steel frames and strong spiral springs, were attached to the end of each vestibule. When the springs pressed the diaphragms together, the resultant friction caused their bearing surfaces to remain firmly in position. These apparatuses welded each train car together, thus forming a wholly connected unit. Flexible passages were not a new concept; they had been used for many years on English mail trains, on at least one English passenger train (the London and South Western Railway), and Russian trains. In addition, several Americans had worked to develop vestibules before 1887, but all such attempts had been experimental, and most had been abandoned after being tried and found wanting.[23]

With the introduction of dining cars, American interest was piqued as railroaders discovered that their less adventurous clients, "especially ladies and invalids," found it most difficult to get from the sleeper seats to the diner, particularly if the train were speeding along. Open platforms between the cars terrified passengers, seeming to threaten death in good weather and assuring them of it during storms.[24]

If dining cars were to succeed, this problem had to be overcome, and Pullman's Palace Car Company employees undertook the task. The resulting vestibule not only eliminated open platforms but eased other irritants, as well. Newspaper accounts noted that the vestibules gave additional strength, preventing a telescope effect — the pushing of cars into each other — in the event of a wreck. The passages also steadied car movement along the track, a feature particularly welcome to occupants of upper berths who tried to pass the time by reading or writing. Vestibules also served as storm doors that sheltered passengers from the sudden drafts experienced when a fellow wayfarer or a train crewman opened the door of an ordinary car. Finally, they deadened noisy car wheels rolling over the rails, permitting passengers to converse without strain. Certainly, Pullman vestibules did away with numerous petty annoyances to which travelers had become inured even on the finest trains. However, the new attachments were both expensive and troublesome to operate. Further, they blocked the circulation of fresh air in summer and did not really alleviate the oscillation of connected cars.[25]

In March 1887, the *Railroad Gazette* noted that a train recently built at Pullman would begin a run on the Pennsylvania Railroad's New York Limited. The new train featured a device that essentially would convert a line of separate carriages into one long vehicle. Apparently ignorant of past attempts to place vestibules on American trains, the article noted that such an improvement was long overdue because open platforms between fast-moving cars were difficult to traverse. This was particularly true on "sharp curves" or when icy conditions caused slippery platforms or cinders rendered handrails gritty.[26]

Pullman employee Henry Howard Sessions designed the new Pullman contrivance, but though it was touted as a boon to railroad users, it was really little more than an improvement over preceding inventions. Sessions received his patent on 15 November 1887 and assigned it to the Pullman Company.[27] The following November, the company promoted Sessions to manager of the Pullman works at Pullman, Illinois. Then, in July 1893, he moved to the Chicago office to assume the new position of chief mechanical engineer.[28]

Americans witnessed the first public exhibition of the Pullman vestibule on 20 April 1887 when a five-car train ran over the Pennsylvania Railroad line between Chicago and New York. The Wagner Palace Car Company imitated Pullman in December 1887, running a special train of vestibuled Wagner cars from New York to Albany on the New York Central and Hudson River Railroad. Wagner's six carriages were constructed especially for use as a limited between New York and Chicago, part of a group of fifty-five vestibuled cars the Vanderbilts had ordered for their roads. They were equipped with Pullman-type vestibules, which prompted the Chicago firm to take the Wagner firm to court.[29]

Pullman had warned both the Wagner Company and the Lake Shore and Michigan Southern Railroad that legal moves would be taken against them if the Sessions buffer were used, and late in December 1887, the Chicago firm asked for an injunction to restrain their infringement. Pullman claimed that the vestibule trains using the Sessions patent had been so successful that the Wagner Company requested a license to run them, which Pullman refused to grant. According to the plaintiff, the Wagner firm then simply appropriated the device for use on their train running over the Lake Shore and Michigan Southern Railroad to New York.[30]

In May 1888, the United States Circuit Court granted the Pullman Company a temporary injunction. Judge Walter Q. Gresham pointed out that after the Pullman vestibule train went into service on the Pennsylvania Railroad, the Wagner Company wasted little time in running trains constructed in a similar fashion. Indeed, their appropriation was so complete that Wagner vestibules seemed to duplicate those on Pullman trains. The judge noted that Wagner "deliberately appropriated every substantial feature which was exhibited in Sessions's invention and the Pullman vestibule train, whether patentable or non-patentable." Gresham believed that such action constituted recognition by Wagner that the Sessions device was a good one. Further, the improvement was practicable because the Pullman Company had substantiated certain statements with affidavits that Pullman vestibule trains reduced car oscillations so passengers slept more comfortably in upper berths, car lamps could be burned with a higher flame, and travelers suffered less nausea than on regular trains.[31]

In 1890, Pullman finally forced the Wagner Company to stop using the Sessions device, which led the New York firm to devise alternate designs for use on the New York Central and Wagner cars. The decision was set aside in 1892, and Pullman lost the monopoly he had obtained on vestibules; however, the following year, the resourceful Chicagoan introduced a similar wide vestibule and matching platform. Vestibules became more a part of the car body, and the design, for all intents and purposes, has remained basically the same during the twentieth century.

The lawsuits George Pullman brought against his competitors were not the only court battles he engaged in as his firm continued

to grow. As noted earlier, he defended his title to lands at the town
of Pullman on at least two separate occasions. Other suits were
brought by passengers discontented with services on his cars. In
one instance, a man sued Pullman because riding backward in a
car during the day had made his wife ill. The court decided in favor
of the plaintiff but awarded him damages amounting to only 1¢.
On another occasion, the court ruled that a passenger who had
been robbed while sleeping on a Pullman car was entitled to $300
in damages because the company had failed to use proper care in
protecting him while asleep.[32] Then there were several actions
brought by individual states (and one by the Dominion of Canada)
that attempted to collect taxes from the railroads or Pullman
himself for the use of sleeping cars within their boundaries.
Pullman defended his firm against these suits with varying degrees
of success. All states had expenses, of course, although many of
them were borne by local communities within their boundaries.
Nevertheless, states taxed corporations or companies within their
borders, particularly banks and railroads. Railroad cars were
highly visible chattel, and property taxes were the main sources of
revenue because, unlike "intangible" assets such as notes, stocks,
or bonds that could be hidden, they could be identified and levied
against when operating within a state. This issue aroused a good
deal of emotion for it was common knowledge that rich men hid a
good percentage of their wealth from tax collectors, and the
nonmonied classes were interested in seeing that the more affluent
paid their just dues. But taxation at the state level was a confused
issue during the 1880s, which doubtless explained why Pullman's
lawyers were able to avoid much taxation on their client's behalf.[33]

Toward the end of the 1870s, the Pullman Southern Car
Company's name surfaced occasionally. Though its business office
was located in Louisville, Kentucky, the general headquarters were
in Chicago because Pullman's Palace Car Company held a majority
of its stock and two of its officers, Pullman and Weinsheimer, were
also president and secretary for the smaller firm. Stock was not
sold on the market, and the company had never paid dividends.
Pullman's Palace Car Company had furnished vehicles and other
necessities for its operations, and the Pullman Southern Car
Company contracted to repay the debt from earnings. At the outset

of the 1880s, Pullman Southern was a prospering organization, although Pullman's Palace Car Company, together with some of its stockholders, still owned and controlled the firm and continued to meet its obligations.[34]

In 1881, a minority group of Pullman Southern stockholders, dissatisfied with Pullman's Palace Car Company's control of their organization, tried to lease the company in an attempt to make its stock pay. The revolt failed, but it led the Pullman Company to buy out three-quarters of the Pullman Southern stockholders through an exchange of stock (one share of Pullman's Palace Car Company for two of Pullman Southern). Pullman's Palace Car Company's directors justified the deal by announcing that it would allow their firm to secure valuable property and contracts to operate its cars upon several important southern railways, thus assuring a large increase in business and revenues. Although the agreement required an additional issue of 6,546 shares of stock, such tactics permitted George Pullman to remain in control and continue as president of Pullman Southern. Over the succeeding years, Pullman's Palace Car Company gradually acquired the remainder of the Pullman Southern stock, so that in December 1894, George Pullman could request dissolution of that company.[35]

Another company Pullman gradually absorbed into his main firm was the Pullman Iron and Steel Company. Organized in October 1883 to produce a patented railroad spike, the original owners held a half interest in the patent; George Pullman and John W. Doane held the other half. The organization invested in plant buildings and machinery at Pullman, Illinois, but defective machinery kept it from profitably producing the quality of goods required by the Pullman Company. Eventually, Pullman Iron and Steel became heavily indebted to the Pullman Loan and Savings Bank and to Pullman's Palace Car Company. And by March 1889, Pullman had purchased Doane's interest in the company and owned over 2,000 of the firm's 5,000 shares of stock.

That month, two stockholders in the Pullman Iron and Steel Company filed suit, charging that George Pullman had bankrupted their firm because he had dictated such low prices on goods sold to his palace car company. According to the complaints, the company should sell its property so proceeds could be distributed on a pro rata basis among the stockholders.[36]

The suit failed, yet the company continued to operate, permitting Pullman, on occasion, to buy shares of its stock until his holdings amounted to 3,092 shares. Then, in November 1893, the Pullman Company directors voted to purchase George's holdings in the Pullman Iron and Steel Company and directed him to buy the firm's outstanding shares at what he determined was the best price.[37]

Another subsidiary firm taken into Pullman's Palace Car Company was the Union Foundry and Pullman Car Wheel Works. Inaugurated during the spring of 1881, the Union Foundry Company of Chicago joined Pullman's company to build a foundry large enough to service both organizations. Pullman's Palace Car board members believed the arrangement was advantageous because they would profit from "the large experience of the Union Foundry Co., in the building and operation of such a foundry." Therefore, they authorized George Pullman to subscribe $150,000 in the name of Pullman's Palace Car Company to the new partnership's capital stock, to be organized as the Union Foundry and Pullman Car Wheel Works.[38]

In June 1882, the new company's stockholders voted to increase its capital stock from $300,000 to $500,000, and Pullman's Palace Car Company subscribed an additional $100,000 as its share. In 1886, both the Union Foundry and Pullman's Palace Car Company owned 2,500 shares of capital stock issued by the foundry firm, which amounted to $250,000 for the par value of each share was $100. At that time, the Union Foundry offered to sell out to Pullman's Palace Car Company for $75 per share, which came to $187,500. The board accepted. This action brought the Union Foundry under the complete control of the Pullman Company, although it was not dissolved until December 1894.[39]

Despite ongoing lawsuits and the absorption of subsidiary firms, Pullman continued to grow as a car manufacturer. In a report to stockholders on 13 October 1887, Pullman stated that seven contracts had been let with railway firms during the fiscal year ending 31 July 1887 and six lines had renewed their contracts, bringing the company's total mileage to 81,384 miles. Fifty-five new cars had been constructed and placed in service, at a cost of $819,000. Additions to the company's manufacturing complex included the purchase and improvement of the Bowers, Dure and Company shops in Wilmington, Delaware; the erection of new repair shops and houses at Pullman; and additions to plants at Detroit and St. Louis, all of which cost $459,265.28. Contract requirements, together with increased business, called for construction of 122 cars, at an estimated total cost of $1,760,000. Such growth led Pullman to request an additional stock issue to pay for these expenditures.[40]

During September 1888, several prominent capitalists and railroad men incorporated the Union Palace Car Company in an effort to keep both the Mann Boudoir Car Company and the Woodruff Sleeping and Parlor Coach Company from going into receivership. The new firm began soliciting railroad companies as their contracts with Pullman's Palace Car Company terminated, offering sleeping car services at prices so low and unprofitable that Pullman decided not to compete for them. Instead, the Chicago firm spent two or three months considering whether to take over this combination of two rivals.[41]

Then on 23 January 1889, at a large meeting on Wall Street attended by numerous prominent railroad magnates (including Pullman and Porter), the contract became a reality. There was little bickering because most of the details had been ironed out prior to the gathering, and those august gentlemen in attendance believed the project very worthwhile. Pullman stated his purchase terms, the deal was finalized, and Pullman paid the full price (just over $2.5 million) the following day. Accordingly, the Union Palace Car Company, together with the Mann Boudoir Car Company and the Woodruff Sleeping and Parlor Coach Company, became a part of the Pullman organization, although the Union Car Company continued a separate corporate existence. Pullman retained many members of the Union Company's board, apparently hoping the takeover would prevent other potential rivals from entering the passenger car field.[42]

There were other advantages connected with the sale in addition to overcoming two erstwhile competitors. For example, Pullman now controlled all the parlor car companies doing business in the United States except the Wagner Company, giving him added influence over the passenger car business on all southern railways, as well as a couple of northern routes.[43]

While bargaining for the Union Palace Car Company, the Pullman Company expanded into another sleeping car area, that of second-class sleeping cars (variously referred to as emigrant or tourist cars). Such carriages had been owned and operated by several individual railroads for many years. Pullman had chosen to ignore them — possibly in the belief that they did not merit his notice — even though they furnished sleeping accommodations at $3, as opposed to the $13 paid by palace car users. Pullman's purchases headed off potential serious dents in his revenues because during heavy travel periods, tourist sleeping cars were in great demand, and, with their comfort and service, they were rapidly reaching a successful, competitive level. If heavy passenger travel continued for a significant period of time, the separate lines might begin to favor their own less-expensive vehicles over Pullman's luxury sleepers and do away with his service entirely. Therefore, it behooved Pullman to take over this traffic and avoid such a risk.[44]

Pullman announced his entry into the second-class sleeping car field at a special meeting of stockholders on 4 March 1889, where the company's growth during that year was summarized. He began by stating that the acquisition of the Union Palace Car Company, the Mann Boudoir Car Company, and the Woodruff Parlor and Sleeping Coach Company had netted 212 cars, at a cost of about $2.55 million. The firm also had purchased a one-half interest in fifty-eight cars it had held jointly with the Atchison, Topeka and Santa Fe for $412,869.46. Furthermore, it had procured sixty tourist or second-class sleeping cars from the Atchison, Topeka and Santa Fe for $261,918.35. The firm also had agreed to buy twenty similar cars from the Atlantic and Pacific Railroad for $97,440 and to purchase a one-fourth interest in seventy second-class sleeping cars from the Union Pacific, at a cost of some $70,000. Pullman continued that, since the start of the current fiscal year (1 August 1888), the company had completed and placed in service "107 sleeping, dining and other cars such as are used in the special vestibuled trains," at a cost of $1,511,842.84. Thirty-two more cars were then being constructed, for an estimated outlay of $378,000. Taken together, he stated, thse investments totaled $5,282,070.52.[45]

He continued by stating that the company had executed additional contracts with the Atchison, Topeka and Santa Fe Railroad Company (including its leased and controlled lines) and the Union Pacific Railway Company for operating second-class sleeping cars on their lines for twenty-five years. It also inherited the Union Palace Car Company's contract with the Richmond and Danville Railroad.

Pullman's lengthy report added that the company had placed standard Pullman cars in operation on the Atchison, Topeka and Santa Fe Railroad (including its leased and controlled lines); the Union Pacific Railway Company; the East Tennessee, Virginia and Georgia Railroad Company; the Central Railroad of New Jersey; and the Jacksonville, Tampa and Key West Railroad Company for operation on their respective lines under the company's standard twenty-five-year contract.

He turned to other matters, informing his audience that the company had paid its debenture bonds amounting to $955,000, which had matured on 15 October 1888. It also had increased its investments in freight and passenger cars held under car trust leases by $1.2 million. Thus far, during the current fiscal year, additions to the Pullman manufacturing plant came to about $70,000. Yet these costs would increase significantly before the close of the year to provide necessary maintenance facilities for the many cars the company recently had added to its inventory. Clearly, Pullman's long hours of hard work and travel were paying off for his firm's growth was due largely to his personal effort as its president. It is understandable, then, that when he concluded his report by asking stockholders to increase the company's capital stock by $5 million to $25 million, they acceded immediately.[46]

During the 1880s, the Pullman Company's business increased overall. Americans began traveling to and from national gatherings, many of which occurred during the clement summer months.

The railroad companies encouraged this trend by decreasing rates and providing side tracking so that such persons, particularly political delegates, could use the cars in lieu of hotels. For example, Pullman's Palace Car Company supplied 125 cars for the Grand Army of the Republic's reunion at San Francisco, plus fifty-three cars for that organization's excursion to Los Angeles. When the Grand Sovereign Lodge of Odd Fellows held their annual meeting in Boston in the final week of September, Pullman ran fifty-five cars, plus a sizable number to the areas in and around Boston. Finally, the triennial enclave of the Knights Templars in St. Louis requested 200 additional cars. All of these demands were promptly met by the Pullman Company.[47]

The Pullman Company enthusiastically promoted the public's interest in car usage, as described in the minutes of a board of directors' meeting on 20 April 1891. The Continental Cantonment and Triennial Parade of the Patriarchs Militant, together with the International Order of Odd Fellows meeting being held in Chicago, always increased travel by large numbers of people from all over the United States. A certain guarantee required in advance that the expenses of the cantonment would be paid promptly. Thomas Wickes, second vice president of the Pullman Company, recommended that the firm be a party to the guarantee because of the advantages that would accrue. George Pullman, in behalf of the company but in his individual name, agreed, and the increased travel that resulted substantially augmented the company's business. Thus, the board resolved that Pullman's action and his liability be accepted by the company.[48]

Industrial capitalists like Pullman changed the economic and social lives of cities as they turned them into modern communities. Chicago during the years following the fire was a good example: Not only did it increase in population, it became the major metropolis of the Midwest. Noted for its industry and commerce, it ranked second only to New York City, with a population of 1,099,850. Thus, as early as 1885, its leaders began considering plans to make it the site for the celebration of the four hundredth anniversary of Columbus's landing in the New World. Their efforts came none too soon, for by 1889, there were three other cities — New York, St. Louis, and Washington, D.C. — vying for the honor.

By the summer of 1889, three hundred Chicagoans, incorporated as the World's Exposition of 1892, were hard at work and issued $5 million worth of stock.[49] These volunteers naturally turned to the city's businessmen and their firms to assist in hosting the celebration. At a director's meeting, on 27 November 1889, John Doane moved (and Marshall Field seconded) that Pullman's Palace Car Company subscribe $100,000 for securing and providing for the proposed world's fair and that the company president be authorized to make the subscription in his own name. The rest of the board adopted the resolution unanimously. Later, in 1893, Pullman also purchased from the World's Columbian Exposition twenty of its 6 percent registered debenture bonds at $5,000 each, and the board quickly approved his actions in that matter also.[50] Thus, the Pullman Company joined the ranks of Chicago organizations that willingly accepted the civic responsibilities thrust upon them by the growing city where they were headquartered.

Chicago was proud of itself: Despite the economic crises of the 1880s, the city had been relatively prosperous and had witnessed great commercial and industrial growth during that decade. The fact that disease, filth, and poor living conditions existed in its poverty-stricken neighborhoods, occupied by recent arrivals from rural areas and from Europe, was depressing, but current thought among the "right sort" was that those who wished to improve themselves would soon leave such areas by their own effort and hard work; those who remained in the slums probably possessed some basic moral or character flaw that prevented them from seeking more desirable residential communities.[51]

As the 1880s slid into the 1890s, Pullman's Palace Car Company's greatest period of expansion under its founder's leadership drew to a close. There was much progress that the firm and chief executive could point to with pride. The 12,367 people on its payroll took home earnings amounting to $6,249,891 per year. Its net earnings, which in the 1880s had totaled $1,416,421, had reached $4,563,731 by 1890. Capital stock had increased from $5,938,200 in 1879 to $25 million in 1890, and stockholders would authorize another $5 million augmentation at their annual meeting on 15 April 1891. At the close of 1890, the Pullman Company had 2,135 vehicles running over 120,686 of the approximately 160,000 miles of railroad track in the United States.[52] Prospects looked even better for the 1890s because of demands for the upcoming Chicago World's Fair; in addition, more Americans appeared to be traveling as the nineteenth century entered its final decade.

To be sure, the 1880s had witnessed some disappointments, such as the less-than-successful European venture (although Pullman Company Limited still maintained a London office). The situation with the Central Transportation Company was still at an impasse, and in spite of the fact that the Pullman Company had absorbed many of its former rivals, the greatest of them all — the Wagner Palace Car Company — still remained unvanquished. Pullman also had received some bad publicity concerning his use of company spies on trains to ensure that his employees did their jobs and comported themselves properly. And there had been several strikes, although such occurrences had not created a great stir because many believed them to have been fomented by malcontents.[53]

Nevertheless, such detractions were little more than unpleasant incidents when offset by the town of Pullman, considered a howling success by most Americans who had heard of it, with a population triumphantly numbering 10,680 souls on 31 July 1890. As a haven to its founder on certain occasions, Pullman was very fond of showing it off to visitors, and its plant was noted for a never-ending stream of inventions designed to keep George Pullman's clientele contented, comfortable, and safe.[54]

In addition, while the company expanded its services into the far West, Canada, and Mexico, its existing customers renewed contracts now executed to last for fifteen to twenty-five years; the ten-year contracts of the 1870s were things of the past. Pullman also had ventured into second-class or tourist cars (with 286 such carriages in operation during 1890). These, together with freight car manufactures, brought more business and more money into the company coffers, which the directors reinvested or paid out as quarterly 2 percent dividends to the firm's satisfied stockholders.[55]

Pullman's Palace Car Company's material prosperity signified success to its founder's generation, which also saw it as an outward manifestation of George Pullman's good morals and strong Christian character. It qualified him as one of the nation's elite, a man whose accomplishments could be pointed to with pride by his fellow Americans. "Right thinking" citizens viewed his absorption of lesser, unprofitable firms as good business, aimed at increasing the efficiency and money-making capacity of his own organization: Such maneuvers *had* to be right, for the United States was surpassing all nations in the western world with its great strides to the top in commerce and industry.[56] The industrial capitalists like George Pullman were reaching the peak of their power and prestige at the close of the 1880s and the opening of the 1890s. Granted, they would be edged out of the limelight by financial capitalists, personified by J. P. Morgan, as a result of the hard times following the panic of 1893. But that eventuality still lay in the future.

Indeed, at fifty-nine, George Mortimer Pullman could afford to feel contented with his business as he left his suite of offices in the Pullman Building to converse with his peers over lunch around the "millionaires table" at the Chicago Club.[57] Yet commercial and financial pressures of the period, together with family concerns, prevented him from becoming complacent about his empire or the world in which it existed.

11

Troubled Times

George Pullman exuded success as he celebrated his sixtieth birthday on 3 March 1891. The head of a nationally known organization, he served as one of its directors and as its president and general manager. According to the company bylaws, set down on 7 September 1882, as the chief executive officer and fiscal agent of the firm, he supervised and controlled its property and business affairs. He appointed other officers, assistants, agents, and employees at will and determined their duties and their pay. Finally, he was responsible for reporting in full the corporation's financial condition at each annual meeting. This latter chore must have been a pleasant one since it put him on center stage as he detailed his company's progress to an appreciative audience.

In addition to directing his company from his offices in Chicago and New York, Pullman also traveled extensively as he executed contracts with numerous railroad companies, which the board would approve at subsequent meetings. He also represented the company at various functions, such as the inaugural run of vestibule cars on the Pennsylvania Railroad in 1887, and acted as its spokesman when the need for publicity arose. Indeed, outsiders considered him to *be* the company; though his titles had changed, he was still its front man.

Ambitious and aggressive, he was one of the top-notch industrialists of his era, established in both Chicago and New York. His company's headquarters in downtown Chicago were housed in a building he had erected and named for himself. His associates were prominent men, leaders in their fields. Wrapped up in his work, Pullman was an efficient manager, attested to by the fact that his firm had survived the numerous financial crises that had ruined many of its contemporaries since 1873. He had been unable to conquer Europe, but he had returned to the United States to buy out or absorb all but one of his competitors. In addition to his main plant at the town of Pullman, he also operated shops in Detroit, St. Louis, Wilmington, and Ludlow, Kentucky, the latter three establishments devoted to repairs, although a few Pullman cars had been built at Wilmington and St. Louis in past years. Pullman's nationally renowned business, together with its acres of shop facilities and blocks of worker residences, were a far cry from the shed near Chicago's Union Depot where he had constructed the *Pioneer* twenty-seven years before. In addition, he had ventured into other types of transportation vehicles, including freight and street railway cars. At the same time, acquisitions like the Allen Paper Wheel Company, coupled with inventions such as the vestibule, increased his income considerably and enhanced his reputation as an industrialist interested in comfort and safety. Seemingly, his tactics were correct: Even though his cars were the most highly sought after, he constantly tried to improve them and his firm's service to customers. His interest in the well-being of his clientele earned him fame and money, which kept his name prominently displayed and permitted the ostentatious way of life he loved.

Pullman's Palace Car Company was well governed. Its board members were leading corporate executives from Boston, Chicago, New York, and Philadelphia who gathered for regular meetings that ran like clockwork. Stockholders kept abreast of company activities by attending meetings and by means of circulars mailed to them. Meanwhile, they were kept happy by quarterly dividends that arrived promptly in their mailboxes. Such details were evidence of a smoothly running establishment.

Pullman exhibited the characteristics of many industrial capitalists, yet he differed from them in certain ways. One notable difference was that, unlike many of the barons, he enjoyed the good life and was anything but frugal in his habits, although he was not a heavy drinker or gambler. He considered himself to be very practical — a straightforward man, hard but fair, who had little use for dreamers. But his cold, unapproachable mien probably helped conceal increasing nervousness and insecurity brought on by incessant corporate cares.

Pullman was a man who comported himself with exaggerated correctness. His associates seldom called him "George"; that was a privilege he accorded only to members of his family. An impeccable dresser, he was never without his coat, even on the hottest days.[1] When in Chicago, he appeared each morning in a dark Prince Albert coat (to which he attached his glasses by means of a gold cord), a white or dark vest (across which he hung a gold watch chain), striped trousers, and patent leather shoes. As he stepped out the door, he completed his outfit by donning a black silk hat. He emerged from his house to be greeted by his liveried, black coachman (the Pullmans were among the few Chicagoans of means to employ black help in preference to English servants) who maintained a tight rein on two blooded black horses anxious to haul their owner and his large Victoria coach to the Pullman Building.[2]

Pullman was accustomed to black servants; blacks had worked as porters on his trains since his firm was incorporated in 1867. There were several probable reasons why he had hired them at the outset. First, they were a cheap source of labor at a time when Pullman possessed limited operating funds. Second, due to the social disparity between blacks and whites in those days, there was little chance that difficulties would arise between passengers and porters during their intimate association while traveling in a palace car. Also, blacks were respectful toward whites, so that their position as servants on board the cars seemed natural to travelers who accepted their ministrations without question. Thus, in addition to the creature comforts they had enjoyed on the palace cars, passengers would recall the cheerful services of the porters, which would do much to enhance the reputation of Pullman's luxurious vehicles.

A freedman's prestige increased once he became a porter, for it was one of a very few nonagricultural positions available to him. Pullman would have taken full advantage of this situation, as it would have made the employee less likely to question the magnate's dictates. Meanwhile, porters had an opportunity to travel and received an income, including gratuities, at least equal to that of other working blacks.[3]

It was George's custom to arrive at his office — one flight up from the street — about 10:00 A.M. each morning. There, he walked through a large, carpeted reception room (whose walls were decorated with handsomely framed engravings) that exuded an atmosphere reminiscent of Pullman palace cars themselves. He passed into a private secretary's office and then into his own, which was dominated by his wonderfully neat, flattopped mahogany desk in the middle of the room. The other office furniture, a massive mahogany sofa and several chairs upholstered with embossed leather, was quiet, solid, and harmonized with the rest of the room. As in the reception area, a few fine engravings graced the walls, along with a picture of Colonel Thomas Scott as a young man. In front of the mantel stood a fine French clock adorned with the plaster head of an Indian.[4]

Once in his office, which was nearly always crowded, Pullman's calm demeanor, correct attire, and flawless manners affected those around him; in an era when American businessmen customarily left their hats on in many places, they invariably doffed them in his office. The many people to whom he granted audiences doubtless kept him preoccupied, for he was so busy that he was often forced to write letters to his wife between appointments and occasionally during interviews. He encountered the same problem in his New York City office.[5]

All of this earned him the reputation of being rather chilly and extremely formal among those not intimately acquainted with him, even in this period noted for strict adherence to social protocol. His close friends, however, considered him quite warmhearted, generous, and hospitable. He constantly sought to be of service to members of his family and others, as well, an ideal that he attempted to instill in his children whenever possible because he believed that helping others was the greatest satisfaction a man could achieve.[6]

Like other wealthy men, Pullman contributed to the welfare of his less fortunate fellows. His intense religious training as a boy must have instilled a sense of moral obligation in him, but the adult George Pullman wanted his benefactions to satisfy *his* will, not *His* will. They had to be used in compliance with Pullman's desires, such as self-help.

Pullman and other Chicagoans also expressed a genuine interest in civic affairs. This interest had begun in their youth when they helped their city grow during and after the Civil War, and it was reinforced when they helped Chicago recover from the fire of 1871. These individuals were expected to share their wealth and donate some of their time to public endeavors. Often, however, it seemed that they made their donations to impress each other, something that would have been natural to Pullman. He made several gifts to the city of Chicago, including a hospital wing and the Massacre Monument. He also began building the Pullman Universalist Church in Albion, New York. Yet such gifts seemed designed to bring personal recognition to Pullman, who wanted full credit for all his charitable acts (for example, donations made with Pullman's Palace Car Company money were made solely in his name). Beyond that, unlike others who knew when to ease into the background, Pullman wanted the spotlight trained on him at all times. Similarly, it was a matter of great importance to him that his signature appear first on a list of public subscribers. A self-conscious man, Pullman's actions definitely showed a desire to be top dog both in business and society. His money and prestige helped him accomplish this status.[7]

As he entered his sixth decade, Pullman spent a good deal of time with his family when his business commitments permitted him to do so. But he was likely to be dictatorial, grouchy, and impatient, probably due to fatigue and an inability to relax. In spite of his bad temper, he was devoted to Hattie and bemoaned his frequent separations from her. A man who loved playing the family patriarch, he presented a different side of his personality when with his brothers Henry and James — with whom he got along well and whom he admired — because both were well educated and highly placed clerics in the Universalist church. George tolerated Albert, who did not choose to run in the same circles but preferred to devote his spare time to the church and his family. Pullman was quite attached to his oldest sister, Helen West, who had made a good marriage, but he saw little of Emma Fluhrer, his younger sister, a physician's wife. George did not get along well with his younger brother Charles, nor had he been too friendly with the youngest sibling, Frank, prior to the latter's death in the late 1870s. He was a caring and dutiful son to his mother, but his relations with his mother-in-law, Mary Catherine Sanger, bordered on open warfare. Thus, even members of his family had to be "achievers" in his eyes before he extended them full recognition.

An ostentatious man, Pullman displayed all the social trappings that signified success to his generation. He saw to it that his family had the best of everything, reflections of his great fortune that showed he was a good provider and thus accrued to his personal glory. His palatial home was said to be the finest on Prairie Avenue, a street noted for its exclusivity and bursting with high-priced and magnificent dwellings. His immaculate dress and fine horses and coaches also advertised his wealth, and his personal palace car was the epitome of traveling elegance in a time when such conveyances provided a measure of their owners' affluence and prestige. Pullman's memberships in the Chicago Club and other prominent organizations, together with the many well-placed figures he counted among his friends, also attested to his eminent position.

He enjoyed entertaining, most of which he had the good sense to leave to his charming wife's taste and direction. A gracious host, he was quite affable with people he considered his equals. Besides, social gatherings permitted him to show off his wealth. As in most Victorian households, his wife and oldest daughter followed his dictates and the prevailing social customs with a rigidity that is unknown today. The younger children, however, chafed at such restrictions and, much to their parents' concern, were beginning to break out of the accepted mold.

George M. Pullman, seated on right, conversing with two unknown persons on a porch at Castle Rest. *Courtesy the Chicago Historical Society.*

Pullman tried to give his sons good formal educations, a start in life that he and his contemporaries agreed was vital, but the boys refused to cooperate. He saw to it, however, that his daughters joined those of other wealthy men at a good New York City finishing school and that they received the requisite grand tour of the European continent. But Pullman differed from several of his wealthy peers in that he had no desire to marry Florence and Harriet to scions of impoverished European nobility.

He acknowledged the sabbath by attending Chicago's Second Presbyterian Church with his wife, who had been raised in that faith. Hattie and the children were regular in their attendance, even when he was away from them. At Castle Rest, George attended religious services that usually were held outdoors and conducted by Henry or James for the benefit of all the Pullmans staying on the island.

Any number of recreational activities were available to him, but few seemed to do the industrialist much good. Pullman particularly enjoyed his weekly card games, where he relaxed with male friends. He liked to attend the theater (there was even a small one on the third floor of his home at 1729 Prairie Avenue), and he enjoyed listening to music played on the organ he had installed in his house. Occasionally, he rode horseback with Hattie or one of the children. But he often wanted to be by himself (as evidenced by his hideaway at the Florence Hotel in Pullman) or with daughter Florence, whom he idolized. Frequently, he forsook his own family and retreated to his mother's apartment in New York City or, when it was open, Castle Rest — interludes that distressed his wife and led to quarrels with her. He sometimes also appeared at Helen's home in Rhode Island. And though he liked to spend summer weekends at Fairlawn with his family, his increasing fatigue caused him to avoid many social affairs. During the winters, he would visit Hattie at Florida resorts, New York sanitariums, or similar spots in California where she sought relief from the bitter cold in Chicago and cures for her various infirmities. But after spending several days with his delighted wife, he nearly always was ready to return to work and never seemed to derive lasting pleasure or real rest at such places.

The Pullman way of life continued into the 1890s — springs spent in the South or California, summers and early autumns in Long Branch and New York, and the social season (with its operas, concerts, dinners, and receptions) in Chicago. In time, however, certain events began to interrupt the smoothly flowing pattern established during the 1880s.

The family became concerned over Emily Pullman, well into her eighties and quite frail as the final decade of the nineteenth century got under way. George, who was very attached to her, maintained his mother for most of the year in an apartment in the Belgravia, an eight-story building at 611 Fifth Avenue (site of today's Saks Fifth Avenue) in New York City; he also saw to it that she spent her summers at Castle Rest. At both places, she welcomed her children and their families, most of whom visited her frequently. George spent many nights at the Belgravia, while Hattie remained at a hotel. For instance, after the Pullmans returned from Europe in 1889, George spent the first five nights back in the United States at his mother's apartment before departing for Pullman Island, while Hattie and the girls stayed at the Windsor: He said he rested better at the Belgravia. At such times, he often rose early and went down to the hotel to breakfast with his family.[8]

The summers at Castle Rest were relaxing for most of Emily Pullman's offspring (especially Henry, her oldest son), who tried to congregate at that spot on 14 August each year to celebrate her birthday. But apparently, they were somewhat stressful for George's family. As noted earlier, he and Hattie quarreled over island visits, which leads one to suspect that he spent more time with his mother and siblings than his wife thought necessary. But Castle Rest also seemed to serve as a haven for him, especially during the summer of 1889 when he spent more time at the island with his mother and her family than he did with his own at Long Branch.[9]

A constant stream of hired companions took care of George's mother, Emily Stuart being particularly noteworthy among them. George's sisters — Helen (Mrs. George West) who lived in Providence, Rhode Island, and Emma (Mrs. William Fluhrer), who lived in New York City — both spent a great deal of time with their mother. George was very solicitous, too, seeing to it that she wanted for nothing. He took her to Chicago on several occasions, where she stayed with Albert and his family when she was not in Harvard visiting her sister, Hanna Maria DaLee. George was in constant

Summer 1891, last photo of all the family together. Mrs. Pullman and all her sons who were living. Top row, left to right: Royal Henry Pullman and Charles Pullman. Seated in the middle, left to right: Albert B. Pullman, George Pullman, Mrs. Lewis Pullman, and Helen West (daughter, eldest). Seated, bottom center: Emma Fluhrer, note daguerreotype, and James Minton Pullman, far right. *Courtesy the Chicago Historical Society.*

attendance during these stays, as were the rest of his siblings in the area — much to Hattie's annoyance, even though she seemed to be quite compatible with her mother-in-law.[10]

Early in March 1891, doctors successfully removed a cancerous wart from Emily Caroline Pullman's face. All her children were in New York during the operation. George suffered from severe mental and nervous stress due to her condition, leaving him very depressed for several days afterward. Later, although she was more or less confined to a wheelchair, Emily enjoyed her customary summer retreat at Castle Rest, where she received long visits from all her offspring and their families. That fall, after her return to New York City, she began to weaken, and by the outset of 1892, she started to fail rapidly. Her extreme nervousness during much of the ordeal distressed her children, particularly George. Hattie,

George M. Pullman and his family at Castle Rest, ca. 1891. Florence is at the top, Hattie is facing George, and Harriet is seated on the steps with twins George, Jr., and Sanger. *Courtesy the Chicago Historical Society.*

herself on a health-seeking trip to Santa Barbara, California (where she had a severe bout with the grippe), urged him not to worry about her because his duty lay with his mother. After several tenuous weeks when her sons and daughters remained constantly alerted for a summons to her bedside, Emily Pullman passed away very quietly on 21 May 1892. The family buried her next to her husband in George's burial plot at Albion, New York.[11]

Another disruption in the Pullman way of life occurred in 1891 as the family started to plan daughter Harriet's marriage to Francis J. ("Frank") Carolan, the son of a San Francisco hardware merchant. Harriet, who would be called "boy crazy" in a later era, had caused her a parents a good deal of worry with her various swains, but the Pullmans considered Frank most acceptable. He was twenty-nine years old, a graduate of Cornell, and a member of the Bohemian and University clubs. According to one report, he was known as "dude" by his western friends because of his close attention to his dress. Harriet was twenty-two, "a tall willowy brunet [sic] with bright coloring, and animated continance [sic]." Both the bride and groom shared good looks, wealth, and social renown.

The wedding, described as the event of Chicago's summer social season, took place on 7 June 1892, less than a month after Emily Pullman's death. For that reason, it was toned down from the magnificent extravaganza originally planned. The reception was originally planned for two thousand people but was changed to include not more than three hundred. Otherwise, the details were much the same, and the brilliant affair was "rich and sumptuous in its every detail." During the months immediately preceding the event, the Pullman home had been enlarged and beautified. A large palm room was added with a brownstone terrace on the Eighteenth Street side of the house, and a little park complete with lawn and palms had been laid out on the south side of that street along Lake Michigan. An immense crowd, interspersed with policemen and carriages, assembled outside the Pullman mansion during the wedding, and the scene was lighted by some twenty calcium lights.

Inside, roses of every color and variety decorated the room. The ceremony took place at the west end of the large drawing room on the Prairie Avenue side. Though the announced hour was 8:00 P.M., the bridal party was not quite on time; however, under the accomplished direction of the Reverend David Swing, the ceremony was still over by 8:15, when the organ boomed forth Mendelssohn's "Wedding March." Florence served as her sister's maid of honor, and Evelyn Carolan was one of the eight bridesmaids. Edgar Carolan, the groom's brother, was his best man, and George, Jr., and Sanger Pullman were among the eight ushers. The remaining bridesmaids and ushers included some of the socially prominant people in the United States.

Once the ceremony was over, the bridal party was treated to a collation served in the new palm room. The group ate amidst dainty white, yellow, and pink decorations, with the large wedding cake forming the centerpiece. Other guests dined in the mansion's large dining room to the music of Johnny Hand's orchestra, the strains of which wafted out to the street, much to the enjoyment of the onlookers.

The Carolans received many beautiful — and costly — gifts, but the most special ones came from George and Hattie, who presented the bride with a diamond necklace, pendant, earrings, bracelets, and rings. The newlyweds left Chicago for New York City very late that evening on board the private palace car just completed for her parents. Once the honeymoon was over, they planned to live in the San Francisco area.[12]

A third rather unsettling factor became the impending Chicago World's Fair. Early in 1892, Hattie learned she had been appointed a lady patroness of the fair's ball, an honor meaning that she and Florence would play prominent parts in the ceremonies. Though they were very active in events leading up to the exposition, they did not attend the grand reception because of Emily Pullman's death earlier that year: Victorian rules of mourning forbade such frivolity.

Nevertheless, the Pullmans celebrated their silver wedding anniversary in their home on 13 June 1892 with a dinner party for forty close friends, from Chicago and beyond, followed by a dance. Their guests arrived early in the evening, to be greeted as they ambled down the mansion corridor by clusters of red and white peonies; in the drawing room, crimson roses were set in stands at strategic spots. At the elaborate 7:00 P.M. dinner, the party was seated at a festive table lighted by several candelabra shaded with rose-colored silk and laden with pink roses. An orchestra, amid a tower of palms and roses, played melodious airs throughout the evening.[13]

After all these events, the Pullmans followed their accustomed pattern at the outset of 1893, spending part of their time in Florida with the boys whom they had withdrawn from school in Pottstown for several weeks due to illness. Sanger returned to school, but Georgie did not, and the family was back in Chicago at the end of April.[14] From then until their departure for Long Branch in July, they were enmeshed in a constant social whirl connected with the World's Fair; among all manner of activities, they spent a morning watching a bicycle race from Chicago to Pullman.[15]

That June, as crowds admired the gleaming display of Pullman cars in the Transportation Building at Jackson Park, Florence and Georgie unveiled a statue commissioned by their father and erected on the site of the Fort Dearborn massacre, close to their home on Prairie Avenue. "Massacre Monument" portrayed an Indian named Black Partridge saving the life of Linai Helm, wife of one of the officers at Fort Dearborn. The statue stood on Prairie Avenue for many years until it was moved to the Chicago Historical Society Museum.[16]

When they arrived at Long Branch that July, the family found a German prince, one of Florence's most ardent admirers, awaiting them in a nearby hotel. They remained in New Jersey until late fall, with George and son Georgie (who had gone to work for Pullman's Palace Car Company) commuting back and forth to New York City. That September, Sanger returned to the Hill School in Pottstown, while Georgie continued working at the Pullman offices in Manhattan. The rest of the family went home to Chicago for a continued round of social activities that did not lessen when the prince, at long last discouraged by Florence, bid them adieu in October. Unlike many of his contemporaries, George Pullman had no desire for a son-in-law from a European family, no matter how distinguished or impressive its pedigree.[17]

By that time, business pressures had begun to tire George to such an extent that the Pullman's started to refuse certain social engagements, although Hattie herself still accepted many.[18] The entire family went to New York City in December 1893, and there, on 18 December, they received news that Albert Pullman had died that morning in Evanston. George probably depended a good deal on Albert, a much kinder man who maintained contact with the employees. More genial and outgoing than his younger brother, Albert could sympathize with the workers' problems, for he had experienced the heartbreak of failure and was himself a craftsman. Yet in spite of his role as an early organizer and molder of Pullman's Palace Car Company, Albert had been relegated to the post of second vice president, the office that supervised car construction and dealt with employees. The more prestigious position of vice president was bestowed upon Horace Porter, whose military title and highly placed connections made him much more acceptable to George. Nevertheless, Albert made his presence felt in the company, and when he left it in 1886, George's last personal relationship with the laboring force was gone. A. B. (as Albert was called) remained in Chicago, where he established a brokerage business that he ran before his wife's death in March 1890 and his own ill health forced him into total retirement. The Prairie Avenue Pullmans rushed back to Chicago to attend his funeral on 21 December 1893.[19]

Possibly because of Albert's recent death, George would not allow Hattie to invite her family to join them on Christmas Day, and that hurt her deeply.[20] Pullman apparently realized he had dealt rather harshly with her, for he was most kind and attentive to his wife for the next several months.

Pullman's constant fatigue, frequent illness, and inability to relax warned that business pressures were starting to take their toll. His increasing irritability and frequent quarrels with his beloved wife indicated his growing frustrations and his inability to solve nagging problems connected with his work. Chief among these problems were recurring financial crises in the commercial world, competition from the Wagner Palace Car Company, and ongoing difficulty with the Central Transportation Company.

Once his town got under way, George acquired an image as an employer who was interested in his workers' welfare, and he maintained that image throughout the 1880s and into the 1890s; it was a characterization he enjoyed in spite of his protestations that the community was not a philanthropic enterprise. True, he had established the industrial complex to benefit his workers, but he had done so with the expectation that it would pay for itself: It was not intended to be a gesture of goodwill, no matter what people said or thought. The town of Pullman was built to improve worker efficiency in order to increase the output and profits of Pullman's Palace Car Company.

Although he had personally supervised his laborers during the company's formative period, Pullman began losing contact with his workers as the 1860s progressed. Now he found himself dealing increasingly with executives such as Carnegie of the Central Transportation Company and Durant of the Union Pacific. The effect of his weakened association with his employees could be seen by 1878, when he extended no mercy to Charles Angell, a formerly loyal member of Pullman's Palace Car Company who obviously was a sick man.

He insisted on respectful, if not obsequious, treatment by those whom he considered beneath him, which gave the impression that he was feared by his minions. But what people under him thought was of no concern; it was his peers and their approbation that mattered to Pullman. Although he remained very paternalistic toward those employees who lived in Pullman, he left them to deal with his managers and shop foremen — men who shielded him from the everyday concerns so vital to his workers. He did not, for example, appear overly worried by the strikes at Pullman during the 1880s. In fact, he sailed for Europe just as one began.

Thus, certain blemishes had begun to appear on the smoothly run organization whose success was based on offering luxury and protection to the traveling public. The strikes at Pullman during the 1880s and 1890s had occurred when various segments of the labor force sought to improve working conditions. However, the Pullman Company's dealings with labor were quite similar to those of contemporary corporations, including the ten- to eleven-hour workday.[21] The majority of work stoppages were responses to periodic wage slashes, with occasional uprisings due to misuse of authority by shop foremen; on one occasion, Pullman workers joined the Knights of Labor in a national movement to secure an eight-hour day. The company successfully combatted such actions in several ways: by making wage cuts selectively, so that all shops were not affected at one time; by resorting to police protection; by firing men who did not return to work within a stated length of time; and by using the obnoxious technique of blacklisting malcontents. An 1886 newspaper article noted that the Knights had known "no more persistent and malignant enemy" than George Pullman, who would not allow them to hold meetings in his town and blacklisted them to hurt their cause in every possible way.[22] Yet each time such a crisis arose, the Pullman Company issued statements to the effect that there was no trouble at the factory and that all was peaceful. As a rule, George Pullman refused to negotiate with unhappy workers, but he allowed them to return to their jobs once they realized he would not heed their complaints nor accede to their demands. Like Armour, Pullman was known as a man who demanded the utmost performance from his employees. But, unlike the meat packer, who was said to be quite easy to get along with, the car builder was generally short-tempered, inaccessible, and dictatorial. When he dealt with employees, he was unyielding in his refusal to accept any opposition to his thinking. Retainers who disagreed with him risked being discharged on the spot.

Both George Pullman and Philip Armour opposed collective bargaining and labor unions.[23] Pullman believed that labor should not dictate the policies of his company, and he was determined to eradicate any vestige of unionism in his organization. He also was convinced that paternalism, if used prudently, would make his employees more amenable to company interests.[24] Yet, the more than half a dozen instances of labor discontent suggested that Pullman's brand of industrial paternalism, no matter how well intentioned or how well thought out, was not totally successful. He reputedly used spies or spotters to check on his employees both in the town of Pullman and on the railroads. And Pullman and other eminent industrialists were accused by the Knights of Labor of boycotting men who organized into unions.

Pullman was among a group of prominent Chicagoans placed on a committee to serve the city in any capacity by the Chicago Citizens Association, in reaction to the Haymarket Square bombing on 4 May 1886. The bombing occurred as Chicago police attempted to break up a labor meeting allegedly composed of anarchists and Communists. After a bomb killed and wounded numerous lawmen, the police opened fire on the demonstrators, eight of whom were later tried and imprisoned or executed on very marginal evidence. The controversial affair did much to harm the labor movement. Like Armour, Marshall Field, Cyrus McCormick, Jr., and other prominent Chicagoans, Pullman favored executing the scapegoat anarchists. His group made a generous contribution of $100,000 to help the families of police officers killed or injured by the bomb, finance official efforts to ferret out more malcontents, and back the prosecution of the eight accused men. For the next few years, these same Chicago leaders donated like amounts to stamp out further subversive movements by workers.

Pullman could not accept the fact that labor's attitudes, like working conditions, had changed since the Civil War, while his own thinking with regard to such matters remained much the same.

217

Employees of the 1890s were not the men with whom he had labored to raise buildings in the 1850s or dealt with in the gold camps and in Chicago during the 1860s. Contemporary laborers, faced by new situations and different treatment by larger, impersonal organizations, worried because they no longer governed their working lives.[25] And those who resided in the community of Pullman sensed their loss of control over much of their personal lives, as well. These were matters that George Pullman, by then far removed from his employees, failed to perceive. Unquestionably, he was in charge of his boardroom, but he had forfeited personal control of his factory.

In November 1890, the London banking firm of Baring Brothers failed. British and European investors began unloading American securities, which caused a minor panic in the American business community. Pullman wrote to his wife, who was in California, that, although the financial depression caused him much anxiety and considerable extra work, he felt that Providence was giving him the strength to meet his increased burdens.[26]

The stock market rallied very quickly, yet overseas money continued to leave the country for several years, a condition that affected Pullman's Palace Car Company. In spite of the fact that he was aging, continually tired, and often sick, George Pullman kept at his work unceasingly, ignoring warnings from his eldest brother, Henry, and his immediate family as he combatted the financial stringencies that lasted throughout most of the 1890s. Pullman continued to operate as though all were well, even though his company's stock fluctuated badly during 1891. Nonetheless, at the company's annual meeting on 15 October, he informed his stockholders that the firm's output for the year ending 31 July amounted to $11,906,977.76, an increase of $2,890,544.78 over the preceding year. At the same time, the company had manufactured a large amount of freight and passenger equipment, which it sold on the car-lease plan favored by many railroad companies. Under this plan, payments were made over a seven- to ten-year period in monthly or quarterly installments. The Pullman Company kept title to the property until final payments were made. Indicators pointed to a large increase in demand for freight and

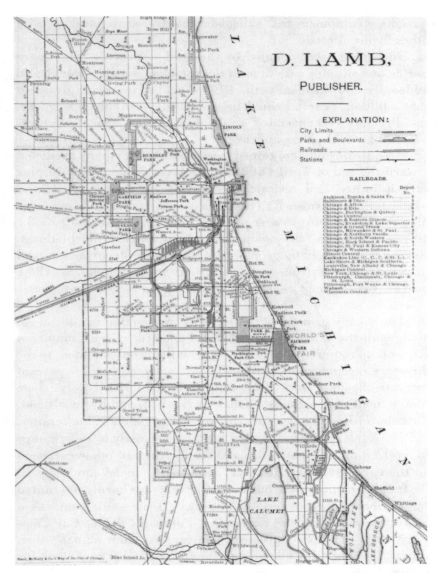

A map of Chicago at the time of the World's Columbian Exposition in 1893. This was the Chicago that Pullman knew so well. *Courtesy the Chicago Historical Society.*

passenger equipment that railroads would want to purchase with other forms of credit.[27]

Such signs, accompanied by the need to provide many more parlor and sleeping cars to meet the company's steady growth and added demands incident to the 1893 World's Fair, made it evident that additional capital could be employed profitably. Therefore, the directors recommended an issue of 50,000 shares of stock, which the stockholders approved.

Because business continued to improve, the company predicted toward the end of April 1893 that its investments in the sleeping cars it owned and operated, plus those in freight, coal, and passenger cars furnished to railway companies under the car-lease plan, would amount to a grand total of $12,413,514.69 by 31 July. In addition, the company had no bonded indebtedness. Revenues rose in both sleeping and parlor car departments, and increased profits from manufacturing since the end of 1891 proved that money realized from stock sales was judiciously invested.[28]

The steady growth of the sleeping and parlor car business, along with the extraordinary demand created by the Columbian Exposition, required a larger investment than contemplated, so the directors recommended and stockholders agreed to a 20 percent increase in capital stock. This was issued on 31 May 1893.[29] Less than a month later, the stock market crashed, and by year's end, the country had plunged into the worst depression of the century.

The 31 May stock issue had been made chiefly to raise money to meet an unanticipated demand for freight and other carriages on the car-lease plan. However, changing financial conditions in the freight and passenger business after that time hardly warranted railway companies materially increasing their equipment. As a result, between May and September, Pullman's Palace Car Company stock could be purchased for far less than actual value. During that period, Pullman purchased 7,615 shares of stock for company use.

In November 1893, the company held about $1 million on deposit above and beyond current expenses, which meant that such funds could be loaned at remunerative rates. In addition, the directors also had felt for several years that part of the company's surplus should be invested in Pullman Land Association real estate "contiguous to and surrounding the town." Such thinking led Pullman's Palace Car Company's president to acquire whatever Pullman Land Association interests he could.[30]

Even though new construction was down, the Pullman Company's repair department stayed very busy. Yet the financial condition of the country continued to be unstable.

Prior to June, the prosperous company paid ample wages, so that workers who lived in Pullman could afford the higher rents charged them. Although employees could not purchase land and build dwellings in the community, evidence showed that the thrifty ones opened and maintained savings accounts in the Pullman Loan and Savings Bank, receiving 4 percent interest per annum.[31] Workers appeared prosperous: One visitor commented on how nicely dressed they looked while walking with wives or sweethearts on Saturday afternoon, a half-holiday. Nevertheless, because they were not able to own their homes, even those Pullman workmen of good character and superior skill never felt any permanent attachment to their community. At the same time, the managers of the corporation's subsidiary, the Pullman Land Association, could fix rents at a level they considered satisfactory, while seeing to it that renters did not violate company rules and standards by such acts as organizing unions.[32]

In August 1893, Pullman lowered the wages of all laborers in every department, whether the departments were losing money or not, in order to cut costs, thanks to the onslaught of the depression. Meanwhile, section foremen became petty tyrants who sought to get the most work for the least pay from those beneath them, including the skilled workers. Despite the wage cuts, the Pullman Land Association did not reduce its rents, and, what was worse, it attempted to collect each payday, leaving workers little to live on until the next paycheck two weeks hence. On occasion, what was left of two weeks' wages after such deductions amounted to less than a dollar.[33]

George Pullman maintained that he had to lower workers' pay in order to keep the shops open and his men employed at a time when contracts were difficult to secure. Unfortunately, he lowered neither his own salary nor those of his executives, nor did he cut the dividends paid by his firm to its stockholders (which he justified by saying that these stockholders contributed to the support of his firm).[34] The workers, who believed that their efforts also contributed to the company's well-being, considered themselves victims of a corporation's hard-heartedness, not only with regard to rents and wages but to working conditions, too.

Finally, in March 1894, Pullman's Palace Car employees, unhappy with their slashed wages, high rents, and harsh shop treatment, began joining the American Railway Union (ARU) in large numbers.[35] This was indicative of their desperation for many had earlier hesitated to join the Knights of Labor for fear of retaliation by Pullman. A new organization, founded in Chicago on 20 June 1893, the ARU advocated negotiation rather than lockouts or strikes. Its membership was open to all white railroad employees below the rank of superintendent. In April 1894, just as Pullman workers were growing totally dissatisfied with their lot, the ARU called a strike against the Great Northern Railroad, which lasted only eighteen days before James J. Hill, head of the railroad, and Eugene V. Debs, president of the union, submitted to an arbitration board. When the arbiters, who were Minneapolis businessmen, decided in favor of the laborers, more Pullman workers placed their names on the union's rolls.[36]

Because the town of Pullman did not have meeting facilities large enough to accommodate their gatherings, the new members of the ARU met outside its borders. The company opposed such actions, although it did not object to the workmen belonging to individual craft unions headquartered in Chicago. Pullman's Palace Car Company preferred to deal with its employees on an individual basis, believing that collective bargaining had forced railroad companies to make extravagant, unwise, or ill-fated concessions to labor.[37]

Discontent continued to mount, until employees protested in May 1894. On 7 May, their representatives met with Thomas Wickes, Pullman Company's second vice president, who informed them he would check into their complaints — especially rent reductions, restorations of wages to pre-depression level, and shop abuses. The laborers were to return on 9 May for another conference and present their grievances in writing.

Pullman was unaccustomed to talking to his shop employees. He was not alone in this, for many industrialists had refused to deal with unions since the 1880s, feeling they could not be bothered to argue with people who had no idea how to run a business.[38] Nevertheless, he was present at the second gathering, where he informed the men that business conditions did not permit wage increases. He professed interest in the welfare of his employees and told those present that he had kept the shops open in spite of company losses. He explained that he could not obtain work at prices based on the wages demanded by the workers and offered to prove this by letting several employees examine the company's books. Pullman continued by stating that the rents were reasonable and had nothing to do with remuneration. He indicated that he was disposed to investigate the complaints about shop conditions, and members of the grievance committee were assured that their participation in such a committee would not militate against them in the shops.

The despairing workers were skeptical about Pullman's protestations of concern for their welfare because they had seen him express little, if any, paternal love toward them. They believed that examining the books would do little good since they probably would have been rigged by that time. They also doubted that their employer was losing money and did not feel that a company investigation into shop conditions would be conducted in good faith. Later, several added that trouble might have been averted by a rent reduction proportionate to the wages paid.[39]

The employees left the meeting "disappointed and chagrined"; they had reached a point where they distrusted the company and its head. Pullman had no conception of the true state of affairs in his shops, nor of the injustices being heaped upon his employees. He was out of touch with his workers, and his lack of understanding, coupled with his brusque mien and refusal to compromise, did little to reinforce his cause with them. Then, the following day, three members of the grievance committee were discharged, fired by shop foremen who claimed there was no work for them. The foremen maintained that they did not discharge the three workers because they were members of the committee, although many employees believed that was the case. Apparently, company management had nothing to do with the dismissals, but workers thought differently. They retaliated by calling a strike on 11 May 1894.[40]

The strikers and their problems had not quite gone unnoticed: Eugene Debs spoke in Pullman on 16 May, and, ten days later, a large group of laborers met in Chicago to formulate plans to obtain financial aid for Pullman workers. The American Railway Union, holding its national convention in Chicago between 12–23 June, also discussed conditions at Pullman. On 15 June, a delegation of ARU members called on Thomas Wickes, spokesman for the Pullman company, who refused to consider any proposition made by the ARU because the Pullman Company had nothing to arbitrate. A week later, on 22 June, the ARU notified Wickes of its decision to refuse to handle Pullman cars as of 26 June, unless the company agreed to do something about worker complaints.[41]

Meanwhile, another organization, the General Managers Association (GMA), composed of leading railroad operators, expressed interest in the activities of the strikers and of the ARU. Both Wickes and Pullman spoke with some of its members, and Wickes attended a GMA meeting in Chicago on 25 June. This group was determined to crush the union and began holding daily meetings to keep its members informed as it schemed to defeat the ARU.[42]

After the boycott of Pullman cars on 26 June, the General Managers Association announced its resistance. A large crowd detained several trains at Grand Crossing in South Chicago but destroyed no property. That evening at 9:00 P.M., Pullman and a party of Illinois Central officers appeared at Chicago's 12th Street station to watch the departure of the "Diamond Special" for St. Louis and to determine the effectiveness of the boycott. Although the train left on time, switchmen refused to handle Pullman cars a short time later.[43] Two days after this, boycotters stopped a mail train at Cairo, Illinois. As a result of such interference, the first deputy U.S. marshals were sworn in and battle lines established by the end of June.

During most of these events, Pullman had been traveling in connection with both business and family matters. That spring, he visited Hattie at a sanitorium in Dansville, New York, before proceeding to California to see Harriet and Frank. Back in Chicago by 19 April, he and he and his wife set off for New York City, where they commissioned artist Eastman Johnson to paint George's portrait.[44] On their return to Chicago, the Pullmans paused at Albion to observe progress on a Universalist church being constructed in memory of his parents. As late as 4 May, Hattie accompanied her spouse to Pullman; then, she and Florence departed for their accustomed spring sojourn at Hot Springs, Arkansas, on 7 May. George M. Pullman left Chicago for New York City and Portland, Maine, five days later.[45]

Hattie and Florence visited Chicago for a few days toward the end of May, before they joined George and Georgie in New York, while Sanger remained in Chicago. The family stayed in the East for over three weeks. During this period, Pullman conducted business from his New York office in the Mills Building, discussed the new church, and visited friends in Washington, D.C. Afterward, he returned to New York while his family continued to travel in the East, but by 21 June, they were reunited in Chicago.[46]

For the next eight days, the Pullmans continued an active social life, seemingly unafraid of repercussions from the strike. The twins, who were not employed by the company at that time, were not bothered when they visited depots to check possible strike damage to trains; and, as noted, George visited the Illinois Central's 12th Street station to observe the effects of the boycott on 26 June.[47]

Three days later, Georgie and the servants left on board the *Keystone* for Elberon, New Jersey. The other Pullmans, except Sanger, departed for Elberon at 5:00 P.M. the next day. Hattie noted in her diary, "Strike situation very serious. Did not take our private car." Instead, they rode in a special car hooked to a regular Pennsylvania train so that George's personal conveyance would not be recognized by mobs along the tracks and either damaged or destroyed. In fact, the family left so quietly that their departure was not discovered until the next day. All arrived at Elberon on 1 July, and Pullman himself went to New York City. He spent most of 4 July 1894 talking with reporters at Fairlawn.[48]

Chicago began to feel the effects of the boycott by 1 July, although lawlessness had not broken out within the city limits. However, that very day, riots began at Blue Island, a suburb south of the city, and continued the following day. The general managers secured an omnibus injunction against interfering with trains, which was read to the Blue Island rioters. Even though four hundred deputy marshals had been sworn in on 1 July, the U.S. marshal requested federal troops from Fort Sheridan. On 3 July, the text of the injunction was published in all Chicago newspapers, and that afternoon, troops at Fort Sheridan were ordered to Chicago to enforce its provisions. Arriving at 12:30 A.M. on 4 July, they were immediately stationed at crucial points in the city. Their presence contributed to the rioting that began that day and continued into the next, with the Rock Island tracks receiving the brunt of the violence. More than a third of the Rock Island employees had voted to back the ARU, which had forced the road to cancel its service to Chicago as early as 1 July. Violence broke out when the company tried to use soldiers to get things moving three days later.

The disorders increased on 5 July when rioters attacked the Chicago stockyards and prevented Rock Island trains from moving. That night, forty-eight cars belonging to the Illinois Central were set afire, one of its passenger trains was boarded, and its locomotives were detached. The next day, Chicago's Mayor John P. Hopkins called for five regiments of the Illinois militia.

Rioters did their worst damage on 6 July when they destroyed $340,000 worth of property, mostly by fire: Some seven hundred cars crowded into the Panhandle yards in South Chicago were burned, although no Pullmans were located there. On 7 July, militiamen clashed with rioters at the 49th Street and Loomis crossing; four rioters were killed, about twenty others (including several women) were wounded, and at least four soldiers and one officer were badly hurt by the rioters' missiles and bullets. This encounter marked the peak of violence in Chicago.[49]

Over the following days, representatives from Mayor Hopkins's office and from labor organizations called at the Pullman Company offices to appeal for arbitration. On another occasion, Mayor Hazen S. Pingree of Detroit journeyed to Chicago, bolstered with telegrams from mayors of some fifty cities, to make a similar plea. All were denied their requests by Pullman officials. Their chief executive was set on exterminating any trace of unionism in his organization so that he could continue his operations free of labor interference.[50]

Nonetheless, by 12 July, trains began moving, and the strike was broken. Debs, who had been arrested and released on bail, also told an American Federation of Labor convention in Chicago that the boycott would be called off if strikers were permitted to return to their jobs.[51] A day later, riots ceased, and trains ran on schedule. Onslaughts by the courts, machinations of the General Managers Association (which had brought in the federal government), interference by the army, and hard times in general had all worn down the workers to a point of surrender.

Throughout the period of unrest, Pullman remained in New York, although he kept in touch with what was happening in Chicago. On 7 July, the day after the worst of the riots, he telegraphed orders to Chicago that all his house servants, especially the women, were to be taken from 1729 Prairie Avenue to places of safety and that the house was to be placed under guard. Much of the valuable plate in the home had already been placed in the vaults of the Pullman Building. His neighbors worried that some sort of violence might occur in the neighborhood, probably because a mob had stopped trains and burned several cars on tracks near the town of Pullman. Once his Chicago dwelling was safe, Pullman, and the Reverend Dr. Charles Eaton, a prominent New York clergyman who was helping him with the church at Albion, traveled to Castle Rest. The strain of the week was starting to show: Helen West reported that her brother looked very badly.[52]

Although Pullman sought to relax at the island, he kept in touch with his offices, and on 10 July, fearing a raid on Pullman stock, he received telegrams throughout the day just to assure himself that all was well. By 12 July, his fears were allayed as the strike failed, and he began to feel better.[53]

Reporters tried to reach him at Castle Rest, but he refused to see them; his brother-in-law, George West, successfully turned them away each time. On 11 July, Robert Lincoln, general counsel for the Pullman Company who had been left in charge of the Chicago office, arrived at the island, and on 12 July, both men traveled to New York City.[54]

Pullman looked rested as he disembarked from a Wagner sleeping car wearing a blue serge suit, straw hat, and flashing patent leather shoes "which glowed as if cared for by one of the

George Pullman, ca. 1894. *Courtesy the Chicago Historical Society.*

most industrious of his own sleeping car porters." The magnate, surrounded almost immediately by reporters, informed them that he would issue a statement concerning the strike later in the day from the Mills Building. The statement finally appeared at 8:00 P.M.

In the release, Pullman explained that the depression had caused customers to cancel orders, which, in turn, had forced the company to lower its working force from six thousand to two thousand by November 1893. The only possible way to recover was to bid for work at prices as low as or lower than those that could be made by other shops. This naturally had necessitated a reduction in the pay of Pullman employees.

George assumed that his plan had been explained to the workers, and he secured enough work to rebuild the working force to forty-six hundred by April 1894. At the beginning of the strike, the Pullman shops had sixty days' worth of car-building work, with little or no prospect of any sizable contracts in the foreseeable future. Secured personally by Pullman at prices below cost, with no consideration for the use of company capital or the plant, such work had been obtained to keep the large force at work and to avoid closing the shops in spite of the depression. The company preferred to operate at a loss, rather than cease operations.

In the midst of this situation, individuals had begun to agitate for a labor organization designed to cover all railway employees "and apparently other industries."[55] Pullman believed his site had been selected not because of worker discontent but due to its prominence. It afforded a medium through which to attack three-quarters of the country's railroads because they had long-term contracts for Pullman sleeping cars, a branch of the Pullman Company's business totally distinct from its manufacture of salable vehicles. Although he did not say so publicly, sources close to Pullman reported that the magnate believed his own employees were generally loyal to the firm and that outside interests, seeking to place gambling dens and brothels in Pullman, were behind the strike and subsequent rioting.[56] Pullman, of course, had barred such institutions, along with drinking establishments, from his town.

Early in May, a committee of workers demanded that wages be restored to the level of the preceding year. Pullman explained that the company was already paying them more than it received for their work and offered to let them examine the company books and contracts on hand. He also promised them "a careful investigation of a number of shop complaints which seemed to end all the trouble." The next day, however, they struck and closed the shops, thereby accomplishing exactly what Pullman had tried to prevent happening because of the depression.

Pullman refused arbitration because, he said, "Arbitration always implies acquiescence in the decision of the arbitrator, whether favorable or adverse." As president of the Pullman Company, he could not agree to a decision made by persons not concerned with stockholders' interests, a ruling that called for him to open the shops and employ men at wages greater than what their finished products sold for on the market. In effect, arbitration could force him to continue a ruinous policy indefinitely or be accused of breach of faith. He refused such a solution.

The car builder then expressed his views concerning the allegedly high rents and excessive water charges in Pullman, stating that they were competitive and fair. Detained in New York City, on 15 July he journeyed to Fairlawn, where, probably because of the pressures of the strike, he treated his wife and favorite daughter to a very harsh lecture.[57]

When the men could no longer hold out, the strike ended. On 18 July, the following notice was posted on the gates of the shops at Pullman: "These shops will be opened as soon as the number of operatives taken on is sufficient to make a working force in all departments." The construction department resumed operations in mid-August, and many of the shops opened before the end of the month. But this did not help many former Pullman employees who faced starvation at a time when public charity's coffers were empty. Illinois governor John Peter Altgeld responded to their desperate plea by inspecting the town and then soliciting — unsuccessfully — George Pullman's help. Thus rebuffed, Altgeld had no choice but to appeal to the generosity of Illinois residents in caring for the vanquished strikers and their families.[58] The industrialist's actions further eroded the notion that he was a philanthropist. Few people ever trusted his motives again.

Although the crisis was nearly over by 31 July, Dr. William Fluhrer visited Pullman at his office in the Mills Building and reported that the sixty-three-year-old magnate "was being very quiet, worn out by the strike."[59] Accounts indicated that Pullman kept himself informed about events through daily contact with his New York office and occasional meetings with high-ranking officers in his organization. He also took precautions to insure his safety and avoid personal harassment, involvement, and loss. Beyond that, he was not overtly active in attempts to curtail the strike; rather, he sat back and followed his customary policy of letting matters settle themselves.

As the strike wound down, the industrialist arranged for Hattie, Florence, and George, Jr., to sail for Europe on 4 August. Sanger remained in Chicago, and Harriet came to stay with him while the others vacationed in France.[60]

Three days after he saw Hattie, Florence, and Georgie off, Pullman returned to Chicago, where he lived quietly, avoiding his company town. Pleading preoccupation with business affairs, he turned down interviews as he prepared to testify before a strike investigation commission appointed by President Cleveland. He and his second vice president, Thomas Wickes, appeared before the commission on 17 August. The commissioners, who had been appointed on 25 July, began taking testimony on both the railroad and Pullman incidents in Chicago on 15 August. They remained there for thirteen days, examining 107 witnesses.

The time Pullman spent under interrogation could not have been pleasant. Many of his responses to questions posed by the commissioners referred his interrogators to other company officials, particularly Wickes. Although there were many specific questions he could not answer, he did express himself forthrightly on company policy — especially that concerning wage reductions and rents. But by and large, he seemed out of touch with the internal operations of his company. After questioning Pullman on matters such as wages, rents, shop abuses, and the strike, the commissioners reached certain conclusions. They noted that since its incorporation in 1867, Pullman's Palace Car Company had been able to put aside a tidy little surplus of $25 million in undivided profits.[61] They also learned (if, indeed, they had not known it before) that employees who dwelt in Pullman were excluded from any role in its management. They concluded that, given the town's system and growth, the 1893 depression morally mandated mutual concessions on wages and rents. Yet the corporation's strong management, bolstered by its great wealth, was able to dictate substantial wage reductions for a multitude of skilled employees (who had no vested rights in the community) while it maintained their high rents. At the same time, because the company did not sanction labor organizations in Pullman and refused to deal with them, it discouraged worker independence and attempts at mediation, arbitration, strikes, and the like. Therefore, a man had two choices: He could work for Pullman, or he could quit. These were the limits of his rights. The commission decided that under such a system, Pullman employees were denied the advantages and protection that they might have enjoyed as members of a union, which indicated that the Pullman Company was behind the times.[62]

When the commission investigated the wage cuts instituted at Pullman, it found that the company had placed a disproportionate amount of its losses on its laborers. Instead of dividing its losses equally with the workers; the commission said, the corporation should have borne three-fourths of the loss and placed one-fourth on the laborers in a fairer division. Company testimony led the commissioners to conclude that some reduction of wages in all departments was proper under the circumstances, but a uniform cut in all sections (including car building, which was losing money, and the repair shops, which were not) was not relatively just and fair to the repair shop employees. Furthermore, they noted that the salaries of officers, managers, and superintendents were not reduced, although such cuts would have been felt less severely, would have shown good faith, would have lessened harshness and tensions, and would have demonstrated genuine sympathy for labor in such disastrous times. The examiners also concluded that if the company had shut down completely, it probably would have lost more money than it did by continuing to operate because

keeping the plant open permitted it to foist some of its losses off
on labor, which was exercising an obvious and unfair advantage.[63]
The commissioners concluded that despite the company's protestations that it stayed in operation to help its labor force — the
tradesmen in Pullman and vicinity — and to spare the public the
annoyance of interrupted travel, its true purpose had been to
benefit itself as a manufacturer. Ultimately, such a scheme prevented plant deterioration, discouraged competitors, kept cars
repaired, and left the company prepared to resume production,
even as it continued to produce revenue.

The commission found that, excluding aesthetics and sanitary
features, rents in Pullman were 20 to 25 percent higher than those
for similar accommodations in Chicago or surrounding towns. It
also found that the company's claim that its workmen did not have
to live in Pullman was incorrect for the company reputedly
preferred to hire its own tenants during slack times. But though
the firm harried its workers for their rent during the hard times,
it had permitted unpaid rent to accumulate for those who could
not afford to pay it and maintain their families. Also, in spite of
its threats, the Pullman Company never evicted a tenant during
that period.

Examining the matter of shop abuses, the commission determined that the company had promised to investigate allegations of
mistreatment promptly and consider corrective measures, actions
that were under way when the workers struck.

Finally, the commissioners stated that employee demands for
a return to the wage scale of June 1893 were clearly unwarranted
because business income in May 1894 could not support such
wages. The commission believed the pay reduction was excessive,
but it felt the company's action was no more unjust than the
demands of the workers. Nonetheless, the three commissioners did
believe that employee requests for lower rent were fair and
reasonable under the circumstances and that a slight concession
in that regard might have averted the strike.[64]

In sum, the picture that emerged from the hearings was that
of a wealthy industrialist who used the depression as an excuse to
make a profit at the expense of his workers. This heartless
characterization was probably not entirely true, but it took very

little imagination to make it appear to be accurate, particularly if one considered Pullman's public reputation. Whether or not it was true, this image continued to haunt George Pullman for the remainder of his life. At the least, the report indicated that Pullman's Palace Car Company had grown so large that its founder and president could no longer control it.

Very few of the findings would have been received kindly by the aging car builder who had instituted the policies investigated by the commission and who had refused to meet with his men or accept arbitration during the strike. In addition, to have many of his contemporaries criticize his actions must have been galling, indeed, to one who brooked no opposition to his opinions and sought the approbation of his peers. One can only imagine the furious outburst that occurred when Pullman learned that the prominent Cleveland industrialist Mark Hanna considered him a fool for not having dealt with his men.[65]

Once the ordeal before the commission was over, Pullman suffered a very severe attack of nervous depression that kept him in bed four days. He was quite ill in September, but he left his sick bed to journey east. By the end of that month, he wrote his wife that, though he was not strong, his health was improving gradually and that everyone kept telling him how much better he looked, which comforted him to some degree.[66]

The strike and boycott brought on by hard times, the arbitrary treatment of workers by management, and the cuts in wages and lack of cuts in rents were now parts of a tragedy that lay in the recent past. Like others of their generation, Pullman workers probably had been goaded into striking by the disheartening realization that they had lost control of their working lives. And those residing in Pullman saw that they had little to say about their personal lives, as well. Their desperation had led them to act in hopes of regaining at least some of their former prestige, along with a few rights.

Seemingly, Pullman was unaware of their feelings. During the 1880s, like other busy industrialists, he left the dealing with unions to hired executives, and uninformed as he was about the state of his company's artisans, he had no reason to doubt the efficacy of such a policy. After all, during his frequent visits to

Pullman, he saw only its bright side as he escorted guests to the theater, the Florence Hotel, the shops, or the residential section. Reports about the community portrayed his workers as happy, well-dressed, contented people who had no quarrel with their jobs or their living conditions. True, the workers had struck in the 1880s when wages had been lowered, but the Pullman managerial staff called the malcontents "chronic kickers" who soon backed down once they saw the futility of their actions.[67] During these crises, Pullman executives (usually backed by police support) always broadcast that the unrest was of little or no consequence.

This time, however, when his men had defied him, Pullman had condescended to let them see his company's books and agreed to investigate shop grievances. But, before these concessions could be implemented, the workers had struck. Once the plant was shut down, Pullman turned to tactics that had served him previously — he relied on hired managers to settle the matter while he left the area and remained away until peace returned. But in this instance, the tactics no longer worked: The effects of the strike reached beyond Pullman and Chicago to touch many Americans who could not understand the industrialist's total resistance to meeting with his men or submitting the problem to arbitration. Although they knew of Pullman, they had little, if any, knowledge of how he had handled similar situations in the past. Many agreed with his philosophy that what a man created was his to do with as he chose. But Pullman's refusal to deal personally with the matter unsettled — and inconvienced — the American public.

One well-known Chicago journalist, George C. Sikes, believed the fundamental cause of the strike had nothing to do with wages; rather, he said, it dealt with the right of a large body of employees to negotiate with their employer through authorized representatives. He also said that Pullman's disinclination to arbitrate was probably correct. Americans did not blame him for standing on his rights, Sikes noted; it was his refusal to relinquish even a modicum of his prerogatives and the resultant suffering that angered the public and besmirched Pullman's name.[68]

Meanwhile, Hattie, Florence, and George, Jr., spent most of their time in France, and George, Jr., also accompanied Nannie Field, the wife of Marshall Field, to Switzerland for several weeks.

As was their custom, George and Hattie communicated with each other almost daily by cable, in code, which was occasionally garbled because French operatives in local offices did not understand their words. Hattie and Florence also received reports of Pullman's activities through clippings from European newspapers sent to them anonymously. Hattie was disgusted by such notices, which insisted that her husband was a German immigrant who had made an enormous fortune. She did her best to cheer him by writing that he should relish the time he and his family spent at Long Branch, a situation that upset her although there was little she could do. Pullman closed Castle Rest early that year and took his siblings to stay at Fairlawn. In spite of misgivings at having them in her home during her absence, Hattie made the best of the matter and bolstered her spouse's spirits by writing him that, within a year, he would enjoy an international reputation as one of the "greatest men of the times."[69]

On 13 October she and her children docked in New York, where George greeted them and took them directly to Fairlawn to see Sanger, who was ill. Pullman and Florence left for Chicago the next day, and by 20 October, the entire family was back at 1729 Prairie Avenue.[70]

The remainder of the year proved less hectic. Hattie returned to the Jackson Sanitorium at Dansville, New York; there, she received treatments for her rheumatism until the end of November, although the medication did her little good. Florence stayed with her mother most of the time, George, Jr., enrolled at Cornell College in Ithaca, New York, and Sanger worked at Marshall Field and Company in Chicago.[71]

The Christmas season of 1894, a relatively pleasant time for the Pullmans, found Florence, her mother, and her father visiting the church in Albion on 19 December but celebrating Christmas Day in Chicago. That afternoon, Frank Lowden, a prominent young Chicago attorney whom Florence had met on the boat to Europe that fall, called and spent the afternoon reading to her.[72]

The rest of the season seemed fairly routine: Pullman treated himself to a new carriage, Hattie entertained but also became ill, and the young people made the usual holiday rounds. But despite the serenity that seemed to follow the end of the strike, financial conditions had not improved, and George Pullman's employees were embittered by his treatment of them. The commission investigating the strike had censured him for refusing to arbitrate the dispute, and matters still remained unsettled. On 11 August, the attorney general of Illinois had filed suit to revoke the Pullman's Palace Car Company charter, alleging that the firm was operating far in excess of what its charter authorized it to do.[73] Although the company fought back, the Supreme Court of Illinois handed down a decision four years later ordering the Pullman Company to divest itself of any real estate not absolutely necessary for the manufacture of railroad cars. Pullman had won the fight, but it was a Pyrrhic victory.

12

The Last Call

A great source of comfort to George Pullman during the strike was the Pullman Memorial Universalist Church being constructed in Albion, New York. The idea for the institution came about during the early summer of 1891 when Charles Danolds, an Albion Universalist, visited Emily Pullman at Castle Rest. George was there also, and during the course of Danolds's stay, the three discussed Universalism in Orleans County and the prominent part Lewis Pullman had played in that movement. As a result, Pullman offered to build the sect a church as a memorial to his parents if the congregation would organize a fund to provide for its care and maintenance. The Universalists accepted the challenge and by December 1892, had raised $5,000 to be used as a maintenance fund. Pullman then purchased a lot for $7,500 at the corner of Main and Madison streets in July 1893, one of the best sites in Albion.[1]

On a very forlorn and stormy Sunday early in December 1893, the Reverend Dr. Henry Pullman delivered a sermon before the congregation crowded into the Albion courthouse. He later wrote his brother that the people interested in forming the church would not shirk their responsibility and that the munificent act would have far-reaching results. Pullman heeded his elder brother's report, and shortly after the start of 1894, construction began on the church, using plans drawn by Solon Beman. By May, George and George, Jr., had observed members of the Masonic Order lay the cornerstone and heard Henry deliver a sermon that he concluded by saying, "The desire of my brother in the erection of this church is to establish a memorial of the father and mother who believed in the doctrines of the Universalist Church and who lived their lives among the people of this community."[2]

During the next two or three months, as the strike dragged on, Pullman spent much of his time at the Belgravia in the company of Helen West and Emily Stuart, with occasional visits from Solon Beman and the Reverend Dr. Charles Eaton to review plans for the edifice at Albion. When Mr. Pullman sought refuge at Castle Rest in July, he took Dr. Eaton with him, presumably to continue their discussions concerning the project.[3]

At the end of October, the Reverend Dr. Charles Fluhrer, pastor of a church in Grand Rapids, Michigan, and a brother of Emma Pullman's husband, Dr. William Fluhrer, accepted the call to serve as minister of the church.[4]

The dedication of the Pullman Memorial Universalist Church took place on 31 January 1895. The new church thronged with spectators, among them members of the Pullman family, including George, Sr., George, Jr., Florence, Emma Fluhrer and Helen West and their children, Frankie Smith (Frankie was Henry Pullman's daughter), the Reverend Henry Pullman, and the Reverend James Pullman. When completed, the church cost $80,000 and boasted both a $5,000 memorial Tiffany window and a $6,000 organ. The English gothic structure's ordinary seating capacity accommodated four hundred people, but this number could be increased to seven hundred by opening the wide doorways between all the rooms. The west transept, facing Albion's Main Street, contained a magnificent memorial window portraying Christ with his arms and hands outstretched; Tiffany, who had contracted for all the church's fifty-six windows, had previously exhibited it in New York City. On the north side of the transept, Beman placed a memorial plaque containing George Pullman's dedication to his parents.

People who entered the main vestibule were greeted by bronze medallion heads of Lewis and Emily Pullman, mounted on the sides of the room. The medallions, executed by Robert Smith of Chicago, were very lifelike, although Lewis Pullman's was said to be the better of the two.[5]

The ceremonies began at 10:00 A.M., with Henry preaching the dedication sermon, and continued until 1:00 P.M. when there was a two-hour break. At 3:00, George delivered his address and heard the response, after which James preached the installation sermon. A reception followed that meeting.[6]

George Pullman considered the dedication services "grand and beautiful in the extreme," but he was very tired at their conclusion. He had been suffering from a prolonged bout of the grippe, and plagued by daily headaches for several weeks. His wife had begun the new year with the same disease, so severe a bout that, soon after Georgie returned to Cornell, she went east with Florence and Sanger, stopping on the way at Jackson Sanitorium in Dansville.[7]

Shortly afterward, on 19 January, Hattie, Mary Logan, and Sanger sailed for Italy. During their trip, Hattie received constant admonitions from her husband to divorce herself entirely "from petty cares and annoyances incident to journeys by entrusting everything of a business nature to Sanger and Mrs. Logan." The group went to Egypt, where Sanger took a tour of the Holy Land before returning to Italy. Sailing from Genoa on 26 March 1895, Hattie did not enjoy the cruise home, although she was pleased that Sanger was a general favorite on board the ship. They reached New York on 5 April, to be greeted by Pullman and other members of the family. After spending a day in New York, they returned to Chicago.[8]

Meanwhile, at the end of February, Pullman and Florence traveled to St. Augustine, Florida; as he wrote his wife, his recent bout with the grippe had left him weaker and more depressed than ever before, making it absolutely necessary for him to get some rest and "horseback exercise in the open air." He had begun to improve and hoped that two or three weeks of rest and proper exercise would enable him to accomplish "the difficult work of the next two months." He took time from his own complaints to comment that Florence was in good health and that she cared for him "in a most delightful manner."[9]

Although Pullman considered his daughter to be in good physical health, her emotional condition, had he taken the trouble to notice, could not have been very satisfactory. He had requested her not to write or see Frank Lowden as often as before, reminding her that she had promised not to marry without his consent. The young couple, very unhappy because of her father's Victorian attitude, had actually arrived at an understanding the preceding January, but their love would be tested for several excruciating months before Pullman relented. Frank managed to see Florence during that time, usually at intervals arranged by Hattie. Lowden spent August 1895 in Europe, and when he returned in early September, he called on the Pullmans at Elberon only to receive a very frosty greeting from his beloved's father, who was not ready to give his consent.[10]

Whether Pullman noticed his daughter's agony during this period is a matter of conjecture, although he probably was aware of it. However, in the course of the years following the strike, he was very busy while the depression lingered and various government bodies continued to examine the town he had created. Much of his time went into securing orders for car construction; he did obtain them but at a loss. Numerous contract renewals and supplements required his personal supervision and kept him in the East much of the time. In addition, he continued to act as the chief director of Pullman's Palace Car Company, although much of the work was now handled by Thomas Wickes and others.[11]

The unsettled financial conditions led the company to close several subsidiaries, such as the Pullman Southern Company, the Union Company, and the Pullman Wheel Works. They also affected the firm's board and stockholders' meetings between 1894 and 1897. Although stockholders' annual meetings were held on the established dates, participants did little more than reelect board members.[12] During the same period, the directors seldom assembled on designated dates because the requisite number needed to establish a quorum were not in Chicago. On the rare occasions that they did gather, they approved payment of quarterly dividends, contracts made by Pullman, reimbursements to Pullman for personal expenditures, and various business and legal matters. Immediately after the 1896 stockholders' meeting, the board convened to elect Pullman president, Wickes vice president (to replace Porter, who had resigned), and Weinsheimer secretary. During 1897, too few directors were available to establish a quorum, even for the directors' meeting customarily held before that of the stockholders on 14 October. At that gathering, the stockholders elected the board and dealt with the company's London branch before adjournment.[13]

George Pullman was absent from Chicago much of the time during early 1895 because of his interest in the church at Albion and the extended vacation he and Florence took in Florida as he recuperated from the grippe. The rest helped, but he still did not look or feel well by the end of April. In fact, Harriet informed him that she wished he could take enough rest to really benefit him so he could continue the work that always awaited him.[14]

During the fall of 1895, two attempts were made on Pullman's life. The first occurred on 12 November when an assistant janitor in the Pullman building, named William B. Graham, threatened to shoot both Pullman and one of his superintendents, J. F. Griffin. Pullman's private policeman, along with city detectives, instituted a search and apprehended Graham after chasing him through the building. Graham declared that Pullman and Griffin were his enemies and that he had been warned to kill them, one by 17 November and the second by 27 November. After his capture, the city physician examined Graham and sent him to the detention hospital for the insane.

The second try came on 16 December when someone sent both Pullman and his neighbor, P. D. Armour, a box containing a pipe bomb. Postal authorities were suspicious of the queerly shaped packages addressed to the two magnates and warned them to hold their mail before they opened it. Also, a man named S. A. Owen appeared twice at both homes, asking to see the two gentleman to warn them of the devices; he stated he had overheard two others discussing them the previous evening. A postal inspector apprehended Owen at the Pullman mansion and took him in for questioning, although the accused man maintained he was innocent of any wrongdoing. The postal authorities found the bombs to be deadly but believed the sender (they suspected Owen) was merely attempting to receive a reward for warning the industrialists of the danger. A second theory was that Owen had intended to assassinate Armour and Pullman but had weakened in his resolve at the last minute.

Although he remained outwardly calm, the threats probably goaded Pullman to become infuriated with his wife just before Christmas over remarks she made in his office before he left for New York City. He departed Chicago thoroughly annoyed with her. Hattie soon made abject apologies for her "unfortunate inspiration" by saying that she always felt as though she stood on the edge of a precipice from which she could be cast into untold misery in an instant.[15] In a letter written two days later, she wondered if the time would ever arrive when business cares would cease and he could enjoy some peace and freedom: Such concerns seemed to multiply, rather than diminish, and there appeared to be nothing bright to look forward to in their future. She knew that if the national financial situation did not improve, Christmas would be a gloomy day for him and sad for her if he were not with her. She added that it might be her last Christmas.[16]

Though his company's affairs caused Pullman much work and worry, he also was involved in other projects, including a scheme in which a group of Chicagoans founded the National Biscuit Company and, between 1895 and 1897, attempted to gain control of the Diamond Match Company. The troubled match firm had to be reorganized as quickly as possible by placing prominent men on its board, and bankers and brokers exerted a great deal of pressure on George Pullman and Philip Armour to become directors of the foundering organization. Armour responded affirmatively, but Pullman did not; instead, he suggested Harlow N. Higginbotham (a member of the Field organization and a Chicago civic leader) and Cyrus McCormick, Jr., as suitable candidates for such office. Pullman admitted the whole affair was an unpleasant situation.[17]

Tiring as they were, Pullman's business affairs continued to improve; by 18 September 1897, Pullman's Palace Car stock stood at 184.5, a tribute to his long hours and hard work. At this point, the exhausted magnate informed Arthur Wells, the major-domo of his private car, that he was cutting back on his various commitments.[18] At long last, the Pullmans might be able to relax and enjoy one another for a prolonged period.

His family maintained a frantic pace, but Pullman was able to unbend and enjoy being with them occasionally during the 1890s, though his periodic outbursts of temper continued. After Hattie returned from Italy and Egypt in 1895, things hummed at 1729 Prairie Avenue: The women of the household took bicycle lessons, bought new horses, and entertained Felicite Oglesby, daughter of a former Illinois governor, who was fast becoming the object of Georgie's affection. Even George, Sr., relaxed enough to take his wife driving and to permit her to give a ball honoring Florence and Harriet, to which she invited 350 guests. Several other social events that spring were hosted by the Pullmans, and the family also journeyed by private car to New York City, stopping at Albion to see the new church, which they all enjoyed a great deal.[19] At the end of June, Hattie, Florence, and Felicite went to Elberon for the season, leaving George and Sanger in Chicago.

But on 19 July, when Hattie was late in picking up her husband at the Long Branch station, he was so angered that he not only treated his family to one of his rages but forbade the twins (both of whom were at Elberon) to ride horses for the entire day. The young people withstood the ordeal, but his wife was very distressed by the matter. For the remainder of the summer, things were strained between George and Hattie, and it was not a happy time for any of the family. Later, toward the end of the season, Pullman tried to make amends for his irritability by taking the family to the theater in New York several times and by spending more time with them at Elberon.[20]

Hattie spent the fall traveling and returned to Chicago on the evening of 14 December to find Florence and Sanger waiting for her, although George had gone to bed. Shortly after her return, Pullman left for New York and, despite his wife's pleadings, did not reappear until Christmas afternoon. A disappointed Hattie and her children dined at her mother's, distressed by the fact that, for the first time in their marriage, Pullman had not given her a Christmas present. Perhaps Florence was the happiest member of the family that season, for her father had finally consented to her marriage to Frank Lowden.[21]

By January 1896, Lowden was an accepted member of the Pullman ménage, and the family made serious plans for the wedding. Although she was absent from Chicago during most of February and March, Hattie was busy ordering furnishings for Florence's new home. She was particularly anxious about the house and table linen because she wanted them to be properly embroidered; in her opinion, these niceties, above all else, bespoke the taste and refinement of the lady of the house and should be the *very best*. She also worried about the exact date of the wedding because it would take at least a month to get Florence ready and she could not do much about her trousseau without her mother's advice. Then, there was the list to be readied and the cards to be sent at least three weeks in advance. Finally, Hattie Pullman was fearful lest she disgrace the family by crying on the night of the wedding.[22] The date was finally set for 29 April, and once she was back in Chicago, Hattie spent most of her time shopping with Florence for the new house. As the wedding day approached, the strain began to tell on the family, and there was an unfortunate scene about linens with George on the eve of one of his trips to New York. Both the Pullmans suffered respiratory ailments, as well, at this time.[23]

In spite of everything, the wedding took place at 8:00 P.M. on the appointed date in the Pullman mansion. It was hailed as a "true wedding feast, in which a splendid type of American girl married the man of her choice, likewise an American." The occasion was grand, indeed, and allowed Chicago's journalists the opportunity to show off their descriptive capabilities. Florence was portrayed as a tall, handsome brunette who was accomplished and gracious and, at the same time, possessed of good sense, charity, and modesty. Her handsome groom boasted many accomplishments, particularly the legal talents and eloquence he used in behalf of many worthy causes. A popular member of Chicago's up-and-coming set, he belonged to numerous prominent social organizations, such as the Calumet, Union League, Washington Park, and Chicago Literary and Law clubs.

The Pullmans' home was decorated with plants and flowers grown in their adjoining conservatory, and the house's "large halls, commodious rooms and high ceilings" made a delightful place for the "green and white wedding," as one writer described the event. A brilliantly lighted terrace greeted guests who walked under a wide awning to enter the home on 18th Street and made their way to the white-enamel-and-gold Louis XVI drawing room. Located in the northwest corner of the house, the room had been stripped of all its furnishings and decorations except for a Bourguereau painting entitled *Happy Moments*, which rested on an easel. For the ceremony, Florence and Frank stood in one of the main alcoves, which was completely bordered and arched with flowers, ferns, and vines. Two hundred guests watched the Reverend Henry Pullman of Baltimore, Maryland, and the Reverend James Pullman of Lynn, Massachusetts, perform the marriage service. Afterward, at 8:30 P.M., one thousand people attended the reception served by Biggs, Chicago's society caterer, in several other large rooms in the mansion. Johnny Hand's orchestra played in the east alcove of the drawing room, while a mandolin orchestra performed on the third floor. Both groups played throughout the evening, and there was dancing as the hour grew later. At 11:30, the young couple left Union Station aboard the Pullman palace car for a ten-day stay in Washington, D.C. Hattie later commented that everything passed off splendidly.[24]

Although Florence's wedding took up much of the family's time, the other children were very much in evidence during the 1890s. But unlike their eldest sister, they continued to be sources of concern and expense to their parents. Harriet and her husband, Frank, lived in San Francisco; when Hattie visited them, she fretted about their dearth of furniture and their need for a house. Rectifying these household shortcomings cost George Pullman a $35,000 check. Harriet did not like San Francisco and, according to at least one report, was not terribly popular in that area, which probably explained why the Carolans built their large home in Burlingame, California. She also spent much of her time with her parents in Chicago, Castle Rest, New York City, and Fairlawn, although she was so preoccupied with her own affairs that she was little comfort or pleasure to her mother and ignored her wishes and desires. In fact, Hattie did not like to be around her.[25]

Then there was the matter of the boys. At the close of 1890, they were fifteen and lived in Chicago with their father and Florence, while their mother stayed at the Hotel del Coronado in San Diego. Pullman did not pay much attention to them and was not even sure where they passed the holidays; he thought it was at their grandmother Sanger's, where the twins often spent time even when Pullman was in Chicago. The industrialist *did* know that they were well, went to the doctor regularly, and enjoyed their Christmas vacation. When he and Florence departed Chicago in early January 1891, he left the twins, who were preparing to return to school, in care of Mattie Smith, the librarian at the town of Pullman.[26]

This appeared to be the standard pattern for the boys. Their parents, busy with their own affairs, were both gone for much of the school year, and they left the boys to fend for themselves under the nominal care of a company or family retainer. They did join their parents at Fairlawn for the summer months, but they usually arrived there unwell. During the fall of 1891, they stayed with their grandmother Sanger, which meant they ate better and more regularly and seemed perfectly happy. They spent that Christmas at home with their father and Florence, while their mother and Harriet visited Santa Barbara. All were sick at the outset of 1892 when the entire family, minus Georgie (who remained in Chicago with jaundice), gathered in St. Augustine. At the end of February, Pullman ordered Sanger home to return to school — much to his mother's distress because Chicago's cold March climate might cause a relapse for the still-weak boy. She added that Sanger was fearful of returning to the cold but would not speak up for himself.[27]

Toward the end of the summer of 1892, Hattie set about finding a suitable school for her sons since her husband was too busy to handle that responsibility. She chose the Hill School at Pottstown, Pennsylvania, which thoroughly pleased George. On 21 September, the Pullmans took Georgie and Sanger there.[28]

The twins made an encouraging start. Professor John Meigs, head of the institution, added chemistry to their studies, hoping to pique their interest. They began to take music lessons — Sanger on the violin and Georgie on the piano. Meigs further encouraged Hattie to lower their allowances to $2 or $3 per week, rather than double or triple that amount. He did, however, approve their expenditures of moderately large sums on athletic equipment.[29]

Late the following February (1893), George and Hattie visited Pottstown to find both twins sick. Taking them to New York, the Pullmans left them at the Windsor Hotel under a doctor's care while they went on to Washington, D.C. Then, at the end of March, Meigs threatened to expel the boys. Realizing the dire consequences of expulsion, Pullman, who could not go himself, sent Samuel Elliott to the school. The upshot was that Sanger remained at Pottstown, and Georgie went to New York City to study under a tutor. Doctors recommended that the twins be separated for at least a year because Georgie had a nervous affliction that, by sympathy, affected Sanger.[30]

That summer, the twins reached eighteen. Sanger remained with his parents when Georgie began work at the Pullman offices in New York, and Georgie stayed in New York when Sanger resumed his studies at Hill School in the fall. Both boys spent a very subdued Christmas at home after their Uncle Albert's death.[31]

Georgie returned to New York City in January 1894, but Sanger accompanied his mother and Florence to the Jackson Sanitorium in Dansville. There he pursued his violin lessons and entered into the active social life of the patients. Both he and Florence attended their mother constantly; Georgie appeared occasionally but only to spend the day.[32]

Sanger left the sanitorium in March with his father. George planned to employ his son in the Pullman Company offices in Chicago, but he also found him quite useful in handling household and stable matters. Sanger continued his violin and devoted the noon hour each day to "elocution and exercise in order to develop himself physically." His father found him to be good company.[33]

Sanger worked in the Pullman Company office throughout 1894, taking time to escort his mother to Hot Springs, Arkansas, in May and to New England in the summer.[34]

While Hattie, Florence, and Georgie were abroad, Harriet and Sanger stayed with their father in Chicago and then accompanied him to Fairlawn to await the arrival of the others from Europe. Sanger returned to Chicago that fall, and Georgie enrolled in Cornell University at Ithaca, New York. Both boys spent Christmas at home.[35]

Between January and April 1895, Sanger escorted his mother and Mary Logan on their trip to Italy and Egypt. During the rough voyage home, Sanger was very attentive to his indisposed mother. Once back in Chicago, he stayed for the rest of the year except for a few weeks at the island and at Fairlawn. He did buy two polo ponies that June: The boys were still most interested in riding and had received riding apparel and equipment on their nineteenth birthdays. Georgie continued to attend Cornell but passed most of the summer with his parents. As was customary, the boys and Florence spent Christmas at home in Chicago. Sanger, who seemed to have inherited his father's love of music and theater, played in several concerts, while Georgie courted Felicite Oglesby, to whom he had become engaged the preceding September.[36]

After Christmas, Georgie withdrew from Cornell. Sick again, he went to Jacksonville and then to Hot Springs with his mother, who wanted him cured before he attempted to return to work. Finally, on 26 March, he began working at the bank at Pullman.[37]

For their twenty-first birthdays in June 1896, each boy received a fine gold watch and chain from their mother. That day, their grandmother Sanger noted that they were "fine handsome boys, both in business."[38] Both seemed well on the way to productive careers at last. Unfortunately, all was far from well.

By September 1896, Hattie, who was staying at Fairlawn, grew very troubled about her sons — especially Sanger, who was lonely and despondent living at home with his father. Sanger was determined to do right and understood why his father ignored him, although he would have given a great deal to be on good terms with his father. According to his mother, he was a strange boy, not bad at heart or vicious but difficult to understand; he troubled her almost beyond endurance. She believed it might take very little to make him go completely bad — or very little in the right direction might make a splendid man of him. Unable to sleep at night for worrying about him, she felt powerless.[39]

In Chicago during January 1897, Hattie was still worried about Sanger, who was doing nothing except waiting at home to report to work at Marshall Field's. Meanwhile, Georgie, between sick spells, continued to spend most of his time with Felicite Oglesby. Later, when Hattie began her usual spring travels, Sanger accompanied her until he and Little Hattie returned to Chicago in March.[40]

Pullman joined his wife in St. Augustine, where he obtained a necessary rest before returning to Chicago. Sanger appeared to be doing very well at Field's, and Georgie expected to go to work at the bank. Hattie was very pleased to learn of Sanger's determination to do a good job at the store and that he appreciated John G. Shedd's kindness to him. (Shedd, a Field partner since 1892, headed the wholesale division.) But shortly afterward, the boys, who were heavy drinkers, gave their father a good deal of trouble, much to their mother's dismay. An exasperated Hattie stated that it did little good to stay at home or sacrifice on the boys' account because if they wanted to go wrong, they would always find a way. She could not restrain them, and it appeared that Pullman could do little with them either. She informed her husband that she would not go home unless he were there because Harriet, who was in Chicago, was no pleasure to her mother and they might just as well have her and the boys together for a while.[41]

That spring, the Pullmans devoted their time to entertaining George, Jr., and Felicite, and George, Sr., spent many of his free hours with Sanger, although the family did not celebrate the boys' twenty-second birthdays. But on 1 July, Sanger left his job at Field's.[42] During the following months, the family was at Fairlawn and the island. By the end of summer, Georgie had returned to Chicago, and Sanger remained at Fairlawn. Neither was gainfully employed.

Although identical twins, they differed in several ways. Georgie was something of an impulsive romantic; Sanger appeared steadier, more calculating, gregarious, and more realistic. Sanger also seemed to possess the most potential and to be stronger physically, although neither was in very good health. Both were fine horsemen and shared an interest in equestrian matters, which the family accepted up to a point. Perhaps if Pullman had permitted his sons to pursue these interests, rather than forcing them into the more prosaic field of business, they would have come closer to fulfilling his expectations. Nevertheless, he did not, and they soon left any positions he gave them or secured for them. Georgie and Sanger, in the fashion typical of rich men's sons of the period, enjoyed the diversions available in Chicago that their father's money afforded them. Georgie mixed with the theater crowd and was a drinker. His associates called him a "true sport," a title he enjoyed as he moved at an ever-increasing pace. His parents, however, urged him to marry and settle down. Sanger was a party boy as well, but he was constantly in and out of love and known as a ladies' man.[43] Yet he liked his home and tried to get along with his parents. He took care of his mother and would have liked to be closer to his father; had he been given any encouragement by that gentleman, he might have turned out a credit to him. At the very least, both boys were immature. And by 1897, Pullman was disgusted with both of them.

Family documents do not disclose specific details of the twins' misconduct, but they shed sufficient light to permit certain conclusions. The most obvious of these is that the boys were victims of too little parental supervision and too much spending money. Pullman made no time for them and seemed only to offer his sons advice; one seldom reads of his doing anything with the twins just to enjoy their company. He was too busy maintaining an image that their antics sullied, and his cold manner and brusque personality undoubtedly added to his disagreeableness when he was with them. As he grew older and grumpier, they received the brunt of his bad temper, so they learned to keep a low profile in his presence and probably were fearful of incurring his wrath when they were around him. Unpleasant feelings doubtless turned to frustration as they entered manhood, possessed of well-established playboy habits.

Although Pullman was not to blame for all their faults, the record shows that his similar treatment of his younger brothers Charles and Frank also met with failure and that they succeeded despite, not because of, his ministrations. He gave his sons spending money, clothing, education, and shelter, but material gifts were not enough; in this regard, his treatment of his sons resembled his actions toward his workmen. Perhaps, had he been able to express a modicum of affection and understanding, the boys' careers might have been more of a credit to him.

In spite of their concerns over their children, George and Hattie Pullman continued their active social lives, which, in 1896, revolved around the theater and the new organ in their home on Prairie Avenue. They went for frequent drives in their Victoria or Stanhope, and they spent an occasional evening at home by themselves, reading and chatting. Hattie left late that spring on short trips to Minnesota, Virginia, Washington, D.C., and New York but did not remain away from Chicago for long.[44]

Their annual trek to Elberon began on 10 July, and, as usual, Pullman spent the remainder of the summer journeying between Castle Rest and Fairlawn, although he complained of being tired most of the time. His wife went to Castle Rest for the annual tree-planting ceremony on her late mother-in-law's birthday but returned to Fairlawn immediately. George spent the better part of a month in Chicago before joining her to host a very successful afternoon tea for seventy guests. He stayed at the cottage for several days and even held a business meeting there.[45] They closed Fairlawn on 25 September and reentered Chicago's active social scene of whist lessons, the theater, dinner parties, and organ recitals in addition to the myriad other activities that appealed to people of their social stature.

They had a pleasant holiday season, and on Christmas Day, they held a party and had a tree for the children of all the family employees. Afterwards, they went to hear the Princeton Glee Club. Felicite arrived the next day, and the boys escorted her to a dinner given by Bertha Palmer. Although Pullman left for New York on 27 December, his wife had an enjoyable dinner for twelve young people in honor of Felicite. The season continued, and Hattie spent New Year's Day 1897 attending two receptions, having her daughter and son-in-law to dine, and then entertaining her neighbors and good friends, the W. W. Kimballs, at cards during the evening. Her social life did not stop in January, although she had an "unhappy scene" with her husband just before leaving for a dinner party, which led her to observe that "these sudden thunder storms out of a clear shine are getting pretty hard to endure."[46]

Then, at 10:30 A.M. on 20 January, a baby arrived at the Lowden home, christened George M. Pullman Lowden. Though the proud grandmother had not received much correspondence from her husband, who was in New York for several days, he answered her wire announcing his grandson's birth and then telephoned her from New York. He called again on 21 January, and upon his return to Chicago on 24 January, he hurried to see the baby before luncheon.[47]

The Pullmans spent much of that spring becoming acquainted with their grandson, attending Pullman's social gatherings for his friends and railroad men, and at Hattie's parties and concerts. They traveled to Washington, D.C., and then to Florida, where Pullman relaxed by riding horseback with his wife or, if she were lame, with other members of the family. They retraced their steps to Richmond and Washington, D.C., before returning to Chicago on 13 May. The next evening, although she did not feel well, Hattie gave a dinner party for eighteen people.[48]

Pullman traveled a good deal during the next month, taking her with him on one excursion into Kansas and Tennessee aboard the private car. It proved to be a miserable trip; the only highlight was an inspection tour of the Kansas City, Pittsburg (Kansas), and Gulf Railroad as guests of the road's president.[49]

The day of their return to Chicago, 13 June, was also their thirtieth wedding anniversary. Hattie gave her husband a silver toilet set as a remembrance, but she received nothing from him. Perhaps Pullman's thoughts were on a higher plane: Soon after, he selected the family burial plot at Graceland Cemetery on Chicago's north side.[50]

After their arrival at Elberon for the summer, Pullman managed to spend more time driving and riding with his wife, though they quarreled as they had all spring. They arrived at Castle Rest on 12 August, where a horde of people awaited the annual celebration. On 14 August (the late Emily Pullman's birthday), they planted the customary tree, christened the baby, and took pictures of four generations of Pullmans. Although George, Hattie,

Summer 1897, Castle Rest. Top, left to right: Florence Lowden, Frank Lowden (holding son Pullman Lowden), portrait of Mrs. Lewis Pullman, the Reverend James Pullman and and unknown person. Seated left to right: Mrs. George Pullman, Royal Henry Pullman and George M. Pullman. *Courtesy the Chicago Historical Society.*

and Georgie left for Bar Harbor on 16 August because Hattie was quite ill and Castle Rock was to be closed in four days, the whole affair had been a great success, and all had had a happy time.

The Pullmans paused at Bar Harbor and Boston on their return to Elberon but cut short this phase of their trip because of Hattie's illness.[51] Pullman left for Chicago but returned immediately, having met with President William McKinley on his way to that city. Later that season, they gave several parties and discussed the remodeling of Fairlawn with architects Beman and Lord. Apparently, they enjoyed each other during these final days of summer and even talked about a trip to Europe in the fall.[52]

They ended their 1897 sojourn at Fairlawn on 8 October when Pullman took his grandson and nurses to the private car for the journey to Chicago. Although he grumbled about the heat in Chicago during the following week, he attended a stockholders' meeting at the Pullman Building on 14 October and then, on the next two days, entertained Frank Thomson and other Pennsylvania Railroad executives in Chicago and Pullman. The aging magnate was so affable that the Pennsylvania men commented on it at their departure.[53] However, the ordeal tired George, and the excessive walking he did at Pullman with his visitors hurt him severely. On 17 October, he notified his wife that he was entirely alone, that he missed her, and that he was not very well.[54] He complained about his indisposition, but most of his associates failed to notice his ill health. However, he knew that he had heart trouble and had been warned that his end might come at any time.[55]

George Pullman spent 18 October working in his office until 5 P.M. He went home and remained there, conversing with the Reverend and Mrs. Charles Eaton, who had arrived for a visit. He retired early, but about 4:30 A.M., he summoned his valet to his bedside, stating that he was uncomfortable. A few minutes later, he sent for Dr. Frank Billings, the family physician. Meanwhile, Dr. Eaton was roused by the commotion of the servants and, learning the nature of the disturbance, hurried to Pullman's bedroom. He found the magnate worsening and put in a second call to Dr. Billings. Shortly after the doctor reached the house, George Pullman died of a massive heart attack.[56]

Hattie and Sanger had stayed at Elberon to close Fairlawn for the year. Afterward, she went to the Holland House in New York and was there when George West appeared at her room very early

George Pullman holding his grandson, Pullman Lowden, at Castle Rest, 1897. *Courtesy the Chicago Historical Society.*

on the morning of Tuesday, 19 October, bearing the sad news of her husband's death. Highly distraught, she left on the Pennsylvania Limited, accompanied by Robert Lincoln and Sanger, and was met at Fort Wayne by a dear friend, Mrs. H. O. Stone, who stayed with her until she reached home. Florence and Georgie were in Chicago, and Harriet was summoned from San Francisco.[57]

257

At funeral services held in the Pullman home on Saturday, 23 October, many out-of-town celebrities joined the prominent Chicagoans in attendance, and the list of honorary and active pallbearers read like a roster of the Chicago social register and the executive force of Pullman's Palace Car Company. The Reverend N. D. Hills and the Reverand C. H. Eaton, the officiating clergy, spoke briefly, after which the Imperial Quartet sang, and the coffin was closed.[58] The cortege began the long journey to Graceland Cemetery where the palace car prince had chosen to be buried.

For some time prior to his death, Pullman had worried that his corpse might be kidnapped by disgruntled former employees; to prevent possible desecration, he had had his grave prepared accordingly.[59] His body lay in a lead-lined box that was wrapped in tar paper and coated with an inch of asphalt. The casket, lowered into a pit thirteen feet long, nine feet wide, and eight feet deep, rested on a concrete flooring eighteen inches thick. Once it was properly positioned, workers filled the space surrounding the casket with concrete to its upper lid. They then built the enclosing walls up to one-half inch above the asphalt coating on the coffin and placed eight heavy T-rails transversely across the top. Resting on the concrete walls at either side, their lower surfaces cleared the asphalt covering by half an inch to allow for settling and to prevent the heavy steel from crushing the casket's top. After the rails were bolted together by two long rods, more tar paper was placed on top to prevent the flow of additional concrete into the half-inch space between the rails and the asphalt surrounding the coffin. Covered by even more concrete, the rods lay like a "wall of stone and steel" between Pullman and would-be grave robbers. At Hattie Pullman's request, Solon Beman designed the monument that stands on the surface of George Pullman's resting place.[60]

After the funeral, John S. Runnells, Pullman's lawyer, read the will to assembled family members at home. Though its contents received no publicity for several days, the instrument contained the usual disposition of properties and monies to Hattie, Florence, and Harriet, with a support bequest of $3,000 per year to each of the twins. Hattie received the home on Prairie Avenue, along with $50,000 and the income from $1.25 million. Florence and Harriet each received the income from $1 million and later inherited an additional $3 million from the residual estate. Florence also received Castle Rest, but there were certain stipulations concerning its use; she also received a $100,000 endowment for its upkeep. Pullman did not forget friends and relatives, dividing some $300,000 among them. He also gave his namesake town $1.25 million with which to build a free manual high school. Pullman also left $10,000 apiece to thirteen public institutions in Chicago. Hattie later contested the will and had it altered so that she could support her sons in better fashion. No one knew the exact size of Pullman's estate, although estimates at the time of death placed it at between $7 million and $8 million. By 1900, however, when the will was probated, the figure rose to $17.5 million.[61]

The boys lived off their mother's largesse for the remainder of their lives. By August 1899, a report stated they had incurred debts amounting to $10,000, which their mother agreed to pay. Sanger went to the northern California peninsula shortly after his father's funeral, with Harriet and Frank Carolan. On 17 March 1898, he married Louise Lander West, one of three daughters of a deceased San Francisco banker. Because their father had lost his wealth, the young women (all said to be beautiful) supported themselves as teachers in the public schools. One newspaper described Louise Lander Pullman as "of medium height, with a profusion of reddish brown hair, blue eyes, and an attractive face." Even though Hattie disapproved of the marriage, which had taken place without her consent, she supported the young couple. But her refusal to accept his wife embittered Sanger, who nevertheless lived a nice life on an estate in Belmont, close to San Mateo.[62]

After his father's death, Georgie worked as a Pullman Car inspector, first in Chicago and then in New Jersey, but resigned in June 1898 to join his mother at the family home in Elberon. There, he courted Lynne Fernald, Sanger's former fiancée and the daughter of J. W. Fernald, who was in the pressed hay business in Chicago. The couple married in New York on 17 August 1898 without their parents' blessing or consent. Hattie Pullman, already upset by Sanger's marriage, was even more distraught by Georgie's trip to the altar.[63]

It was not long before Georgie took up with Blanche Bowers, a former childhood playmate who had married a New York composer. Bowers obtained a divorce from her and sued Georgie for alienating his wife's affections. Lynne Pullman then divorced Georgie in September 1901, receiving alimony of $1,000 per year. While all this was going on, Georgie, according to one report, spent a summer at Long Branch, consuming nearly $5,000 worth of cigars and wine, all purchased on credit. (During the summer of 1899, Georgie had reconciled with his mother, probably by taking the Keeley cure, a treatment for alcoholism.) He remained at Elberon, very ill and barely escaping pneumonia, throughout the first half of 1901 and then joined Sanger in California that June. A month later, Georgie was in Redwood City, California, the proprietor of the short-lived San Mateo Polo Pony Company. He was heavily in debt.

He soon became infatuated with Louise Pullman's older sister, Sarah Lander Brazell, whom he married in Carson City, Nevada, on 30 September 1901, just two weeks after his divorce from Lynne. His thirty-year-old bride had divorced her first husband, Colonel Jim Brazell, a well-known stock entrepreneur on Nevada's Comstock Lode during its bonanza days.

Shortly after the newlyweds returned to their home near San Mateo, Georgie contracted a cold that turned into acute pneumonia; he died on 28 November 1901 at twenty-six years of age. Sanger refused to allow his brother's remains to be returned to Chicago, so Georgie was buried at Cypress Lawn Cemetery, San Mateo. Georgie's will, executed on 25 November 1901, just days before his death, left everything to his wife. Actually, there was very little in his estate because his horses, carriages, and motor cars were mortgaged to a San Francisco liveryman. In the meantime, his mother notified his personal secretary that all claims against him would be paid. Rumors abounded that she would resist any attempt by her daughter-in-law, of whom she did not approve, to secure a portion of the Pullman estate. Sanger and his wife, of course, supported Sarah's efforts.[64] Sanger, who survived his brother by only four years, met his death in a coaching accident in August 1905. He was buried beside Georgie.[65]

By that time, Pullman's surviving brothers — Henry, James, and Charles — were dead, and his sisters — Helen and Emma — were gone by the time World War I broke out. Hattie continued to live in Chicago, dividing her time between travel, social events, and charities. Her greatest charitable interests focused on Chicago's destitute children, but during the war, she donated much time to war relief efforts. She was seventy-nine years old when she died of pneumonia in Pasadena, California, on 28 March 1921. She was laid to rest beside her husband at Graceland Cemetery in Chicago.[66]

After Frank Carolan's death in 1923, Harriet moved to New York City where, two years later, she married a childhood sweetheart, Colonel Arthur Frederic Schermerhorn. She continued to live in New York following his demise in 1933. During her final years, Harriet served as an officer in the Outdoor Cleanliness Association and won several awards for her flower arrangements at the organization's annual flower mart. She was eighty-seven when she died on 20 October 1956; she, too, was buried in the Pullman plot in Chicago's Graceland Cemetery.[67]

Florence and Frank Lowden moved to a farm at Oregon, Illinois, where they raised their four children. Florence also helped her husband in his political and agricultural careers — assistance that he came to depend on a great deal. Lowden enjoyed a distinguished political career, serving as a congressman from Illinois between 1906 and 1911 and as governor of Illinois from 1917 to 1921. As the governor's wife, Florence was a very active participant in the state's war effort during World War I. And like her mother, she was interested in numerous charities, including St. Luke's Hospital and the Visiting Nurse Association. After her husband's retirement from active politics in 1928, they spent their summers abroad and at Castle Rest and their winters in Chandler, Arizona. Florence was sixty-eight when she died unexpectedly in her sleep at the family farm, Sinnissippi, on 5 July 1937. Both Lowden and she are buried in the plot next to her parents in Graceland Cemetery.[68]

In later years, Pullman's name never received the accolades it had before the strike. George Mortimer Pullman was not a lovable man — although many people would have admired or envied him because of his money, prestige, and status. He was cold and aloof, a posture that carried over into his dealings with employees. In fact, as years passed, his name became almost synonymous with industrial tyranny. Pullman would have brushed aside such a reputation, believing his intent, as exemplified by his actions, was totally misinterpreted. He failed to perceive that he had lost contact with his employees because success had removed him from their sphere. A student of his life cannot fail to notice that growth changed him from a respected employer accustomed to supervising his hired hands to one whom they disliked and distrusted because he was far removed from them. Here, he personified the changes occurring in American industry during the years immediately following the Civil War, as businesses expanded to a point where their owners no longer shared workbenches with employees and instead grew more detached from them. The alteration in George Pullman's status and attitude probably began when he went to Colorado and was forced to turn his Chicago interests over to men he could trust. Later, his prolonged visits from Colorado to the States led him to relinquish the day-to-day management of his mercantile and mining operations to others who were equally or better versed in those skills. After his return to Chicago, he was able to concentrate on acquiring contracts for his company because Albert Pullman could handle the production side and deal with the workers. This arrangement permitted George to impress prospective investors and customers and to pour champagne for hordes of thirsty journalists who would advertise his palace cars in glowing terms. Certainly, George Pullman was far beyond the reach of his men at the outset of the 1880s, as demonstrated by the early strikes at Pullman and the way management handled them.

Pullman remained concerned about his employees, but his paternalism would not permit him to recognize them as productive members of the firm. He possessed foresight and vision enough to try to assist his workers, but the desire for profit eventually soured that attempt; in the end, it tarnished his image. He never lied about his intentions, for he always maintained that the town of Pullman was not a philanthropic endeavor. Nevertheless, his publicized treatment of his workers did nothing to enhance his reputation. Ultimately, Pullman was a man of his time who stood by his decisions even when a majority of his peers disapproved of them. He firmly believed that what he had earned was due principally to his own efforts, assisted by stockholders who had risked their money in his firm. Why should he — or any man of his caliber, for that matter — explain his actions to people who were unfamiliar with his business and who had not accumulated the capital to place themselves on his level? Pullman and others like him recognized that not all success was based on money, and they contributed to worthy causes in the arts, education, medicine, and religion. But when it came to business, they spelled achievement with dollar signs alone. Pullman donated to private charities, helped his mother, brothers, and sisters, and supported his immediate family, but he did so with a modicum of publicity, in the manner of most gentlemen. Therefore, people outside his personal circle knew only the autocrat, not the philanthropist. Even in death, he hardly appealed to the public for his grave, designed to frustrate vandals, resembled the sepulchers of Egyptian pharaohs.

Pullman's wife, whom he adored in spite of their quarreling, eased his way into the nation's social world. The lives of the Pullmans as they circulated among Chicago's monied coterie were much more fulfilling thanks to Hattie's management. And the three homes and one office building he constructed during his lifetime probably would have been more ostentatious had it not been for his spouse's tempering influence. Yet, typical of the successful men of his era, Pullman believed that whatever he erected — church, home, or office — should mirror his accomplishments. The castle-like houses built for Marshall Field and Potter Palmer, both nabobs of Chicago's gilded age, certainly were monuments that reflected the affluence of their owners. And their structures, both commercial and domestic, and others like them added a great deal to Chicago's prestige and skyline during the Victorian age.

Pullman was willing to take risks as he built his empire. Most of his peers in Chicago had, like him, been daring enough to leave their eastern homes for careers in a town still only one step removed from the frontier in the 1850s. Yet he outdid many of them by crossing the Great Plains to seek a fortune in the Pike's Peak goldfields. Once his cars succeeded in the United States, he did not hesitate to try placing them overseas, although the venture proved unsuccessful. Unlike his foremost competitors in the sleeping car business, Webster Wagner (who enjoyed the support of the Vanderbilts) and Theodore Woodruff (backed by Carnegie),

George Pullman relied on Pullman's Palace Car Company stock-holders and satisfied customers for his backing. He also differed from many other industrial captains because he never attempted to undercut his competition; instead, he provided an excellent product and efficient service for which he asked and obtained full value. He preferred not to share credit with others but chose to buy out people, which enabled him to accept the accolades for himself.

Although his competitors could never best him, his employees eventually called him to account and dealt him his most serious blow. They found the chink in his armor. Their strike exposed him as an autocrat and opened him to criticism, something he could not abide. His style of life was jarred by the incident: Not only were his actions questioned, his own stockholders, angered by his attitude and conduct in the matter, discussed removing him as the company's head. This state of affairs, which he could not control, irritated him greatly. It seemed financial upheaval, ungrateful workers, unknowledgeable investors, and an unsympathetic governmental bureaucracy had combined to menace the empire he had constructed so lovingly. Indeed, one observes a definite decline in Pullman after the strike, as he devoted his final energy to combat various threatening elements. Americans were changing their attitudes about business and labor. Unfortunately, Pullman had not accepted the new ways of thinking.

George Pullman came to be remembered as an inventor, which he was not; rather, he was an astute businessman who sold his generation sumptuous and comfortable railroad accommodations. His brother Albert was more the inventor, devoting his skills to designing the posh interiors of the early Pullman palace cars.

George M. Pullman accumulated a fortune selling a superior product because he recognized the benefits to be derived from good publicity; tragically, he did not perceive its value in representing *himself* to the public. Because he died so soon after the strike ended, he never had an opportunity to change his image through public bequests and donations, as Carnegie and Rockefeller had. Yet despite his tarnished reputation, Americans remembered him as long as train travel was a major part of the national way of life. Indeed, many Americans still fondly recall at least one ride on a "Pullman."

APPENDIX

Members of the Board of Directors, Pullman's Palace Car Company, 1867–1897:

E.L.S. Benzon (London), 1873
John Crerar (Chicago), 1867–1889
John W. Doane (Chicago), 1881–1897
J. N. DuBarry (Philadelphia), 1876–1879
Marshall Field (Chicago), 1877–1897
R. P. Flower (New York), 1879–1881
Amos T. Hall (Chicago), 1870–1881
Charles G. Hammond (Chicago), 1871–1883
Robert Harris (Chicago), 1867–1876
Ira Holmes (Chicago), 1868
Henry C. Hulbert (New York), 1882–1897
Robert T. Lincoln (Chicago), 1880
J. Pierpont Morgan (New York), 1874–1878
Henry R. Pierson (Chicago), 1870
George M. Pullman (Chicago), 1867–1897
Henry R. Reed (Boston), 1890–1897
Homer E. Sargent (Chicago), 1867–1872
Thomas A. Scott (Philadelphia), 1870–1871
Edmund Smith (Philadelphia), 1872–1875
O.S.A. Sprague (Chicago), 1884–1897
Norman Williams, Jr. (Chicago), 1867, 1882–1897

NOTES

Introduction

1. John H. White, Jr., *The American Railroad Passenger Car* (Baltimore, Md: Johns Hopkins University Press, 1978), p. 353.

2. Ibid., p. 660.

3. Paul Avrich, *The Haymarket Tragedy* (Princeton, N.J.: Princeton University Press, 1984), pp. 17, 33, 223, and 365.

4. George C. Sikes to Madeline Wallin, 24 July 1894, Madeline Wallin Sikes Collection, Box 6, Chicago Historical Society, Chicago, Ill.

5. See, for instance, Rev. C. H. Eaton, "The Pullman Strike," in *The Christian Leader,* ca. late summer 1894, clipping, The Pullman Company, Series 1, Box 10, Chicago Public Library, Special Collection Division, Chicago, Ill.

6. Almont Lindsey, "Paternalism and the Pullman Strike," *American Historical Review* 45 (January 1939): 288.

Preface

1. The only article concerning his career in the Colorado gold camps that I located was Peter D. Vroom, "George M. Pullman and the Colorado Tradition," *The Colorado Magazine* 17 (May 1940): 113–115. This short essay simply denied that Pullman had developed the sleeping car as a result of his stay in the Rockies.

Chapter 1

1. This genealogical material is from a manuscript entitled "Pullman," which was commissioned by Harriet Pullman Schermerhorn in memory of her parents. It is in the Mrs. C. Phillip Miller Collection, Chicago Historical Society, Chicago, Ill. Additional information may be obtained by scanning the Pullman Genealogy Collection in the Manuscript Section of the Chicago Historical Society, Chicago, Ill.

2. Isaac S. Signor, *Landmarks of Orleans County, N.Y.*, Part 3 (Syracuse, N.Y.: D. Mason, 1894), p. 76. George N. McGinnis, closely related to the Pullmans and interested in genealogy, noted that Psalter Pullman's main occupation was carpenter/joiner, so his son's choice of carpentry as his life's career was natural. George N. McGinnis to author, 18 September 1983. Andrew W. Young, *History of Chautauqua County New York, From Its First Settlement to the Present Time, With Numerous*

Biographical and Family Sketches. (Buffalo, N.Y.: Matthews & Warren, 1875), p. 647; H. C. Taylor, *Historical Sketches of the Town of Portland, Comprising Also the Pioneer History of Chautauqua County, With Biographical Sketches of the Early Settlers* (Fredonia, N.Y.: W. McKinstry and Son, 1873), pp. 98–105.

3. Royal H. Pullman, D.D., "Dedication Sermon," dedication of the Pullman Memorial Universalist Church, 31 January 1895, Albion, N.Y., p. 19, Mrs. C. Phillip Miller Collection, Chicago Historical Society, Chicago, Ill.; Taylor, *Historical Sketches,* p. 434. The origin of George Pullman's middle name remains unknown.

4. Douglass C. North, *The Economic Growth of the United States: 1790–1860* (New York: W. W. Norton, 1966), pp. 196–197.

5. Ray Allen Billington, *Westward Expansion: A History of the American Frontier,* 3rd ed. (New York: Macmillan, 1967), pp. 301 and 334; Arthur Cecil Bining and Thomas C. Cochran, *The Rise of American Economic Life* (New York: Charles Scribner's Sons, 1964), p. 191.

6. Billington, *Westward Expansion,* p. 334.

7. Robert E. Riegel, *Young America: 1830–1840* (Westport, Conn.: Greenwood Press, 1973), pp. 5 and 131; Royal H. Pullman, "Dedication Sermon," p. 19. Royal H. Pullman to George M. Pullman, 23 October 1893, Mrs. C. Phillip Miller Collection, Chicago Historical Society, Chicago Ill.; Emily C. Pullman to Fanny Pomroy, 10 March 1830, Emily Caroline Minton Pullman Correspondence, Chicago Historical Society, Chicago, Ill.

8. Royal H. Pullman to George M. Pullman, 15 December 1892, 12 December 1893, and 30 April 1897, Mrs. C. Phillip Miller Collection, Chicago Historical Society, Chicago, Ill.

9. Royal H. Pullman, "Dedication Sermon," p. 18; Emily Caroline Minton Pullman Correspondence, 1830–1850s, Chicago Historical Society, Chicago Ill. See also, George N. McGinnis to author, 12 November 1983; Signor, *Landmarks of Orleans County,* p. 76.

10. Royal H. Pullman, "Dedication Sermon," pp. 20 and 22; Taylor, *Historical Sketches,* pp. 164–166; Royal H. Pullman to George M. Pullman, 12 December 1893, Mrs. C. Phillip Miller Collection, Chicago Historical Society, Chicago, Ill.

11. Edmund Burke, comp., *List of Patents for Inventions and Designs, Issued by the United States From 1790–1847 With the Patent Laws and Notes of Decisions of the Courts of the United States for the Same Period* (Washington, D.C.: J. and G. S. Gideon, 1847), p. 240; *In Memorian, Emily Caroline Pullman* (n.p., n.d.), booklet in the Office of the County Historian, Orleans County Courthouse, Albion, N.Y.

12. Royal H. Pullman to George M. Pullman, 27 March 1895, Mrs. C. Phillip Miller Collection, Chicago Historical Society, Chicago, Ill.; Young, *History of Chautauqua County,* pp. 605–606; see also Joseph Husband, *The Story of the Pullman Car* (1917; reprint ed., Grand Rapids, Mich.: Black Letter Press, 1974), p. 24; Emily C. Pullman to Lewis Pullman, 1 June 1845, Emily Caroline Minton Pullman Correspondence, Chicago Historical Society, Chicago, Ill.

13. Arad Thomas, *Pioneer History of Orleans County, New York* (Albion, N.Y.: H. A. Bruner, Orleans American Steam Press Print, 1871), pp. 59, 180–183, and 447.

14. Emily C. Pullman to Lewis Pullman, 1 June 1845, Emily Caroline Minton Pullman Correspondence, Chicago Historical Society, Chicago, Ill.

15. George M. and Albert B. Pullman to Lewis and Emily C. Pullman, 14 December 1845, Pullman Collection, Chicago Historical Society, Chicago, Ill.; Royal H.

Pullman to George M. Pullman, 27 March 1895, Mrs. C. Phillip Miller Collection, Chicago Historical Society, Chicago, Ill.; Lewis E. Atherton, *The Frontier Merchant in Mid-America* (Columbia: University of Missouri Press, 1971), p. 29.

16. Emily C. Pullman to her mother, brothers, and sister, 9 January 1848, Emily Caroline Minton Pullman Correspondence, Chicago Historical Society, Chicago, Ill.

17. Ibid.

18. George M. Pullman to Theodosia R. Minton, 2 October 1848, George M. Pullman Correspondence, Chicago Historical Society, Chicago, Ill.

19. Signor, *Landmarks of Orleans County*, pp. 76, 265, and 266; Emily C. Pullman to her mother, brothers, and sister, 9 January 1848, Emily Caroline Minton Pullman Correspondence, Chicago Historical Society, Chicago, Ill.; George M. Pullman to Theodosia R. Minton, 2 October 1848, George M. Pullman Correspondence, Chicago Historical Society, Chicago, Ill.

20. Royal H. Pullman, "Dedication Sermon," p. 23; Whitney R. Cross, *The Burned-Over District: The Social and Intellectual History of Enthusiastic Religion in Western New York, 1800–1850* (New York: Harper Torchbooks, 1950), pp. 44 and 324; Russel Blane Nye, *Society and Culture in America: 1830–1860* (New York: Harper and Row, 1974), p. 299.

21. Royal H. Pullman, "Dedication Sermon," pp. 23–24; Ernest Cassara, ed., *Universalism in America, A Documentary History* (Boston: Beacon Press, 1971), p. 39; see also Pullman Company, Miscellaneous Scrapbooks, Series A, vol. 18, 1894–1895 and Series B, vol. 7, 1899–1903, Newberry Library, Chicago, Ill.

22. Royal H. Pullman to George M. Pullman, 12 December 1894, Mrs. C. Phillip Miller Collection, Chicago Historical Society, Chicago, Ill.

23. Signor, *Landmarks of Orleans County*, p. 76; Hannah M. DaLee to Emily C. Pullman, 17 March 1850, Emily Caroline Minton Pullman Correspondence, Chicago Historical Society, Chicago, Ill.; Albert B. Pullman to Lewis and Emily C. Pullman, 27 August 1852 (?), Emily Caroline Minton Pullman Correspondence, Chicago Historical Society, Chicago Ill.

24. Lewis and Emily C. Pullman to Theodosia R. Minton, 21 November 1852, Emily Caroline Minton Pullman Correspondence, Chicago Historical Society, Chicago, Ill.

25. *Rochester Post Express*, 21 September 1894, clipping, in the Office of the County Historian, Orleans County Courthouse, Albion, N.Y. clipping, ca. 12 November 1927, in file titled "Famous People, G. W. [sic] Pullman," Office of the County Historian, Orleans County Courthouse, Albion, N.Y.

26. Signor, *Landmarks of Orleans County*, p. 76; Royal H. Pullman to Emily C. Pullman, 21 March 1879, Emily Caroline Minton Pullman Correspondence, Chicago Historical Society, Chicago, Ill.; Richard W. and Hanna M. DaLee to Lewis and Emily C. Pullman, 13 February 1853, Emily Caroline Minton Pullman Correspondence, Chicago Historical Society, Chicago, Ill.; Signor, *Landmarks of Orleans County*, p. 76; Royal H. Pullman, "Dedication Sermon," p. 24.

27. Riegel, *Young America*, p. 6, 7, and 15; see also Frances W. Gregory and Irene D. Neu, "The American Industrial Elite in the 1870's: Their Social Origins," in *Men in Business: Essays in the History of Entrepreneurship*, ed. William Miller (Cambridge, Mass.: Harvard University Press, 1952), pp. 193–211.

28. North, *Economic Growth of the United States*, pp. 204–209.

29. John F. Stover, *Iron Road to the West: American Railroads in the 1850s* (New York: Columbia University Press, 1978), pp. 45–46.

30. Taylor, *Historical Sketches*, p. 434; *Chicago Evening Post*, 18 December 1893, p. 3; *Chicago Tribune*, 19 December 1893, p. 6; Harriet Pullman Schermerhorn, "Pullman." Manuscript in the Mrs. C. Phillip Miller Collection, Chicago Historical Society, Chicago, Ill.; "In Memoriam, George M. Pullman," *Chicago Morning News*, 19 October 1897, clipping, Chicago Historical Society, Chicago, Ill.

31. *Biographical Sketches of the Leading Men of Chicago* (Chicago, Ill.: Wilson and St. Clair, 1868), *Chicago Morning News*, 19 October 1897, clipping, in volume titled "In Memoriam, George M. Pullman," Chicago Historical Society, Chicago, Ill.; *Pullman Ill. Journal*, 14 January 1893, p. 1 (reprint in author's possession), *Chicago Morning News*, 19 October 1897; Ronald E. Shaw, *Erie Water West: A History of the Erie Canal 1792–1854* (Lexington: University of Kentucky Press, 1966), pp. 379–396.

32. Clipping, ca. 12 November 1927, in file titled "Famous People, G. W. [sic] Pullman," Office of the County Historian, Orleans County Courthouse, Albion, N.Y.; Signor, *Landmarks of Orleans County*, p. 226.

33. *Weekly Time Book, for Contractors, Workingmen and Others* (Philadelphia, Pa.: Troutman & Hayes, n.d.), Mrs. C. Phillip Miller Collection, Chicago Historical Society, Chicago, Ill.; *Chicago Morning News*, 19 October 1897. Other accounts state that he made several thousand dollars. See "Albion Points with Pride to G. M. Pullman," clipping, Office of the County Historian, Orleans County Courthouse, Albion, N.Y.; Signor, *Landmarks of Orleans County*, p. 77; George M. Pullman to Emily C. Pullman, 2 April 1857, George M. Pullman Correspondence, Chicago Historical Society, Chicago, Ill.

34. *Chicago Morning News*, 19 October 1897, clipping, in volume titled "In Memorium, George M. Pullman," Chicago Historical Society, Chicago, Ill.

35. George M. Pullman to Emma Pullman, 18 January 1859, and George M. Pullman to Helen Pullman, 20 January 1859, George M. Pullman Correspondence, Chicago Historical Society, Chicago Ill.

36. George M. Pullman to Emily C. Pullman, 30 January 1859, George M. Pullman Correspondence, Chicago Historical Society, Chicago, Ill.

37. George M. Pullman to Emily C. Pullman, 20 February 1859, George M. Pullman Correspondence, Chicago Historical Society, Chicago, Ill.

38. *Chicago Daily Press and Tribune*, 28 February 1859, p. 1.

Chapter 2

1. *Chicago Daily Press and Tribune* 28 February 1859, p. 1; A. T. Andreas, *History of Chicago, From the Earliest Period to the Present Time*, 3 vols. (1886; reprint ed., New York: Arno Press, 1975), 1: 637 and 2: 504; Frank A. Randall, *History of the Development of Building Construction in Chicago* (Urbana: The University of Illinois Press, 1949), p. 120; *Chicago Daily Press and Tribune*, 28 February 1859, p. 1, and 22 March 1859, p. 1; *Chicago Daily Herald*, 26 March 1859, p. 3, and 3 April 1859, p. 3; Elizabeth Hoon Cawley, ed., *The American Diaries of Richard Cobden*, (New York: Greenwood Press, 1969), p. 163.

2. Bessie Louise Pierce, *A History of Chicago*, vol. 2, *From Town to City 1848–1871* (New York: Alfred A. Knopf, 1940), p. 37.

3. Ibid., pp. 37, 77, 78, 80, and 90.

4. Douglas C. North, *The Economic Growth of the United States, 1790–1860* (New York: W. W. Norton, 1966), pp. 211-214; Arthur Cecil Bining and Thomas C.

Cochran, *The Rise of American Economic Life* (New York: Charles Scribner's Sons, 1964), pp. 225–226.

5. North, *Economic Growth of the United States*, pp. 213–214.

6. Pierce, *A History of Chicago*, pp. 127–128 and 156–157; Elias Colbert and Everett Chamberlin, *Chicago and the Great Conflagration* (Chicago: J. S. Goodman, 1871), p. 96.

7. Pierce, *A History of Chicago*, pp. 128 and 140; Colbert and Chamberlin, *Chicago*, pp. 95–97.

8. Pierce, *A History of Chicago*, pp. 316–318; Colbert and Chamberlin, *Chicago*, pp. 97–99.

9. *Chicago Morning News*, 19 October 1897, clipping, in volume titles "In Memorium, George M. Pullman," Chicago Historical Society, Chicago, Ill.; *Chicago Press and Tribune*, 17 May 1859, p. 1; *Chicago Daily Democrat*, 4 August 1859, p. 1, 16 August 1859, p. 1, and 18 August 1859, p. 1.

10. *Chicago Daily Democrat*, 2 January 1860, p. 2, 5 January 1860, p. 1, and 23 March 1860, p. 1; *Chicago Press and Tribune*, 6 January 1860, 1, and 24 March 1860, 1; George M. Pullman, diary, 3 January 1860, Chicago Historical Society, Chicago, Ill.

11. George M. Pullman diary, 21 February 1860, Chicago Historical Society, Chicago, Ill.

12. George M. Pullman diary, 17 March 1860, Chicago Historical Society, Chicago, Ill.

13. George M. Pullman diary, 2 March 1860. Chicago Historical Society, Chicago, Ill.; *Chicago Press and Tribune*, 9 March 1860, p. 1, 2 April 1860, p. 1, 14 April 1860, p. 1, 16 April 1860, p. 4, 12 May 1860, p. 1, and 17 May 1860, p. 4; *Chicago Daily Democrat*, 24 March 1860, p. 1.

14. *Chicago Morning News*, 19 October 1897, clipping, in volume titled "In Memoriam, George M. Pullman," Chicago Historical Society, Chicago, Ill.; "Raising the Grade," *Chicago History* 3 (Fall, 1953): 263–270.

15. Negotiations for this project, begun in April 1860, took almost a year. *Chicago Press and Tribune*, 14 April 1860, p. 1. For further developments, see Ibid., 12 May 1860, p. 1; George M. Pullman to Emily C. Pullman, 21 January 1861, George M. Pullman Correspondence, Chicago Historical Society, Chicago, Illinois; *Tribune*, 28 January 1861, p. 1, 12 February 1861, p. 1, 25 February 1861, p. 1, 26 February 1861, p. 1, and 27 February 1861, p. 1; *Rocky Mountain News*, 13 February 1861, 2; George M. Pullman to Emily C. Pullman, 17 March 1861, George M. Pullman Correspondence, Chicago Historical Society, Chicago, Ill.

16. *Pullman* (Illinois) *Journal*, 7 January 1893 pp. 1–2 (reprint in author's possession); George Grantham Bain, "George M. Pullman, He Had Promised to Write a History of His Cars," *Philadelphia Evening Star*, 1 November 1897, clipping, and *Chicago Morning News*, 19 October 1897, clipping, in volume titled "In Memoriam, George M. Pullman," Chicago Historical Society, Chicago, Ill.; Pullman [Ill.] Journal, 14 January 1893, p. 2.

17. Early family correspondence intimates that George traveled constantly. See various letters in the Emily Caroline Minton Correspondence, 1840s and 1850s, Chicago Historical Society; Royal H. Pullman to George M. Pullman, 13 May 1889, Mrs. C. Phillip Miller Collection, Chicago Historical Society, Chicago, Ill.: "I recall a firm which was pressed for money when one of the partners was about to sail on the Erie Canal for New York."

18. *Chicago Morning News,* 19 October 1897, and Bain, "Pullman," clippings in volume titled "In Memoriam, George M. Pullman," Chicago Historical Society, Chicago, Ill.

19. Bain, "Pullman," clipping in volume titled "In Memoriam, George M. Pullman," Chicago Historical Society, Chicago, Ill.

20. Frederick Clifton Pierce, *Field Genealogy: Being the record of All the Field Family in America Whose Ancestors Were in This Country Prior to 1700,* 2 vols. (Chicago: W. B. Conkey, 1901), 2: 675–676; *Philadelphia Evening Star,* 30 October 1897, clipping, in volume titled "In Memoriam, George M. Pullman," Chicago Historical Society, Chicago, Ill. Joseph Husband, *The Story of the Pullman Car* (1917; reprint ed., Grand Rapids, Mich.: Black Letter Press, 1974), pp 28–32; *Railroad Gazette,* 6 April 1877, p. 153.

21. John H. White, Jr., *The American Railroad Passenger Car* (Baltimore, Md.: The Johns Hopkins University Press, 1978), p. 247. *Pullman* (Ill.) *Journal* published a description of the Car No. 9 replica as it appeared at a fair held in Nashville during the summer of 1897. *Pullman* (Ill.) *Journal,* ca. May 1897, clipping, Pullman Company, Miscellaneous Scrapbooks, Series B, vol. 4, 1893–1899, Newberry Library, Chicago, Ill. Husband, *The Story of the Pullman Car,* 28–32, relied on two accounts of cars 9 and 19 as they appeared following their conversion to sleepers, one by Leonard Seibert, the mechanic who performed most of the work on them, and the other by Jake Barnes, the conductor on the first car run from Bloomington to Chicago on the Chicago and Alton line. Seibert's account seems to be more valid because he actually helped convert the carriages. Barnes's description appears to confuse these cars with the earlier sleepers that Pullman would have slept on during his journey from Buffalo to Westfield before departing for Chicago. Journalists who rode the converted cars of the period were careful to point out that the supports for upper berths on older sleepers were absent from the Field-Pullman conversions; Barnes maintained they were still present. In addition, the journalist's reports may have been made more enthusiastic as a result of the libations liberally poured by Pullman and Field on the trial trip of 16 August 1859. Their impressions, written shortly after the excursion, were probably more correct than those of Barnes, who apparently described the cars from memory.

22. Husband, *The Story of the Pullman Car,* pp. 28–32; *Chicago Daily Herald,* 17 August 1859, p. 3; *Chicago Press and Tribune,* 17 August 1859, p. 1.

23. *Chicago Daily Herald,* 17 August 1859, p. 3; *Chicago Daily Democrat,* 17 August 1859, p. 1; Husband, *The Story of the Pullman Car,* p. 29.

24. *Chicago Daily Democrat,* 17 August 1859, p. 1; *Chicago Press and Tribune,* 17 August 1859, p. 1; *Chicago Daily Herald,* 17 August 1859, p. 3.

25. George M. Pullman diary, 20 January 1860, 26 January 1860, 30 January 1860, 22 February 1860, 13 April 1860, 10 May 1860, and 11 June 1860, Chicago Historical Society, Chicago, Ill.; Pierce, *A History of Chicago,* pp. 51 and 147.

26. George M. Pullman diary, 1 January–18 June 1860, passim, Chicago Historical Society, Chicago, Ill.

27. George M. Pullman diary, 1 January 1860 to 18 June 1860, passim, and 26 March 1860, Chicago Historical Society, Chicago, Ill.

28. Ibid. See also George M. Pullman to Emily C. Pullman, 13 February 1860, George M. Pullman Correspondence, Chicago Historical Society, Chicago, Ill.; Pierce, *A History of Chicago,* pp. 474 and 476. Note, however, that Professor Pierce stated on p. 376 that the 1857 panic caused many Chicagoans to turn to religion.

29. George M. Pullman diary, 1 January 1860 to 18 June 1860, passim. and 9 May 1860, Chicago Historical Society, Chicago, Ill.

Notes

30. The Greeley, Richardson, and Villard report, dated 9 June 1859, has been reprinted many times. For example, see Wilbur Fiske Stone, ed., *History of Colorado*, 4 vols. (Chicago: S. J. Clarke, 1918), 1:240–245. The report also appeared in the *Chicago Press and Tribune*, 24 June 1859, p. 2.

31. *Chicago Daily Herald*, 11 August 1859, p. 3, and 12 August 1859, p. 1; *Chicago Press and Tribune*, 15 August 1859, p. 2, 11 January 1860, p. 2, 16 January 1860, p. 2, 24 January 1860, p. 1, and 9 March 1860, p. 2.

32. Otis E. Young, Jr., *Western Mining* (Norman: University of Oklahoma Press, 1970), pp. 69–70.

33. Samuel Cushman and J. P. Waterman, The Gold Mines of Gilpin County, Colorado (Central City, Colo.: Register Steam Printing House, 1876), p. 21; *Rocky Mountain News*, 1 December 1859, p. 3 and 14 March 1860, p. 3.

34. *Rocky Mountain News*, 1 December 1859, p. 3, 14 February 1860, p. 1, 4 April 1860, p. 2, 11 April 1860, p. 3, and 11 July 1860, p. 2; *Western Mountaineer* (Golden, Colo.), 11 January 1860, p. 2; *Chicago Press and Tribune*, 20 March 1860, p. 1, 21 March 1860, p. 1, 3 April 1860, p. 1, 1 May 1860, p. 2, and 5 May 1860, p. 2; C. M. Clark, M.D., *A Trip to Pike's Peak and Notes by the Way*, ed. Robert Greenwood (San Jose Calif.: Talisman Press, 1958), p. 99; Hiram A. Johnson, "A Letter from a Colorado Mining Camp in 1860," *Colorado Magazine*, 7 (September 1930):193.

35. *Chicago Press and Tribune*, 28 September 1859, p. 1, 13 December 1859, p. 2, 10 January 1860, p. 2, 3 February 1860, p. 2, 28 February 1860, p. 1, and 21 March 1860, p. 1; *Rocky Mountain News*, 14 March 1860, p. 3.

36. George M. Pullman diary, 5 May 1860 and 9 May 1860, Chicago Historical Society, Chicago, Ill.

37. Colbert and Chamberlin, *Chicago*, p. 97.

38. George M. Pullman diary, 17 May 1860 to 7 June 1860, passim, Chicago Historical Society, Chicago, Ill.

39. George M. Pullman diary, 14 June 1860 to 19 June 1860; Chicago Historical Society, Chicago, Ill. *Chicago Press and Tribune*, 21 June 1860, p. 1; George M. Pullman to Emily C. Pullman, 20 June 1860, George M. Pullman Correspondence, Chicago Historical Society, Chicago, Ill.

40. A. D. Richardson, "The Pike's Peak Region," *Chicago Press and Tribune*, 3 March 1860, p. 2, and "The Pike's Peak Hegira," *Chicago Press and Tribune*, 30 May 1860, p. 2; Margaret Louise Fitzsimmons, "Missouri Railroads During the Civil War and Reconstruction," *Missouri Historical Review*, 35 (January 1941): 188–189.

41. George M. Pullman diary, 21 June 1860, Chicago Historical Society, Chicago Ill.

42. Dwight L. Smith, ed., *John D. Young and the Colorado Gold Rush*, (Chicago: R. R. Donnelley and Sons, 1969), pp. 7–8; Chris. L. Rutt, ed. and comp., *History of Buchanan County and the City of St. Joseph and Representative Citizens, 1826–1904*, (Chicago: Biographical Publishing, 1904), p. 251.

43. George M. Pullman diary, 21–23 June 1860, and George M. Pullman to Emily C. Pullman, 23 June 1860, George M. Pullman Correspondence, Chicago Historical Society, Chicago, Ill.

44. Sir Richard Burton, *The Look of the West, 1860: Across the Plains to California* (Lincoln: University of Nebraska Press, n.d.), pp. 15–18.

45. George M. Pullman diary, 23 June 1860 to 30 June 1860, Chicago Historical Society, Chicago, Ill.

46. Jerome C. Smiley, *History of Denver* (1901; reprint ed., Evansville, Ind.: Unigraphic, 1971), p. 326; *Weekly Rocky Mountain News*, 25 January 1860, p. 3, and 3 February 1860, p. 2; *Chicago Press and Tribune*, 11 April 1860, p. 1 and 10 May 1860, p. 2; The Society of Colorado Pioneers, "Colorado Pioneer Register," Maria Davis McGrath Collection, Denver Public Library, Western History Department, Denver, Colo.; George M. Pullman to Emily C. Pullman, 31 October 1860, George M. Pullman Correspondence, Chicago Historical Society, Chicago, Ill.; see also entries for 9 July and 10 July 1860.

47. Lewis E. Atherton, *The Frontier Merchant in Mid-America* (Columbia: University of Missouri Press, 1971), pp. 115–118.

Chapter 3

1. George M. Pullman to Emily C. Pullman, 2 July 1860 and 15 July 1860, and George M. Pullman diary, 3 July 1860, Chicago Historical Society, Chicago, Ill.

2. George M. Pullman diary, 10 July 1860 to 18 July 1860; see also George M. Pullman to Emily C. Pullman, 15 July 1860, Chicago Historical Society, Chicago, Ill.; Caroline Bancroft, *Gulch of Gold: A History of Central City, Colorado* (Denver, Colo.: Sage Books, 1958), p. 57.

3. Frank Hall, *History of the State of Colorado*, 4 vols. (Chicago: Blakely Printing, 1889–1895), 3:408–409. Hall went through the area that would become Central City in June 1860. Frank Fossett, *Colorado: A Historical, Descriptive and Statistical Work on the Rocky Mountain Gold and Silver Mining Region* (Denver, Colo.: Daily Tribune Printing House, 1876), p. 173.

4. George M. Pullman diary, 7 July 1860, Chicago Historical Society, Chicago, Ill. Mrs. Lane was the widow of a Chicago man.

5. George M. Pullman diary, 10 July 1860 to 18 July 1860, and George M. Pullman to Emily C. Pullman, 15 July 1860, George M. Pullman Correspondence, Chicago Historical Society, Chicago, Ill.

6. Preemption notice, Gilpin County Mining Records, 1859–1864, Russell District, Book E, p. 125, Colorado State Archives, Denver, Colo.

7. George M. Pullman to his mother, sisters, and brother, 17 September 1860, George M. Pullman Correspondence, and George M. Pullman diary, 4 August 1860 to 12 August 1860, Chicago Historical Society, Chicago, Ill.

8. George M. Pullman to his mother, sisters, and little brother, 17 September 1860; and George M. Pullman to Emily C. Pullman, 23 September 1860, George M. Pullman Correspondence, Chicago Historical Society, Chicago, Ill.

9. George M. Pullman to Emily C. and Emma Pullman, 31 October 1860, George M. Pullman Correspondence, Chicago Historical Society, Chicago, Ill.; see also Robert Graham to George M. Pullman, deed, 19 October 1860, Gilpin County Mining Records, 1859–1864, Russell District, Book D, pp. 326–327, Colorado State Archives, Denver, Colo.; Robert Graham to George M. Pullman, power of attorney, 19 October 1860, Colorado State Archives, Gilpin County Mining Records, 1859–1864, Book D, p. 327. Colorado State Archives, Denver, Colo.; both documents were filed 27 October 1860. Lynn I. Perrigo, ed., "H. J. Hawley's Diary, Russell Gulch in 1860," *Colorado Magazine*, 30 (April 1953): 149.

10. See Duane A. Smith, *Rocky Mountain Mining Camps: The Urban Frontier* (Bloomington: Indiana University Press, 1967), pp. 169–171.

11. George M. Pullman to Emily C. and Emma Pullman, 31 October 1860, George M. Pullman Correspondence, Chicago Historical Society, Chicago, Ill.

12. George M. Pullman to his sisters and brother, 22 July 1860, and George M. Pullman to Emily C. Pullman, 23 September 1860, George M. Pullman Correspondence, Chicago Historical Society, Chicago, Ill.

13. George M. Pullman to Emily C. Pullman, 23 September 1860, and 31 October 1860, George M. Pullman Correspondence, Chicago Historical Society, Chicago, Ill.

14. Ovando J. Hollister, *The Mines of Colorado* (Springfield, Mass.: Samuel Bowles, 1867), p. 80; Charles L. Brown to Lyon, Pullman and Company, bill of sale, 5 November 1860, Teller Collection, University of Colorado Library, Boulder, Colo.

15. George M. Pullman to Emily C. Pullman, 9 October 1860, George M. Pullman Correspondence, Chicago Historical Society, Chicago, Ill.; *Rocky Mountain News*, 14 November 1860, p. 3. Pullman reported twenty-eight wagons, and the *Rocky Mountain News* listed twenty-six. George M. Pullman to Emily C. Pullman, 23 November 1860, George M. Pullman Correspondence, and George M. Pullman, Folder 72:34, Chicago Historical Society, Chicago, Ill.; *Rocky Mountain News*, 12 December 1860, p. 4; George M. Pullman to Helen Pullman, 2 December 1860, George M. Pullman Correspondence, Chicago Historical Society, Chicago, Ill.

16. *Denver Republican*, 8 June 1861, p. 3 (courtesy of Clement M. Silvestro). The exact transaction for this piece of property has not been uncovered; however, Lyon, Pullman and Company had rented it by early November 1861. Lyon, Pullman and Company to C. H. Morgan, lease, 10 October 1861, Teller Collection, University of Colorado Library, Boulder, Colo.

17. Lyon, Pullman and Company and G. A. Fox and H. Higgins, building contract, 2 May 1861, Teller Collection, University of Colorado Library, Boulder, Colo.

18. Margery Chase to Lyon, Pullman and Company, lease, 5 November 1861, Teller Collection, University of Colorado Library, Boulder, Colo.

19. C. B. Clark and Company (C. B. Clark, George Sears, Daniel Curran, and Robert D. Thompson) to A. J. Williams, H. L. Wright, R. H. Hill, W. T. Welborn, N. Peloney, and J. H. Alexander, bill of sale, 31 March 1860, Teller Collection, University of Colorado Library, Boulder, Colo.; *Rocky Mountain News*, 4 April 1860, p. 2, and 6 June 1860, p. 2.

20. *Rocky Mountain News*, 12 September 1860, p. 2; Joseph W. Bowles to Lyon, Pullman and Company, sheriff's sale, 24 January 1861, Teller Collection, University of Colorado Library, Boulder, Colo.

21. *Rocky Mountain News*, 27 March 1861, p. 3.

22. James E. Lyon, et al. v. James Brown, bill for injunction, 27 May 1862, General Docket no. 142, Colorado State Archives, Denver, Colo.

23. The partners never seemed to realize a great deal from their mining claim ventures. For example, see the summary of their experience with the west half of Claim Number Five on the Gregory Lode in Hollister, *Mines of Colorado*, pp. 63–65. Mention of their banking enterprise appears in Hall, *History of the State Of Colorado*, vol. 1, p. 363. See George M. Pullman's letters to his family, dated 17 September 1860, and 16 February 1861; see also *Rocky Mountain News*, 2 January 1861, p. 1.

24. George M. Pullman to Emily C. Pullman, 20 August 1860, George M. Pullman Correspondence, Chicago Historical Society, Chicago, Ill.; John F. Vandevanter to J. W. Medberry, undated and unsigned contract, Teller Collection, University of Colorado Library, Boulder, Colo.

25. See George M. Pullman diary, 15 September 1860, and George M. Pullman to his mother, sister, and brother, 17 September 1860. George M. Pullman Correspondence, Chicago Historical Society, Chicago, Ill.

26. John F. Vandevanter to George M. Pullman, release, 19 May 1861, Teller Collection, University of Colorado Library, Boulder, Colo.; Lyon, Pullman and Company, judgment against John S. Harris, Charles H. Wheeler, and John W. Medberry, 26 May 1862, Property Book A, p. 434, Office of the Clerk and Recorder, Gilpin County, Central City, Colo.; Lyon, Pullman and Company to Benjamin O. Russell, lease, 9 June 1862, Teller Collection, University of Colorado Library, Boulder, Colo.; Lyon, Pullman and Company to J. H. Hayford, quitclaim deed, 15 April 1863, Property Book 3, p. 481, and Lyon, Pullman and Company to James W. Richards, quitclaim deed, 15 April 1863, Property Book 3, p. 482, Office of the Clerk and Recorder, Gilpin County, Central City, Colo.

27. *Rocky Mountain News*, 8 August 1860, p. 2; S. C. Field to George M. Pullman, receipt, 17 September 1860, George M. Pullman Collection, Miscellaneous Documents, Chicago Historical Society, Chicago, Ill.; S. C. Field to John Smith, Esq., 26 November 1860, in ibid.; George M. Pullman to his mother, sisters, and brother, 17 September 1860, George M. Pullman Correspondence, Chicago Historical Society, Chicago, Ill.; *Rocky Mountain News*, 27 February 1861, p. 3.

28. See, for instance, George M. Pullman to his sisters and brother, 22 July 1860, George M. Pullman to his mother, sisters, and brother, 17 September 1860, George M. Pullman to Helen Pullman, 2 December 1860, George M. Pullman to Emily C. Pullman, 21 January 1861, George M. Pullman to Emma Pullman, 16 February 1861, and George M. Pullman to Emily C. Pullman, 17 March 1861, George Pullman Correspondence, Chicago Historical Society, Chicago, Ill.

29. George M. Pullman to Emily C. Pullman, 20 August 1860, George Pullman Correspondence, Chicago Historical Society, Chicago, Ill.

30. George M. Pullman to Emily C. Pullman, 23 September 1860; George M. Pullman to Emily C. and Emma Pullman, 31 October 1860, and George M. Pullman to Helen Pullman, 2 December 1860, George Pullman Correspondence, Chicago Historical Society, Chicago, Ill.

31. George M. Pullman to Emily C. Pullman, 21 January 1861, George Pullman Correspondence, Chicago Historical Society, Chicago, Ill.

32. George M. Pullman to Emily C. Pullman, 28 January 1861; George M. Pullman to Emma Pullman, 16 February 1861, George Pullman Correspondence, Chicago Historical Society, Chicago, Ill.

33. George M. Pullman to Emma Pullman, 16 February 1861, and George M. Pullman to Emily C. Pullman, 17 March 1861, George Pullman Correspondence, Chicago Historical Society, Chicago, Ill.

34. George M. Pullman to Emily C. Pullman, 17 March 1861, and 19 April 1861, George M. Pullman to Emma Pullman, 16 February 1861, George M. Pullman Correspondence, Chicago Historical Society, Chicago, Ill.; *Weekly Rocky Mountain News*, 13 February 1861, p. 4; *Rocky Mountain News*, 11 May 1861, p. 3.

35. George M. Pullman to Emily C. Pullman, 17 March 1861, 19 April 1861, and 28 May 1861, and George M. Pullman to Helen Pullman, 11 May 1861, George M. Pullman Correspondence, Chicago Historical Society, Chicago, Ill.; *Rocky Mountain News*, 22 June 1861, p. 3; George T. Clark diary, 22 June 1861, p. 82, Denver Public Library, Western History Department, Denver, Colo.

Notes

36. George M. Pullman to Emily C. Pullman, 11 May 1862, George M. Pullman Correspondence, Chicago Historical Society, Chicago, Ill.; *Rocky Mountain News,* 20 March 1862, p. 3, 31 March 1862, p. 3, and 30 April 1862, p. 4.

37. George M. Pullman to Emily C. Pullman, 11 May 1862, George M. Pullman Correspondence, Chicago Historical Society, Chicago, Ill.; Moore's reluctance to continue dealing with James E. Lyon is evident in his letters to George M. Pullman, 29 November 1861, 2 May 1862, and 9 July (?) 1862. Mrs. C. Phillip Miller Collection, Chicago Historical Society, Chicago, Ill.

38. James E. Lyon to George M. Pullman, 31 July 1862, 5 August 1862, 10 August 1862, 12 September 1862, 21 September 1862, 15 October 1862, and 7 December 1862, Mrs. C. Phillip Miller Collection, Chicago Historical Society, Chicago, Ill.

39. Charles H. Moore to George M. Pullman, 24 June 1862, Mrs. C. Phillip Miller Collection, Chicago Historical Society, Chicago, Ill.

40. H. D. Towne to George M. Pullman, 21 October 1862, Mrs. C. Phillip Miller Collection, Chicago Historical Society, Chicago, Ill.

41. George M. Pullman to Emily C. Pullman, 11 May 1862, and 15 April 1863, George M. Pullman Correspondence, Chicago Historical Society, Chicago, Ill.; *Rocky Mountain News,* 28 July 1862, p. 2 and 29 July 1862, p. 3; George M. Pullman to Emily C. Pullman, telegram from Atchison, Kansas, 1 January 186[3], Chicago Historical Society, Chicago, Ill.

42. Carroll R. Harding, *George M. Pullman (1831–1897) and the Pullman Company* (New York: The Newcomen Society in America, 1951), p. 12; James E. Lyon to George M. Pullman, 10 May 1880, Mrs. C. Phillip Miller Collection, Chicago Historical Society, Chicago, Ill.

43. Smith, *Rocky Mountain Mining Camps,* p. 159.

44. Chalkley J. Hambleton, *A Gold Hunter's Experience* (Chicago: privately printed, 1898), p. 91; George M. Pullman to Emily C. Pullman, 23 September 1860, 31 October 1860, and 28 January 1861, George M. Pullman Correspondence, Chicago Historical Society, Chicago, Ill.

45. George M. Pullman to his mother and sisters, 28 January 1861, George M. Pullman Correspondence, Chicago Historical Society, Chicago, Ill.; Lynn I. Perrigo, ed., "H. J. Hawley's Diary, Russell Gulch in 1860," *Colorado Magazine* 30 (April 1953):149.

46. George M. Pullman to Emily C. Pullman, 9 November 1863, George M. Pullman Correspondence, Chicago Historical Society, Chicago, Ill.; Office of the Clerk and Recorder, Gilpin County, Central City, Colo., Property Book 4, pp. 614–615; Office of the Clerk and Recorder, Gilpin County, Central City, Colo. Property Book A, p. 346; George W. Hall and Lyon, Pullman and Company, agreement dated 26 May 1862 to remodel and update the Milwaukee Mill, Teller Collection, University of Colorado Library, Boulder, Colo.; *Tri-Weekly Miner's Register,* 5 September 1862 (courtesy of Clement M. Silvestro).

47. Announcement of the Eagle Gold Company, George M. Pullman Collection, Chicago Historical Society, Chicago, Ill.; *Daily Mining Journal* (Black Hawk, Colo.), 26 March 1864, p. 2, contains a detailed description of this company; *Railway Register,* 18 June 1892, clipping, Pullman Company, Miscellaneous Scrapbooks, Series B, vol. 3, 1891–1893, Newberry Library, Chicago, Ill.

Chapter 4

1. George M. Pullman to Emily C. Pullman, 15 April 1863, George M. Pullman Correspondence, Chicago Historical Society, Chicago, Ill.

2. Elias Colbert and Everett Chamberlin, *Chicago and the Great Conflagration* (Chicago: J. S. Goodman, 1871), pp. 107–116; Bessie Louise Pierce, *A History of Chicago*, vol. 2 (New York: Alfred A. Knopf, 1940), p. 272.

3. Colbert and Chamberlin, *Chicago*, p. 117–122.

4. Limited amounts of material concerning the Eagleton Wire Manufacturing Company are included in the Pullman materials at the Chicago Historical Society. He also was called the "principal owner" of that organization in *Biographical Sketches of the Leading Men of Chicago* (Chicago, Ill.: Wilson and St. Clair, 1868), p. 475; George M. Pullman to Emily C. Pullman, 9 November 1863, George M. Pullman Correspondence, Chicago Historical Society, Chicago, Ill.

5. *Chicago Times*, 9 September 1864, 3. General descriptions of hiring substitutes for military service appear in Pierce, *A History of Chicago*, pp. 273–276; Colbert and Chamberlin, *Chicago*, pp. 107–109; A. T. Andreas, *History of Chicago*, 3 vols. (1884; reprint ed., New York: Arno Press, 1975), 2:167–168.

6. John F. Stover, *Iron Road to the West: American Railroads in the 1850s* (New York: Columbia University Press, 1978), p. 103.

7. Stover, *Iron Road*, pp. 141, 221–227, and 230; John F. Stover, *History of the Illinois Central Railroad* (New York: Macmillan, 1975), pp. 97–105.

8. Richard C. Overton, *Burlington Route: A History of the Burlington Lines* (New York: Alfred A. Knopf, 1965), pp. 82–84; Arthur M. Johnson and Barry E. Supple, *Boston Capitalists and Western Railroads: A Study in the Nineteenth-Century Railroad Investment Process* (Cambridge, Mass.: Harvard University Press, 1967), pp. 189–190.

9. Benjamin Field to George M. Pullman, 23 January 1863, and George M. Pullman to Emily C. Pullman, 29 May 1863, Mrs. C. Phillip Miller Collection, Chicago Historical Society, Chicago, Ill.

10. *Western Railroad Gazette*, 18 July 1863, quoted in John H. White, Jr., *The American Railroad Passenger Car* (Baltimore, Md.: Johns Hopkins University Press, 1978), p. 248.

11. George M. Pullman to Emily C. Pullman, 29 May 1863, and 20 July 1863, Mrs. C. Phillip Miller Collection, Chicago, Ill.; White, *American Railroad*, p. 248.

12. D. W. Youngmeyer, "An Excursion Into the Early History of the Chicago and Alton Road," *Journal of the Illinois State Historical Society* 38 (March 1945): 7–37.

13. Stanley Buder, Pullman: *An Experiment in Industrial Order and Community Planning 1880–1930* (New York: Oxford University Press, 1967), p. 10; Frank Pullman to Emma C. Pullman, 16 May 1864, Emily Caroline Minton Pullman Correspondence, Chicago Historical Society, Chicago, Ill.

14. *Daily Illinois State Register* (Springfield), 26 May 1865, clipping, and *St. Louis Dispatch*, 26 May 1865, clipping, Pullman Company Miscellaneous Scrapbooks, Series A, vol. 1–3, 1865–1875, Newberry Library, Chicago, Ill. *Daily Illinois State Register* (Springfield), 26 May 1865; *St. Louis Dispatch*, 26 May 1865; *Daily Missouri Democrat* (St. Louis), 27 May 1865; *Daily Missouri Republican* (St. Louis), 27 May 1865; *Illinois Journal* (Springfield, Illinois), 30 May 1865; all are clippings in the Pullman company Miscellaneous Scrapbooks, Series A, vol. 1, March 1865–

September 1867, Newberry Library, Chicago, Ill.; White, *American Railroad*, 248–249.

15. Joseph Husband, *The History of the Pullman Car* (1917; reprint ed., Grand Rapids, Mich.: Black Letter Press, 1974), pp. 33–34 and 43–44. Husband also wrote that the car, without its equipment, cost $18,239.31. By the time it was fully equipped and ready to go on the road, the price had risen to $20,178.14; ibid., p. 32; see also White, *American Railroad*, p. 248.

16. *Daily Illinois State Register* (Springfield), 26 May 1865, *St. Louis Dispatch*, 26 May 1865, *Daily Missouri Democrat* (St. Louis), 27 May 1865, *Daily Missouri Republican* (St. Louis), 27 May 1865, and *Illinois Journal* (Springfield), 30 May 1865, clippings, Pullman Company, Miscellaneous Scrapbooks, Series A, vol. 1, March 1865–September, 1867, Newberry Library, Chicago, Ill.; White, *American Railroad*, pp. 248–249.

17. Husband, *History of the Pullman Car*, pp. 33–34. See also Horace Porter, "Railway Passenger Travel," in *The American Railway: Its Construction, Development, Management, and Appliances* (1892; reprint ed., New York: Bramhal House, n.d.), pp. 241–242; White, *American Railroad*, p. 249; *Album of Genealogy and Biography Cook County, Illinois*, 11th ed., rev. and impr. (Chicago: LaSalle, 1899), p. 232; Charles Long, "*Pioneer* and the Lincoln Funeral Train: The Making of a Pullman Myth?" *Railway World*, in press.

18. *Boston Daily Globe*, 5 March 1888, clipping, p. 65, Pullman Company, Miscellaneous Scrapbooks, Series B, vol. 1, 1883–1903, Newberry Library, Chicago, Ill.; Brian Haresnape to author, 8 November 1986; *Biographical Sketches of the Leading Men of Chicago*, pp. 489–493.

19. *Illinois Journal* (Springfield), 30 May 1865, and *Daily Missouri Democrat* (St. Louis), 27 May 1865, clippings, Pullman Company, Miscellaneous Scrapbooks, Series A, vol. 1, Newberry Library, Chicago, Ill..

20. *Times* (no city), 19 June 1865, clipping, Pullman Company, Miscellaneous Scrapbooks, Series A, vol. 1, Newberry Library, Chicago, Ill.

21. *St. Louis Dispatch*, 26 May 1865, and *Daily Missouri Democrat*, (St. Louis), 27 May 1865, clippings, Pullman Company, Miscellaneous Scrapbooks, Series A, vol. 1, The Newberry Library, Chicago, Ill.

22. *Pullman* (Ill.) *Journal*, 7 January 1893, p. 2 (reproduction of an article based on an interview with George Pullman, in the *New York World*, 23 December 1892); Buder, *Pullman*, pp. 12–13. See also Frank Pullman to Emily C. Pullman, 13 September 1865, Emily Caroline Minton Pullman Correspondence, Chicago Historical Society, Chicago, Ill.; *Report of the Directors of the Chicago Burlington and Quincy Railroad Company: Annual Meeting, June 22d 1866* (Chicago, Ill.: Garden City Printing, 1866), p. 39.

23. *Republican* (Chicago?), 21 May 1866, clipping, Pullman Company, Miscellaneous Scrapbooks, Series A, Newberry Library, Chicago, Ill. One of the menus used at the outing is owned by the Chicago Historical Society.

24. Almont Lindsey, *The Pullman Strike* (Chicago, Ill.: University of Chicago Press, Phoenix Books, 1964), p. 22; White, *American Railroad*, pp. 250 and 252.

25. Robert Ramsey to George M. Pullman, 10 March 1866, Mrs. C. Phillip Miller Collection, Chicago Historical Society, Chicago, Ill.; "Illinois," vol. 30, p. 213, R. G. Dun and Company Collection, Baker Library, Harvard University Graduate School of Business Administration, Soldiers Field, Boston, Mass.; White, *American Railroad*, p. 252.

26. White, *American Railroad*, p. 252; Martin B. Hayes to George M. Pullman, 13 April 1862, Charles H. Moore to George M. Pullman, 8 May 1862, Albert B. Pullman to George M. Pullman, 8 January 1863, Albert B. Pullman to George M. Pullman, 21 January 1863, Martin B. Hayes to George M. Pullman, 27 January 1863, Martin B. Hayes to George M. Pullman, 3 February 1863, Charles H. Moore to George M. Pullman, 8 February 1863, Albert B. Pullman to George M. Pullman, 10 February 1863, Albert B. Pullman to George M. Pullman, 2 March 1863, Benjamin Field to George M. Pullman, 12 August 1867, and William Angell to George M. Pullman, 14 January 1867, Mrs. C. Phillip Miller Collection, Chicago Historical Society, Chicago, Ill.

27. Pullman's Palace Car Company, Record Book A, p. 2, Newberry Library, Chicago, Ill.; Edward Chase Kirkland, *Industry Comes of Age: Business, Labor and Public Policy, 1860–1897* (Chicago: Quadrangle Books, 1967), pp. 196–197.

28. Arthur Cecil Bining and Thomas C. Cochran, *The Rise of American Economic Life*, 4th ed. (New York: Charles Scribner's Sons, 1964), p. 481; Kirkland, *Industry Comes of Age*, p. 197.

29. N.S.B. Gras, *Business and Capitalism: An Introduction to Business History* (1939; reprint ed., New York: Augustus M. Kelley, 1971), pp. 185 and 192–193.

30. Pullman's Palace Car Company, Record Book A, p. 2, Newberry Library, Chicago, Ill.

31. Herman Kogan, *Traditions and Challenges: The Story of Sidley and Austin* (Chicago: R. R. Donnelley & Sons, 1983), pp. 10–14; Andreas, *History of Chicago*, pp. 155–156 and 503; Overton, *Burlington Route*, pp. 96, 105, and 147.

32. Pullman's Palace Car Company, Record Book A, p. 3, Newberry Library, Chicago, Ill.

33. Ibid., pp. 7–10.

34. Ibid., pp. 11–12, 58, and 60.

35. Ibid., pp. 63, 65, 67, 69, 70, 78, 86, and 92.

36. Ibid., pp. 70, 76-77.

37. Ibid., p. 80.

38. Ibid., pp. 89 and 94.

39. *Chicago Republican*, 21 March 1867, clipping; unidentified newspaper clipping; *Chicago Times*, 21 March 1867, clipping; *Leavenworth Evening Bulletin*, 16 August 1867, clipping, Pullman Company, Miscellaneous Scrapbooks, Series A, vol. 1, March 1865–September 1867, Newberry Library, Chicago, Ill.

40. *St. Louis Daily Times*, 3 April 1868, clipping; *New York Stockholder*, 19 May 1868, clipping; *Leavenworth Daily Conservative*, 14 April 1869, clipping, Pullman Company, Miscellaneous Scrapbooks, Series A, vol. 2, March 28, 1868–June 26, 1870, Newberry Library, Chicago, Ill. See also White, *American Railroad*, p. 317.

41. *St. Louis Daily Times*, 3 April 1868, clipping, and *New York Stockholder*, 19 April 1868, clipping, Pullman Company, Miscellaneous Scrapbooks, Series A, vol. 2, March 28, 1868–June 25, 1870, Newberry Library, Chicago, Ill.

42. White, *American Railroad*, p. 317; *St. Louis Daily Times*, 3 April 1868, clipping; *New York Stockholder*, 19 May 1868, clipping; *Council Bluffs Daily Nonpareil*, 10 June 1868, clipping, Pullman Company, Miscellaneous Scrapbooks, Series A, vol. 2, 1868–1870, Newberry Library, Chicago, Ill.

43. White, *American Railroad*, p. 317.

44. *Springfield* (Ill.) *Republican*, 7 June 1869, clipping, Pullman Company, Miscellaneous Scrapbooks, Series A, vol. 2, 1868–1870, Newberry Library, Chicago, Ill.; Charles W. Angell to George M. Pullman, 18 August 1870, and 15 September 1870, W. C. Ralston to George M. Pullman, 20 July 1870, Charles W. Angell to George M. Pullman, 10 September 1870, Mrs. C. Phillip Miller Collection, Chicago Historical Society, Chicago, Ill.

45. Pullman's Palace Car Company, Record Book A, pp. 65, 67, 75, 80, and 97, Newberry Library, Chicago, Ill.

46. Ibid., p. 97.

47. White, *American Railroad*, p. 363.

48. Lucius Beebe, *Mr. Pullman's Elegant Palace Car*, (Garden City, N.Y.: Doubleday, 1961), p. 142; Husband, *History of the Pullman Car*, p. 52; Porter, "Railway Passenger Travel," p. 242.

49. *Sacramento Daily Union*, 17 July 1869, clipping, Pullman Company, Miscellaneous Scrapbooks, Series A, vol. 2, 1868–1870, Newberry Library, Chicago, Ill.

50. Unidentified newspaper clipping, 25 July 1870, Pullman Company, Miscellaneous Scrapbooks, Series A, vol. 2, 1868–1870, Newberry Library, Chicago, Ill.

51. *Worcestershire* (England) *Advertizer*, 22 March 1873, clipping, Pullman Company, Miscellaneous Scrapbooks, Series A, vol. 3, 1871–1875, Newberry Library, Chicago, Ill.

52. Helen Pullman to Frank Pullman, 28 February 1865, and 22 March 1865, Emily Caroline Minton Pullman Correspondence, Chicago Historical Society, Chicago, Ill.

53. T. M. Halpin, comp., *Halpin and Bailey's Chicago City Directory for the Year 1862–63* (Chicago, Ill.: Halpin and Bailey, 1862), p. 325; T. M. Halpin, comp., *Halpin and Bailey's Chicago City Directory for the Year 1863–64* (Chicago, Ill.: Halpin and Bailey, 1863), p. 369; *John C.W. Bailey's Chicago City Directory for the Year 1864–65* (Chicago, Ill.: John C.W. Bailey, 1864), p. 456.

54. Emily C. Pullman to Emma Pullman, 23 April 1865, Frank Pullman to Emily C. Pullman, 7 June 1865, Emily Caroline Minton Pullman Correspondence, Chicago Historical Society, Chicago, Ill.

55. Frank Pullman to Emily C. Pullman, 13 September 1865, 16 November 1865, and 11 October 1868, Emily Caroline Minton Pullman Correspondence, Chicago Historical Society, Chicago, Ill.

56. Florence Lowden Miller, "The Pullmans of Prairie Avenue: A Domestic Portrait From Letters and Diaries," *Chicago History* 1 (1971): 142–155; Nellie B. Earl to Hattie Sanger, 22 February 1867, Mrs. C. Phillip Miller Collection, Chicago Historical Society, Chicago, Ill.

57. Isabelle O'Keefe, "Mrs. Pullman," clipping, and James Y. Sanger obituary, clipping, Harriett S. Pullman scrapbook, Chicago Historical Society, Chicago, Ill.

58. "Extracts From Mrs. John A. Logan's Tribute to Mrs. Pullman," *Journal of the Illinois State Historical Society* 14 (April, 1921): 210–211; Miller, "The Pullmans of Prairie Avenue," p. 144.

59. James Y. Sanger obituary, clipping, Harriett S. Pullman scrapbook, Chicago Historical Society, Chicago, Ill.

60. Harriett S. Pullman diary, 1867, passim, and George M. Pullman to Hattie Sanger, 1 February 1867, Mrs. C. Phillip Miller Collection, Chicago Historical Society, Chicago, Ill.

61. Harriett S. Pullman diary, 13 June 1867, 14 June 1867 to 20 June 1867, and 3 July 1867, Mrs C. Phillip Miller Collection, Chicago Historical Society, Chicago, Ill.

Chapter 5

1. *Pullman Palace Car Patents*, a bound book of patents owned by Pullman's Palace Car Company, Mrs. C. Phillip Miller Collection, Chicago Historical Society, Chicago, Ill.

2. Joseph Frazier Wall, *Andrew Carnegie* (New York: Oxford University Press, 1970), pp. 140–142.

3. Ibid., pp. 199–201.

4. Among several summaries of this celebration are: John F. Stover, *The Life and Decline of the American Railroad* (New York: Oxford University Press, 1970), p. 51; Charles Edgar Ames, *Pioneering the Union Pacific: A Reappraisal of the Builders of the Railroad* (New York: Appleton, Century, Crofts, 1969), pp. 152–154; Wesley S. Griswold, *A Work of Giants: Building the First Transcontinental Railroad* (New York: McGraw-Hill, 1962), pp. 182–183.

5. Ames, *Pioneering the Union Pacific*, p. 159; Edwin L. Sabin, *Building the Pacific Railway* (Philadelphia, Pa.: J. B. Lippincott, 1919), p. 282.

6. *Chicago Republican*, 21 March 1867, clipping; unidentified newspaper clipping; *Chicago Times*, 21 March 1867, clipping, Pullman Company, Miscellaneous Scrapbooks, Series A, vol. 1, March 1865–September 1867, Newberry Library, Chicago, Ill.

7. *Chicago Times*, 21 March 1867, clipping, Pullman Company, Miscellaneous Scrapbooks, Series A, vol. 1, March 1865–September 1867, Newberry Library, Chicago, Ill.

8. *Rochester Daily Union and Advertiser*, 10 April 1867, clipping; *Chicago Republican*, 17 April 1867, and 18 April 1867, clippings; *Western Railroad Gazette*, 20 April 1867, clipping; *Detroit Commercial Advertiser*, 1 June 1867, clipping, Pullman Company, Miscellaneous Scrapbooks, Series A, vol. 1, March 1865–September 1867, Newberry Library, Chicago, Ill.

9. *New York Times*, 18 April 1867, p. 5; Ames, *Pioneering the Union Pacific*, p. 159.

10. Wall, *Andrew Carnegie*, pp. 203–205; Harold C. Livesay, *Andrew Carnegie and the Rise of Big Business* (Boston, Mass.: Little, Brown, 1975), pp. 66–67.

11. Pullman's Palace Car Company, Record Book A, pp. 97–102 and 461–463; Newberry Library, Chicago, Ill. Wall, *Andrew Carnegie*, 205–211. See also H. W. Schotter, *The Growth and Development of the Pennsylvania Railroad Company* (Philadelphia, Pa.: Allen, Lane and Scott, 1972), pp. 87–88 and 129.

12. Helen Hunt Jackson, *Bits of Travel at Home* (Boston, Mass.: Roberts Brothers, 1880), pp. 28–36; David Lavender, *The Great Persuader* (Garden City, N.Y.: Doubleday, 1970), p. 410n; Lucius Beebe, *Mr. Pullman's Elegant Palace Car* (Garden City, N.Y.: Doubleday, 1961), p. 115; John H. White, Jr., *The American Railroad Passenger Car* (Baltimore, Md.: Johns Hopkins University Press, 1978), p. 253. See also Dogo (?) Tevis to George M. Pullman, 4 July 1870, Mrs. C. Phillip Miller Collection, Chicago Historical Society, Chicago, Ill.

13. White, *American Railroad*, pp. 219 and 253; *Railroad Gazette*, 15 June 1883, p. 394; Pullman's Palace Car Company, Record Book A, pp. 425–426, Newberry Library, Chicago, Ill.

14. Pullman's Palace Car Company, Record Book A, p. 127, Newberry Library, Chicago, Ill.

15. Julius Grodinsky, *Transcontinental Railway Strategy, 1869–1893: A Study of Businessmen* (Philadelphia: University of Pennsylvania Press, 1962), p. 21.

16. James A. Ward, *J. Edgar Thomson: Master of the Pennsylvania* (Westport, Conn.: Greenwood Press, 1980), p. 200; Grodinsky, *Transcontinental Railway Strategy*, p. 21.

17. Ward, *J. Edgar Thomson*, pp. 200–204; Grodinsky, *Transcontinental Railway Strategy*, p. 22; Ames, *Pioneering the Union Pacific*, pp. 416, 425, and 560.

18. Harriett S. Pullman to George M. Pullman, 12 March 1872, Mrs. C. Phillip Miller Collection, Chicago Historical Society, Chicago, Ill.

19. White, *American Railroad*, p. 253.

20. Samuel Bowles, *A Summer Vacation in the Parks and Mountains of Colorado* (Springfield, Mass.: Samuel Bowles, 1869), pp. 9–21; Bowles also described the journey by Pullman coach in another book, *Our New West* (Hartford, Conn.: Hartford Publishing, 1869), p. 48.

21. Grace Greenwood, *New Life in New Lands; Notes of Travel* (New York: J. B. Ford, 1873), p. 34.

22. *Mechanic Inventor*, 18 November 1869, clipping, Pullman Company, Miscellaneous Scrapbooks, Series A, vol. 2, 1868–1870, Newberry Library, Chicago, Ill.

23. *Boston Advertizer*, 18 February 1870, clipping, Pullman Company, Miscellaneous Scrapbooks, Series A, vol. 2, March 28, 1868–June 25, 1870, Newberry Library, Chicago, Ill.

24. Harriett S. Pullman diary, 23 May 1870, Mrs. C. Phillip Miller Collection, Chicago Historical Society, Chicago, Ill.; Stuart H. Holbrook, *The Story of American Railroads* (New York: Crown Publishers, 1947), pp. 347–348; Beebe, *Mr. Pullman's Elegant Palace Car* pp. 143–144; Lucius Beebe, *Mansions on Rails; the Folklore of the Private Railway Car* (Berkeley, Calif.: Howell-North, 1959), pp. 94–96.

25. Harriett S. Pullman diary, 24 May 1870, Mrs. C. Phillip Miller Collection, Chicago Historical Society, Chicago, Ill.; Holbrook, *Story of American Railroads*, p. 348.

26. Beebe, *Mr. Pullman's Elegant Palace Car*, p. 144. Readers seeking the passenger list for this party may find it in Joseph Husband, *The History of the Pullman Car* (1917; reprint ed., Grand Rapids, Mich.: Black Letter Press, 1974), pp. 56 and 57.

Chapter 6

1. Harriett S. Pullman diary, 26 March 1871, Mrs. C. Phillip Miller Collection, Chicago Historical Society, Chicago, Ill.

2. Bessie Louise Pierce, *A History of Chicago*, vol. 2, *From Town to City, 1848–1871* (New York: Alfred A. Knopf, 1940), pp. 476–478; Harriett S. Pullman diary, 8 October 1871, 9 October 1871, 23 November 1871, 25 November 1871, 30 November 1871, 4 December 1871, and 5 December 1871, Mrs. C. Phillip Miller Collection, Chicago Historical Society, Chicago, Ill.; Florence Lowden Miller, "The Pullmans of Prairie Avenue: A Domestic Portrait from Letters and Diaries," *Chicago History* 1 (Spring 1971): 143–145; George M. Pullman, Folder 2 in Box A 1 298a, Chicago Historical Society, Chicago, Ill.; A. T. Andreas, *History of Chicago From*

the Earliest Period to the Present Time, 3 vols. (Chicago, Ill.: A. T. Andreas, 1886), 3: 608–609 and 416–417.

3. Harriett S. Pullman to George M. Pullman, 4 March 1872 (?), and 11 March 1872, Mrs. C. Phillip Miller Collection, Chicago Historical Society, Chicago, Ill.

4. George M. Pullman, Folder 2 in Box A 1, Chicago Historical Society, Chicago, Ill. There are two pieces connected with this matter, the first a statement of costs from Jaffray to Pullman dated 1 February 1872 and the second a letter from Jaffray to Pullman dated 15 May 1872. See also Andreas, *History of Chicago*, p. 79.

5. Harriett S. Pullman diary, 11 September 1875, 29 October 1875, 1 January 1876, 13 January 1876, 3 April 1876, and 6 April 1876, Mrs. C. Phillip Miller Collection, Chicago Historical Society, Chicago, Ill.

6. Harriett S. Pullman diary, 1 January 1877, Mrs. C. Phillip Miller Collection, Chicago Historical Society, Chicago, Ill. William T. Hutchinson, *Lowden of Illinois: The Life of Frank O. Lowden*, vol. 2 (Chicago, Ill.: University of Chicago Press, 1957), p. 488.

7. Harriett S. Pullman diary, 5 July to 9 July 1871, 1 September 1873 to 27 September 1873, and 18 June 1874 to 27 September 1874; Mrs. C. Phillip Miller Collection, Chicago Historical Society, Chicago, Ill. Karl Baedeker, ed., *The United States With an Excursion Into Mexico* (Leipsie: Karl Baedeker, 1893), p. 224.

8. Harriett S. Pullman diary, 18 June to 2 October 1874. Mrs. C. Phillip Miller Collection, Chicago Historical Society, Chicago, Ill. Hattie added a list of "cottage visitors" at the end of this diary. She also included names of people brought to Fairlawn by her husband throughout her diaries.

9. *Inter Ocean* (Chicago), 12 September 1886, clipping, Pullman Company, Miscellaneous Scrapbooks, Series A, vol. 10, 1886–1887, Newberry Library, Chicago, Ill.

10. Royal H. Pullman to George M. Pullman, 29 August 1872, Mrs. C. Phillip Miller Collection, Chicago Historical Society, Chicago, Ill.

11. Baedeker, *The United States*, pp. 206–207.

12. Emily C. Pullman mentioned Albert Pullman and his family in their new cottage in her diary, Emily C. Pullman diary, 14 July 1881, Chicago Historical Society, Chicago, Ill.

13. Emily C. Pullman diary, 12 August 1888, Chicago Historical Society, Chicago, Ill.; Royal H. Pullman to George M. Pullman, 5 September 1895, Mrs. C. Phillip Miller Collection, Chicago Historical Society, Chicago, Ill.

14. Harriett S. Pullman diary, 5 June 1878 to 6 August 1878, Mrs. C. Phillip Miller Collection, Chicago Historical Society, Chicago, Ill.

15. *Chicago Evening Journal*, 21 October 1881, clipping, Pullman Company, Miscellaneous Scrapbooks, Series A, vol. 6, 1881–1882, Newberry Library, Chicago, Ill.

16. *New York Times*, 15 February 1882, p. 2, and 16 February 1882, p. 5.

17. George M. Pullman to Harriett S. Pullman, 15 May 1882, Mrs. C. Phillip Miller Collection, Chicago Historical Society, Chicago, Ill.; Emily C. Pullman diary, 5 June 1882, Chicago Historical Society, Chicago, Ill.

18. Harriett S. Pullman diary, 18 June 1887, Mrs. C. Phillip Miller Collection, Chicago Historical Society, Chicago, Ill.

19. George M. Pullman to Harriett S. Pullman, 17 June 1887, and 29 June 1887, Mrs. C. Phillip Miller Collection, Chicago Historical Society, Chicago, Ill.

20. George M. Pullman to Harriett S. Pullman, 7 July 1887, and 9 July 1887, Mrs. C. Phillip Miller Collection, Chicago Historical Society, Chicago, Ill.

21. Harriett S. Pullman diary, 16 July 1887, and 25 July 1887, Mrs. C. Phillip Miller Collection, Chicago Historical Society, Chicago, Ill.

22. Harriett S. Pullman diary, 24 October 1888, and 25 October 1888, Mrs. C. Phillip Miller Collection, Chicago Historical Society, Chicago, Ill.

23. Harriett S. Pullman diary, 7 September 1887, and 8 September 1887, Mrs. C. Phillip Miller Collection, Chicago Historical Society, Chicago, Ill. There was another explosion in January 1888, just as Hattie and Florence departed Chicago for Jacksonville, Florida. Harriett S. Pullman to George M. Pullman, 27 January 1888, Mrs. C. Phillip Miller Collection, Chicago Historical Society, Chicago, Ill.

24. George M. Pullman to Harriett S. Pullman, 15 December 1888, Mrs. C. Phillip Miller Collection, Chicago Historical Society, Chicago, Ill.

25. George M. Pullman to Harriett S. Pullman, 22 March 1889, Mrs. C. Phillip Miller Collection, Chicago Historical Society, Chicago, Ill.

26. Harriett S. Pullman diary, 16 April–5 June 1889, Mrs. C. Phillip Miller Collection, Chicago Historical Society, Chicago, Ill.

27. Harriett S. Pullman diary, 1 January 1890 to 18 June 1890, passim. See also diary entries for 13 July–19 July 1890, Mrs. C. Phillip Miller Collection, Chicago Historical Society, Chicago, Ill.

28. George M. Pullman to Harriett S. Pullman, 15 July 1890, and 17 July 1890, Mrs. C. Phillip Miller Collection, Chicago Historical Society, Chicago, Ill.

29. Harriett S. Pullman diary, 19 July–31 July 1890; George M. Pullman to Harriett S. Pullman, 25 July 1890, Mrs. C. Phillip Miller Collection, Chicago Historical Society, Chicago, Ill.

30. Harriett S. Pullman diary, 1 August 1890 to 10 August 1890, Mrs. C. Phillip Miller Collection, Chicago Historical Society, Chicago, Ill.

31. Harriett S. Pullman diary, 15 April 1879 (on this occasion, she stayed at the Baldwin Hotel in San Francisco), 21 March 1881, and 30 May 1881, Mrs. C. Phillip Miller Collection, Chicago Historical Society, Chicago, Ill.

32. Harriett S. Pullman diary, 27 June–28 June 1873, 22 May–26 May 1883, Mrs. C. Phillip Miller Collection, Chicago Historical Society, Chicago, Ill.

33. Harriett S. Pullman diary, 20 April 1881, 7 March 1886, 3 April 1887, and 23 February 1888, Mrs. C. Phillip Miller Collection, Chicago Historical Society, Chicago, Ill.

34. Harriett S. Pullman diary, 13 September 1872, 19 January 1881, 23 October 1885, and 30 October 1885, Mrs. C. Phillip Miller Collection, Chicago Historical Society, Chicago, Ill.

35. Baedeker, ed., *The United States*, pp. 7–8; Russell Lynes, *The Tastemakers* (New York: Grosset and Dunlap, 1954), p. 86. The American plan included a daily fixed charge for food and lodging; the European plan included charges for rooms only, and guests took their meals separately. Baedeker, *The United States*, XXVI.

36. Harriett S. Pullman diary, 3 February 1871, 22 February 1871, and 27 February 1871, see also entries for 5 July–9 July 1871, and 15 January–18 January 1872, Mrs. C. Phillip Miller Collection, Chicago Historical Society, Chicago, Ill.

37. Harriett S. Pullman diary, 2 October 1871, 2 August-7 August 1872, 7 May 1873, and 8 August 1885, Mrs. C. Phillip Miller Collection, Chicago Historical Society, Chicago, Ill.

38. W. T. Stead, *Chicago To-day: Or The Labour War in America* (1894; reprint ed., New York: Arno Press and the *New York Times*, 1969), p. 113; see George M.

Pullman to Harriett S. Pullman, 12 September 1890, and 24 March 1891, and Harriett S. Pullman diary, 26 March 1892, Mrs. C. Phillip Miller Collection, Chicago Historical Society, Chicago, Ill.

39. George M. Pullman to Harriett S. Pullman, 12 September 1890, 24 March 1891, and 21 September 1890, Mrs. C. Phillip Miller Collection, Chicago Historical Society, Chicago, Ill.; *Railroad Gazette*, 24 April 1891, p. 292.

40. Caroline Kirkland, *Chicago Yesterdays: A Sheaf of Reminiscences* (Chicago, Ill.: Daughaday, 1919), 202–203; Andreas, *History of Chicago* 3: 152–153, 392–393, and 542; Pierce, *History of Chicago* 3: 405 and 459–460.

41. Andreas, *History of Chicago* 3: 649–650; Pierce, *History of Chicago*, 3: 493–494.

42. Andreas, *History of Chicago* 2:615 and 3:404–405; Pierce, *History of Chicago* 3: 197, note 14, and 203.

43. Harriett S. Pullman diary, 25 January 1883, 27 May 1887, 1 June 1888, 19 September 1888, 14 September 1889, 18 September 1889, and 21 September 1892, Mrs. C. Phillip Miller Collection, Chicago Historical Society, Chicago, Ill. See also "Record of George Pullman, Jr.," at the Hill School, Pottstown, Pa.; *Chicago Times*, 24 March 1889, clipping, Pullman Company, Miscellaneous Scrapbooks, Series A, vol. 12, 1889, Newberry Library, Chicago, Ill.

44. Harriett S. Pullman diary, 20 March 1883, 24 March 1883, and 27 March 1883, Mrs. C. Phillip Miller Collection, Chicago Historical Society, Chicago, Ill. See also, *Inter Ocean* (Chicago), 6 April 1888, clipping, Pullman Company, Miscellaneous Scrapbooks, Series A, vol. 11, 1889, Newberry Library, Chicago, Ill.

45. George M. Pullman to Harriett S. Pullman, 24 March 1893, and George M. Pullman, Jr., diary, 16 June 1894, Mrs. C. Phillip Miller Collection, Chicago Historical Society, Chicago, Ill.

46. Frank Pullman to George M. Pullman, 14 May 1872, Mrs. C. Phillip Miller Collection, Chicago Historical Society, Chicago, Ill. Frank went on to become a lawyer whose career seemed to show a great deal of promise. He died very suddenly of pneumonia on 21 March 1879. *New York Times*, 23 March 1879, p. 7, and 25 March 1879, p. 3. Charles Pullman, the only brother to serve in the Civil War, emerged from that conflict a captain. He moved his family to a farm in Kansas following the war but was unable to make a go of it. He returned to Chicago and worked for George for several years before embarking on a career as an entrepreneur.

47. Harriett S. Pullman diaries, 1886–1887, passim, Mrs. C. Phillip Miller Collection, Chicago Historical Society, Chicago, Ill.

Chapter 7

1. *Chicago Railway Review*, 21 May 1869, clipping, Pullman Company, Miscellaneous Scrapbooks, Series A, vol. 2, 29 March 1868 to 25 June 1869, Newberry Library, Chicago, Ill.

2. This summary of the Pullman trip to England and the Continent is based on entries in Harriett S. Pullman diary, 10 August 1870 to 22 October 1870, Mrs. C. Phillip Miller Collection, Chicago Historical Society, Chicago, Ill.

3. Pullman's Palace Car Company, Record Book A, pp. 195, 215–224, 235, 272, 296, and 319, Newberry Library, Chicago, Ill.

4. Many summaries of James Allport's visit to America exist, all saying about the same thing. This account came from the following sources: *Railway Times* (London), 22

February 1873, p. 171, and 20 February 1875, p. 182; Hamilton Ellis, *Nineteenth Century Railway Carriages in the British Isles–From the Eighteen-thirties to the Nineteen-hundreds* (London: Modern Transport Publishing, 1949), p. 83; Hamilton Ellis, *The Midland Railway* (London: Ian Allan, 1953), p. 70.

5.   *Railway Times* (London), 22 February 1873, p. 171.

6.   Ellis, *Midland Railway*, pp. 70–71; *Railway Times* (London), 20 February 1875, p. 182; George Behrend, *Pullman in Europe* (London: Ian Allan, 1962), p. 22; Ellis, *Nineteenth Century Railway Carriages*, pp. 83–84; *Philadelphia Ledger and Transcript*, 19 April 1873, clipping, *The National Car Builder*, May 1873, clipping, *Derbyshire Times*, 22 February 1873, clipping, Pullman Company, Miscellaneous Scrapbooks, Series A, vol. 3, 1871–1875, Newberry Library, Chicago, Ill., *New York Times*, 29 March 1873, p. 12.

7.   *Railway Times* (London), 25 October 1873, p. 1085, and 1 March 1873, p. 237; *The Commercial*, 10 March 1873, clipping, Pullman Company, Miscellaneous Scrapbooks, Series A, vol. 3, 1871–1875, Newberry Library, Chicago, Ill.

8.   *New York Times*, 29 March 1873, p. 12; *Railway Times* (London), 21 November 1874, p. 1154, and 20 February 1875, p. 182; Ellis, *Nineteenth Century Railway Carriages*, p. 83; *Philadelphia Ledger and Transcript*, 19 April 1873, clipping, Pullman Company, Miscellaneous Scrapbooks, Series A, vol. 3, 1871–1875, Newberry Library, Chicago, Ill.

9.   Behrend, *Pullman in Europe*, p. 22; Ellis, *Nineteenth Century Railway Carriages*, p. 83; *New York Times*, 29 March 1873, p. 12; *National Car Builder*, May 1873, clipping, *Philadelphia Ledger and Transcript*, 19 April 1873, clipping, Pullman Company, Miscellaneous Scrapbooks, Series A, vol. 3, 1871–1875, Newberry Library, Chicago, Ill.

10.   *New York Times*, 29 March 1873, p. 12; Behrend, *Pullman in Europe*, p. 22.

11.   *Railway Times* (London), 20 February 1875, p. 182; *Philadelphia Ledger and Transcript*, 19 April 1873, clipping, *National Car Builder*, May 1873, clipping, Pullman Company, Miscellaneous Scrapbooks, Series A, vol. 3, 1871–1875, Newberry Library, Chicago, Ill.

12.   The Pullmans sailed from New York on Christmas Day 1872. George's avowed purpose for the journey was to introduce his palace cars on European railroads. Clipping from a British newspaper, Pullman Company, Miscellaneous Scrapbooks, Series A, vol. 3, 1871–1875, Newberry Library, Chicago, Ill. *Tribune* (Chicago), 8 December 1872, p. 11, and 21 December 1872, p. 3; *New York Times*, 27 December 1872, p. 8.

13.   Pullman Company Limited, Board Minute Book, p. 2, 6 February 1875, Newberry Library, Chicago, Ill.

14.   Clipping from a British newspaper, Pullman Company, Miscellaneous Scrapbooks, Series A, vol. 3, 1871–1875, Newberry Library, Chicago, Ill.; Emily C. Pullman diary, 26, 27, and 28 March 1873, Chicago Historical Society, Chicago, Ill.

15.   Pullman's Palace Car Company, Record Book A, p. 162, Newberry Library, Chicago, Ill.

16.   Ibid., pp. 165–168.

17.   *Philadelphia Ledger and Transcript*, 19 April 1873, clipping, Pullman Company, Miscellaneous Scrapbooks, Series A, vol. 3, 1871–1875, and Pullman's Palace Car Company, Record Book A, p. 126, Newberry Library, Chicago, Ill.; Harriett S. Pullman diary, 2 July 1873, Mrs. C. Phillip Miller Collection, Chicago Historical Society, Chicago, Ill. Albert Pullman remained in England for nearly a year. He

returned to the United States with his wife, Nellie, on 9 July 1874. He sailed again for England on 26 October 1874 and returned to the United States on 21 April 1875. Emily C. Pullman, diary, 9 July 1874, 26 October 1874, and 21 April 1875, Chicago Historical Society, Chicago, Ill.

18. *Railway Times* (London), 2 August 1873, p. 789; *National Car Builder,* August 1873, clipping, Pullman Company, Miscellaneous Scrapbooks, Series A, vol. 3, 1871–1875, Newberry Library, Chicago, Ill.; Ellis, *Midland Railway,* p. 71; Ellis, *Nineteenth Century Railway Carriages,* p. 84. Although Behrend (p. 22) mentions that A. Rapp was the first superintendent of the reassembly at Derby, later information shows that Albert Pullman and another man, Aaron Longstreet (from the Detroit shops), were the first to supervise the reassembly of the sectioned vehicles. Rapp went over later and managed the Pullman assembly plant in Turin, Italy. A civil engineer, he got his start in the Pullman shops in Elmira, New York, and Detroit. See *National Car Builder,* August 1873, clipping, and *Elmira Daily Gazette,* 10 May 1873, clipping, Pullman Company, Miscellaneous Scrapbooks, Series A, vol. 3, 1871–1875, Newberry Library, Chicago, Ill.

19. Ellis, *Nineteenth Century Railway Carriages,* pp. 84–85.

20. Ibid., pp. 72 and 86; Behrend, *Pullman in Europe,* pp. 24–25.

21. Ellis, *The Midland Railway,* pp. 72–73; Ellis, *Nineteenth Century Railway Carriages,* p. 86.

22. *Railway Times* (London), 21 November 1874, p. 1154.

23. *Railway Times* (London), 20 February 1875, p. 182.

24. *Chicago Times,* 10 June 1875, clipping, Pullman Company, Miscellaneous Scrapbooks, Series A, vol. 3, 1871–1875, Newberry Library, Chicago, Ill. Harriett S. Pullman diary, 12 December 1874, and 13 February 1875, Mrs. C. Phillip Miller Collection, Chicago Historical Society, Chicago, Il.; *Inter Ocean,* (Chicago), 10 June 1875, clipping, Pullman Company, Miscellaneous Scrapbooks, Series A, vol. 3, 1871–1875, Newberry Library, Chicago, Ill. Pullman also had cars running on Italian lines by that time.

25. Jack Simmons, *The Railway in England and Wales 1830–1914: The System and Its Working,* vol. 1 (Leister, England: Leister University Press, 1978), p. 197, notes 26 and 27.

26. Harriett S. Pullman diary, 5 June 1878 to 17 June 1878, Mrs. C. Phillip Miller Collection, Chicago Historical Society, Chicago, Ill.

27. Florence Pullman to Emily C. Pullman, 21 June 1878, Emily Caroline Minton Pullman Correspondence, 1877–1882, Chicago Historical Society, Chicago, Ill.

28. Harriett S. Pullman diary, 27 June–11 July 1878; George M. Pullman to Harriett S. Pullman, 13 July 1878, 15 July 1878, and 16 July 1878, Mrs. C. Phillip Miller Collection, Chicago Historical Society, Chicago, Ill.

29. Harriett S. Pullman diary, 9 July 1878 to 19 July 1878; Harriett S. Pullman to George M. Pullman, 15 July 1878, Mrs. C. Phillip Miller Collection, Chicago Historical Society, Chicago, Ill.

30. *Railroad Gazette,* 27 September 1878, p. 467.

31. Harriett S. Pullman diary, 18 July 1878, and 19 July 1878, Mrs. C. Phillip Miller Collection, Chicago Historical Society, Chicago, Ill.

32. Anthony J. Bower (James Bower's grandson) to the author, 10 March 1984; Harriett S. Pullman diary, 20 July 1878, and 21 July 1878, Mrs. C. Phillip Miller Collection, Chicago Historical Society, Chicago, Ill.

33. Harriett S. Pullman diary, 22 July 1878 to 25 July 1878, Mrs. C. Phillip Miller Collection, Chicago Historical Society, Chicago, Ill.

34. Harriett S. Pullman diary, 26 July 1878 to 6 August 1878, Mrs. C. Phillip Miller Collection, Chicago Historical Society, Chicago, Ill.

35. A. J. Bower, "Dining on Wheels: Part 1 — The Prince of Wales," Transport History 10 (Spring 1979): 41–62.

36. Ellis, Nineteenth Century Railway Carriages, p. 85; Simmons, The Railway in England and Wales, p. 197; Behrend, Pullman in Europe, p. 24.

37. Ellis, Nineteenth Century Railway Carriages, pp. 84–85; Railroad Gazette, 11 November 1892, p. 850, and 18 November 1892, p. 867; Behrend, Pullman in Europe, p. 24.

38. Ellis, Midland Railway, p. 71.

39. Ibid., p. 72; Ellis, Nineteenth Century Railway Carriages, p. 88.

40. Simmons, The Railway in England and Wales, p. 197; Frederick S. Williams, William's Midland Railway: Its Rise and Progress, A Narrative of Modern Enterprise (1888; reprint ed., New York: Augustus M. Kelley, 1968), pp. 490–492.

41. Behrend, Pullman in Europe, pp. 39–41; Railroad Gazette, 9 November 1883, p. 745; Bower, "Dining on Wheels," pp. 42–43; Ellis, The Midland Railway, p. 73; Simmons, The Railway in England and Wales, p. 197.

42. Behrend, Pullman in Europe, p. 21; Julian Morel, Pullman: The Pullman Car Company — Its Services, Cars and Traditions (North Pomfret, Vt.: David and Charles, 1983), p. 32.

43. Behrend, Pullman in Europe, p. 28.

44. Ibid.; New York Times, 16 June 1874, p. 1.

45. Railway Times (London), 21 June 1873, pp. 645–646, and 12 June 1875, p. 577.

46. Morel, Pullman, p. 19. Pullman bought out Mann in the United States at the outset of 1889.

47. George M. Pullman to Harriett S. Pullman, 13 July 1878, Mrs. C. Phillip Miller Collection, Chicago Historical Society, Chicago, Ill.; Morel, Pullman, p. 24; New York Times, 4 March 1877, p. 1 and 6 March 1887, p. 9; Railroad Gazette, 5 August 1887, p. 518.

48. Pullman's Palace Car Company, Record Book B, p. 14, Newberry Library, Chicago, Ill.; Morel, Pullman, p. 19.

49. Mary C. Sanger diary, 1 June 1881, 25 June 1881, 31 July 1881, 9 August 1881, 26 October 1881, and 6 November 1881, Mrs. C. Phillip Miller Collection, Chicago Historical Society, Chicago, Ill.; Chicago Evening Journal, 21 October 1881, clipping, Pullman Company, Miscellaneous Scrapbooks, Series A, vol. 6, 1881–1882, Newberry Library, Chicago, Ill.

50. New York Times, 13 February 1882, p. 8; Harriett S. Pullman diary, 23 February 1882 to 26 February 1882, Mrs. C. Phillip Miller Collection, Chicago Historical Society, Chicago, Ill.

51. Harriett S. Pullman diary, 10 March 1882 to 2 April 1882, Mrs. C. Phillip Miller Collection, Chicago Historical Society, Chicago, Ill.

52. Actually, the British Pullman Palace Car Company had been registered on 2 June 1882 as a subsidiary of the Pullman's Palace Car Company. Morel, Pullman, p. 24. Pullman Company Limited, Board Minute Book, Newberry Library, Chicago, Ill.

53. Behrend, *Pullman in Europe*, pp. 37–38; Ellis, *Nineteenth Century Railway Carriages*, pp. 119–120.

54. Harriett S. Pullman diary, 6 April 1882, 10 April 1882, 11 April 1882, and 21 April 1882, Mrs. C. Phillip Miller Collection, Chicago Historical Society, Chicago, Ill.

55. No entries appear in Harriet Pullman's 1882 diary between 22 April and 14 July. Her entries following that period indicate that she was at Elberon in the Pullman summer home.

56. Harriett S. Pullman diary, 18 June–25 July 1887, George M. Pullman to Harriett S. Pullman, 29 June 1887, 7 July 1887, and 9 July 1887, Mrs. C. Phillip Miller Collection, Chicago Historical Society, Chicago, Ill.; Behrend, *Pullman in Europe*, p. 39.

57. Behrend, *Pullman in Europe*, p. 39–40.

58. Morel, *Pullman*, pp. 29–30.

Chapter 8

1. See Vincent P. DeSantis, *The Shaping of Modern America: 1877–1916* (Port, N.Y.: Forum Press, 1977), pp. 1–10.

2. Pullman's Palace Car Company, Record Book A, pp. 97–102, 170–172, Newberry Library, Chicago, Ill. The Southern Transportation Company was controlled by the Central Transportation Company.

3. Pullman's Palace Car Company, Record Book A, pp. 103, 108, 111, and 112, Newberry Library, Chicago, Ill.

4. *Edwards' Annual Directory to the Inhabitants, Institutions, Incorporated Companies, Manufacturing Establishments, Business, Business Firms, Etc., in the City of Chicago for 1869–70* (St. Louis and New York: Edwards, n.d.). Pierson's name appeared in the city directory for the following year, but he probably left Chicago after that time. See ibid., 1870–1871 edition, p. 658; Harriett S. Pullman diary, 10 June 1870, Mrs. C. Phillip Miller Collection, Chicago Historical Society, Chicago, Ill. Pullman's Palace Car Company, Record Book A, pp. 110 and 118, Newberry Library, Chicago, Ill.

5. Pullman's Palace Car Company, Record Book A, p. 114, Newberry Library, Chicago, Ill.; Charles W. Angell to George M. Pullman, 18 August 1870, 10 September 1870; Henry R. Pierson to George M. Pullman, 13 September 1870, Mrs. C. Phillip Miller Collection, Chicago Historical Society, Chicago, Illinois.

6. Charles W. Angell to George M. Pullman, 15 September 1870, Mrs. C. Phillip Miller Collection, Chicago Historical Society, Chicago, Ill.

7. Ibid.

8. Henry R. Pierson to George M. Pullman, 13 September 1870, Mrs. C. Phillip Miller Collection, Chicago Historical Society, Chicago, Ill.

9. Harriett S. Pullman diary, 22 October 1870, Mrs. C. Phillip Miller Collection, Chicago Historical Society, Chicago, Ill.; Pullman's Palace Car Company, Record Book A, pp. 124, 126, and 152, Newberry Library, Chicago, Ill.

10. R. H. Titherington, "General Horace Porter," *Munsey's Magazine* 17 (April 1897): 120–121; *New York Times*, 30 November 1872, p. 1.

11. Pullman's Palace Car Company, Record Book A, pp. 341–342, Newberry Library, Chicago, Ill. Dumas Malone, ed., *Dictionary of American Biography*, vol. 15 (New York: Charles Scribner's Sons, 1935), pp. 92–93.

12. *Railroad Gazette*, 30 December 1881, p. 747.

13. Bessie Louise Pierce, *A History of Chicago*, vol. 3, *The Rise of the Modern City, 1871–1893* (New York: Alfred A. Knopf, 1940), pp. 3–6; Pullman's Palace Car Company, Record Book A, pp. 138–142; Newberry Library, Chicago, Ill.; Elias Colbert and Everett Chamberlin, *Chicago and the Great Conflagration* (Chicago: J. S. Goodman, 1871), pp. 341 and 425.

14. Pierce, *History of Chicago*, pp. 9–17.

15. Walter T.K. Nugent, *From Centennial to World War: American Society, 1876–1917* (Indianapolis, Ind.: Bobbs-Merrill, 1977), pp. 26–27; Walter T.K. Nugent, *Money and American Society, 1865–1880* (New York: Free Press, 1968), p. 176; Arthur Cecil Bining and Thomas C. Cochran, *The Rise of American Economic Life* (New York: Charles Scribner's Sons, 1964), p. 410.

16. Bining and Cochran, *Rise of American Economic Life*, pp. 411–412; Nugent, *Money and American Society*, p. 177.

17. Pullman's Palace Car Company, Record Book A, p. 120, Newberry Library, Chicago, Ill.

18. Ibid., pp. 120–123.

19. The details of this transaction are discussed in Chapter 5.

20. Pullman's Palace Car Company, Record Book A, p. 127, Newberry Library, Chicago, Ill.

21. Ibid., pp. 145, 148, 181, 185, 202, and 211.

22. Ibid., pp. 215–224, 236, and 246.

23. Ibid., pp. 250–251.

24. *New York Times*, 15 October 1875, p. 8; "Illinois," vol. 30, p. 353, R. G. Dun and Company Collection, Baker Library, Harvard University Graduate School of Business Administration, Soldiers Field, Boston, Mass.

25. Pullman's Palace Car Company, Record Book A, pp. 286–287, Newberry Library, Chicago, Ill..

26. Ibid., pp. 309–310.

27. Ibid., pp. 130 and 167.

28. Ibid., pp. 192–193 and 264–265.

29. Ibid., pp. 337–338.

30. Ibid., pp. 343.

31. Ibid., pp. 169–170.

32. "Illinois," vol. 30, p. 353, R. G. Dun and Company Collection, Baker Library, Harvard University Graduate School of Business Administration, Soldiers Field, Boston, Mass.

33. *New York Times*, 18 August 1878, p. 1; Charles W. Angell to George M. Pullman, 18 February 1871, 19 April 1871, and 29 May 1871, Mrs. C. Phillip Miller Collection, Chicago Historical Society, Chicago, Ill.

34. Caroline Kirkland, *Chicago Yesterdays; A Sheaf of Reminiscences* (Chicago: Daughaday, 1919), pp. 165 and 174; Harriett S. Pullman diary, 2 June 1875, 3 June

1875, and 6 June 1875, Mrs. C. Phillip Miller Collection, Chicago Historical Society, Chicago, Ill.; *New York Times*, 18 August 1878, p. 1.

35. "Illinois," vol. 30, p. 353. Dun and Company Collection, Baker Library, Harvard University Graduate School of Business Administration, Soldiers Field, Boston, Mass.

36. *New York Times*, 18 August 1878, p. 1; Herbert Asbury, *Gem of the Prairie: An Informal History of the Chicago Underworld* (1940; reprint ed., DeKalb: Northern Illinois University Press, 1986), pp. 135–138.

37. *New York Times*, 18 August 1878, p. 1, 22 August 1878, p. 1, 30 November 1878, p. 3. The Chicago Historical Society possesses several copies of the reward circulars issued by the Pullman Company for Angell's apprehension. They were accompanied by a letter from Horace Porter, dated 20 September 1878, together with a description of the sixty bonds Angell had taken.

38. *Railroad Gazette*, 10 January 1879, p. 21, 28 February 1879, p. 118; *New York Times*, 25 February 1879, p. 1.

39. *Railroad Gazette*, 7 March 1879, p. 133; *New York Times*, 1 March 1879, p. 1, and 18 July 1883, p. 1; *Chicago Times*, 1 March 1879, p. 3.

40. *Railroad Gazette*, 20 September 1878, p. 464; Pullman's Palace Car Company, Record Book A, p. 321, Newberry Library, Chicago, Ill.

41. Palace Car Company Record Book A, pp. 343–344.

42. Henry V. Poor, *Manual of the Railroads of the United States*, vol. 13, *Showing Their Mileage, Stocks, Bonds, Cost, Earnings, Expenses, and Organizations . . . Together With an Appendix* (New York: H. V. & H. W. Poor, 1880), pp. 1004–1005.

Chapter 9

1. John Tebbel, *The Marshall Fields: A Study in Wealth* (New York: E. P. Dutton, 1947), p. 25.

2. Pullman's Palace Car Company, Record Book B, p. 33, Pullman's Palace Car Company, Record Book A, pp. 349 and 366, Newberry Library, Chicago, Ill.; *The Story of Pullman* (n.p., n.d.), p. 18, copy in author's possession.

3. See Tebbel, *The Marshall Fields*, p. 68; Harper Leech and John Charles Carroll, *Armour and His Times* (New York: D. Appleton-Century, 1938), pp. 75 and 110–111.

4. Stanley Buder, *Pullman: An Experiment in Industrial Order and Community Planning, 1880–1930* (New York: Oxford University Press, 1970), pp. 37–44; Edward Chase Kirkland, *Industry Comes of Age: Business, Labor and Public Policy, 1860–1897* (Chicago: Quadrangle Books, 1967), p. 334.

5. *Pullman* (Ill.) *Journal*, 14 January 1893, p. 2 (reproduction of an article based on an interview with George Pullman in the *New York World*, 23 December 1892); see also Buder, *Pullman*, p. 44.

6. Buder, *Pullman*, p. 45; Tebbel, *The Marshall Fields*, pp. 68–70.

7. Pullman's Palace Car Company, Record Book A, p. 349, Newberry Library, Chicago, Ill.

8. Ibid., p. 350; Almont Lindsey, *The Pullman Strike* (Chicago, Ill.: University of Chicago Press, 1964), p. 38; *The Story of Pullman*, p. 20.

9. Pullman's Palace Car Company, Record Book A, pp. 350–351, Newberry Library, Chicago, Ill.

10. Buder, *Pullman*, p. 50.

11. M. N. Forney, "American Locomotives and Cars," in *The American Railway: Its Construction, Development, Management, and Appliances* (1892; reprint ed., New York: Bramhall House, n.d.), p. 145; *Railroad Gazette*, 30 April 1880, p. 235.

12. Carlton J. Corliss, *Main Line of Mid-America: The Story of the Illinois Central Line* (New York: Creative Age Press, 1950), p. 352; Buder, *Pullman*, pp. 50–53.

13. Pullman's Palace Car Company, Record Book A, p. 365, Newberry Library, Chicago, Ill.

14. Mary C. Sanger diary, 2 April 1881, and 5 April 1881, Mrs. C. Phillip Miller Collection, Chicago Historical Society, Chicago, Ill.; Buder, *Pullman*, p. 54; *Chicago Journal of Commerce*, 6 April 1881, clipping, Pullman Company, Miscellaneous Scrapbooks, Series A, vols. 6–7, pp. 1881–1883, Newberry Library, Chicago, Ill.; George M. Pullman to Harriett S. Pullman, 31 March 1881, and Harriett S. Pullman diary, 5 April 1881, Mrs. C. Phillip Miller Collection, Chicago Historical Society, Chicago, Illinois.

15. Mrs. Duane Doty, *The Town of Pullman* (1893; reprint ed., Chicago, Ill.: Pullman Civic Organization, 1974), p. 31; Buder, *Pullman*, pp. 70–71.

16. Doty, *Town of Pullman*, pp. 51 and 125; Kirkland, *Industry Comes of Age*, p. 334.

17. Pullman's Palace Car Company, Record Book A, pp. 366–367, Newberry Library, Chicago, Ill.

18. Ibid., pp. 371 and 373–374.

19. Ibid., pp. 374–392.

20. Ibid., pp. 394–396; Raymond R. Mohl, *The New City: Urban America in the Industrial Age, 1860–1920* (Arlington Heights, Ill.: Harlan Davidson, 1985), p. 25.

21. Stewart H. Holbrook, *The Story of American Railroads* (New York: Crown, 1947), p. 93; Matthew Josephson, *The Robber Barons: The Great American Capitalists, 1861–1901* (New York: Harcourt, Brace and World, 1962), pp. 186, 295–300; Frederick Lewis Allen, *The Great Pierpont Morgan* (New York: Harper and Row, 1965), pp. 39–44; Joseph R. Daughen and Peter Binzen, *The Wreck of the Penn Central* (Boston: Little, Brown, 1971), pp. 21–24; Joseph Frazier Wall, *Andrew Carnegie* (New York: Oxford University Press, 1970), pp. 510–514; George H. Burgess and Miles C. Kennedy, *Centennial History of the Pennsylvania Railroad Company, 1846–1946* (Philadelphia, Pa.: Pennsylvania Railroad, 1949), pp. 408–411.

22. *Railroad Gazette*, 8 January 1886, p. 32; Pullman's Palace Car Company, Record Book A, pp. 436–437; and Record Book B, pp. 37–42, Newberry Library, Chicago, Ill.

23. Pullman's Palace Car Company, Record Book B, p. 33, Newberry Library, Chicago, Ill.

24. *New York Times*, 19 February 1884, p. 5; George M. Pullman to Harriett S. Pullman, 12 February 1884, and 16 February 1884, Mrs. C. Phillip Miller Collection, Chicago Historical Society, Chicago, Ill.

25. George M. Pullman to Harriett S. Pullman, 22 July 1882, Mrs. C. Phillip Miller Collection, Chicago Historical Society, Chicago, Ill.; Pullman's Palace Car Company, Record Book A, pp. 425–426, Newberry Library, Chicago, Ill. *Railroad Gazette*, 5 June 1883, p. 394.

26. Harriett S. Pullman to George M. Pullman, 26 August 1882, George M. Pullman to Harriett S. Pullman, 7 January 1882, 6 September 1882, 8 April 1884, and 9 July 1884, Mrs. C. Phillip Miller Collection, Chicago Historical Society, Chicago, Ill.

27. *New York Times*, 16 August 1883, p. 2, and 30 July 1885, p. 5.

28. Pullman's Palace Car Company, Record Book A, p. 402, Newberry Library, Chicago, Ill.

29. *Chicago Journal of Commerce*, 4 April 1884, and 25 April 1883, clippings, Pullman Company Miscellaneous Scrapbooks, Series A, vols. 8–9, 1883–1886, Newberry Library, Chicago, Ill.; Frank A. Randall, *History of the Development of Building Construction in Chicago* (Urbana: University of Illinois Press, 1949), p. 159; *Western Manufacturer* (Chicago), 31 March 1884, clipping, Pullman Company, Miscellaneous Scrapbooks, Series B, vol. 1, 1883–1903, Newberry Library, Chicago, Ill.; A. T. Andreas, *History of Chicago*, 3 vols. (1884; reprint ed., New York: Arno Press, 1975) 3: 72. The Pullman Building was demolished in 1956 to make way for the Borg-Warner Building.

30. *Western Manufacturer* (Chicago), 31 March 1884, clipping, Pullman Company, Miscellaneous Scrapbooks, Series B, vol. 1, 1883–1903, Newberry Library, Chicago, Ill.

31. Finis Farr, *Chicago: A Personal History of America's Most American City* (New Rochelle, N.Y.: Arlington House, 1973), p. 283; *Western Manufacturer* (Chicago), 31 March 1884, undated clipping, ca. January 1886, Pullman Company, Miscellaneous Scrapbooks, Series A, vol. 9, 1885–1886, Newberry Library, Chicago, Ill.; *Chicago Journal of Commerce*, 7 April 1886, clipping, Pullman Company, Miscellaneous Scrapbooks, Series B, vol. 1, 1883–1903, Newberry Library, Chicago, Ill.

32. According to tradition, Pullman, Washington, was named for George M. Pullman. He supposedly sent the town, on its citizens' request, a check for $50 with which to celebrate 4 July 1881; the grateful residents are said to have memorialized his act by naming the town in his honor. Unfortunately, this interesting bit of memorabilia cannot be verified because historians of the town cannot agree on how it received its name. For more on this controversy, see Lawrence R. Stark, "The Founding of Pullman: A Local Folktale," and Esther Pond Smith, "The Development of the Postal Service in Pullman," in *Bunchgrass Historian, Whitman County* (Washington) *Historical Society Quarterly* 9 (Summer 1981): 4–24. I am indebted to Mr. Henry A. Pullman of Long Beach, California, for bringing this matter to my attention.

Chapter 10

1. "Illinois," vol. 30, p. 346, R. G. Dun and Company Collection, Baker Library, Harvard University Graduate School of Business Administration, Soldiers Field, Boston, Mass.

2. Ibid.

3. Pullman's Palace Car Company, Record Book A, pp. 394 and 430, Newberry Library, Chicago, Ill.

4. Almont Lindsey, *The Pullman Strike* (Chicago, Ill.: University of Chicago Press, 1964), pp. 28–30; *New York Times*, 15 February 1882, p. 2, 16 February 1882, p. 5, 30 September 1885, p. 5, 7 May 1886, p. 1, 23 August 1887, p. 5.

5. *New York Times*, 26 September 1880, p. 2, and 19 October 1880, p. 1.

Notes

6. *New York Times*, 26 September 1880, p. 1, and 21 June 1888, p. 3; *Railroad Gazette*, 14 January 1881, pp. 16–17.

7. Pullman's Palace Car Company, Record Book B, pp. 24–25, Newberry Library, Chicago, Ill.

8. Ibid., p. 25; *Railroad Gazette*, 20 March 1885, p. 192.

9. *Railroad Gazette*, 27 March 1885, p. 208, and 24 April 1885, p. 272; Pullman's Palace Car Company, Record Book B, p. 25, Newberry Library, Chicago, Ill.

10. A handwritten copy of this letter was entered into Pullman's Palace Car Company, Record Book B, pp. 26–30, Newberry Library, Chicago, Ill.

11. *Railroad Gazette*, 15 May 1885, p. 320.

12. The letter appeared in *New York Times*, 22 August 1885, p. 2.

13. Ibid. Stevens' reply to Pullman also appeared in *New York Times*, 23 August 1885, p. 7, and 28 August 1885, p. 2.

14. *New York Times*, 3 September 1885, p. 2; *Railroad Gazette*, 29 April 1887, p. 295, and 6 May 1887, p. 311.

15. *New York Times*, 19 December 1894, p. 1, 25 January 1896, p. 15, and 3 July 1898, p. 7.

16. *The National Cyclopaedia of American Biography* (New York: James T. White, 1907), 9: 208–209.

17. Alvin F. Harlow, *The Road of the Century: The Story of the New York Central* (New York: Creative Age Press, 1947), p. 177; John H. White, Jr., *The American Railroad Passenger Car*, (Baltimore, Md.: Johns Hopkins University Press, 1978), pp. 235–238.

18. *New York Times*, 3 February 1880, p. 8. Hattie also noted in her diary that George had spent the evening with Webster Wagner; Harriett S. Pullman diary, 14 December 1877, Mrs. C. Phillip Miller Collection, Chicago Historical Society, Chicago, Ill.

19. *New York Times*, 6 January 1882, p. 1.

20. *New York Times*, 20 January 1882, p. 50, and 23 January 1882, pp. 3 and 8; *National Cyclopaedia*, 9: 209.

21. Railroad Gazette, 30 December 1881, p. 748, and 28 April 1882, p. 262; *New York Times*, 10 January 1882, p. 2.

22. *Railroad Gazette*, 11 December 1885, p. 792.

23. White, *American Railroad*, p. 447; Horace Porter, "Railway Passenger Travel," in *The American Railway: Its Construction, Development, Management, and Appliances* (1892; reprint ed., New York: Bramhall House, n.d.), p. 249; *Railroad Gazette*, 18 March 1887, p. 182.

24. *New York Times*, 23 May 1888, p. 5.

25. White, *American Railroad*, p. 450.

26. *Railroad Gazette*, 18 March 1887, p. 182.

27. *Railroad Gazette*, 2 March 1894, p. 153, and 11 May 1888, p. 308. Pullman also obtained a patent for vestibules that he likewise assigned to the company in order to bring suit against Wagner Palace Car Company and the Boston and Albany Railroad. Pullman's Palace Car Company, Record Book B, p. 62, Newberry Library, Chicago, Ill.; *New York Times*, 10 October 1890, p. 2.

28. *Railroad Gazette*, 25 November 1887, p. 272, and 21 July 1893, p. 556.

29. *Railroad Gazette*, 9 March 1894, p. 173.

30. *Railroad Gazette*, 23 December 1887, p. 829.

31. *New York Times*, 3 May 1888, p. 1.

32. *New York Times*, 10 October 1890, p. 2, 21 October 1890, p. 2, 27 October 1895, p. 1, and 13 November 1883, p. 2.

33. *Railroad Gazette*, 23 December 1881, p. 736, 21 January 1887, p. 52, 4 March 1887, p. 154; *New York Times*, 21 April 1887, p. 5; James Bryce, *The American Commonwealth*, 2d. rev. ed., 2 vols. (London and New York: Macmillan, 1891) 1: 490–498.

34 "Illinois," vol. 43, p. 18, R. G. Dun and Company Collection, Baker Library, Harvard University Graduate School of Business Administration, Soldiers Field, Boston, Mass.; *New York Times*, 16 March 1881, p. 2.

35. Pullman's Palace Car Company, Record Book A, pp. 407, 414–415, and 417, and Pullman's Palace Car Company, Record Book B, p. 146, Newberry Library, Chicago, Ill.

36. *New York Times*, 5 March 1889, p. 5.

37. Pullman's Palace Car Company, Record Book B, p. 136, Newberry Library, Chicago, Ill.

38. Pullman's Palace Car Company, Record Book A, pp. 373–374, Newberry Library, Chicago, Ill.

39. Ibid., pp. 403 and 460; Pullman's Palace Car Company, Record B, p. 147, Newberry Library, Chicago, Ill.

40. Pullman's Palace Car Company, Record Book B, p. 5, Newberry Library, Chicago, Ill.

41. Ibid., pp. 48–49; White, *American Railroad*, p. 230.

42. *New York Times*, 24 January 1889, p. 1, and 25 January 1889, p. 2.

43. *New York Times*, 24 January 1889, p. 1.

44. Pullman's Palace Car Company, Record Book B, pp. 50–51, Newberry Library, Chicago, Ill.; *Railroad Gazette*, 1 March 1889, pp. 151–152, and 25 October 1889, p. 698; White, *American Railroad*, p. 260.

45. Pullman's Palace Car Company, Record Book B, p. 52, Newberry Library, Chicago, Ill.

46. Ibid., pp. 52–59, Newberry Library, Chicago, Ill.

47. *Railroad Gazette*, 1 October 1886, p. 681, and 12 August 1892, p. 601.

48. Pullman's Palace Car Company, Record Book B, p. 83, Newberry Library, Chicago, Ill.

49. Raymond A. Mohl, *The New City: Urban America in the Industrial Age, 1860–1920* (Arlington Heights, Ill.: Harlan Davidson, 1985), pp. 13–16; Bessie Louise Pierce, *A History of Chicago*, vol. 3 *The Rise of a Modern City, 1871–1893* (Chicago, Ill.: The University of Chicago Press, 1957), p. 501.

50. Pullman's Palace Car Company, Record Book B, p. 71 and 113, Newberry Library, Chicago, Ill.

51. Mohl, *The New City*, pp. 16–19; Samuel P. Hays, *The Response to Industrialism, 1885–1914* (Chicago, Ill.: University of Chicago Press, 1957), p. 38.

52. *Railroad Gazette*, 24 October 1890, p. 746, and 28 October 1891, p. 756; Henry V. Poor, *Manual of Railroads of the United States . . . Showing Their Mileage, Stocks, Bonds, Cost, Earnings, Expenses, and Organizations . . .Together With an Appendix* (New York: H. V. and H. W. Poor, 1891), p. 1087.

53. *Poor's Manual,* p. 1088; *New York Times,* 15 February 1882, p. 2, 16 February 1882, p. 5, 30 September 1885, p. 5, 6 February 1886, p. 3, 7 May 1886, p. 1, 19 May 1886, p. 3, 23 August 1887, p. 5, and 15 July 1888, p. 1.

54. *Railroad Gazette,* 20 December 1889, p. 837, 14 February 1890, p. 107, and 24 October 1890, p. 746.

55. *Railroad Gazette,* 24 October 1890, p. 746.

56. Hays, *Response to Industrialism,* p. 22; Robert H. Wiebe, *The Search for Order, 1877–1920* (New York: Hill and Wang, 1967), p. 46; Katharine Coman, *The Industrial History of the United States,* new and rev. ed. (New York: Macmillan, 1910), pp. 328 and 355.

57. Caroline Kirkland, *Chicago Yesterdays: A Sheaf of Reminiscences* (Chicago, Ill.: Daughaday, 1919), pp. 212–213.

Chapter 11

1. Arthur A. Wells, *Reminiscences of Mr. and Mrs. George M. Pullman,* printed pamphlet, and Benjamin Harrison to George M. Pullman, 7 February 1896, Mrs. C. Phillip Miller Collection, Chicago Historical Society, Chicago, Ill.

2. Ernest Poole, *Giants Gone: Men Who Made Chicago* (New York: McGraw-Hill, 1943), pp. 198–199; George Ade, "The Glory of Being a Coachman," in *Chicago Stories,* ed Franklin J. Meine (1941; reprint ed., Chicago, Ill: Henry Regnery, 1963), pp. 148–149.

3. Brailsford Reese Brazel, *The Brotherhood of Sleeping Car Porters, Its Origins and Development* (New York: Harper and Brothers, 1946), pp. 1–2.

4. *Pullman* (Ill.) *Journal,* 7 January 1893, pp. 1–2.

5. Bessie Louise Pierce, comp. and ed., *As Others See Chicago: Impressions of Visitors, 1673–1933* (Chicago, Ill.: University of Chicago Press, 1933), p. 27; George M. Pullman to Harriett S. Pullman, 19 February 1892, 24 March 1893, 25 February 1894, and 22 March 1894, Mrs. C. Phillip Miller Collection, Chicago Historical Society, Chicago, Ill.

6. George M. Pullman, Jr., diary, 29 May 1894, and 2 June 1894, and Wells, *Reminiscences,* Mrs. C. Phillip Miller Collection, Chicago Historical Society, Chicago, Ill.

7. John Tebbel, *The Marshall Fields: A Study in Wealth* (New York: E. P. Dutton, 1947), p. 47.

8. Harriett S. Pullman diary, 10 June 1889, Mrs. C. Phillip Miller Collection, Chicago Historical Society, Chicago, Ill.

9. Harriett S. Pullman diary, 30 August 1887, and entries between 10 June 1889 and 26 September 1889, Mrs. C. Phillip Miller Collection, Chicago Historical Society, Chicago, Ill.

10. See, for instance, Harriett S. Pullman diary, 5 November 1889, Mrs. C. Phillip Miller Collection, Chicago Historical Society, Chicago, Ill.

11. George M. Pullman to Harriett S. Pullman, 11 March 1891; Harriett S. Pullman to George M. Pullman, 24 January 1892; Harriett S. Pullman diary, 21 May 1892, and 23 May 1892, Mrs. C. Phillip Miller Collection, Chicago Historical Society, Chicago, Ill.; *New York Times,* 22 May 1892, p. 5.

12. The description of the Carolan wedding came from several sources: Harriett S. Pullman to George M. Pullman, 23 December 1891, Harriett S. Pullman diary, 7

June 1892, Mrs. C. Phillip Miller Collection, Chicago Historical Society, Chicago, Ill.; see also clipping, Pullman Company, Miscellaneous Scrapbooks, Series B, vol. 3, 1891–1893, p. 52, Newberry Library, Chicago, Ill.; *Inter Ocean* (Chicago), 7 June 1892, 5:5, and 8 June 1892, 5:1.

13. Harriett S. Pullman diary, 5 February 1892, 13 June 1892, and 19 October 1892, Mrs. C. Phillip Miller Collection, Chicago Historical Society, Chicago, Ill.; *Inter Ocean*, (Chicago), 14 June 1892, clipping, Pullman Company, Miscellaneous Scrapbooks, Series B, vol. 3, 1891–1893, Newberry Library, Chicago, Ill.

14. Harriett S. Pullman diary, 23 February 1893, 24 February 1893, 21 April 1893, and 29 April 1893, Mrs. C. Phillip Miller Collection, Chicago Historical Society, Chicago, Ill.

15. Harriett S. Pullman diary, 30 May 1893, Mrs. C. Phillip Miller Collection, Chicago Historical Society, Chicago, Ill. The bicycle races at Pullman were held each Memorial Day. *Chicago History*, 8 (Summer 1967): 107.

16. Harriett S. Pullman diary, 22 June 1893, Mrs. C. Phillip Miller Collection, Chicago Historical Society, Chicago, Ill.; A. Milo Bennett, "The Building of a State — The Story of Illinois," *Journal of the Illinois State Historical Society* 13 (October 1920): 324–354; Bessie Louise Pierce, *A History of Chicago*, vol. 3, *The Rise of a Modern City 1871–1893* (Chicago, Ill.: University of Chicago Press, 1957), pp. 498–499.

17. Harriett S. Pullman diary, 16 July 1893, 21 August 1893, 21 September 1893, and 10 October 1893, Mrs. C. Phillip Miller Collection, Chicago Historical Society, Chicago, Ill.; *New York Times*, 13 September 1893, p. 8, 22 August 1894, p. 1, and 22 March 1896, p. 26.

18. Harriett S. Pullman diary, 30 July 1893, 2 December 1893, and 5 December 1893, Mrs. C. Phillip Miller Collection, Chicago Historical Society, Chicago, Ill.

19. Emily C. Pullman diary, 8 March 1890, Chicago Historical Society, Chicago, Ill.; Harriett S. Pullman diary, 18 December 1893 and 21 December 1893, Mrs. C. Phillip Miller Collection, Chicago Historical Society, Chicago, Ill.; *New York Times*, 19 December 1893, p. 4; *Inter Ocean* (Chicago), 19 December 1893, p. 5.

20. Harriett S. Pullman diary, 24 December 1893, Mrs. C. Phillip Miller Collection, Chicago Historical Society, Chicago, Ill.

21. Almont Lindsey, *The Pullman Strike: The Story of a Unique Experiment and of a Great Labor Upheaval* (Chicago, Ill.: University of Chicago Press, 1942), p. 28.

22. Ibid., pp. 28–30 and 95; *Herald*, 3 September 1886, clipping, Pullman Company, Miscellaneous Scrapbooks, Series A, vol, 1885–1886, Newberry Library, Chicago, Ill.

23. Pierce, *As Others See Chicago*, p. 273; Ray Ginger, *Altgeld's America: The Lincoln Ideal Versus Changing Realities* (Chicago: Quadrangle Books, 1965), pp. 148–149; Lindsey, *Pullman Strike*, p. 30; Harper Leech and John Charles, *Armour and His Times* (New York: D. Appleton-Century, 1938), pp. 75, 217–218.

24. Almont Lindsey, "Paternalism and the Pullman Strike," *American Historical Review* 45 (January 1939): 287; Lindsey, *Pullman Strike*, pp. 34–35.

25 *New York Times*, 15 August 1888, p. 1; Ray Ginger, *Eugene V. Debs: A Biography* (New York: Collier Books, 1970), p. 124; see also Ginger, *Altgeld's America*, pp. 147–148; Pierce, *History of Chicago*, p. 290; Paul Avrich, *The Haymarket Tragedy* (Princeton, N.J.: Princeton University Press, 1984), pp. 223 and 365; Robert H. Wiebe, *The Search for Order, 1877-1920* (New York: Hill and Wang, 1967), p. 47.

26. George M. Pullman to Harriett S. Pullman, 22 December 1890, Mrs. C. Phillip Miller Collection, Chicago Historical Society, Chicago, Ill.

27. Royal H. Pullman to George M. Pullman, 6 November 1890, and 20 January 1891, Mrs. C. Phillip Miller Collection, Chicago Historical Society, Chicago, Ill.; Pullman's Palace Car Company, Record Book B, pp. 87–91, Newberry Library, Chicago, Ill.

28. Ibid., pp. 117–120.

29. Ibid., pp. 131.

30. Ibid., pp. 131–137.

31. *United States Strike Commission Report*, Senate Executive Document no. D3276 7/53 Cong., 3d Sess. (Washington, D.C.: Government Printing Office, 1895), pp. XXII, XXXII, 535–536, 555, and 624–625.

32. Pierce, *As Others See Chicago*, pp. 270–271; *United States Strike Commission Report*, pp. XXIII.

33. *United States Strike Commission Report*, pp. XXXIV and XXXVI; Reverend William H. Carwardine, *The Pullman Strike* (1894; reprint ed., Chicago: Charles H. Kerr, 1973), p. 69 and chapter 10.

34. *United States Strike Commission Report*, pp. XXXIV, 554, and 567.

35. Ibid., p. XXV.

36. Lindsey, *Pullman Strike*, pp. 29 and 110–113.

37. *United States Strike Commission Report*, pp. XXV and 621–622.

38. Norman J. Ware, *The Labor Movement in the United States, 1860–1895: A Study in Democracy* (New York: Vintage Books, 1929), p. 124.

39. Lindsey, *Pullman Strike*, pp. 103–105.

40. *United States Strike Commission Report*, pp. XXXVII-XXXVIII; Carwardine, *Pullman Strike*, pp. 35–36.

41. Lindsey, *Pullman Strike*, pp. 129–130.

42. Ibid., pp. 136–137.

43. Ibid., pp. 134.

44. Harriett S. Pullman diary, 30 March 1894, 19 April 1894, and 27 April 1894, Mrs. C. Phillip Miller Collection, Chicago Historical Society, Chicago, Ill.

45. Harriett S. Pullman diary, 1 May 1894, 4 May 1894, 7 May 1894, 12 May 1894, Mrs. C. Phillip Miller Collection, Chicago Historical Society, Chicago, Ill.; Stanley Buder, *Pullman: An Experiment in Industiral Order and Community Planning, 1880–1930* (New York: Oxford University Press, 1970), p. 169.

46. Harriett S. Pullman diary, 23 May 1894 to 21 June 1894, and George M. Pullman, Jr., diary, 24 May 1894 to 20 June 1894, Mrs. C. Phillip Miller Collection, Chicago Historical Society, Chicago, Ill.

47. Lindsey, *Pullman Strike*, p. 134; Wells, *Reminiscences*; George M. Pullman, Jr., diary, 26 June 1894 and 28 June 1894, Mrs. C. Phillip Miller Collection, Chicago Historical Society, Chicago, Ill.

48. George M. Pullman, Jr., diary, 29 June 1894, and Harriett S. Pullman diary, 30 June 1894 and 4 July 1894, Mrs. C. Phillip Miller Collection, Chicago Historical Society, Chicago, Ill.; Buder, *Pullman*, p. 190.

49. Lindsey, *Pullman Strike*, pp. 163, 173, 197–198, and 204–209.

50. *United States Strike Commission Report*, p. XXXIX; Lindsey, *Pullman Strike*, p. 231.

51. *United States Strike Commission Report*, pp. XLI and 58; Lindsey, *Pullman Strike*, pp. 226–227.

52. *New York Times,* 9 July 1894, p. 2; Lindsey, *Pullman Strike,* p. 232; Helen Pullman (West) to Emma Pullman (Fluhrer), 12 July 1894, Fluhrer Family Papers, Chicago Historical Society, Chicago, Ill.

53. Helen Pullman (West) to Emma Pullman (Fluhrer), 12 July 1894, Fluhrer Family Papers, Chicago Historical Society, Chicago, Ill.

54. Ibid. See also Buder, *Pullman,* p. 191; Harriett S. Pullman diary, 12 July 1894 and 13 July 1894, Mrs. C. Phillip Miller Collection, Chicago Historical Society, Chicago, Ill.

55. *New York Times,* 14 July 1894, p. 1.

56. Julian Morel, Kent, England, provided this interesting insight into George Pullman's thinking. Morel interviewed Edgar Mayer, a resident of London who had worked as a private secretary to Pullman during the last several years of his life. Apparently, Mayer spent a substantial amount of time with the Pullman family (Hattie Pullman mentioned Edgar with some frequency in her diaries, as did her husband in several pieces of correspondence). In addition to stating that he had happy recollections of them, Mr. Mayer also mentioned the subversive elements who were trying to infiltrate the town of Pullman in his memories of the Pullman family. Julian Morel to Author, 15 November 1983.

57. *New York Times,* 14 July 1894, p. 1. His statement also appeared in the *United States Strike Commission Report,* p. 584; Harriett S. Pullman diary, 15 July 1894, Mrs. C. Phillip Miller Collection, Chicago Historical Society, Chicago, Ill.

58. *United States Strike Commission Report,* p. 586; Lindsey, "Paternalism and the Pullman Strike," p. 288.

59. Dr. William Fluhrer to Emma Pullman (Fluhrer), 31 July 1894, Fluhrer Family Papers, Chicago Historical Society, Chicago, Ill.

60. Harriett S. Pullman diary, 30 July 1894, and 4 August 1894, and George M. Pullman, Jr., diary, 3 August 1894, and 4 August 1894, Mrs. C. Phillip Miller Collection, Chicago Historical Society, Chicago, Ill.

61. Buder, *Pullman,* pp. 196–197; *United States Strike Commission Report,* pp. XVII, XXI, and 528–630.

62. *United States Strike Commission Report,* p. XXVII.

63. Ibid., pp. XXXII-XXXV.

64. Ibid., pp. XXXV-XXXVIII.

65. Edward Chase Kirkland, *Industry Comes of Age: Business, Labor and Public Policy, 1860–1897* (Chicago: Quadrangle Books, 1967), p. 397.

66. Mary C. Sanger diary, 14 September 1894 and 18 September 1894; George M. Pullman to Harriett S. Pullman, 2 September 1894 and 28 September 1894, Mrs. C. Phillip Miller Collection, Chicago Historical Society, Chicago, Ill.

67. *Chicago Times,* 5 March 1884, p. 8.

68. George C. Sikes to Madeline Wallin, 24 July 1894, Madeline Wallin Sikes Collection, Box 6, Chicago Historical Society, Chicago, Ill.

69. Harriett S. Pullman to George M. Pullman, 31 August 1894, and 6 September 1894; George M. Pullman, Jr., diary, 30 August 1894 to 19 September 1894; Mary C. Sanger diary, 31 August 1894, Mrs. C. Phillip Miller Collection, Chicago Historical Society, Chicago, Ill.

70. Harriett S. Pullman diary, 13 October 1894, 14 October 1894, and 20 October 1894, Mrs. C. Phillip Miller Collection, Chicago Historical Society, Chicago, Ill.

71. Mary C. Sanger diary, 10 November 1894, and 27 November 1894; Harriett S. Pullman diary, 4 November 1894 and 19 December 1894, Mrs. C. Phillip Miller Collection, Chicago Historical Society, Chicago, Ill.

72. Florence Pullman Lowden diary, 19 December 1894, 25 December 1894, and 31 December 1894, Harriett S. Pullman diary, 7 August 1894, 12 August 1894, 14 August 1894, and 18 December 1894, Mrs. C. Phillip Miller Collection, Chicago Historical Society, Chicago, Illinois;; William T. Hutchinson, *Lowden of Illinois: The Life of Frank O. Lowden*, 2 vols. (Chicago, Ill.: University of Chicago Press, 1957), vol. 1, pp. 41–44.

73. *New York Times*, 12 August 1894, p. 9, 15 August 1894, p. 9, 9 October 1894, p. 2, 25 October 1894, p. 7, and 14 February 1895, p. 7.

Chapter 12

1. Isaac S. Signor, *Landmarks of Orleans County, N.Y.*, part 3 (Syracuse, N.Y.: D. Mason, 1894), pp. 290–291.

2. Royal H. Pullman to George M. Pullman, 12 December 1893, Mrs. C. Phillip Miller Collection, Chicago Historical Society, Chicago, Ill.; Signor, *Landmarks of Orleans County*, pp. 290–291; see also George M. Pullman, Jr., diary, 22 May 1894, Mrs. C. Phillip Miller Collection, Chicago Historical Society, Chicago, Ill.

3. George M. Pullman, Jr., diary, 24 May 1894, 10 June 1894, and 15 June 1894; Harriett S. Pullman diary, 26 May 1894, 1 June 1894, 2 June 1894, 3 June 1894, and 10 June 1894, Mrs. C. Phillip Miller Collection, Chicago Historical Society, Chicago, Ill. Helen Pullman West to Mrs. William Fluhrer, 12 July 1894, Fluhrer Family Papers, Chicago Historical Society, Chicago, Ill.

4. Charles Fluhrer to William Fluhrer, 30 October 1894, Fluhrer Family Papers, 1890–1899, Chicago Historical Society, Chicago, Ill.; Florence Pullman diary, 1 November 1894, and 2 November 1894, Mrs. C. Phillip Miller Collection, Chicago Historical Society, Chicago, Ill.

5. *New York Times*, 1 February 1895, p. 10; Florence Pullman diary, 20 October 1894, Mrs. C. Phillip Miller Collection, Chicago Historical Society, Chicago, Ill.; Caroline Jefferds to Emma Pullman (Fluhrer), 15 February 1895, Fluhrer Family Papers, 1890–1899, Chicago Historical Society, Chicago, Ill.

6. *New York Times*, 29 January 1895, p. 10; Florence Pullman diary, 20 October 1894; George M. Pullman to Harriett S. Pullman, 4 February 1895, George M. Pullman, Jr. to Mrs. George M. Pullman, 1 February 1895, Mrs. C. Phillip Miller Collection, Chicago Historical Society, Chicago, Ill.; *Dedication of the Pullman Memorial Universalist Church* (Albion, N.Y.: 31 January 1895), booklet in author's possession; Signor, *Landmarks of Orleans County*, pp. 290–291.

7. George M. Pullman, Jr., to Harriett S. Pullman, 1 February 1895; George M. Pullman to Harriett S. Pullman, 4 February 1895; Harriett S. Pullman diary, 1 January 1895 to 19 January 1895, Mrs. C. Phillip Miller Collection, Chicago Historical Society, Chicago, Ill.

8. George M. Pullman to Harriett S. Pullman, 22 January 1895, Harriett S. Pullman diary, 14 February 1895 to 7 April 1985, Mrs. C. Phillip Miller Collection, Chicago Historical Society, Chicago, Ill.

9. George M. Pullman to Harriett S. Pullman, 22 February 1895, Mrs. C. Phillip Miller Collection, Chicago Historical Society, Chicago, Ill.

10. Harriett S. Pullman diary, 9 April 1895, 15 April 1895, 28 April 1895, 5 May 1895, 17 June 1895, 22 June 1895, 6 August 1895, 7 August 1895, 7 September 1895, 9 September 1895, and 27 October 1895, Mrs. C. Phillip Miller Collection, Chicago Historical Society, Chicago, Ill.; William T. Hutchinson, *Lowden of Illinois: The Life of Frank O. Lowden*, 2 vols. (Chicago, Ill.: University of Chicago Press, 1957) 1: 45–46.

11. Stanley Buder, *Pullman: An Experiment in Industrial Order and Community Planning, 1880–1930* (New York: Oxford University Press, 1970), pp. 207–208; Pullman's Palace Car Company, Record Book B, pp. 152–167, Newberry Library, Chicago, Ill. Although one author noted that stockholders, angered by Pullman's handling of the strike, were anxious to reorganize the company, no indications of such a revolt appeared on the pages of the Pullman Company record book for that period. See John Tebbell, *The Marshall Fields: A Study in Wealth* (New York: E. P. Dutton, 1947), pp. 57–58.

12. Pullman's Palace Car Company, Record Book B, pp. 146–150, 157–158, and 161–163, Newberry Library, Chicago, Ill.

13. Ibid., pp. 142, 152, 155–156, 159, and 161–163.

14. Harriet Pullman (Carolan) to George M. Pullman, 20 April 1895, Mrs. C. Phillip Miller Collection, Chicago Historical Society, Chicago, Ill.

15. *New York Times*, 13 November 1895, p. 5, and 17 December 1895 p. 1; Harriett S. Pullman to George M. Pullman, 19 December 1895, Mrs. C. Phillip Miller Collection, Chicago Historical Society, Chicago, Ill.

16. Harriett S. Pullman to George M. Pullman, 21 December 1895, Mrs. C. Phillip Miller Collection, Chicago Historical Society, Chicago, Ill.

17. Hutchinson, *Lowden*, pp. 51–54; George M. Pullman to Harriett S. Pullman, 29 August 1896, Mrs. C. Phillip Miller Collection, Chicago Historical Society, Chicago, Ill.

18. Harriet Pullman (Carolan) to George M. Pullman, 19 September 1897; Arthur Wells, *Reminiscences of Mr. and Mrs. George M. Pullman*, printed pamphlet, Mrs. C. Phillip Miller Collection, Chicago Historical Society, Chicago, Ill.

19. Harriett S. Pullman diary, 9 April 1895 to 7 May 1895 and 17 May–24 May 1895, Mrs. C. Phillip Miller Collection, Chicago Historical Society, Chicago, Ill.

20. Harriett S. Pullman diary, 19 July 1895 and 26 August 1895 to 6 October 1895, passim, Mrs. C. Phillip Miller Collection, Chicago Historical Society, Chicago, Ill.

21. Harriett S. Pullman diary, 9 October 1895 to 21 October 1895, 6 November 1895 to 14 December 1895, and 25 December 1895; Harriett S. Pullman to George M. Pullman, 19 December 1895, and 21 December 1895, Mrs. C. Phillip Miller Collection, Chicago Historical Society, Chicago, Ill.; Hutchinson, *Lowden*, p. 47.

22. Harriett S. Pullman to George M. Pullman, 10 March 1896, and Harriett S. Pullman diary, 27 February 1896, Mrs. C. Phillip Miller Collection, Chicago Historical Society, Chicago, Ill.

23. Harriet S. Pullman diary, 3 April 1896 to 23 April 1896, Mrs. C. Phillip Miller Collection, Chicago Historical Society, Chicago, Ill.

24. Florence Pullman scrapbook, wedding invitation; Harriett S. Pullman diary, 29 April 1896, Mrs. C. Phillip Miller Collection, Chicago Historical Society, Chicago, Ill. Descriptions of the wedding appear in Florence Lowden Miller, "The Pullmans of Prairie Avenue: A Domestic Portrait From Letters and Diaries," *Chicago History* 1 (Spring 1971): 153–154; Hutchinson, *Lowden*, vol. 1, pp. 48–49; see also *Inter Ocean* (Chicago), 30 April 1896, p. 2; *Tribune* (Chicago), 30 April 1896, p. 13.

25. Harriett S. Pullman to George M. Pullman, 21 November 1895, 26 March 1897, and 5 April 1897; Harriett S. Pullman diary, 18 November 1896, Harriet Pullman (Carolan) to George M. Pullman, 1 October 1897, and Florence Pullman scrapbook, 1893, clipping, p. 32, Mrs. C. Phillip Miller Collection, Chicago Historical Society, Chicago, Ill.

26. George M. Pullman to Harriett S. Pullman, 2 January 1891, 6 January 1891, 11 March 1891, and 24 March 1891, Mrs. C. Phillip Miller Collection, Chicago Historical Society, Chicago, Ill.

27. Harriett S. Pullman to George M. Pullman, 11 June 1891, 2 October 1891, 6 October 1891, 30 December 1891, 24 January 1892, 27 January 1892, and 27 February 1892, and Harriett S. Pullman diary, 23 January 1892 to 27 February 1892, Mrs. C. Phillip Miller Collection, Chicago Historical Society, Chicago, Ill.

28. George M. Pullman to Harriett S. Pullman, 9 September 1892 and 14 September 1892; Harriett S. Pullman diary, 13 September 1892 and 21 September 1892. Mrs. C. Phillip Miller Collection, Chicago Historical Society, Chicago, Ill. Charles C. Watson, headmaster at Hill School, stated that he had very little information on the Pullman sons because they did not graduate. However, Sanger was a member of the school's gun club in 1893, and he played violin for the orchestra in 1892–1893. Hill School also possesses young George's application, in which he stated he had spent one school year each at Dobbs Ferry, the University School of Chicago, and the Chicago Manual Training School. Presumably, Sanger had the same record. Charles C. Watson to the author, 20 November 1984.

29. Professor John Meigs to Harriett S. Pullman, 10 October 1892, Mrs. C. Phillip Miller Collection, Chicago Historical Society, Chicago, Ill.

30. Harriett S. Pullman diary, 23–24 February 1893; George M. Pullman to Harriett S. Pullman, 24 March 1893, Mrs. C. Phillip Miller Collection, Chicago Historical Society, Chicago, Ill.

31. Harriett S. Pullman diary, 25 June 1893, and 29 June 1893 to 29 December 1893, passim, Mrs. C. Phillip Miller Collection, Chicago Historical Society, Chicago, Illinois.

32. George M. Pullman to Harriett S. Pullman, 25 February 1894, Harriett S. Pullman diary, 4 January 1894 to 10 March 1894, Mrs. C. Phillip Miller Collection, Chicago Historical Society, Chicago, Ill.

33. Harriett S. Pullman diary, 10 March 1894; George M. Pullman to Harriett S. Pullman, 22 March 1894, Mrs. C. Phillip Miller Collection, Chicago Historical Society, Chicago, Ill.

34. George M. Pullman to Harriett S. Pullman, 30 March 1894, Harriett S. Pullman to George M. Pullman, 19 July 1894, Mary Catherine Sanger diary, 12 May 1894, and 3 June 1894, Harriett S. Pullman diary, 14 May–19 May 1894, and 18 July–23 July 1894, Mrs. C. Phillip Miller Collection, Chicago Historical Society, Chicago, Ill.

35. Harriett S. Pullman to George M. Pullman, 31 August 1894, Harriett S. Pullman diary, 13 October 1894, and 20 October 1894 to 31 December 1894, passim, Mrs. C. Phillip Miller Collection, Chicago Historical Society, Chicago, Ill.

36. Harriett S. Pullman diary, 3 June 1895, 25 June 1895, 7 January 1895, 30 June 1895 to 2 August 1895, Harriet Pullman (Carolan) to George M. Pullman, 19 September 1895, Harriett S. Pullman to George M. Pullman, 21 December 1895, Mrs. C. Phillip Miller Collection, Chicago Historical Society, Chicago, Ill.

37. Harriett S. Pullman diary, 9 February 1896 to 19 March 1896, and 26 March 1896, Harriett S. Pullman to George M. Pullman, 20 February 1896 and 26 February 1896, Mrs. C. Phillip Miller Collection, Chicago Historical Society, Chicago, Ill.

38. Harriett S. Pullman diary 25 June 1896, Mary Catherine Sanger diary, 25 June 1896, Mrs. C. Phillip Miller Collection, Chicago Historical Society, Chicago, Ill.

39. Harriett S. Pullman to George M. Pullman, 11 September 1896, Mrs. C. Phillip Miller Collection, Chicago Historical Society, Chicago, Ill.

40. Harriett S. Pullman diary, 15 January 1897, 23 January 1897, 10 February 1897, 21 February 1897, 25 February 1897, and 26 February 1897 to 15 March 1897, Mrs. C. Phillip Miller Collection, Chicago Historical Society, Chicago, Ill.

41. Harriett S. Pullman diary, 4 March 1897 to 21 March 1897, Mrs. C. Phillip Miller Collection, Chicago Historical Society, Chicago, Ill.; Lloyd Wendt and Herman Kogan, *Give the Lady What She Wants! The Story of Marshall Field and Company* (Chicago: Rand McNally, 1952), pp. 199–200; George M. Pullman to Harriett S. Pullman, 27 March 1897, and 31 March 1897, Harriett S. Pullman to George M. Pullman, 28 March 1897, 1 April 1897, and 5 April 1897, Mrs. C. Phillip Miller Collection, Chicago Historical Society, Chicago, Ill.

42. Harriett S. Pullman diary, 22 May 1897, 25 May 1897, 31 May 1897, and 1 July 1897, Mrs. C. Phillip Miller Collection, Chicago Historical Society, Chicago, Ill.

43. *Inter Ocean*, (Chicago), 27 November 1901, clipping, Pullman Company, Miscellaneous Scrapbooks, Series B, vol. 7, 1899–1901, p. 82, Newberry Library, Chicago, Ill.; Florence Pullman scrapbook, clipping, p. 32, Mrs. C. Phillip Miller Collection, Chicago Historical Society, Chicago, Ill.

44. Harriett S. Pullman diary, 27 May 1896 to 10 July 1896, passim, and 25 September 1896, 28 October 1896, 8 November 1896, 15 November 1896, 22 November 1896, 5 December 1896, and 10 December 1896, Mrs. C. Phillip Miller Collection, Chicago Historical Society, Chicago, Ill.

45. Harriett S. Pullman diary, 5 August 1896, 13 August 1896 to 17 August 1896, 18 September 1896, and 21 September 1896 Mrs. C. Phillip Miller Collection, Chicago Historical Society, Chicago, Ill..

46. Harriett S. Pullman diary, 25 December 1896, 27 December 1896, 30 December 1896, 1 January 1897, and 15 January 1897, Mrs. C. Phillip Miller Collection, Chicago Historical Society, Chicago, Ill.

47. Harriett S. Pullman diary, 20 January 1897, 21 January 1897, and 24 January 1897, Mrs. C. Phillip Miller Collection, Chicago Historical Society, Chicago, Ill.

48. Harriett S. Pullman diary, 1 February 1897 to 20 March 1897, 17 April 1897, 19 April 1897, and 14 May 1897, Mrs. C. Phillip Miller Collection, Chicago Historical Society, Chicago, Ill.

49. *Poor's Manual of the Railroads of the United States, 1897*, 30th annual ed. (New York: H. V. and H. W. Poor, 1897), p. 1337; Harriett S. Pullman diary, 9 June to 13 June 1897, Mrs. C. Phillip Miller Collection, Chicago Historical Society, Chicago, Ill.

50. Harriett S. Pullman diary, 28 June 1897, Mrs. C. Phillip Miller Collection, Chicago Historical Society, Chicago, Ill.

51. Harriett S. Pullman diary, 8 July 1897, 12 August–16 August 1897, 21 August 1897, 23 August 1897 to 31 August 1897, Harriet Pullman (Carolan) to George M. Pullman, 19 September 1897, Mrs. C. Phillip Miller Collection, Chicago Historical Society, Chicago, Ill.

52. Harriett S. Pullman diary, 8 September 1897, 17 September 1897, 24 September 1897, 28 September 1897, and 3 October, 1897, Harriet Pullman (Carolan) to George M. Pullman, 19 September 1897, Mrs. C. Phillip Miller Collection, Chicago Historical Society, Chicago, Ill.

53. Harriett S. Pullman diary, 8 October 1897, and 15 October 1897, Mrs. C. Phillip Miller Collection, Chicago Historical Society, Chicago, Ill. See also Pullman's Palace Car Company, Record Book B, p. 161, Newberry Library, Chicago, Ill.; Ernest Poole, *Giants Gone: Men Who Made Chicago* (New York: McGraw-Hill, 1943), p. 208.

54. Harriett S. Pullman diary, 16 October 1897, Mrs. C. Phillip Miller Collection, Chicago Historical Society, Chicago, Ill. Hattie noted that she made this entry in 1898. George M. Pullman to Harriett S. Pullman, telegram, 17 October 1897, Mrs. C. Phillip Miller Collection, Chicago Historical Society, Chicago, Ill.

55. *New York Times*, 20 October 1897, p. 4; see also *Rocky Mountain News*, 20 October 1897, pp. 1–2; *Inter Ocean* Chicago), 24 October 1897, p. 14.

56. *New York Times*, 20 October 1897, p. 4; *Inter Ocean* (Chicago), 20 October 1897, p. 1.

57. Harriett S. Pullman diary, 19 October 1897 (entered in September 1898) and 20 October 1897, Mrs. C. Phillip Miller Collection, Chicago Historical Society, Chicago, Ill.; *New York Times*, 20 October 1897, p. 4.

58. *New York Times*, 24 October 1897, p. 24; see also Harriett S. Pullman diary, 23 October 1897, Mrs. C. Phillip Miller Collection, Chicago Historical Society, Chicago, Ill.; *Inter Ocean* (Chicago), 24 October 1897, p. 14.

59. There had been instances of grave molestation in the past, including that involving the corpse of A. T. Stewart, the New York merchant, whose body was kidnapped from its resting place and held for ransom.

60. *Tribune* (Chicago), 24 October 1897, p. 1; *New York Times*, 25 October 1897, p. 7; Buder, *Pullman*, p. 210.

61. *New York Times*, 25 October 1897, p. 7; Harriett S. Pullman diary, 23 October 1897, Mrs. C. Phillip Miller Collection, Chicago Historical Society, Chicago, Ill.; Hutchinson, *Lowden*, vol. 1, p. 64–65; "The Last Will and Testament of George M. Pullman," a copy of which is deposited in the Chicago Historical Society, Chicago, Ill.

62. *Inter Ocean* (Chicago), 16 August 1899, clipping, Pullman Company, Miscellaneous Scrapbooks, Series B, Vol. 6, 1899–1903, Newberry Library, Chicago, Ill.; *New York Times*, 18 March 1898, p. 1; Minnie Demarest to Harriett S. Pullman, 2 March 1902; Harriett S. Pullman to Harriet Pullman (Carolan), 27 August 1905, Frank O. Lowden to Harriett S. Pullman, rough draft of a letter dated 22 March (1899?), Mrs. C. Phillip Miller Collection, Chicago Historical Society, Chicago, Ill.

63. *New York Times*, 7 February 1898, p. 2; Harriett S. Pullman to Harriet Pullman (Carolan), 17 August 1898. Mrs. C. Phillip Miller Collection, Chicago Historical Society, Chicago, Ill.; *New York Times*, 17 August 1898, p. 7, and 18 August 1898, p. 7.

64. *Inter Ocean* (Chicago), 27(?) November 1901, clipping, Pullman Company, Miscellaneous Scrapbooks, Series B, vol. 7, 1899–1903, p. 82, Newberry Library, Chicago, Ill. Accounts of young George's marriages, divorce, death, and the subsequent controversy over his estate and place of burial also appear in this scrapbook volume, pp. 45, 73, and 75–86, as well as in vol. 6, 1899–1903, pp. 32, 144, and 218 of the same series.

65. Harriett S. Pullman to Harriet Pullman (Carolan), 22 August 1905, 27 August 1905, and 31 August 1905, Mrs. C. Phillip Miller Collection, Chicago Historical Society, Chicago, Ill.

66. *New York Times*, 29 March 1921, p. 15.

67. *New York Times*, 23 October 1956, p. 33.

68. *New York Times*, 6 July 1937, p. 19; Hutchinson, *Lowden*, vol. 2, pp. 708 and 742.

BIBLIOGRAPHY

COLLECTIONS

Albion, N.Y. Office of the County Historian, Orleans County Courthouse. G. W. [sic] Pullman file and clipping files.

Chicago, Illinois. Miller, Mrs. C. Phillip Collection. This collection, located at the Chicago Historical Society, includes: correspondence between George M. and Harriett S. Pullman; other family correspondence, including that of Royal H. Pullman to George M. Pullman; George M. Pullman's diary fragment, 1874; Harriett S. Pullman's diaries and scrapbook; Mary Catherine Sanger's diaries; George M. Pullman, Jr.'s 1894 diary; Florence Pullman Lowden's diaries and scrapbooks; Pullman family genealogical materials, including "Pullman," a genealogy commissioned by Harriet Pullman Schermerhorn in memory of her parents, George Mortimer Pullman and Harriett Amelia (Sanger) Pullman; *Pullman Palace Car Patents*, a bound book of patents owned by Pullman's Palace Car Company; and *Weekly Time Book, for Contractors, Workingmen and Others*. Philadelphia, Pa.: Troutman & Hayes, n.d.

Chicago, Ill. Chicago Public Library, Special Collections Division. Pullman Collection, Boxes 1–10.

Chicago, Ill. Chicago Historical Society. Pullman Collection. This collection includes: "Pullman Enterprises," a folder; "In Memoriam, George M. Pullman," a collection of obituaries bound into a volume presented to Harriett S. Pullman shortly after her husband's death; "The Last Will and Testament of George M. Pullman"; George M. Pullman Correspondence; George M. Pullman's diary for 1860; Emily C. Pullman's diary; Pullman Genealogy Collection; Harriett S. Pullman's scrapbook; Emily Caroline Minton Pullman Correspondence; Fluhrer Family Papers; and Madeline Wallin Sikes Collection, Box 6.

Chicago, Ill. The Newberry Library. Pullman Company Limited, Board Minute Book. Pullman's Palace Car Company, Record Book A. Pullman's Palace Car Company, Record Book B. Pullman Company, Miscellaneous Scrapbooks, Series A. Pullman Company, Miscellaneous Scrapbooks, Series B.

Boulder, Colo. University of Colorado Library, Western History Section. Henry M. Teller Collection.

Boston, Mass. Baker Library, Harvard University Graduate School of Business Administration. R. G. Dun and Company Collection. "Illinois," vols. 30 and 43.

307

Bibliography

Denver, Colo. Denver Public Library, Western History Department. "Colorado Pioneer Register," Maria Davis McGrath Collection. George T. Clark's diary.

Fort Collins, Colo. Author's collection. George N. McGinnis correspondence to author.

Pottstown, Pa. The Hill School. Record of George Pullman, Jr.

DIRECTORIES

Bailey, John C.W. *John C.W. Bailey's Chicago City Directory for the Year 1864–1865.* Chicago, Ill.: John C.W. Bailey, 1864.

Edward's Annual Directory to the Inhabitants, Institutions, Incorporated Companies, Manufacturing Establishments, Business, Business Firms, Etc. in the City of Chicago for 1869–70. St. Louis, Mo. and New York: Edwards and Company, n.d.

Halpin, T. M., Comp. *Halpin and Bailey's Chicago City Directory for the Year 1863–64.* Chicago, Ill.: Halpin and Bailey, 1863.

————. *Halpin and Bailey's City Directory for the Year 1862–63.* Chicago, Ill.: Halpin and Bailey, 1862.

Poor, Henry V., comp. *Poor's Manual of United States Railroads, 1880.* New York: H. V. and H. W. Poor, 1880.

————. *Poor's Manual of United States Railroads, 1883.* New York: H. V. and H. W. Poor, 1883.

————. *Poor's Manual of United States Railroads, 1891.* New York: H. V. and H. W. Poor, 1893.

————. *Poor's Manual of the Railroads of the United States, 1897.* 30th annual ed. New York: H. V. and H. W. Poor, 1897.

GOVERNMENT DOCUMENTS

Burke, Edmund, commissioner of patents, comp. *List of Patents for Inventions and Designs, Issued by the United States From 1790–1847 With the Patent Laws and Notes of the Decisions of the Courts of the United States for the Same Period.* Washington, D.C.: J. and G. S. Gideon, 1847.

U.S. Congress, Senate. *United States Strike Commission Report.* Senate Executive Document no. D3276# 7/53 Cong., 3d Sess. Washington, D.C.: Government Printing Office, 1895.

Bibliography

PUBLIC DOCUMENTS

Central City, Colo. Office of the Clerk and Recorder, Gilpin County. Property Books A, 3, 4, and 21.

Denver, Colo. Colorado State Archives. General Docket No. 142, Bill for Injunction, 27 May 1862.

Denver, Colo. Colorado State Archives., Gilpin County Mining Records, 1859–1864, Russell District, Books D and E.

BOOKS

Album of Genealogy and Biography: Cook County, Illinois. 11th ed., rev. and impr. Chicago, Ill.: LaSalle, 1899.

Allen, Frederick Lewis. *The Great Pierpont Morgan.* New York: Harper and Row, 1965.

Ames, Charles Edgar. *Pioneering the Union Pacific: A Reappraisal of the Builders of the Railroad.* New York: Appleton, Century, Crofts, 1969.

Andreas, A. T. *History of Chicago, From the Earliest Period to the Present Time.* 3 vols. Chicago, Ill.: A. T. Andreas, 1886, vol. 3.

——. *History of Chicago, From the Earliest Period to the Present Time.* 3 vols. 1886. Reprint. New York: Arno Press, 1975, vol. 2.

Asbury, Herbert. *Gem of the Prairie: An Informal History of the Chicago Underworld.* 1940. Reprint. DeKalb: Northern Illinois University Press, 1986.

Atherton, Lewis E. *The Frontier Merchant in Mid-America.* Columbia: University of Missouri Press, 1971.

Avrich, Paul. *The Haymarket Tragedy.* Princeton, N.J.: Princeton University Press, 1984.

Baedeker, Karl, ed. *The United States With an Excursion Into Mexico.* Leipsic, Germany: Karl Baedeker, 1893.

Bancroft, Caroline. *Gulch of Gold: A History of Central City, Colorado.* Denver, Colo.: Sage Books, 1958.

Beebe, Lucius. *Mansions on Rails; The Folklore of the Private Railway Car.* Berkeley, Calif.: Howell-North, 1959.

——. *Mr. Pullman's Elegant Palace Car.* Garden City, N.Y.: Doubleday, 1961.

Behrend, George. *Pullman in Europe.* London: Ian Allan, 1962.

Billington, Ray Allen. *Westward Expansion: A History of the American Frontier.* 3d. ed. New York: Macmillan, 1967.

Bining, Arthur Cecil, and Cochran, Thomas C. *The Rise of American Economic Life.* New York: Charles Scribner's Sons, 1964.

Biographical Sketches of the Leading Men of Chicago. Chicago, Ill.: Wilson and St. Clair, 1868.

Bowles, Samuel. *A Summer Vacation in the Parks and Mountains of Colorado*. Springfield, Mass.: Samuel Bowles, 1869.

———. *Our New West*. Hartford, Conn.: Hartford Publishing, 1869.

Brazeal, Brailsford Reese. *The Brotherhood of Sleeping Car Porters: Its Origin and Development*. New York: Harper and Brothers, 1946.

Bryce, James. *The American Commonwealth*. 2d. rev. ed. 2 vols. London and New York: Macmillan 1891, vol. 1.

Buder, Stanley. *Pullman: An Experiment in Industrial Order and Community Planning, 1880–1930*. New York: Oxford University Press, 1970.

Burgess, George H., and Kennedy, Miles C. *Centennial History of the Pennsylvania Railroad Company, 1846–1946*. Philadelphia, Pa.: Pennsylvania Railroad, 1949.

Burt, S. W. and Berthoud, E. L. *The Rocky Mountain Gold Regions, Containing Sketches of Its History, Geography, Mineralogy and Gold Mines and Their Present Operations*. Denver City, Jefferson Territory: Rocky Mountain News, 1861.

Burton, Sir Richard. *The Look of the West: 1860; Across the Plains to California*. Lincoln: University of Nebraska Press, n.d.

Carroll, John Charles. *Armour and His Times*. New York: D. Appleton-Century, 1938.

Carwardine, Rev. William H. *The Pullman Strike*. 1894. Reprint. Chicago, Ill.: Charles H. Kerr, 1973.

Cassara, Ernest, ed. *Universalism in America, A Documentary History*. Boston, Mass.: Beacon Press, 1971.

Clark, C. M. *A Trip to Pike's Peak and Notes by the Way*. Edited by Robert Greenwood. San Jose, Calif.: Talisman Press, 1958.

Cobden, Richard. *The American Diaries of Richard Cobden*. Edited by Elizabeth Hoon Cawley. New York: Greenwood Press, 1969.

Colbert, Elias, and Chamberlin, Everett. *Chicago and the Great Conflagration*. Chicago: J. S. Goodman, 1871.

Coman, Katharine. *Industrial History of the United States*. rev. ed. New York: Macmillan, 1910.

Corliss, Carlton J. *Main Line of Mid-America: The Story of the Illinois Central Line*. New York: Creative Age Press, 1950.

Cross, Whitney R. *The Burned-Over District: The Social and Intellectual History of Enthusiastic Religion in Western New York, 1800–1850*. New York: Harper Torchbooks, 1950.

Cushman, Samuel, and Waterman, J. P. *The Gold Mines of Gilpin County, Colorado*. Central City, Colo.: Register Steam Printing House, 1876.

Bibliography

Daughen, Joseph R., and Binzen, Peter. *The Wreck of the Penn Central*. Boston, Mass.: Little, Brown, 1971.

DeSantis, Vincent P. *The Shaping of Modern America, 1877–1916*. Port, N.Y.: Forum Press, 1977.

Doty, Mrs. Duane. *The Town of Pullman*. 1893. Reprint. Chicago: Pullman Civic Organization, 1974.

Ellis, Hamilton. *Nineteenth Century Railway Carriages in the British Isles — from the Eighteen-thirties to the Nineteen-hundreds*. London: Modern Transport Publishing, 1949.

————. *The Midland Railway*. London: Ian Allan, 1953.

Farr, Finis. *Chicago, A Personal History of America's Most American City*. New Rochelle, N.Y.: Arlington House, 1973.

Fossett, Frank. *Colorado: A Historical, Descriptive and Statistical Work on the Rocky Mountain Gold and Silver Mining Region*. Denver, Colo.: Daily Tribune Printing House, 1876.

Ginger, Ray. *Altgeld's America: The Lincoln Ideal Versus Changing Realities*. Chicago, Ill.: Quadrangle Books, 1965.

————. *Eugene V. Debs: A Biography*. New York: Collier Books, 1970.

Gras, N.S.B. *Business and Capitalism: An Introduction to Business History*. 1939. Reprint. New York: Augustus M. Kelley, 1971.

Greenwood, Grace. *New Life in New Lands: Notes of Travel*. New York: J. B. Ford, 1873.

Griswold, Wesley S. *A Work of Giants: Building the First Transcontinental Railroad*. New York: McGraw-Hill, 1962.

Grodinsky, Julius. *Transcontinental Railway Strategy, 1869-1893: A Study of Businessmen*. Philadelphia: University of Pennsylvania Press, 1962.

Hall, Frank. *History of the State of Colorado*. 4 vols. Chicago, Ill.: Blakely Printing, 1889–1895.

Hambleton, Chalkley J. *A Gold Hunter's Experience*. Chicago, Ill.: privately printed. 1898.

Harding, Carroll R. *George M. Pullman (1831–1897) and the Pullman Company*. New York: Newcomen Society in America, 1951.

Harlow, Alvin F. *The Road of the Century: The Story of the New York Central*. New York: Creative Age Press, 1947.

Hays, Samuel P. *The Response to Industrialism, 1885–1914*. Chicago, Ill.: University of Chicago Press, 1957.

Holbrook, Stuart H. *The Story of American Railroads*. New York: Crown, 1947.

Hollister, Ovando J. *The Mines of Colorado*. Springfield, Mass.: Samuel Bowles, 1867.

Husband, Joseph. *The History of the Pullman Car*. 1917. Reprint. Grand Rapids, Mich.: Black Letter Press, 1974.

311

Bibliography

Hutchinson, William T. *Lowden of Illinois: The Life of Frank O. Lowden*. 2 vols. Chicago, Ill.: University of Chicago Press, 1957.

Jackson, Helen Hunt. *Bits of Travel at Home*. Boston, Mass.: Roberts Brothers, 1880.

Johnson, Arthur M., and Supple, Barry E. *Boston Capitalists and Western Railroads: A Study in the Nineteenth-Century Railroad Investment Process*. Cambridge, Mass.: Harvard University Press, 1967.

Josephson, Matthew. *The Robber Barons: The Great American Capitalists*. New York: Harcourt, Brace and World, 1962.

Kirkland, Caroline. *Chicago Yesterdays: A Sheaf of Reminiscences*. Chicago: Daughaday, 1919.

Kirkland, Edward Chase. *Industry Comes of Age: Business, Labor and Public Policy, 1860–1897*. Chicago, Ill.: Quadrangle Books, 1967.

Kogan, Herman. *Traditions and Challenges: The Story of Sidley and Austin*. R. R. Donnelley & Sons, 1983.

Lavender, David. *The Great Persuader*. Garden City, N.Y.: Doubleday, 1970.

Lindsey, Almont. *The Pullman Strike.The Story of a Unique Experiment and of a Great Labor Upheaval*. Chicago, Ill.: University of Chicago Press, Phoenix Books, 1964.

Livesay, Harold C. *Andrew Carnegie and the Rise of Big Business*.

Boston, Mass.: Little, Brown, 1975.

Lynes, Russell. *The Tastemakers*. New York: Grosset and Dunlap, 1954.

Malone, Dumas. *Dictionary of American Biography*. Vol. 15. New York: Charles Scribner's Sons, 1935.

Mohl, Raymond A. *The New City: Urban America in the Industrial Age, 1860–1920*. Arlington Heights, Ill.: Harlan Davidson, 1985.

Morel, Julian. *Pullman: The Pullman Car Company — Its Services, Cars and Traditions*. North Pomfret, Vt.: David and Charles, 1983.

The National Cyclopaedia of American Biography. Vol. 9. New York: James T. White, 1907.

North, Douglass C. *The Economic Growth of the United States, 1790–1860*. New York: W. W. Norton, 1966.

Nugent, Walter T.K. *Money and American Society, 1865–1880*. New York: Free Press, 1968.

———. *From Centennial to World War: American Society, 1876-1917*. Indianapolis, Ind.: Bobbs-Merrill, 1977.

Nye, Russel Blaine. *Society and Culture in America, 1830–1860*. New York: Harper and Row, 1974.

Overton, Richard C. *Burlington Route: A History of the Burlington Lines*. New York: Alfred A. Knopf, 1965.

Pierce, Bessie Louise, comp. and ed. *As Others See Chicago: Impressions of Visitors, 1673–1933*. Chicago, Ill.: University of Chicago Press, 1933.

————. *A History of Chicago: From Town to City, 1848–1871*. vol. 2. New York: Alfred A. Knopf, 1940.

————. *A History of Chicago: The Rise of a Modern City, 1871–1893*. Vol. 3. Chicago, Ill.: University of Chicago Press, 1975.

Pierce, Frederick Clifton. *Field Genealogy: Being the Record of All the Field Family in America Whose Ancestors Were in This Country Prior to 1700*. 2 vols. Chicago: W. B. Conkey, 1901, vol. 2.

Poole, Ernest. *Giants Gone: Men Who Made Chicago*. New York: McGraw-Hill, 1943.

Randall, Frank A. *History of the Development of Building Construction in Chicago*. Urbana: The University of Illinois Press, 1949.

Report of the Directors of the Chicago, Burlington and Quincy Railroad Company: Annual Meeting, June 22d, 1866. Chicago: Garden City Printing, 1866.

Riegel, Robert E. *Young America, 1830–1840*. Westport, Conn.: Greenwood Press, 1973.

Rutt, Chris. L., comp. and ed. *History of Buchanan County and the City of St. Joseph and Representative Citizens*. Chicago: Biographical Publishing, 1904.

Sabin, Edwin L. *Building the Pacific Railway*. Philadelphia, Pa.: J. B. Lippincott, 1919.

Schotter, H. W. *The Growth and Development of the Pennsylvania Railroad Company*. Philadelphia, Pa.: Allen, Lane and Scott, 1927.

Shaw, Ronald E. *Erie Water West: A History of the Erie Canal, 1792–1854*. Lexington: University of Kentucky Press, 1966.

Signor, Isaac S. *Landmarks of Orleans County, N.Y.* New York: D. Mason, 1894.

Simmons, Jack. *The Railway in England and Wales, 1830–1914: The System and Its Working*. Vol. 1. Leicester, England: Leicester University Press, 1978.

Smiley, Jerome C., ed. *History of Denver With Outlines of the Earlier History of the Rocky Mountain Country*. 1901. Reprint. Evansville, Ind.: Unigraphic, 1977.

Smith, Duane A. *Rocky Mountain Mining Camps: The Urban Frontier*. Bloomington: Indiana University Press, 1967.

Smith, Dwight L., ed. *John D. Young and the Colorado Gold Rush*. Chicago, Ill.: R. R. Donnelley & Sons, 1969.

Stead, W. T. *Chicago To-Day: Or The Labour War in America*. 1894. Reprint. New York: Arno Press and the *New York Times*, 1969.

Bibliography

Stone, Wilbur Fiske, ed. *History of Colorado*. 4 vols. Chicago, Ill.: S. J. Clarke, 1918, vol. 1.

Stover, John F. *The Life and Decline of the American Railroad*. New York: Oxford University Press, 1970.

————. *History of the Illinois Central Railroad*. New York: Macmillan, 1975.

————. *Iron Road to the West: American Railroads in the 1850s*. New York: Columbia University Press, 1978.

Taylor, H. C. *Historical Sketches of the Town of Portland, Comprising Also the Pioneer History of Chautauqua County, With Biographical Sketches of the Early Settlers*. Fredonia, N.Y.: W. McKinstry and Son, 1873.

Tebbel, John. *The Marshall Fields: A Study in Wealth*. New York: E. P. Dutton, 1947.

Thomas, Arad. *Pioneer History of Orleans County, New York*. Albion, N.Y.: H. A. Bruner, Orleans American Steam Press Print, 1871.

Villard, Henry. *The Past and Present of the Pike's Peak Gold Regions*. Edited by LeRoy R. Hafen. 1932. Reprint. New York: DaCapo Press, 1972.

Wall, Joseph Frazier. *Andrew Carnegie*. New York: Oxford University Press, 1970.

Ward, James A. *J. Edgar Thomson: Master of the Pennsylvania*. Westport, Conn.: Greenwood Press, 1980.

Ware, Norman J. *The Labor Movement in the United States, 1860–1895: A Study in Democracy*. New York: Vintage Books, 1929.

Wendt, Lloyd, and Kogan, Herman. *Give the Lady What She Wants! The Story of Marshall Field and Company*. Chicago: Rand McNally, 1952.

White, John H., Jr. *The American Railroad Passenger Car*. Baltimore, Md.: Johns Hopkins University Press, 1978.

Wiebe, Robert H. *The Search for Order, 1877–1920*. New York: Hill and Wang, 1967.

Williams, Frederick S. *Williams's Midland Railway: Its Rise and Progress, A Narrative of Modern Enterprise*. 1888. Reprint. New York: Augustus M. Kelley, 1968.

Young, Andrew W. *History of Chautauqua County, New York, From Its First Settlement to the Present Time, With Numerous Biographical and Family Sketches*. Buffalo, N.Y.: Matthews & Warren, 1875.

Young, Otis E., Jr. *Western Mining*. Norman: University of Oklahoma Press, 1970.

BOOKLETS

In Memoriam, Emily Caroline Pullman. N.p., n.d. Booklet in the Office of the County Historian, Orleans County, Albion, N.Y.

Bibliography

Pullman, Rev. Royal H., D.D. "Dedication of the Pullman Memorial Universalist Church, January Thirty-First, 1895. Albion, N.Y." N.p., n.d.

The Story of Pullman. N.p. n.d. Copy in author's possession.

Wells, Arthur A. *Reminiscences of Mr. and Mrs. George M. Pullman.* Privately printed pamphlet in the Mrs. C. Phillip Miller Collection, Chicago Historical Society, Chicago, Ill.

ARTICLES/CHAPTERS

Ade, George. "The Glory of Being a Coachman." *Chicago Stories.* Edited by Franklin J. Meine. 1941. Reprint. Chicago, Ill.: Henry Regnery, 1963, pp. 148 –149.

Bennett, A. Milo. "The Building of a State — The Story of Illinois." *Journal of the Illinois State Historical Society* 13 (October 1920): 324–354.

Bower, A. J. "Dining on Wheels: Part 1 — *The Prince of Wales.*" *Transport History* 10 (Spring 1979): 41–62.

Chicago History 8 (1967): 107.

"Extracts From Mrs. John A. Logan's Tribute to Mrs. Pullman." *Journal of the Illinois State Historical Society* 14 (April–July 1921): 210–211.

Fitzsimmons, Margaret Louise. "Missouri Railroads During the Civil War and Reconstruction." *Missouri Historical Review* 35 (January 1941): 188–189.

Forney, M. N. "American Locomotives and Cars." *The American Railway: Its Construction, Development, Management, and Appliances.* pp. 100–148. ca. 1892. Reprint. New York: Bramhall House, n.d.

Gregory, Frances W., and Neu, Irene D. "The American Industrial Elite in the 1870s: Their Social Origins." Edited by William Miller. *Men in Business: Essays in the History of Entrepreneurship.* Cambridge, Mass.: Harvard University Press, 1952, 193–211.

Johnson, Hiram A. "A Letter From a Colorado Mining Camp in 1860."

Colorado Magazine 7 (September 1930): 192–195.

Lindsey, Almont. "Paternalism and the Pullman Strike." *American Historical Review* 45 (January 1939): 272–289.

Long, Charles. "*Pioneer* and the Lincoln Funeral Train: The Making of a Pullman Myth?" *Railway World.* In press.

Miller, Florence Lowden. "The Pullmans of Prairie Avenue: A Domestic Portrait From Letters and Diaries." *Chicago History* 1 (Spring 1971): 142–155.

Perrigo, Lynn I., ed. "H. J. Hawley's Diary, Russell Gulch in 1860." *Colorado Magazine* 30 (April 1953): 133–149.

Porter, Horace. "Railway Passenger Travel." *The American Railway: Its Construction, Development, Management, and Appliances.* pp. 228–266. ca. 1892. Reprint. New York: Bramhall House, n.d.

315

"Raising the Grade." *Chicago History* 3 (Fall 1953): 263–270.

Smith, Esther Pond. "The Development of the Postal Service in Pullman." *Bunchgrass Historian: Whitman County* (Washington) *Historical Society Quarterly* 9 (Summer 1981): 13–20.

Stark, Lawrence R. "The Founding of Pullman: A Local Folktale." *Bunchgrass Historian: Whitman County* (Washington) *Historical Society Quarterly* 9 (Summer 1981): 4–12.

Titherington, R.H. "General Horace Porter." *Munsey's Magazine* 17 (April 1897): 120–121.

Vroom, Peter D. "George M. Pullman and the Colorado Tradition." *The Colorado Magazine* 17 (May 1940): 113-115.

Youngmeyer, D. W. "An Excursion Into the Early History of the Chicago and Alton Road." *Journal of the Illinois State Historical Society* 38 (1945): 7–37.

NEWSPAPERS

Chicago Daily Press and Tribune

Chicago Morning News

Chicago Evening Post

Chicago Times

Daily Democrat (Chicago, Ill.)

Daily Herald (Chicago, Ill.)

Daily Mining Journal (Black Hawk, Colo.)

Denver Republican

Inter Ocean (Chicago, Ill.)

New York Times

Pullman (Ill.) Journal

Railroad Gazette

Railway Times (London)

Rocky Mountain News (Denver, Colo.)

Tribune (Chicago, Ill.)

Tri-Weekly Miner's Register (Central City, Colo.)

The Western Mountaineer (Golden, Colo.)

INDEX

Abbott, A. D., 39
Abbott, Charles S., 62
Allen, R. V., 167
Allen Paper Wheel Company, 167
Allport, James, 129-31
Altgeld, John Peter, 6, 230
American Federation of Labor, 227
American Railway Union (ARU), 222, 224, 226
Ames, Oliver, 100, 102
Angell, Charles W., 84, 149, 215; absconds, 159-61
Angevine, Frank H., 62
Armour, Charles Lee, 60
Armour, Philip D., 165, 216-17, 243-44
Ashbury, James, 131
Atchison, Topeka and Santa Fe Railroad, 194-95
Atlantic Pacific Railroad, 194

Baltimore and Ohio Railroad (B&O), 117, 181-82
Barclay, Richard D., 147
Barney and Smith (car company), 182
Barrett, Nathan F., 167
Beatrice drawing room car, 143
Beer, Julius, 133
Beman, Solomon Spencer, 167, 169, 176, 240, 258
Benjamin, Schuyler S., 83
Benzon, Ernest, 133
Billings, Frank, 256
Blackstone, Timothy, 75
Blaine, James G., 116, 122
Bowen, James H., 77-78

Bower, James, 137-38
Bowers, Blanche, 259
Bowers, Dure and Company, 193
Bowles, Samuel, 105
British Pullman Palace Car Company, 143
Bross, William, 99
Brown, Charles L., 57
Brown, Dan, 91
Brown, James P., 59
Brown and Hollingsworth (contractors), 33
Bushnell, Cornelius S., 104

Caird, Robert and James, 116
Calumet Club, 122
Car A. *See Pioneer* sleeping car
Car 40. *See Springfield* sleeping car
Carnegie, Andrew, 81-82, 97-98, 101-4
Carolan, Francis J. (husband of Harriet Pullman), 211-13, 261
Carter, Timothy J., 100
Carter and Bauer (architects), 33
Central City, Colorado, 53; Pullman's activities in, 58-61
Central Pacific Railroad, 103, 174, 180
Central Railroad of New Jersey, 195
Central Transportation Company (CTC), 81, 90, 97-98, 101-2, 146-48, 182-84, 198
Cessford, William, 38
Chase, Margery, 58
Cheesman, Walter Scott, 120
Chemical National Bank, 123
Chicago: in the 1800s, 30-32, 71-72; great fire of, 109, 151-52; postfire growth of, 196-97

Chicago, Alton and St. Louis Railroad,
   37, 46, 74-75, 77-78, 83, 85, 88
Chicago and Great Eastern Railway, 85
Chicago and North Western Railway, 81,
   85, 149
Chicago Baseball Club, 123
Chicago, Burlington and Quincy Railroad
   (CB&Q), 30, 80-81, 83, 85, 87,
   92, 99, 101, 158
Chicago Citizens Association, 217
Chicago Citizens League, 122
Chicago Club, 122, 199
Chicago College of Dental Surgery, 122
Chicago Manual Training School, 122
Chicago, Milwaukee and St. Paul
   Railroad, 180
Chicago Musical Festival Association,
   122-23
Chicago Orchestra, 123
Chicago Relief and Aid Society, 109, 152
Chicago World's Fair (1893), 213, 220.
   See also Columbian Expositon
City of Detroit hotel car, 99
City of New York sleeping car, 81
Clark, C. B., 43-44. See also Lyon,
   Pullman and Company
Clark, George T., 59
Cleveland, Grover, 231
Cobb, S. B., 29
Columbian Exposition (1893, Chicago),
   38, 123. See also Chicago World's
   Fair
Commercial Club, 123
Commissary cars, 91
Compagnie Internationale des Wagons-
   Lits, 140-41
Consolidated Gregory Company, 70
Corporations, 82
Crerar, John, 83, 170
Crocker, Charles, 103

DaLee, Hannah Maria (sister of Emily
   Pullman), 92, 209
DaLee, Richard R.W., 26
Danolds, Charles, 239
Davis, Noah, 24
Debs, Eugene V., 222, 224, 227
Delmonico dining car, 86-88
Depression (1870s), 152-53

Detroit Car and Manufacturing Company,
   88-89; purchased by Pullman, 149
Diamond Match Company, 244
Dillon, Sidney, 100
Dining cars, 86-88. See also Prince of
   Wales dining car; Southern dining
   car
Dixon Air Line, 39
Doane, John W., 191, 197
Drawing room cars, 86-87, 90-91. See
   also Beatrice drawing room car;
   City of Detroit hotel car; Western
   World hotel car
Drexel, Morgan and Company, 104
Drummond, Thomas, 80
Duff, John, 100
Dun credit rating agency. See R. G. Dun
   and Company
Dunphy, John M., 110
Durant, Thomas C., 98, 100

Eagle Gold Company, 70
Eagle Iron Works, 43-45
Eagleton Wire Manufacturing Company,
   72
Earl, Dan and Nellie, 120
East Tennessee, Virginia and Georgia
   Railroad, 195
Eaton, Charles, 227, 256, 258
Eaton, Timothy C., 15
Elliott, Samuel, 116-17, 119, 143, 249
Ely and Smith (contractors), 33, 35
Emigrant cars. See Second-class
   sleeping cars
Erie Canal, 12-13
Excelsior sleeping car, 134

Farmers Loan and Trust Company (New
   York), 151, 153-55
Field, Benjamin C., 36-39, 45, 74, 81,
   95
Field, Marshall, 165-66, 197
Field, Nannie (wife of Marshall Field),
   235
Field, Spafford C., 61
Fluhrer, Charles, 240
Fluhrer, Emma. See Pullman, Emma
Fluhrer, William (husband of Emma
   Pullman), 231, 240

Foster, Sophie (wife of George C. Symes), 120

Gage, David A., 70
Galena Air Line. *See* Dixon Air Line
Galena and Chicago Union Railroad, 30, 39
Gill, S. H., 62
Gold: strike in Colorado, 42-43; milling techniques for, 43-44
General Managers Association (GMA), 224, 227
Globe parlor car, 137-38
Gould, Jay, 186
Gouraud, Georges, 116, 119, 127-29, 138, 140-41
Graham, Robert, 45, 49, 69; with Pullman in Colorado, 54-56
Graham, William B., 243
Grand Trunk Railway Company, 149
Grant, Ulysses S., 111, 121, 150-51
Great Northern Railroad, 222
Great Northern Railway (England), 136-38
Great Western Railway (Canada), 80, 85, 101, 149
Green, Edward Henry, 133
Greenwood, Grace, 105
Gregory, John Hamilton, 43
Gresham, Walter Q., 189
Griffin, J. F., 243

Hall, Amos T., 150, 170
Hall, Frank, 53
Hammond, Charles G., 150, 166, 170
Hanna, Mark, 234
Hannibal and St. Joseph Railroad, 89, 148
Harris, John S., 60
Harris, Robert, 83, 185
Harrison, Benjamin, 121-22
Hayford, J. H., 61
Haymarket Square bombing, 217
Higginbotham, Harlow N., 244
Hill, James J., 222
Hill, Nathaniel P., 64
Hills, N. D., 258
Hollister, Cady, 59, 64, 66, 70
Honore, Laura, 128

Hopkins, John P., 226
Hopkins, Mark, 103
Hotel cars. *See* Drawing room cars
Hudson River Railroad, 100
Huntington, Collis P., 103, 174

Illinois Central Railroad, 30, 73, 168, 224, 226
India railway car, 139
International Railroad Commission, 122
Iona railway car, 139
Iron Mountain Railroad, 186

J. H. Alexander and Company, 58-59
J. S. Morgan Company (London), 154
Jackson, Huntington W., 167
Jacksonville, Tampa and Key West Railroad, 195
Jaffray, Henry S., 110, 112
Jay Cook and Company, 152
Johnson, Eastman, 225
Johnson, L. M., 115
Joy, James F., 80

Kansas Pacific Railway Company, 149
Kimball, H. I., 81
Knights of Labor, 181, 216-17, 222

Lake Shore and Michigan Southern Railroad, 189
Lincoln, Abraham, 77
Lincoln, Robert, 119, 227
Logan, John A., 121
Logan, Mary (wife of John A. Logan), 93, 117-18, 121, 241, 250
London and South Western Railway, 136, 144, 187
London, Brighton and South Coast Railway, 136, 143
London, Chatham and Dover Railway, 136
Louisville and Nashville Railroad, 180
Lowden, Frank (husband of Florence Pullman), 236, 242-47, 261
Lyman, David B., 167
Lyon, James E., 48-49, 57-59, 65-66, 70
Lyon, Pullman and Company, 48-49, 60-61, 63-65, 72; store in Central City, 57-58; acquires Clark-Vandevanter crushing mill, 58-59

McCormick, Cyrus, Jr., 244
McGinnis Brothers and Fearing brokers (New York), 173-74
McKinley, William, 256
Mann, William D'Alton, 140-41
Mann Boudoir Car Company, 193-94
Massacre Monument (Chicago), 205, 213-14
Matteson House (Chicago), 26; constructed, 29-30
Medberry, John W., 60
Meigs, John, 248-49
Mendel, Edward, 33
Merchants Loan and Trust Company, 123
Meridionale Railway Company (Italy), 142
Metropolitan Bank (New York), 65
Michigan Central Railroad, 80, 83, 85, 87, 92, 101, 149, 155, 158, 185
Midland Railway (England), 116, 129-33, 139-40, 143-44; introduces Pullman cars, 135-36
Midland sleeping car, 134; displayed on the Continent, 141
Minton, William, 46
Missouri Pacific Railroad, 186
Moore, Charles Henry, 24, 29, 48-49, 63, 65, 70
Morgan, J. P. (son of Junius S. Morgan), 130, 172, 199
Morgan, Junius Spencer, 128, 130
Morris, J. W., 55
Mountain City. See Central City, Colorado

Nagelmackers, Georges, 140-42
National Biscuit Company, 244
New York Central and Hudson River Railroad, 188
New York Central Railroad, 23, 80, 104, 172, 184-85
New York Central Sleeping Car Company. *See* Wagner Car Company
New York Elevated Railroad Company, 159
New York Railroad Bureau, 39
New York, West Shore and Buffalo Railway Company, 118, 172-73, 186
Nichols, Grace, 118

Noble, Gilbert C., 54, 62
Nord Railway (France), 140-41
North Eastern Railway (England), 137
Northern Central Railway, 104
Northern Pacific Railway, 152, 172-73
North Missouri Railroad, 46, 89, 148

Oglesby, Felicite, 245, 250-51, 253
Omaha sleeping car, 81
Owen, S. A., 243-44

P. W. Gates and Company, 43-45, 65
Pacific Railroad Act (1862), 98
Palmer, Potter and Bertha, 128, 253
Parmalee, Franklin, 70
Pearce, J. Irving, 83
Pennsylvania Central Railroad. *See* Pennsylvania Railroad Company
Pennsylvania Railroad Company, 89, 97-98, 101-2, 104, 146-48, 172, 182-83; Sessions's vestibule used on, 188
Pierson, Henry R., 149-50
Pingree, Hazen S., 226
Pintsch lamps, 163
Pioneer sleeping car, 76-80, 95
Porter, Horace, 111, 150-51, 172, 185, 193, 214, 243
Price, W. P., 130
Prince of Wales dining car, 138
Pullman, Albert (brother of George M.), 23-24, 26, 42, 76, 84, 90, 92, 95, 100, 107, 133-34, 149, 206; dies, 214-15. *See also* Pullman and Moore; Pullman family
Pullman, Charles (brother of George M.), 16, 92, 124, 206
Pullman, Emily (cousin of George M.), 116-17, 119
Pullman, Emily (mother of George M.), 113, 209-11; moves to Chicago. *See also* Pullman, George; Pullman family
Pullman, Emma (sister of George M.), 18-19, 45, 92, 94, 206, 240
Pullman, Florence (daughter of George M.), 112-13, 168, 213-14, 225, 235-36, 240-42; born, 94; tours Europe, 117-18; education and

childhood of, 123-24, 136-37;
marries, 245-47; son born to, 254;
last years of, 261

Pullman, Frank (brother of George M.),
19-21, 45, 76, 92, 134, 206

Pullman, George M.: family life of, 7-9,
91-92, 111-13, 123-25, 175;
birth and early life of, 11-16, 24-
25; moves to Chicago, 26-27; early
interest of, in sleeping cars, 36-38;
life of, in Chicago, 41-42; moves
west to goldfields, 45-48; partnerships of, 48-49; in Colorado, 51-
53, 61-70; in Central City, 53-61;
returns to Chicago, 71; builds
Springfield car, 74-75; builds and
exhibits *Pioneer*, 75-81; branches
out into different types of cars, 86-
87; turns to manufacturing, 88-90;
courtship and marriage of, 92-94;
married life of, 94-95; competes
for Union Pacific contract, 98-
103; joins Union Pacific board,
philanthropies and public service
of, 109, 122-23, 205; 104; 109-
11; business climate during life of,
107, 23, 145-46; travels in Europe, 114-18, 127-29, 136-38,
142-44; marital relations of, 117-
18; travels of, in U.S.A., with Harriet, 120-22; builds home on
Prairie Avenue, relations of, with
children, 124, 206-8; finances Midland contract, 133; knighted by
King Humbert of Italy, 141-42; experiments with electric lighting,
143; in 1891, 201-5; relations of,
with blacks, 203-4; family life of,
205-15, 245-56; attempts on life
of, 243-44; dies, 256; funeral of,
258; last will and testament of,
258-59; reputation after death,
261-64. *See also* Pullman's Palace
Car Company

Pullman, George, Jr. (son of George M.),
214, 225, 235-36, 240, 248-52,
259-60; born, 94; education and
childhood of, 123-24

Pullman, Harriet (Little Hattie; daughter of George M.), 112, 247-48;
born, 94; tours Europe, 117-18;
education and childhood of, 123-

24; married, 211-13; marries second husband, 261

Pullman, Harriet Sanger (Hattie; wife of
George M.), 92-93, 104, 107,
117, 213, 224-25, 235-36, 241,
244; courtship of, 94; married life
of, 94, 109-13, 117-18; in Europe,
114-15, 118-19, 127-29, 136-38,
142-43; travels in U.S.A., 120-22;
sons and, 250-51; notified of
George's death, 256-57; last years
of, 260-61

Pullman, Helen (sister of George M.),
16, 21, 45, 92, 94, 113, 116-17,
206, 227, 240

Pullman, Henry (brother of George M.),
23-24, 113, 119, 206, 239-41,
247. *See also* Pullman family

Pullman, James (brother of George M.),
16, 20-21, 24, 169, 206, 240-41,
247

Pullman, Lewis (father of George M.).
See Pullman, George; Pullman
family

Pullman, Louise Lander (wife of Walter
Sanger), 259

Pullman, Lynne Fernald (first wife of
George, Jr.), 259-60

Pullman, Sarah Lander Brazell (second
wife of George, Jr.), 260

Pullman, Walter Sanger (son of George
M.), 214, 225, 236, 241, 248-52,
259-60; born, 94; education and
childhood of, 123-24

Pullman and Field, 37, 48, 75, 81, 101

Pullman and Moore, 24, 29, 32-36;
earnings of, 41; branches out to
Colorado, 45, 49

Pullman Building (Chicago), 176-77

Pullman family: origins of, 11-12;
moves westward, 12-13; religious
beliefs of, 14-15, 19-20, 22-23; in
Albion, 16-20; children move
away, 21; father dies, 22-24

Pullman, Illinois, 198; founded, 164-
68; described, 168-69; expenditures on, 170-71; visitors to, 174

Pullman Iron and Steel Company, 191-
92

Pullman Island, 113, 119

Pullman, Kimball and Company, 81

Pullman Land Association, 167, 221

Pullman Loan and Savings Bank, 191, 221

Pullman Pacific Palace Car Company, 101, 103, 105, 146, 153-54

Pullman sleeping cars, 90-91; early models of, 38-40; travelers' comments on, 105-7; English reaction to, 139-40; Italian reaction to, 141-42. *See also City of New York* sleeping car; *Excelsior* sleeping car; *Midland* sleeping car; Omaha sleeping car; *Pioneer* sleeping car; Second-class sleeping cars; *Springfield* sleeping car

Pullman Southern Car Company, 151, 190-91

Pullman, Sweet and Company, 59

Pullman Universalist Church (Albion, N.Y.), 205, 239-41

Pullman's Pacific Ca. Company. *See* Pullman Pacific Palace Car Company

Pullman's Palace Car Company, 85-86, 95, 102-3, 117-18; incorporated, 81-84; early growth of, 88-90; labor relations at, 114-15, 180-81, 215-18, 221-31, 234-35; expands into England, 131-32; competition of, with Central Transportation Company, 146-49, 182-84; Pierson assumes vice presidency of, 149-50; Porter assumes vice presidency of, 150-51; during 1870s depression, 153-59; growth of, during 1880s, 179-80, 195-98; lawsuit against B&O, 181-82; vestibule designed for, 187-88; litigation against, 189-90; absorbs rivals, 192-94; in 1891, 202-3; 1890s depression and, 218-21, 242-43; strike commission hearings on, 231-34, 237; suit against, by State of Illinois, 237. *See also* Gouraud, Georges; Pullman, Illinois; Pullman Iron and Steel Company; Pullman Southern Car Company; Union Foundry and Pullman Car Wheels Works; Wagner Car Company

Pullman's Palace Eating Car (PPEC) monogram, 87

Pullman's Sleeping Car Lines, 81

R. G. Dun and Company, 179-80

Railroads, expansion of, during and after Civil War, 73-74

Ramsey, Robert, 81

Rice, George, 81

Richards, James W., 61

Richmond and Danville Railroad, 195

Roberts, H. S., 137, 143

Rock Island Railroad, 226

Runnells, John S., 258

Russell, Benjamin O., 61

Russell, William Green, 54

Sanger, James (father of Harriet Pullman), 92-94

Sanger, Mary Catherine (mother of Harriet Pullman), 91, 206

Sanger, Steel and Company, 93

Sargent, Homer E., 83, 85, 133

Schermerhorn, Arthur Frederic (second husband of Harriet Pullman Carolan), 261

Scott, Thomas A., 81, 98, 104

Second-class sleeping cars, 194-95, 198

Seibert, Leonard, 37

Sessions, Henry Howard, 188-89

Shaw, C. A., 60

Shedd, John G., 251

Sheridan, Philip, 177

Shield, David, 38

Sikes, George C., 6, 235

Sleeping cars. *See* Pullman sleeping cars

Smith, Mattie, 248

Smith, Robert, 241

South Pennsylvania Railroad, 172

Southern dining car, 86

Southern Pacific Railroad, 103, 173, 180. *See also* Huntington, Collis P.

Southern Railroad Company (Italy), 141

Southern Transportation Company, 148

Springfield sleeping car, 74-75

Stagecoach travel, 46-47

Stanford, Leland, 103, 174

Starring, F. A., 129

Stevens, John S., 183-84

Stockton, J. W., 77-78

Stuart, Emily, 119, 240
Sweet, Emory J., 59, 66, 70
Swing, David, 212
Symes, George C., 120

Terre Haute and Alton Railroad, 97
Third National Bank (Chicago), 72, 78, 92
Thomas, Theodore, 123
Thomson, Frank, 256
Thomson, J. Edgar, 97, 104
Tourist cars. *See* Second-class sleeping cars
Towne, Henry D., 65-66, 70
Tremont dining car, 86

Union Foundry and Pullman Car Wheel Works, 170, 192
Union League Club, 151
Union Pacific Railroad, 98-102, 105, 108, 145, 153, 180, 194-95; fiscal crisis of, 103-4
Union Palace Car Company, 118, 193-95
Union Soldiers of the Sanitary Commission, 93
Upper Italy Railway, 141
Utica and Schenectady Railroad, 184

Vanderbilt, Cornelius, 81, 155. *See also* New York Central Railroad; Wagner Car Company

Vandevanter, John F., 43-45, 60-61. *See also* Lyon, Pullman and Company

Wagner, Webster T., 76, 97, 184-86
Wagner Car Company, 81, 117, 155, 184-86, 194, 198; competes for vestibulated train, 188-89
Waite, William H., 65
Ward, A. G. Dudley, 91
Wason Car Company, 74
Weinsheimer, A. S., 161, 180, 190, 243
Wells, Arthur, 245
West, George (husband of Helen Pullman), 227, 256
West, Helen. *See* Pullman, Helen
Western Marine and Fire Insurance Company, 65
Western World hotel car, 98-100
Wheeler, Charles H., 60
Wickes, Thomas, 196, 222, 224, 231, 242-43
Williams, Norman, Jr., 83
Woodruff, Theodore T., 76, 97-98
Woodruff Sleeping and Parlor Coach Company, 193-94
World's Exposition (1893), 197. *See also* Chicago World's Fair

Young America commissary car, 91
Young Men's Christian Union of Chicago, 110